D0414609
30107 005 105 504

# FROM GRUB STREET TO FLEET STREET

This book is dedicated to the memory of
Lucille Bogan (1897–1948),
who recorded a gloriously filthy blues in 1935

# From Grub Street to Fleet Street

## An Illustrated History of English Newspapers to 1899

BOB CLARKE

ASHGATE

© Bob Clarke 2004

All rights reserved. No part of this publication may be reproduced, stored in a retrieval system, or transmitted in any form or by any means, electronic, mechanical, photocopying, recording, or otherwise without the prior permission of the publisher.

Bob Clarke has asserted his moral right under the Copyright, Designs and Patents Act, 1988, to be identified as the author of this work.

Published by

Ashgate Publishing Limited
Gower House, Croft Road
Aldershot, Hants
GU11 3HR
England

Ashgate Publishing Company
Suite 420
101 Cherry Street
Burlingon, VT 05401–4405
USA

Ashgate website: http://www.ashgate.com

**British Library Cataloguing in Publication Data**
Clarke, Bob
From Grub Street to Fleet Street: an illustrated history of the English newspaper to 1899
1. Newspapers – Great Britain – History
I. Title
072'.09

**US Library of Congress Cataloging-in-Publication Data**
Clarke, Bob, 1949–
From Grub Street to Fleet Street: an illustrated history of English newspapers to 1899 / Bob Clarke.
p. cm.
Includes bibliographical references and index. (alk. paper)
1. English newspapers – History. 2. Journalism – England – History.
I. Title.

PN5114.C58 2004
072–dc22

2004001782

ISBN 0 7546 5007 3

This book is printed on acid-free paper

Typeset in Garamond by Bournemouth Colour Press, Parkstone, Poole.

Printed and bound in Great Britain by MPG Books Ltd, Bodmin, Cornwall.

# Contents

BARCODE No. 5105504
X
CLASS No. 072.09 CLA
BIB CHECK ✓
4 NOV 2004
PROC CHECK ✓
FINAL CHECK
lA 11/04
OS
SYSTEM No.
LOAN CATEGORY
S/L

# List of Illustrations

# PART ONE
# Grub Street

## Chapter 1

# Grub Street: an Introduction

> Grub-street: a street near Moorfields in London, much inhabited by writers of small histories, dictionaries, and temporary poems, whence any mean production is called grubstreet.
>
> Johnson's *Dictionary*, 1755

Grub Street (Figure 1.1) was a real place, as real as Fleet Street. Its name came from the refuse ditch (grub) that ran alongside. Built on marshy ground, Grub Street was a notoriously unhealthy place, prone to epidemics. Cripplegate had the highest death rate during the 1665 Plague, with over 6,000 killed by the plague in three months alone. As the land commanded a poor price, cheap lodgings were easy to find. It was an area of poverty and vice, teeming with disreputable tenements, mean courts, low alehouses and dark alleys, that Fielding could have been describing when he wrote:

> Whoever indeed considers ... the great irregularity of their buildings; the immense number of lanes, alleys, courts, and bye-places; must think, that, had they been intended for the very purpose of concealment, they could scarce have been better contrived. Upon such a view, the whole appears as a vast wood or forest, in which a thief may harbour with as great security, as wild beasts do in the deserts of Africa or Arabia; for by *wandering* from one part to another, and often shifting his quarters, he may almost avoid the possibility of being discovered.[1]

Jonathan Wild set up his first thieving den just round the corner[2] and Mrs Habbiger ran a bawdy house in Turks Head Alley, which led into Grub Street.[3] *The Wandring Whore*, Number 2, 5 December 1660, lists Mrs Bull, Mrs Halfpenny and Mrs Harrison as Crafty Bawds operating from the Three Sugar-loaves, Grub-street, and 'Mrs Wroth, Grub-street' as a Common Whore. Grub Street was a place to hide from one's creditors, or the law, and was not safe at night: 'On Monday Night a Journeyman Shoemaker was set on by two Footpads in Grub-street, who knock'd him down and robb'd him of 3s.6d. and two Knives.'[4]

Grub Street also had a crude sense of humour. Ned Ward reported the existence of a Farting Club in Grub Street, 'established by a Parcell of empty *Sparkes* about thirty years since in a Publick House in Cripplegate Parish and

## 1.1 Grub Street

meet once a Week to poyson the Neighbourhood, and with their Noisy *Crepitations* attempt to outfart each other'.[5]

Unfortunately, there is little evidence to support the picturesque myth that the garrets of Grub Street played host to a colony of impoverished writers. It is known that some of the more destitute writers and printers of 'mean publications' lived in the area around Grub Street. Journalists too: Defoe was born just round the corner in Fore Street and died in Ropemakers Alley, one of the many dark passages that fed into Grub Street; and John Dunton lived not far away in Jewen Street. Little Britain, the book-publishing centre of the seventeenth and early eighteenth centuries, was only half a mile away. In the 1640s and 1650s, with the explosion of newsbooks and other unlicensed publications, the warrens surrounding Grub Street were the hiding places of fugitive printers lugging their moonshine presses from one garret to the next, trying to keep one step ahead of the authorities.

## Grub Street Hacks

The term Grub Street was first recorded in its non-geographical sense in 1630. It became more prevalent during the Civil War when both sides paid the authors of newsbooks to fight a paper war on their behalf. With the formation of political parties after the Restoration, the term became established to describe journalists, political pamphleteers and other writers of ephemeral publications who, with neither a private income nor a wealthy patron, wrote for money.

Grub Street is a metaphor for the hack writer. The word 'hack' derives from Hackney, originally meaning a horse for hire and later a prostitute, a woman for hire. Finally, it was applied to a writer for hire, a newspaper writer or a literary drudge. Paid by the line, scratching a precarious living from the lower reaches of literature, including journalism, the Grub Street hack received no public acclaim, other than the sneers and jibes of his more successful contemporaries who, by a mixture of ability and sycophancy, had found the security of a patron. His life was pictured by Hogarth in the *Distrest Poet* (Figure 1.2). His condition was described by Ned Ward as

> very much like that of a Strumpet … and if the reason be requir'd, why we betake our selves to be so Scandalous a Profession as Whoring or Pamphleteering, the same excusive Answer will serve us both, viz. that the unhappy circumstances of a Narrow Fortune, hath forced us to do that for our Subsistence.[6]

And his fate was described by Macaulay:

> To lodge in a garret up four pairs of stairs … to translate ten hours a day for the wages of a ditcher, to be haunted by bailiffs from one haunt of beggary and pestilence to another, from Grub Street to St George's Fields, and from St George's Fields to the alleys behind St Martin's Church, to sleep in a bulk in June and amidst the ashes of a glass-house in December, to die in an hospital, and to be buried in a parish vault.[7]

**1.2** *The Distrest Poet*: Hogarth's portrait of the Grub Street hack

The traditional view of the Grub Street hack as feckless, living in a garret, and scribbling furiously by rush-light to earn the next bottle of gin and to get his belongings out of pawn – the eighteenth-century equivalent of the jazz musician – is exemplified by Samuel Boyse, who wrote for the *Gentleman's Magazine*. Boyse, by all accounts a thoroughly dishonest and disreputable rogue, was generally paid by the line for his efforts as a poet, translator and literary jack-of-all-trades. He was said to be 'intoxicated whenever he had the means to avoid starving' and, 'after squandering away in a dirty manner any money which he had acquired', was known to 'pawn all his apparel'. On at least one occasion he was found shivering in his garret, naked in bed with two holes cut in his blanket so that he could write. Whenever he pawned his shirt, 'he fell upon an artificial method of supplying one. He cut some white paper in slips, which he tyed round his wrists, and in the same method supplied his neck. In this plight he frequently appeared abroad, with the added inconvenience of want of breeches.'[8]

Accounts of his death at the early age of 41 vary. One story has it that he was run over by a coach while lying drunk in the street. If this is true, it was perhaps a fitting end. I like the man, and I hope he did not suffer.

Unable to secure the custom and favour of the great, journalists stood outside polite society. In the eyes of the establishment, they were a semi-criminal class. They were vulnerable to the law, especially the law of seditious libel, and their uncertain way of life, with its irregular payment and lack of security, compelled them to live in the lower quarters of the city, such as the Grub Street area. They could only make their living in a hackney kind of way by prostituting their pens to the highest bidder: Tories one day, Whigs the next, and all the time suffering harassment from authority.

We know tantalizingly little about the anonymous journalists who wrote for the eighteenth-century newspapers. Perhaps the description of journalists in a letter to the printer in *Say's Weekly Journal* for 25 April 1767 contains some degree of fictionalized truth. The writer explains that he was sitting in the Camden coffee-house in Mitre-court, 'a house that I use because there are more news-papers taken in than at any other coffee-house in England', when his attention was drawn to two other customers:

> They seemed to be about thirty, and were dressed in that manner which is generally termed the *shabbily genteel* … that is, every article in their dress was in the newest taste, but had undergone a great deal of service, and appeared to be somewhat worse for wearing … the black stock about the neck of the shirt, rather sable at the wristbands, supported a strong supposition, that it was worn to the full as much as from necessity as inclination; as for the coat, nothing could be better brushed, the threads might be counted without the least assistance of spectacles, and it buttoned amazingly close about the body of the owner, as to do the highest credit to the taylor's ingenuity; the breeches, which formerly were a black knit, had been newly inked over, to refresh the colour, and the baging of the stockings about the ankles, easily declared, that the gentlemen were proficients in economy … [the writer describes his mounting horror when he overhears one of the customers ask the other] … how he had amused himself in the course of the week, 'Why', replied the other, 'I picked a few pockets in Fleet-street, broke open a house in High-Holborn; this evening I purpose to commit a murder in the neighbourhood of Newington, in the morning I shall set a stable on fire, and burn half a dozen horses in Ratcliffe-highway.' … the person who asked the first question, being interrogated in turn, he thus gave his companion an account of his pretty performances. 'As for me I have done a great deal more, on Monday, I ravished a girl of seven years old in Chancery-lane, and thrust out a publican's eye with a roasting-fork, in Barbican; on Tuesday I stole a child from its parents in Smithfield, and after stripping it, got five shillings from a beggar-woman for my theft, who broke its back immediately, to excite the compassion of the public; the consequences are admirable; for, on Thursday the mother cut her throat in a fit of despair, for the loss of her infant, which gave the father so terrible a shock that he is raving mad in a private repository near Islington; the same day also, I robbed a

western mail; stole the communion plate out of a church; and formed a conspiracy for an unnatural crime against a dignified clergyman' … There was no hearing any thing further, I started from my seat, and there being a good deal of company in the room, cried out, 'Gentlemen, I demand your assistance in the King's name, to apprehend the two desperate villains at this table; I can charge them both with robbery and murder, on their own confession.' … [Having secured the two men, the writer repeated to the company what he had overheard, when one of the accused exclaimed] … 'Lord, Sir, you are certainly out of your senses, or strangely mistaken in the nature of our conversation. We commit robberies and murders – no, no Sir, – we only commit them with pen and ink. We are paragraph-makers, and were merely telling each other in our usual way, what inventions we had used to gratify the curiosity of the public, during the last week, with extraordinary intelligence. Here to convince you', continued he, pulling out a parcel of papers from his pocket, full of robberies, murders, adulteries, rapes, impositions, political squibs, theatrical puffs, broken bones, and inferior casualties.

Journalism was not an honourable profession in the eyes of the establishment, nor, indeed, in the eyes of their fellow hacks, especially in Walpole's time when the newspapers entertained their readers with a glorious display of personal abuse, hack versus hack, in the battles between the ministerial and the opposition presses:

The *Common Sense* of last Saturday tells the *Daily Post* that he is a *Pyrate*, a *Pick-pocket*, and a *Highwayman* and treats his Brother-Scribler in almost as many Names, as he would do a Minister of State, a Privy Counsellor, or a Bishop … this egregious Blunderer has, in the Violence of his Passion, pulled off his Mask and discover'd himself … that he means nothing more by what he writes, than to *earn a Penny*, and get *Bread*, which he would otherwise be obliged to *steal* or *work for* … a Retailer of Scandal! a Disperser of Lies! a common Defamer! a hired, hackney, abandon'd, profligate Scribler … a Fellow that is known to be bigoted, avow'd, determined IRISH PAPIST … an infamous Vagrant … a contemptible Out-cast of Faction.[9]

By the sputtering Virulence of the Stile, I scruple not to pronounce this *Gazetteer* the Handy-Work of the political Merry-Andrew, or Jack-pudding Balance-Master … a Man might as well pretend to answer the Barking of a mad Dog, which has about as much Sense or Argument in it as can be found in this *Paper* … if we should have the Honour of hearing from thee in the same Blackguard Stile, as Rogue, Rascal or Son of a Whore, which cannot be properly answered in Print, we shall take some other Method of letting thee know a Piece of our Mind.[10]

That the little, low Emissaries of Faction, and the Hackney-Sciblers who are of no Faction, but write merely that they may Eat, should be as scurrilous and abusive as if there was not an Oaken Stick, a Blanket, or a Horse-Pond in the World; and should, from their Garrets and lurking Holes, pelt even Persons of the Highest Rank with all the Dirt and Excrement that they can rake out of their Kennels … when I saw to what a Height of Impudence the Fellow that writes the Journal, most improperly called *Common Sense*, was arrived … I can't say I was at all

> surprised … it was no more than what might be expected from an infamous Miscreant, who has spent his whole Life in the very Sink of Scandal; who has wallowed in the Mire of Calumny and Defamation ever since he left the *Bogs* where he was ingender'd, and came naked and starved, to seek his Fortune in this Country, as a Knight of the Post, a Bully to a Brothel, a Puff to a Gaming-Table, or a Hackney-Writer, as Chance and Time should direct.[11]

Even in the relative calm after the fall of Walpole, the rough and tumble of Grub Street infighting continued. Henry Fielding, who used the *Jacobite's Journal* (1747–48) to attack opposition journalists, received a taste of his own medicine when an opposition journal described him as

> A needy vagrant, who has long hunted after fortunes, lived on kept mistresses, scored deep at taverns, pox'd them all round, hackney'd for booksellers and news papers; lampoon'd the virtuous, ridicul'd all the inferior clergy in the dry unnatural character of parson *Adams*, related the adventures of footmen and wrote the lives of thief-catchers, bilked every lodging for 10 years altogether, and every alehouse and every chandler's shop in every neighbourhood, defrauded and reviled all his acquaintance, and meriting and possessing universal infamy and contempt.[12]

The view from outside Grub Street was no more respectful. In May 1756 an anonymous pamphleteer described journalists as

> dastardly mongrel insects, scribbling incendiaries, starveling savages, human shaped tygers, senseless yelping curs, blushless caitliffs, common plunderers, grovelling and treacherous, heartless thieves, vipers, doubly malignant wretches, ribbalds, growling groveling bipeds, scandal yelping crew, varlets lavish of falsehood, rogues, drones, logger-heads, journalistical fire-eaters, superlative coxcombs, crack-brained dealers in absurdity, drivellers, oafs, cubs, jack a lanterns, hounds, pragmatical ghosts of entity, crawling vermin, unnatural fry of *barbarous insects*, one is a heartless witling that choaks himself by *swallowing a flight*, another is a little griping understrapper with a dirt raking mind, and *spurious* breast. It is no wonder that by creatures so strange, strange crimes have been committed, that they should be guilty of cannibal *libertinism*, that they should *gall a reeking wound*, and produce horrorous effects, that they should throw out *random hints* which *appear* to a man's *bowels* and *brains* to be the transports of savages, that they should be big with their own *downfall*, and commit *intellectual mendicity* in *buffoonist* terms.[13]

Perhaps Samuel Johnson, a journalist himself, should have the last word:

> A news-writer is a man without virtue who writes lies at home for his own profit. To these compositions is required neither genius nor knowledge, neither industry nor sprightliness, but contempt of shame and indifference to truth are absolutely necessary.[14]

Although maligned, venal and brimful of human failings, the men and women of Grub Street are the heroes of this book. Risking prison, the pillory and even death to publish the events of the day, they entertained and informed their readers and enraged the Establishment by having the audacity to make free with their opinions, the audacity to criticize the powerful and the audacity to behave as if the conduct of government was any of their business. The pioneers of Grub Street laid the foundations of Fleet Street and the modern newspaper.

## Requiem

Sadly, Grub Street is no more. Probably due to the connotations surrounding its name it was rechristened Milton Street in 1830 – named after a builder, not the poet. Most of it now lies beneath the Barbican, which buries the symbol of the noisy, squabbling, scribbling, vibrant community of hack writers and transient printers that once was Grub Street. All that remains of the original street plan is a bland hundred yards or so of concrete and glass office blocks. The only buildings left on a human scale are St Paul's Tavern and the wall of Whitbread's brewery – some small, but appropriate, consolation for the drunken ghosts of Grub Street.

## Notes

1 Fielding, Henry (1751), *An Enquiry into the Causes of the late Increase in Robbers.*
2. Hanson, Gerald (1970), *Thief-Taker General,* London: Hutchinson.
3. Burford, E. J. (1990), *London: The Synfulle Citie,* London: Hale.
4. *Chester Weekly-Journal,* 6 October 1731.
5. Ward, Ned, *The Secret History of Clubs,* 1709.
6. Ward, Ned, *A Trip to Jamaica,* 1698.
7. Macaulay drew heavily on Johnson's *Life of Savage* for some of these images.
8. Cibber, Theophilus (1753), *The Lives of the Poets of Great Britain and Ireland.*
9. *Daily Gazetteer,* 24 March 1739.
10. *Common Sense,* 7 April 1739.
11. *Daily Gazetteer,* 17 April 1739.
12. *Old England,* 3 March 1748.
13. *A satyrical review of the manifest falsehoods and absurdities hitherto published, concerning the earthquake at Lisbon, to which is annexed an authentic account of it, and the present state of that capital. By a Man of Business.* Author unknown, May 1756.
14. From the issue of the *Idler* printed in *Payne's Universal Chronicle* for 11 November 1758.

# Chapter 2

# The Beginnings of the English Newspaper, 1513–1695

There is no humour in my Countrymen which I am more inclined to wonder at, than in their general thirst after News.

The *Spectator*, 8 August 1712

Before the invention of printing, and for many years afterwards, people got what news they could by word of mouth. From London and the ports, returning soldiers and sailors, merchants and other travellers spread their news inland. Their stories were picked up by pedlars, ballad singers, travelling players and drovers who added their own gloss as they travelled from town to town. Eventually, distorted beyond recognition, the news slowly made its uncertain way down country tracks through villages and hamlets to the cottage hearth.

The wealthy were slightly better informed. If they had friends at court, those friends were expected to keep them regularly in touch with the latest court gossip and the news of foreign wars. Some families even employed their own news-writers – embryo journalists – to send them news from the court to their country estates.

On the continent there was a commercial trade in handwritten newsletters, notably those produced by the Augsburg banking house of Fugger in the sixteenth century. These newsletters provided political and economic information. They circulated between the headquarters and branch offices of the major trading organizations and to others who were willing to pay for this service.

In the very early years of printing, the audience for books was limited to the Court, lawyers, clerics and scholars. Their law books, liturgical works, plays, romances and grammars posed no threat to authority.[1] However, by the early sixteenth century, there was a wider range of material for audiences outside that limited circle. This coincided with the impact of the new ideas of the Reformation that were spreading in from Europe, and the political, religious and social upheaval as society was evolving from feudalism to capitalism.

By increasing the number of bibles available for individual study, printing had made Protestantism possible. Protestantism, with its emphasis on literacy, education and the individual conscience, gave rise to a theoretical resistance to constitutional authority. Later, the puritan ideology of literacy led to a new class of reader, free from the orthodoxies of a university, or even a grammar school, education. By the middle of the seventeenth century, around 80 per cent of the male population in London and 30 per cent elsewhere are estimated to have been literate.[2] They interpreted the Bible and other printed material by their own lights. Believing in the priesthood of every believer, they began actively to question and challenge political and religious authority.[3]

## Early Press Controls

The printing press was a relatively cheap and portable piece of equipment. With literacy fast expanding beyond the narrow confines of Caxton's day, a press in the wrong hands could be a powerful force for subversion. From Henry VIII's time onwards, the state began to regard the printing press as a dangerous weapon. It imposed such stringent controls that, from the time William Caxton established his press in the precincts of Westminster Abbey in 1476, it took nearly 150 years before the first regular news publication was started.

In 1534 printing was restricted to English subjects. This emphasized that printing was firmly within the royal jurisdiction. Strict controls were imposed on imported books to prevent the distribution of material that was unacceptable to the Crown on political or religious grounds. As the religious settlement of the country at any one time was determined by the government of the day, works of religious controversy were automatically regarded as works of political criticism. In 1538 Henry VIII decreed that all printed matter had to be approved by the Privy Council or its deputies before publication. By 1581 the publication of seditious material had become a capital offence.

However, the most effective form of control was to use the trade itself. Queen Mary granted a Royal Charter to the Company of Stationers in 1557, which restricted the right of owning a press to a member of the Company. Under Queen Elizabeth the Company became a partner with the state in assisting with pre-publication licensing.[4] The stationers derived great advantages from these arrangements. The record of licences in the register at Stationers' Hall led to the practice, and thus to the law, of copyright, which was reinforced by the Stationers' powers of search. The ruling oligarchy of the Company benefited from the restrictions on the number of presses by subsequent Star Chamber decrees. This kept the profitable business of printing in the hands of the fortunate few. With their privileges derived directly from the state, they were less likely to publish material that would disturb this cosy relationship.

The trade in printed news was subject to even tighter controls. To publish news was seen as an interference with the affairs of state which would expose the workings of government to the giddy multitude and undermine the relationship between governors and governed. Even 'spoken news or rumour' was prohibited by Edward VI's proclamations of 1547 and 1549. Printed news was regarded as a matter of the royal prerogative, and royal permission had to be obtained before any news could be published. This view was reinforced as late as 1680 when the judges ruled 'that his Majesty may by law prohibit the printing and publishing of all newsbooks and pamphlets of news whatsoever not licensed by his Majesty's authority as manifestly tending to the breach of the peace and the disturbance of the kingdom'.[5]

## 'Wonderful and Strange Newes'

The only form of printed news that was permitted was the 'relation', a rather stale narrative of a single event. For over a hundred years single pamphlets, ballads and broadsides containing news of domestic or foreign affairs appeared at uncertain intervals and were sold at the north door of St Paul's Cathedral and at the major country fairs. Relations fell into two categories: government propaganda; and items of 'Wonderful and Strange Newes', which steered clear of religion and politics.

The first category included the earliest known relation, the illustrated pamphlet *Hereafter ensue the trewe encountre or Batayle lately don betwene Englade and Scotlande*, a contemporary account of the Battle of Flodden 'emprynted by me Richard Faques dwllyng near poulys church-yerde' in September 1513. Other titles in this category included:

*Answere made by the Kynges Hyghness to the petitions of the rebelles in Yorkshire* (1536)

*A declaration conteynyng the just causes of the present warre with the Scottis* (1542)

*The passage of our most drad soveraign lady Quene Elyzabeth to Westminster the daye before her coronacion* (1558).

The second category of relations, with its sensational subject matter and eye-catching titles, was designed to tempt the reader to part with his groat:

*Hevy newes of an horryble earthquake* (1542)

*A straunge and terrible wunder wrought in the parish church of Bongay* (1577) (in a great tempest of violente raine, lightning, and thunder … an horrible shaped thing [was] sensibly perceived of the people then and there assembled, which in the twinkling of an eye, mortally wrung the necks of several worshippers)

*Wonderful and Strange Newes out of Suffolke and Essex where it Rayned Wheat the Space of Six or Seven Miles* (1583)

*Strange newes of a monster borne at Adlington in Lancashire* (1613)

*True and wonderfull, A discourse relating to a strange and monstrous serpent (or dragon) Lately discovered, and yet living… In Sussex, two miles from Horsam… this present Month of August, 1614*
(which slaughtered 'Men and Cattell, by his strong and violent Poyson').

This last title was published by the enterprising John Trundle, a prolific purveyor of newsbooks concerning the supernatural. Not content with publishing unbelievable stories that must have stretched the credibility of even the most superstitious reader, Trundle was not averse to rehashing old stories in the guise of up-to-date, or at least very recent, news. His *A Miracle, of Miracles* (1614) contained three reports: a miraculous prophesy by 'a pore Countrey Maide … at Rostorphe in Germanie … the first of October last, 1613', which was undoubtedly based on *A moste Strange and Rare example of a maide, happeninge at a Towne called Rostorphe in Jermanie*, published in 1580; a woman possessed of the devil, which was copied virtually word for word from *A true and most Dreadfull discourse of a woman possessed with the Devill*, published in 1584 (the devil in the shape of a headless bear 'did thrust the womans hed betwixt her legges, and so roulled her in a rounde compasse like an Hoope … thorow three Chambers, and downe a high paire of staiers'); and an account of a flood in Lincolnshire that Trundle had already covered in his newsbook, *Lamentable Newes out of Lincolne-shire*.

Another of Trundle's efforts was *Anthony Painter the Blaspheming Caryer. Who sunke into the ground up to the neck, and there stood two days and two nights, and not to bee drawne out by the strength of Horses or digged out by the help of Man: and there dyed the 3. of November, 1613. Also the punishment of Nicholas Mesle a most wicked blasphemer. Reade and Tremble.* This was one of many newsbooks that gave examples of God's wrath against blasphemers or drunkards or Sabbath breakers, or dreadful warnings that God will avenge the sinfulness of the nation. In many cases the catchpenny title promised more than the text delivered, and the brief news story was almost completely smothered by acres of pious moralizing.

## The First Newsbooks

Despite their entertainment value, these irregular and uncontroversial publications were not sufficient to satisfy the 'general thirst after News' from the strong and ambitious merchant class that came into being with England's rise as a maritime and commercial power. This was especially so after the start of the Thirty Years War in 1618.

The war, seen as a struggle between Protestant and Catholic for the domination of Europe, was of intense interest to the new, and overwhelmingly Protestant, middle class. A number of English volunteers went over to fight for the Protestant cause. Those at home were frustrated by the lack of news of what was going on. They looked with envy at their continental neighbours who had for some time enjoyed a regular news service from a number of weekly publications, known as corantos, mainly from Holland and Germany. They wanted the same over here.

This was initially supplied from Holland. On 2 December 1620 George Veseler, an Amsterdam printer, produced the first of a number of irregular corantos for the English market. Untitled, it began, '*The new tydings out of Italie are not yet com.*' They were English-language translations of Dutch corantos but with the English news omitted to make them acceptable to authority. Coranto, from the French *Courante* – running – meant a publication with different items of news running together to describe the events of a given period of time, also a publication of news which is current or running on – in other words, a periodical.

Although no copies have survived, it is likely that Thomas Archer of Pope's Head Alley, Cornhill produced the first coranto printed in England in early 1621 as we know that he was sent to prison that year for publishing a coranto without a licence.

The earliest surviving copy of an English coranto is Nathaniel Butter's *Corante, or, News from Italy, Germany, Hungarie, Spaine and France* dated 24 September 1621 and 'printed for N.B.', either Nathaniel Butter or Nicholas Bourne. This was the first of a series of six single-sheet corantos, the last of which was dated 'October the 22. 1621'. The next year saw the publication by Nicholas Bourne and Thomas Archer of the first regular weekly coranto, the *Weekely Newes from Italy, Germanie, Hungaria, Bohemia, the Palatinate, France and the Low Countries.* From its miscellaneous contents and periodicity of production, it is regarded as the true forerunner of the English newspaper. Its first issue was dated 'The 23. of May. 1622.' Subsequent issues appeared in a numbered series. Numbering helped to maintain sales by creating the sense of news as a continuing activity. Later items in the sequence would develop and qualify what had gone before. Yet each issue would report that something new had happened. In order to keep informed, the reader had to maintain the sequence:

> A coranto-coiner … ever leaves his pages doubtfull, as if they were some more intimate secrecies of State, closing his sentence abruptly with – hereafter you shall heare more. Which words, I conceive, hee onely useth as baites, to make the appetite of the Reader more eager for the next week's pursuit.[6]

The *Weekely Newes* and its competitors were pamphlets conforming to the style of the printed book, and are thus known as 'newsbooks'. Under the tight censorship of Archbishop Laud and the Star Chamber newsbooks were only allowed to print foreign news – domestic news was forbidden. At a time when religion was politics, and politics religion, the newsbooks had to tread very carefully. People who published opinions contrary to those of the archbishop were heavily fined and imprisoned, and, in some cases, were branded or suffered some other form of mutilation. William Prynne and was branded SL (Seditious Libeller) on both cheeks and had his ears sawn off.

During the period 1620–42, it is reckoned that about one thousand corantos were issued by the same combination of stationers – Archer, Butter, Bourne, William Sheffard, Nathaniel Newberry and Bartholomew Downes – sometimes working together, other times in competition. Although they were regular serial publications, the corantos did not always appear on the same day of each week. If the ships containing the Dutch newsbooks were delayed by high seas, the printers would defer the publication day; if there was little to report, they would miss a week altogether; and if news was plentiful they would issue two or three numbers in the same week.

According to Ben Jonson's *Staple of News* (1626), corantos cost a groat (4d.). Purchasers were therefore restricted to a narrow class who could afford to buy weekly copies on a regular basis and were sufficiently interested in the affairs of Europe to do so. Their circulation may have been as low as 200 per issue.[7] However, it has been argued that conventional estimates of the circulation of corantos are too conservative. The evidence of the expansion of the businesses of those involved in coranto making during the 1620s from the records of the Stationers' Company and the employment of Captain Thomas Gainsford as a news editor points to their commercial success. References to news from corantos in journals and diaries indicate that corantos were regularly distributed outside London.[8]

The corantos had such low sales because people were more interested in the political and religious tensions at home. There was an increasing political awareness amongst all classes, particularly in London, and a popular suspicion of the king and his bishops. King Charles had been ruling without a parliament since 1629 and had introduced illegal taxes. He had taken a French Catholic wife and appointed William Laud as Archbishop of Canterbury. Laud imposed innovations in the ritual of the Church that seemed to be taking England closer to Catholicism. To many, the king, the court and the bishops seemed to be riding roughshod over the rest of the country.

The tensions in society at large were mirrored by tensions within the Stationers' Company. On the one hand there were the master printers and the copy owning booksellers whose control of the trade rested on the authority of the Crown expressed through the Star Chamber. Understandably, most were royalist sympathizers. On the other hand, there was everybody else, especially the journeymen printers and apprentices who had no hope of legally owning a press while the restrictions on the number of presses were still in place.

## Civil War Newsbooks

The abolition of the Star Chamber and the Court of High Commission in July 1641, and the breakdown of royal authority at the onset of the Civil War, shattered the chains of censorship. Without the authority of the Star Chamber, the Stationers' Company was powerless to control the moonshine presses that seemed to have sprung out of nowhere. Copyright melted into thin air and the Stationers' register was virtually ignored. With one bound the press was free.

The first person to take advantage of this new freedom was one John Thomas, a publisher of cheap pamphlets. He produced the first newsbook to contain domestic news, *The Heads of Severall Proceedings in this Present Parliament*, on 29 November 1641, later renamed *A Perfect Diurnall of the Passages in Parliament*. The use of the word 'Diurnall' does not mean that it was a daily publication. It was a weekly summary of the daily proceedings in Parliament. The *Perfect Diurnall* was written by Samuel Pecke. Unlike his predecessors, who were mere translators of continental newsbooks, Pecke actually had to go out and find his own news. He can, therefore, be acclaimed as the first English diurnalist, or journalist. He was described as 'a bald-headed buzzard … with a Hawks nose, a meagre countenance and long runagate legs, constant in nothing but wenching, lying and drinking… you may meet with him late in the night … and seldom walks without his she-intelligencer'[9] – the Lunchtime O'Booze of the seventeenth century.

As with all new industries, a crowd of entrepreneurs will leap in and try to grab a slice of the action. Many will be eliminated fairly early on in the game, leaving the remaining players to consolidate their market share. So it was with the newsbooks. In 1642 there were 64 separate titles, of which 30 appeared for only one issue. In 1643 the number of titles had reduced to 39, and by 1645 there was less than 30 titles in circulation.[10]

The *Perfect Diurnall* gave rise to a number of pirates wishing to cash in on its success by stealing its title for their own publications. By August 1642 there were seven different *Perfect Diurnalls* and one *True and Perfect Diurnal*. In the issue of the *Perfect Diurnall* for 26 December 1642 to 2 January 1643 it was felt necessary to issue the following warning: 'Courteous Reader, take heed of a false and scandalous Diurnal which is this day printed & fashioned with such a modell like this, by a company of Grub-street mercenary fellowes.'

Unlike the news in the corantos, which was of direct importance to only a very restricted group, the events recorded in the Civil War newsbooks affected everybody. At a penny or twopence per copy, they were available to a much wider class of reader. Nehemiah Wallington, a wood turner, recorded in his journal, 'these little pamphlets of weekly news about my house … were so many thieves that had stolen away my money before I was aware of them'.[11] The average print run is thought to have been 500 copies – at least twice that of the corantos – and some titles sold 1,500 copies.[12]

Pressures to get the newsbooks printed in time for publication day and the print runs needed to meet the demand for the more popular titles were such that one press could not cope on its own. Differences in the typesetting of two copies of the same issue of Samuel Pecke's *Perfect Diurnall* and certain other titles were quite common. These indicate either that the papers were printed simultaneously on two presses or that another printer was producing pirate copies as soon as the first issues hit the streets, before that week's news went stale.

The next stage in the development of the newsbook was the introduction of collections of reports from a number of different sources. These were known as 'passages' after the title of the first of its kind, *Some Speciall and Considerable Passages from London, Westminster, Portsmouth, Warwicke, Coventry, and other places. Collected for the use of all those that desire to be truely informed*, dated 16 August 1642 (Figure 2.1).

This is the paragraph of news datelined 'Randevous at Worcester, Septemb. 24.' from the issue of *Speciall Passages* for 27 September 1642:

> The unseasonablenesse of the weather in our march with the Artillery, extreamly retarded our comming to *Worcester*, which prevented us of taking the Cavaliers, though not of the City of *Worcester*, which our Horse obtained with much Honour, though with great difficulty, and disadvantage; for (as I have it from my Comrade that was in the fight) Prince *Robert* with 11. Troopes came to Worcester, and joyned with Sir *John Byron*: We had about ten Troopes neere the City, though not in a body, Prince *Robert* sallies out of the City, and puts his Horse in Battalia, on a faire Meadow, and seemed to challenge an Encounter; Colonell *Sandis* with his Regiment of Horse, Captaine *Wingate*, and Captaine *Hales*, were about halfe a quarter of a mile, and had no passage to the Enemy, but in a Lane, where they could not march five a breast: yet so keene Colonell *Sandis* was, that he adventured to march up, and charged the Prince, which he did so effectually, that eleven of them quickly fell: Prince *Rupart*, or Prince *Maurice* being sore wounded in the head or on his hand: Commissary Wilmott he comes and relieves Prince *Robert*, and Colonell *Sandis* and he had a single Encounter, Colonell *Sandis* received a sore wound, but we hope not mortall: and run his Sword up to the Hilts in Commissary *Wilmots* body, as it is reported, then Captaine *Wingates* Troope came on, and did most desperate service, and after him Captaine *Fines* and Captaine *Hale*, then came up Captaine *Austins* Troope, who could not all this while get out

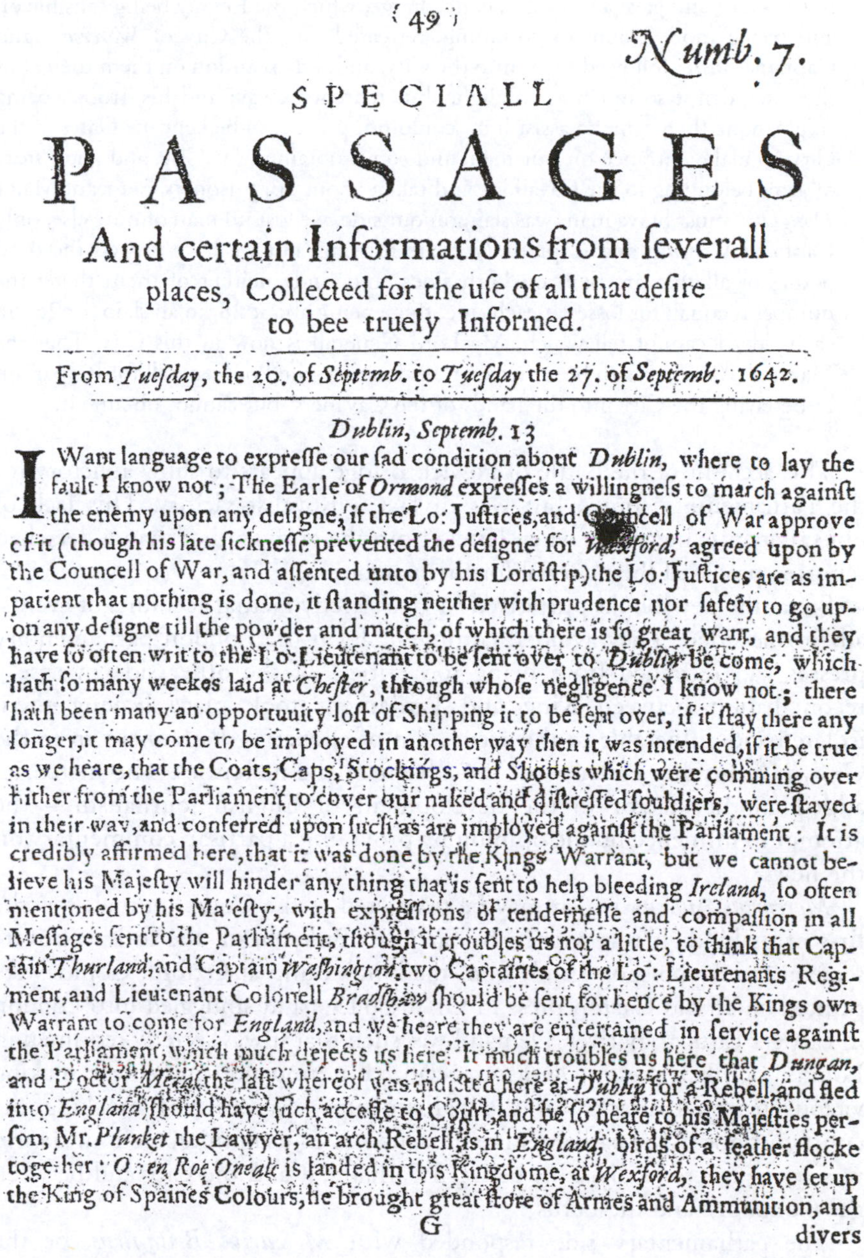

(49)

*Numb.* 7.

SPECIALL

# PASSAGES

And certain Informations from ſeverall places, Collected for the uſe of all that deſire to bee truely Informed.

From *Tueſday*, the 20. of *Septemb.* to *Tueſday* the 27. of *Septemb.* 1642.

*Dublin, Septemb.* 13

I Want language to expreſſe our ſad condition about *Dublin*, where to lay the fault I know not; The Earle of *Ormond* expreſſes a willingneſs to march againſt the enemy upon any deſigne, if the Lo: Juſtices, and Councell of War approve of it (though his late ſickneſſe prevented the deſigne for *Wexford*, agreed upon by the Councell of War, and aſſented unto by his Lordſhip) the Lo: Juſtices are as impatient that nothing is done, it ſtanding neither with prudence nor ſafety to go upon any deſigne till the powder and match, of which there is ſo great want, and they have ſo often writ to the Lo: Lieutenant to be ſent over to *Dublin* be come, which hath ſo many weekes laid at *Cheſter*, through whoſe negligence I know not; there hath been many an opportuuity loſt of Shipping it to be ſent over, if it ſtay there any longer, it may come to be imployed in another way then it was intended, if it be true as we heare, that the Coats, Caps, Stockings, and Shooes which were comming over hither from the Parliament to cover our naked and diſtreſſed ſouldiers, were ſtayed in their way, and conferred upon ſuch as are imployed againſt the Parliament: It is credibly affirmed here, that it was done by the Kings Warrant, but we cannot believe his Majeſty will hinder any thing that is ſent to help bleeding *Ireland*, ſo often mentioned by his Ma'eſty, with expreſſions of tenderneſſe and compaſſion in all Meſſages ſent to the Parliament, though it troubles us not a little, to think that Captain *Thurland*, and Captain *Waſhington*, two Captaines of the Lo: Lieutenants Regiment, and Lieutenant Colonell *Bradſhaw* ſhould be ſent for hence by the Kings own Warrant to come for *England*, and we heare they are entertained in ſervice againſt the Parliament, which much dejects us here. It much troubles us here that *Dungan*, and Doctor *Meca* (the laſt whereof was indicted here at *Dublin* for a Rebell, and fled into *England*) ſhould have ſuch acceſſe to Court, and be ſo neare to his Majeſties perſon, Mr. *Plunket* the Lawyer, an arch Rebell, is in *England*, birds of a feather flocke together: *Owen Roe Oneale* is landed in this Kingdome, at *Wexford*, they have ſet up the King of Spaines Colours, he brought great ſtore of Armes and Ammunition, and

G

divers

**2.1** *Speciall Passages*, an early Civil War newsbook

> of the Lane, and gave a most desperate charge, which the Enemy being sensible of, and seeing more Troopes a comming, retreated into the City of *Worcester*, and Captaine *Austin* followed them into the City, and did execution on them there, but they stayed not so much as to alight, but marched away; and his Troope being single, none then came to assist him, could not pursue, so he kept the Gates of the City, to make entrance for our men, and so we obtained the City, and good store of arms belonging to the Cavaliers, and taken about 26. prisoners: Sergeant Major *Douglas*, a most brave man, was slain on our side, we lost no man of note else, only Captaine *Wingate*, and Captain *Fines* are missing, but we have viewed the dead bodies of all that are slain on both sides, and finde neither of them there; the number is equall for losse on each side, there being about 28. in all slain, or 28. on each side, I cannot tell which: My Lord Generall is now in this City. That the Maior of *Worcester* hath been twice on his knees to the Lo. Generall for his pardon in betraying the City into the hands of the Cavaliers, but cannot obtaine it.

This account of the Battle of Powick Bridge appears to show a victory for the Parliamentary forces, but was in fact a Royalist victory. This lack of objectivity was inevitable when letters from the army, rather than a detached reporter, provided the material for the newsbooks.

So far the newsbooks purported to give strictly factual accounts of events, albeit one-sided. They avoided comment. Even the London parliamentary presses had refrained from being too critical of the other side in case a reconciliation between King and Parliament took place leaving them isolated and vulnerable to the accusation of alienating Parliament from the Crown. Neutrality ended with the advent of the mercuries. The mercuries added another factor to the development of English journalism – the attempt to influence public opinion by providing a partisan commentary on the news.

*Mercurius Aulicus*, which may be translated as the Court Journal, was the first of its kind. It was written by Sir John Birkenhead, the former private secretary to Archbishop Laud, from the king's camp at Oxford. Copies were printed on an old Caxton press in Oriel College and smuggled into London in carriers' carts or by river. Demand was such that it was secretly reprinted in London on illicit presses. *Aulicus* specialized in innuendo and smear, making vicious personal attacks on the parliamentary leaders and mocking the contradictions in the parliamentary newsbooks. In its opinion section, *Aulicus* was trying to create divisions between Parliament and the City and between the Commons and the Lords.

The parliamentary side responded with *Mercurius Britanicus*, or the People's Paper. Originally edited by Captain Thomas Audley, it was soon taken over by his assistant, Marchamont Nedham, 'a tall, gaunt figure, perpetually stooping from shortness of sight, with a hook nose, and two rings dangling from his pierced ears when not in pawn', who had 'a publique Brothel in his Mouth'.[13] John Goodwin, the puritan preacher, described

Nedham as having 'a foul mouth, which Satan hath opened against the truth and mind of God', and being 'a person of an infamous and unclean character'.

From 1643 to 1645 the public were entertained by the exchange of insults between Nedham and Birkenhead. Here is Nedham addressing Birkenhead:

> Thou mathematicall liar, that framest lies of all dimensions, long, broad and profound lies … the quibling pricklouse every weeke … I tell thee thou art a knowne notorious forger: and though I will not say thou art (in thine own language, the sonne of an Egyptian whore), yet all the world knowes thou art an underling pimpe to the whore of Babylon, and thy conscience an arrant prostitute for base ends.[14]

The most famous example of Nedham's malicious style was his hue and cry after King Charles:

> If any man can bring any tale or tiding of a wilfull King, which has gone astray these foure yeares from his Parliament, with a guilty Conscience, bloody Hands, a Heart full of broken Vowes and Protestations: if these marks be not sufficient, there is another in the Mouth; for bid him speak, and you will soon know him.[15]

The reference to the mouth was a cruel dig at the king's stammer.

When *Aulicus* ceased publication in 1645, Nedham was lost without Birkenhead to do battle with. Frustrated that his powers of invective were no longer in demand, lacking the tact and agility to satisfy the competing factions of Commons, Lords, Army, Independents and Presbyterians, he continued *Britanicus* for another year. In 1646 he was jailed by the House of Lords and prohibited from writing any pamphlet in the future, for publishing 'divers passages between the two Houses of Parliament, and other scandalous particulars not fit to be tolerated' – calling the king to a 'strict account' for the blood shed in the Civil War. Unable to make a living from journalism on the Parliamentary side, and fearing (incorrectly) that the Presbyterians would gain the upper hand over the Independents and subject the country to a more rigorous religious discipline than even that of the hated bishops, he changed sides and appeared in Oxford in 1647 editing *Mercurius Pragmaticus* for the king. Following the defeat of the Royalists, he was arrested in 1649. Despite having called Cromwell 'Coppernose', 'Nose Almighty' and 'the Town bull of Ely' in *Pragmaticus*, he was forgiven and changed sides yet again. He wrote two official newsbooks, *Mercurius Politicus* (1650–60; Figure 2.2), for which John Milton acted as overseeing editor in its first two years, and the *Publick Intelligencer* (1655–60). At the Restoration Nedham fled to Holland. But a few months later he obtained his pardon 'for money given to a hungry courtier', and was allowed to return to England where he disappeared from public view. There was, however, a surprising sequel. During the Exclusion

[981] **Numb.62.**

# *Mercurius Politicus.*

## Comprising the summe of all Intelligence, with the Affairs and Designs now on foot in the three Nations of *England*, *Ireland*, and *Scotland*.

### In defence of the Common-wealth, and for Information of the People.

——*Ita vertere Seria.* {Hor. de Ar. Poet

From *Thursday* August 7. to *Thursday* August 14. 1651.

SEE now the fruits of Mr *Love's* godly Ministry! for he hath lived to see the day, and receiv tydings of his *yong Masters* being mounted, and upon a march in *England*; for which wee are very much bound to him, and all the Fellow-labourers of his *Faction*; for, they were the men, by whose perswasions the *Tyrant*, and his *Scotish Retinue*, were drawn to an union for the ruine of *England*, as appeared to all the World upon the late Tryals of the *Conspirators*. But whatsoever the issue of things may bee, neither they nor their Friends will receive comfort by the bargain, should they survive the decision, to see a successe answerable to their hopes and wishes: For, however, they may flatter themselves with Phansies of Favor from that *accursed Family*; yet (if the Fury take its course) the *Cloud* that is now gathering, will showre down an equall portion of *Revenge*, upon Them and their For-

Hhhhh tunes

**2.2** Marchamont Nedham's *Mercurius Politicus*

crisis, the government paid Nedham to write five pamphlets attacking Shaftesbury's republicanism.

The 1640s and 1650s were exciting times in the history of journalism. A number of developments took place very quickly. Freed from the shackles of press restrictions, a great jumble of assorted *Diurnalls*, *Passages*, *Mercuries*, *Intelligencers*, *Posts*, *Spies* and *Scouts* appeared on the streets. Over 300 different titles came into existence during this period, some just for one issue, and others of quite long duration. Thirty-three titles lasted a year or more. This great vitality in the press was spurred on by the events of the war and by the fragmentation of opinion into opposing political factions and religious sects, each with different and fresh ideas about how society should be organized.

This fragmentation of opinion was reflected in the organization of the press. The Royalist viewpoint was represented by *Mercurius Aulicus*, *Mercurius Melancholicus* ('The King shall enjoy his owne againe and the Royall throne shall be arraied with the glorious presence of that mortall Deity'), *Mercurius Elencticus* ('Communicating the Unparallell'd Proceedings of the Rebels at West-minster, The Head Quarters and other Places, Discovering their Designs, Reproving their Crimes, and Advising the Kingdome'), *Mercurius Rusticus* and others.

Most London newsbooks supported Parliament, but from different viewpoints. By identifying and then appealing to specific audiences, journalists aimed to generate such brand loyalty that their readers would buy the next weeks' issues. In the way that papers nowadays will label a story 'Exclusive' to try to attract buyers, newsbooks attempted to flatter their readers that they were privy to special information that had taken great pains to acquire. Newsbooks reflected this in their titles. The *Spie* had gone under cover to obtain the news. The *Parliament Scout*, the *Faithful Scout*, the *Impartial Scout* and the *Kingdomes Weekly Scout* had been sent ahead at great danger to scout out the news and bring it back to their readers.

Even the Levellers had a newsbook: the *Moderate* (?July 1648–September 1649). It was produced by Gilbert Mabbott who was also, incredibly, a licenser. John Harris, formerly a stage-player, ran a travelling press following the army on its campaigns. He wrote and printed a newsbook, *Mercurius Militaris* (10 October – 21 November 1649) for the Agitators, the Leveller faction in the army. According to John Crouch, Harris was convicted in 1654 of forging Cromwell's signature and seal and of obtaining £900 by it, and lived to tell the tale.[16] He was hanged for theft and burglary at St Mary Axe in September 1660.

Finally, there was the series of semi-pornographic newsbooks produced by John Crouch: *The Man in the Moon* (1649–50); *Mercurius Democritus* (1652–53); and *Mercurius Fumigosus* (1654–55), which contained a mixture of genuine news and dirty jokes disguised as news.

Although the content of the Civil War newsbooks had moved on considerably from the rather staid productions of Bourne, Butter and Archer, their physical appearance remained broadly the same – small-format, book-like pamphlets, usually of eight pages. The only significant physical development was that a masthead followed by news on the front page replaced the title page of the old corantos.

Their conformity with the established book format extended to continuous pagination. For example, the pages of *Perfect Occurrences* for 3 August to 10 August 1649 are numbered 1209 to 1216. This was for those who wanted to keep their copies and have them bound at the end of the year as a history of their own times.

Newsbooks were sold on the streets by semi-destitute female hawkers, known as Mercury Women. One of the most famous characters of early journalism was the spy, Elizabeth Alkin, otherwise known as 'Parliament Joan'. She acted the part of a Mercury Woman, but in addition she actually wrote and produced her own newsbook. This had a Royalist title, *Mercurius Scoticus; or, the Royal Messenger*. She hawked this on the streets and, having won the confidence of her customers, she got them to reveal the whereabouts of Royalist moonshine presses. When the gullible purchasers got home they found to their chagrin that the *Royal Messenger* contained nothing but praise for Cromwell. Other titles printed for Elizabeth Alkin included the *Impartial Scout*, the *Moderne Intelligencer* and *Mercurius Anglicus*.

Not everyone was delighted with the new freedom of the press. As early as 1642, the author of *A Presse full of Pamphlets* remarked that this new breed of journalists 'perceiving their wits must be the chief means of their livelihood' and fearing that their wits

> were grown somewhat rusty, they conceived it were the safest way to scour them with wine, beer, and tobacco in some ale-house or tavern. They fill'd the pan so full of liquor that they drown'd their wits, and so producing them uncapable of good action, betook themselves to fabulous invention.

*Mercurius Anti-Mercurius* in 1648 described journalists as 'this filthy Aviary, this moth-eating crew of News-mongers … every Jack-sprat that hath but a pen in his ink-horn is ready to gather up the Excrements of the Kingdom'. Lucy Hutchinson in her *Memoirs* said they would deliberately write up a soldier's reputation for money.

Once the genie of press freedom was out of the bottle, the authorities found it very difficult to get it back in. The Stationers tried to persuade Parliament to restrict the number of presses and to reinstate their powers of prosecution to enforce copyright. They argued that 'printing is as inherent a Prerogative to the Crowne as Coining of Money', to which William Prynne replied, 'it being a blessing to all in generall from God, it ought not to be restrained to particular Companies'.[17]

Largely as a reaction to the popularity of *Mercurius Aulicus*, Parliament tried to reintroduce pre-publication licensing by making the Licensing Order of 14 June 1643

> for suppressing the great late abuses and frequent disorders in printing many false, forged, scandalous, seditious, libellous and unlicensed Papers, Pamphlets and Books, to the great defamation of religion and government … [calling for the apprehension of] … all Authors, Printers and other Persons whatsoever employed in compiling, printing, stitching, binding, publishing and dispersing of the said scandalous, unlicensed and unwarrantable Papers, Books and Pamphlets.

In the confusion of the times the Order was impossible to enforce, but it stung John Milton into writing *Areopagitica*,[18] an eloquent plea for the freedom of the press. He compared the Licensing Order with censorship in Catholic countries and the hated Star Chamber decrees:

> It will be primely to the discouragement of all learning, and the stop of Truth … by hindring and cropping the discovery that might bee yet further made in civill Wisdom … hee who kills a Man, kills a reasonable creature, God's Image; but hee who destroyes a good Booke, kills reason it selfe, kills the Image of God … if it comes to inquisitioning again and licensing, and that we are so timorous of our selvs, and so suspicious of all men, as to fear each book and the shaking of every leaf, before we know what their contents are … Lords and Commons of England, consider what Nation it is whereof ye are, and whereof ye are the governours; a Nation not slow and dull, but of a quick, ingenious and piercing spirit, acute to invent, suttle and sinewy in discours, but beneath the reach of any point the highest that human capacity can soar to … What could a man require more from a Nation so pliant and so prone to seek after knowledge? What wants there to such a towardly and pregnant soile, but wise and faithfull labourers, to make a knowing people, a Nation of Prophets, of Sages, and of Worthies? … Methinks I see in my mind a noble and puissant Nation rousing herself like a strong man after sleep, and shaking her invincible locks … Give me the liberty to know, to utter, and to argue freely according to conscience … Let [Truth] and Falshood grapple; who ever knew Truth put to the wors in a free and open encounter?

Despite Milton's rhetoric, Parliament continued its attempts to control the press. The Act against Unlicensed and Scandalous Books and Pamphlets and for the Better Regulation of Printing in 1649 and the Printing and Printers Act of 1653 had some success. But it was not until the Ordinance issued by the Protector in 1655 that the presses were finally silenced, leaving only Nedham's official newsbooks in place. After Richard Cromwell recalled the

Rump Parliament in January 1659, unofficial newsbooks sprung up again, taking sides in the struggles between the army leaders and the Commons.

The importance of the Civil War newsbooks cannot be overstated. Newsbooks of both sides demonized the other with stories of atrocities. By recording the divisions between King and Parliament, they added to them. After the advent of the mercuries, no one, however detached, reading the newsbooks could ever imagine that England was a nation at peace with itself. The reader was compelled to take sides.

## Restoration Censorship

The absolute freedom of the press in the 1640s and the relative freedom of the 1650s came to an end with the Restoration. Charles introduced the Printing Act of 1662 for 'preventing the frequent Abuses in printing seditious, treasonable, and unlicenced Books and Pamphlets, and for regulating of Printing and Printing Presses'. The 1662 Act restricted printing to the Universities of Oxford and Cambridge and to the master printers of the Stationers' Company in London. No new master printer was permitted to be created until their numbers had reduced to twenty. The Act permitted only four type-founders. (The Act is also known as the Licensing Act because it appointed licensers to assess the political loyalty of all printed material. Copy had to be submitted to the licenser for approval before it could be printed.)

In 1660 Henry Muddiman,[19] General Monck's newswriter, took Marchamont Nedham's post as official newswriter. Muddiman's *Mercurius Publicus* (Figure 2.3) and the *Parliamentary Intelligencer*[20] replaced Nedham's publications.

The problem with official newsbooks 'Published by Authority' is that they were primarily the voice of government rather than a medium for the spread of news. The 16-page *Mercurius Publicus* for 31 January to 7 February 1661 demonstrates their distorted news values. It began with the Proclamation for the Restraint of Killing, Dressing and Eating of Flesh in Lent or on Fish-Days to secure the 'sparing and increase of *Flesh-victuals* … [and the] … maintenance of the Navy and Shipping of this Realm by encouragement of *Fishermen*'. It continued with a note of the sermons preached before the Scottish Parliament, the text of two Acts of Parliament and a Proclamation by the Lords and Council in Ireland for a Solemn Humiliation on 30 January, a letter from Dorchester expressing sorrow that the Proclamation for observing 30 January as a fast day was not received, a page of advertisements for books and 'those so famous lozanges or Pectorals' made by Theophilus Buckworth of Mile-end Green as a 'soverain Antidote against the Plague', and the text of a Proclamation given at the Council-chamber in Dublin 'against the Meetings

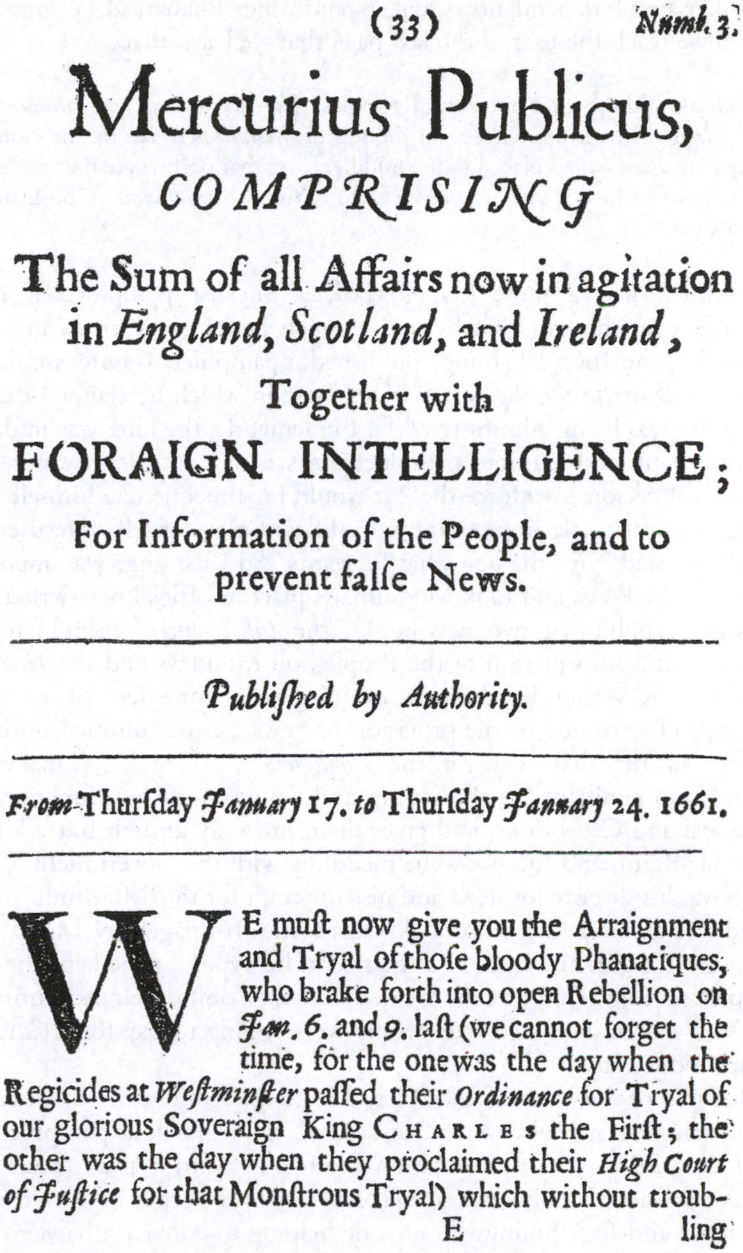

(33) *Numb.* 3.

# Mercurius Publicus,

*COMPRISING*

The Sum of all Affairs now in agitation in *England*, *Scotland*, and *Ireland*, Together with

FORAIGN INTELLIGENCE;

For Information of the People, and to prevent falſe News.

*Publiſhed by Authority.*

*From*-Thurſday *January* 17. *to* Thurſday *January* 24. 1661.

WE muſt now give you the Arraignment and Tryal of thoſe bloody Phanatiques, who brake forth into open Rebellion on *Jan.* 6. and 9. laſt (we cannot forget the time, for the one was the day when the Regicides at *Weſtminſter* paſſed their *Ordinance* for Tryal of our glorious Soveraign King CHARLES the Firſt; the other was the day when they proclaimed their *High Court of Juſtice* for that Monſtrous Tryal) which without troub-

E ling

2.3 Henry Muddiman's *Mercurius Publicus*

of Presbiterians, Independants, Quakers and other Phanatical Persons'. It is not until we reach the foot of the last page that we learn that

> The Heads of those three notorious Regicides, *Oliver Cromwell*, *John Bradshaw* and *Henry Ireton*, are set upon Poles on the top of *Westminster-Hall* by the Common Hangman: *Bradshaw* is placed in the middle, (over that part where that monstrous High Court of Justice sate) *Cromwell* and his Son in Law *Ireton* on both sides of *Bradshaw*.

Muddiman had a most jealous rival, a Royalist pamphleteer, Roger L'Estrange, who thought that he had a much better claim to Muddiman's position. In June 1663 L'Estrange published a pamphlet, *Considerations and Proposals in Order to the Regulation of the Press*, in which he claimed that the Printing Act was being administered far too leniently, the king was in danger from treasonable and seditious pamphleteers, stricter controls were necessary, and the ideal person to enforce the Act would be someone like himself. King Charles was sufficiently impressed by this blatant piece of self-advertisement. 'We will', he said, 'give the dog what he wants.' So L'Estrange was appointed Surveyor of the Press, and took Muddiman's place as official newswriter.

L'Estrange published two newsbooks: the *Intelligencer*, 'Printed for the Satisfaction and Information of the People', on Mondays and the *Newes* on Thursdays.[21] It would be difficult to imagine anyone less fit to run a newspaper. His attitude to the provision of news can be summed up by his statement in the first issue of the *Intelligencer*: '[News] … makes the Multitude too familiar with the actions and Counsels of their superiors, too pragmatical and Censorious, and gives them not only an itch but a kind of Colourable Right, and License to be meddling with the Government.'

Such was his distaste for news and his contempt for the 'Multitude' that he reduced the size of the newsbooks from the 16 pages in Muddiman's newsbooks to eight, and increased the size of his type. But he kept the price at twopence a copy. Despite this, the news-buying habit developed during the Civil Wars was so ingrained that people were willing to pay for L'Estrange's inferior productions.

In his role of Surveyor of the Press, L'Estrange scoured the bookstalls of Little Britain and St Paul's Churchyard searching for libellous pamphlets. He offered a reward of £5 for information about 'any printing press erected and being in a private place, hole or corner, contrary to the tenor of the late act of parliament', and five shillings for anyone helping to convict a hawker of an unlicensed publication. Acting on information received as a result of these bribes, he raided the home of a printer called John Twyn and seized his types. Twyn was torn from his family, carted off to Newgate and hung, drawn and quartered. Twyn's crime, in the eyes of the authorities, was compounded by his heroic refusal to divulge the name of the author.

### *The London Gazette*

L'Estrange's monopoly of printed news lasted until 1665 when the king and his court fled to Oxford to escape the plague and took Muddiman with them. L'Estrange remained in London to enforce the licensing system. As a result of his distance from the court, the unpopular *Intelligencer* had even less to report. Besides, King Charles and his courtiers were reluctant to touch his newsbooks for fear of getting the plague. Muddiman was therefore asked to write an official newsbook, the *Oxford Gazette*. Its first issue was dated 16 November 1665. When the plague abated and the court returned to London, the *Gazette* moved with it. From issue number 24 on 5 February 1666, its title changed to *The London Gazette* (Figure 2.4), the name it has retained ever since.

The *Gazette* is generally regarded by newspaper historians as the first English newspaper. This is due to its physical appearance more than its content. Printed on a single sheet of paper with the news divided into two columns, it was the first news periodical to break with the format of the newsbook. Unlike the newsbooks with eight or 16 pages that needed turning, *The London Gazette* allowed the busy merchant to see at a glance the events in Europe and could be held in one hand by the man about town in the new coffee-houses that were springing up all over London. It gave rise to the word 'newspaper', which was first recorded in 1670.

Published 'by authority', the *Gazette* gave the official presentation of foreign news that had been provided by diplomats, merchants and spies and then screened by the government. Samuel Pepys described the *Gazette* as 'very pretty, full of news with no folly in it'.[22] For all that, it was a most unsatisfactory newspaper. Bereft of domestic news, apart from royal proclamations, official announcements and shipping movements, it was a dull read whose only saving grace was its brevity.

The late Stuart regime used *The London Gazette* to help maintain social and political order. The *Gazette* projected the image of a nation at peace with itself again after the upheaval of the Civil War and the uncertainties of the Interregnum; but a nation vigilant against threats to its stability from without or within, whether from highwaymen, papists or dissenters; and most of all, as evidenced from the number of Loyal Addresses printed in the *Gazette*, a nation united in loyalty to its king and government. It referred to the king as 'his sacred Majesty' and emphasized his powers by the frequent notices announcing the arrangements for curing disease by the Royal Touch.

The virtual monopoly of the tame *London Gazette* produced a need for other news outlets. These were provided by handwritten newsletters and by the proliferation of coffee-houses that became centres for gossip and the exchange of information. Despite their great expense (an annual subscription cost about £5), the newsletters were very popular. They contained

Numb. 770.

# The London Gazette.

**Published by Authority.**

From Thursday April 3. to Munday April 7. 1673.

Whitehall, April 5.

*WE are Commanded by the Lords of His Majesties most Honourable Privy Council, appointed a Committee for the Redemption of Captives, to Publish this Ensuing List of His Majesties Subjects, who have been redeemed out of Captivity from* Algiers, Salley, &c. *by the Monies Collected within this Kingdom, by vertue of His Majesties Letters Patents, Dated the* 10th *of* August, 1670. *viz.*

*From* Algiers.

Edward Castle
Nathaniel Brown, *Carpent.*
Leonard Bing
Thomas Lange, *Gunner*
Richard Draper
Henry Tryers
Stephen Hazwell
Benj. Barefoot, *Cooper*
Samuel Hammond
William Whitcomb
Zachary Archer
Richard Nelson
John Milton
Peter Stukeley
John Day, *Carpent.*
Thomas Pitman
John Collins
Daniel Coachman
John Greeves
John Argent *Boatesw.*
Henry Nance
John Tonstal
Jeremy Armiger
John Snel
George Swedeland
Thomas Stollard, *Commander*
William Orchard
John Keeble, *Master*
John Wilds
Thomas Foreman, *Master*
George Coney
John Kiddle
William Mosely, *Capt.*
Caleb Cock, *Capt.*
Bartholemew Clements, *Capt.*
Edward Day
Nicholas Churchwood, *Mate*
John Saunders
Edward Clements,
John Dawney,
Gilbert Hurfoll, *Mate*
Joachim Paget } *of* Fowey
Paget }
John Sprye, *Mate*
Bernard Bligh, *Mate*
Jasper Goodman
Henry Mitcham, *Jun.*
Thomas Robinson, *Chyrur.*
James Blake
Richard Mabit
John Morley
David Bernard
George Shale
William Sowell
John Hall
William Heydon
Lawrence Hulson
Samuel Lawson
John Hazelwood
James Wells
Richard Hounsley
John Zouch
Phillip Guppy, *Chirurgeon*
James Smythborne
Richard Maye
Daniel Masterson
Richard Mason
John Towers

John Nye
Nicholas Braxton
Francis Lake
Henry Pettis
John Claydon
Thomas Smith
Richard Cunnet
George Linum
Christopher Brecknell
John Mayor
Simon Comfort
Nicholas Lash, *Cook*
John Smith
George Mason
Peter Rowland
Henry Bull
Richard Baker
William Dixon
Nicholas Brooking
Lionel Day
William Purser
Edward Horton
John Bunce
George Russel
William Key
John Limbrey, *Mate*
Ambrose Taylor
John Violl
Stephen Beere, *Mate*
John Benson
Thomas Thomson
Robert Lambly
Thomas Fox
Richard Wakeham, *Mate*
Richard Tarling
Stephen Bantick
William Cleer
Richard Villiers
William Osborne
Thomas Waterson
James Loveday
James Mason
John Jones
Henry Webb
George Martin
Peter Towers
Tho. Wilcox Boatswain
Simon Gudging
Samuel Dawkes
Nicholas Burgesse
William Jerrot
Tho. Scoyls Gunner
Tho. Sylvester Carpenter
Abraham Harman Carpenter
Tho. Richards Cook
John Keevel
William Winter
William Ensley
Peter Tydder
Robert Ellison
John Bradford
John Robarts
Abraham Mason, *Chirurgeon*
Lawrence Nelson
William Paddicum
Henry Mitcham, *Senior*
Philip Gibs
Matthew Garwood

Thomas Bayly
Richard Eggerton
James Rogers
George Triplet
Richard Miller
Matthew Sayers
Henry Archer
Robert Randol, *Cook*
Charles Hyat
Henry Symmons, *Gunners Mate*
John Nowell, *Boatsw.*
Philip Ninum
John Evans
Henry Chub
Griffin Skinner
Richard Fleek
John Crow

John Filer
John Liste
Richard Broome
Daniel Cleribut‍
Hercules Mullet
William Rounsdale
Thomas Body.
Ed: Jones, Quartermaster.
Jeremy Lestock
William Stokes
Henry Dryer
Peter Bennet
Dunkin Davis
Francis Brewster
Thomas Mudd, Master.
John Fletcher, Master.
John Covant, Master.

*From* Salley.

John Kingcome
Richard Mogg, *Cook*
Ambrose Richards
Andrew Norcoat
Edward Tongkin
George Dalmon, *Mate*
John Welchman
James Goodridge
Roger Matthews
Thomas Winter
John Russell
Matthew Valpe
Samuel Swaine
John Williams
Martin Johnson
John Lange
John Pierce
Arthur Cloke
John Sheppard, *Carpenter*
William Boswan
Gregory Derry
Edward Hodder, *Master*
Abraham Moone, *Boatesw.*
Leonard Symons
Robert Penwarden
John Hutchins,
Gregory Martin
Michael Humbling
Nicholas Berry
William Dollingen
Israel Symons
Henry Manning
Edward Roy
Richard Kingcome
Francis Demster
Daniel Hardick
Thomas Tenning
Thomas Dixon

John Cox
Robert Pattison
William Rainbow
Nathaniel Row
William Lewis
Samuel Wyat
Robert Smyth
William Row
Anthony Harwood
William Burnet
William Browne
Thomas Row
John Guin
Thomas Edgecomb
Samuel Ford
Samuel Brely
Michael Harman
William Dollen
Edmond Finny
Richard Hoar
Peter Mitchell
William Symons
Francis Lawson
John Clarke
Thomas Cragg
Robert Bramble
William Pepper
Walter Elliot
Daniel French
Anthony Burgesse
George Bowen
Jacob Perry, *Mate*
Nicholas Haye
Thomas Whitney, *Master*
Benjamin Lenton
Richard Birt
William Price
John Johnson
Thomas Browne.

*We are likewise to give Notice, that the whole Collection upon the said Brief, that hath been paid into the Chamber of* London, *amounts unto Twenty Thousand and five hundred pounds, and that there hath been issued thence, towards the Redemption of the aforesaid Two hundred forty seven Persons, the sum of fifteen thousand, one hundred and seventy pounds.*

*That the Remainder is imprested and actually employing towards the carrying on the said Redemption, with all the Expedition that may be.*

*And we are likewise to desire all Persons who have any Monies in their hands, Collected upon His Majesties said Letters Patents, that they forthwith pay the same, as they are directed by the said Brief, to the end it may be brought into the Chamber of* London; *there yet remaining some hundreds of His Majesties Subjects in Turkish Captivity, more then the Moneys hitherto come in will redeem.*

*Brussels, April 8.* From *Holland* we have advice, that they are using all the diligence possible to get their Fleet to Sea, which however will not be so soon as some thought; They of *Amsterdam* seem to be the forwardest, but we certainly hear, that the Ships fitted out by the Admiralties of *Zealand, Friesland* and *North-Holland*, are very backward, especially occasioned through the want of Men. The French make great

UNIVERSITY OF CENTRAL LANCASHIRE LIBRARY

**2.4** *The London Gazette*, 7 April 1673

information about the proceedings of Parliament and the latest political gossip the *Gazette* would not print. The newswriters employed armies of scribes to copy out their works, which were then hawked around the London coffee-houses and posted to country subscribers.

Macaulay, in his *History of England*, gives the following description of these early journalists:

> The newswriter rambled from coffee room to coffee room, collecting reports, squeezed himself into the Sessions House at the Old Bailey if there was an interesting trial, nay, perhaps, obtained admission to the gallery at Whitehall, and noticed how the King and Duke looked. In this way he gathered materials for his weekly epistles destined to enlighten some country town or some bunch of rustic magistrates. Such were the sources from which the inhabitants of the largest provincial cities, and the great body of the gentry and clergy, learned almost all that they knew of the history of their own time.

**Popish Plot Papers**

In the alarms and confusion surrounding the allegations of a Popish Plot, there was a brief interlude of press freedom when, forgetting that the Printing Act had not been renewed, the king dissolved Parliament in May 1679 to prevent the passing of the Exclusion Bill that would have barred James II from the throne. Between 1679 and 1685, when the controls were reimposed, a number of unlicensed newssheets appeared. One of the first was Benjamin Harris's pro-Whig, *Domestick Intelligence.* When issue No. 16 was published on 26 August 1679, another *Domestick Intelligence* appeared on the streets, also numbered 16, but written in the Tory interest. This 'spoiler' was the work of Nathaniel Thompson, otherwise known as 'Popish Nat'. To distinguish his paper from the interloper, Harris renamed it *The Protestant (Domestick) Intelligence: or, News from both City and Country. Published to prevent False Reports* (Figure 2.5). Popish Nat then rather misleadingly renamed his paper *The Loyal Protestant, and True Domestic Intelligence, or, News from both City and Countrey. Published to prevent False, Scandalous and Seditious Reports.*

Thereafter came a confusion of similar sounding titles from both Whig and Tory presses, each trying to decoy their rivals' readers. In addition to Harris's and Thompson's *Domestick Intelligences,* T. Benskin produced a *Domestick Intelligence; or, News from both City and Country impartially related* (from 13 May 1681 to 16 November 1682). Confusion was also caused by Langley Curtis's *True Protestant Mercury* (from 28 December 1680) and R. Janeway's *True Protestant Mercury* (from 27 April 1681); Thomas Vile's *London Mercury* (from 6 April 1682), the *Loyal London Mercury; or, the Moderate Intelligencer* (from 14 June 1682) and the *Loyal London Mercury; or, the Currant*

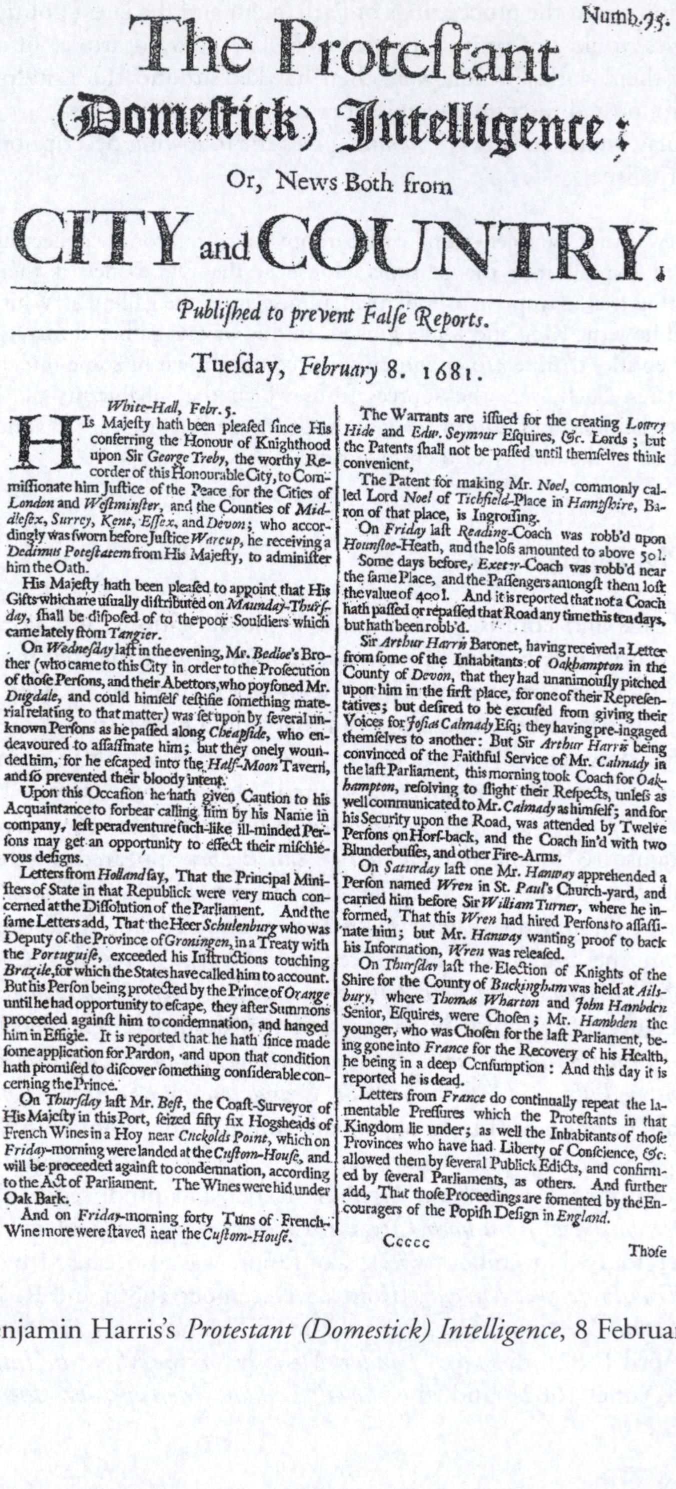

Numb. 95.

# The Protestant (Domestick) Intelligence;

Or, News Both from

# CITY and COUNTRY.

*Published to prevent False Reports.*

Tuesday, *February* 8. 1681.

*White-Hall, Febr.* 5.

HIs Majesty hath been pleased since His conferring the Honour of Knighthood upon Sir *George Treby*, the worthy Recorder of this Honourable City, to Commissionate him Justice of the Peace for the Cities of *London* and *Westminster*, and the Counties of *Middlesex, Surrey, Kent, Essex*, and *Devon*; who accordingly was sworn before Justice *Warcup*, he receiving a *Dedimus Potestatem* from His Majesty, to administer him the Oath.

His Majesty hath been pleased to appoint that His Gifts which are usually distributed on *Maunday-Thursday*, shall be disposed of to the poor Souldiers which came lately from *Tangier*.

On *Wednesday* last in the evening, Mr. *Bedloe's* Brother (who came to this City in order to the Prosecution of those Persons, and their Abettors, who poysoned Mr. *Dugdale*, and could himself testifie something material relating to that matter) was set upon by several unknown Persons as he passed along *Cheapside*, who endeavoured to assassinate him; but they onely wounded him, for he escaped into the *Half-Moon* Tavern, and so prevented their bloody intent.

Upon this Occasion he hath given Caution to his Acquaintance to forbear calling him by his Name in company, lest peradventure such-like ill-minded Persons may get an opportunity to effect their mischievous designs.

Letters from *Holland* say, That the Principal Ministers of State in that Republick were very much concerned at the Dissolution of the Parliament. And the same Letters add, That the Heer *Schulenburg* who was Deputy of the Province of *Groningen*, in a Treaty with the *Portuguise*, exceeded his Instructions touching *Brazile*, for which the States have called him to account. But his Person being protected by the Prince of *Orange* until he had opportunity to escape, they after Summons proceeded against him to condemnation, and hanged him in Effigie. It is reported that he hath since made some application for Pardon, and upon that condition hath promised to discover something considerable concerning the Prince.

On *Thursday* last Mr. *Best*, the Coast-Surveyor of His Majesty in this Port, seized fifty six Hogsheads of French Wines in a Hoy near *Cuckolds Point*, which on *Friday*-morning were landed at the *Custom-House*, and will be proceeded against to condemnation, according to the Act of Parliament. The Wines were hid under Oak Bark.

And on *Friday*-morning forty Tuns of French-Wine more were staved near the *Custom-House*.

The Warrants are issued for the creating *Lowry Hide* and *Edw. Seymour* Esquires, &c. Lords; but the Patents shall not be passed until themselves think convenient.

The Patent for making Mr. *Noel*, commonly called Lord *Noel* of *Tichfield*-Place in *Hampshire*, Baron of that place, is Ingroising.

On *Friday* last *Reading*-Coach was robb'd upon *Hounsloe*-Heath, and the loss amounted to above 50l.

Some days before, *Exeter*-Coach was robb'd near the same Place, and the Passengers amongst them lost the value of 400l. And it is reported that not a Coach hath passed or repassed that Road any time this ten days, but hath been robb'd.

Sir *Arthur Harris* Baronet, having received a Letter from some of the Inhabitants of *Oakhampton* in the County of *Devon*, that they had unanimously pitched upon him in the first place, for one of their Representatives; but desired to be excused from giving their Voices for *Josias Calmady* Esq; they having pre-ingaged themselves to another: But Sir *Arthur Harris* being convinced of the Faithful Service of Mr. *Calmady* in the last Parliament, this morning took Coach for *Oakhampton*, resolving to slight their Respects, unless as well communicated to Mr. *Calmady* as himself; and for his Security upon the Road, was attended by Twelve Persons on Horse-back, and the Coach lin'd with two Blunderbusses, and other Fire-Arms.

On *Saturday* last one Mr. *Hanway* apprehended a Person named *Wren* in St. *Paul's* Church-yard, and carried him before Sir *William Turner*, where he informed, That this *Wren* had hired Persons to assassinate him; but Mr. *Hanway* wanting proof to back his Information, *Wren* was released.

On *Thursday* last the Election of Knights of the Shire for the County of *Buckingham* was held at *Ailsbury*, where *Thomas Wharton* and *John Hambden* Senior, Esquires, were Chosen; Mr. *Hambden* the younger, who was Chosen for the last Parliament, being gone into *France* for the Recovery of his Health, he being in a deep Consumption: And this day it is reported he is dead.

Letters from *France* do continually repeat the lamentable Pressures which the Protestants in that Kingdom lie under; as well the Inhabitants of those Provinces who have had Liberty of Conscience, &c. allowed them by several Publick Edicts, and confirmed by several Parliaments, as others. And further add, That those Proceedings are fomented by the Encouragers of the Popish Design in *England*.

Cccc Those

**2.5** Benjamin Harris's *Protestant (Domestick) Intelligence*, 8 February 1681

*Intelligence* (from 23 August 1682); and John Smith's *Currant Intelligence* (from 14 February 1680) and Allen Banks's *Currant Intelligence* (from 13 March 1680).

They were all similar in appearance to *The London Gazette* except that, free from the self-imposed shackles of the *Gazette*, they carried domestic news. Some of the domestic stories highlighted the eccentric nature of some of the radical Protestant sects of the period:

> *Edenburgh. May 5.* As some of our Lords were Returning yesterday from Council, attended by the Horse and Foot-Guards, nine Women (who call themselves the Sweet Singers of *Israel*) that are imprisoned here for their Extravagancies, threw down stones out of the Prison windows, upon their Coaches, upon which an Officer ran to the Lords, and desired to know what should be done to them; but their Lordships looking upon them to be distracted, commanded him not to meddle with them, and so went on; however the Officer went into the Prison, where he found them singing, and could not interrupt them till he had taken away their books; he highly threatned them for what they had done, and asked them how they durst abuse Authority after such an insolent manner; to which they replyed, that they did Reverence Lawful Authority, but did not look upon those Lords to be so qualified, and so went on with their singing.
>
> The Privy Council met again in the Afternoon, as they did also this *Monday*, and made an Order, that all the aforesaid Women should be removed from that Prison, to the House of Correction, where they are to be set to work, and fed only on bread and water; and one of our Bailiffs is appointed to go twice a week to visit them, and see them Receive Twenty Stripes a piece each time; They are to be treated after this manner, till a conveniency can be found of transporting them either to *Virginia or Barbadoes.*[23]

These Scottish Sweet Singers of Israel should not be confused with the English Sweet Singers of Israel who 'met in ale-houses and ate, drank and smoked' in the belief that the death of Christ had abolished sin, they were therefore sinless, and it was God's will that they should devote their lives to eating, drinking and making merry. The Scottish Sweet Singers of Israel, a much grimmer lot, were the followers of John Gibb, 'a sailor of great stature', whom they believed to be the second King Solomon. After Gibb was transported to America, it was said that he 'caused much awe to the Indians by his intercourse with the devil'.[24]

This period also saw the birth of the dialogue paper. Dialogue papers provided a commentary on the politics of the day in the form of a conversation between two speakers. The first of its kind, *Heraclitus Ridens; or, a discourse between Jest and Earnest, where many a true Word is spoken in opposition to all Libellers against the Government*, was started on 1 February 1681. It contained attacks on the Whig presses, particularly those of Benjamin Harris and Frank Smith, the dissenting preacher and printer of *Smith's*

*Protestant Intelligence*, who was nicknamed Elephant Smith from the name of his sign, the Elephant and Castle:

> *Earn.* Well! and what news from the Press?
> *Jest.* What would you be at? Here's a spick and span *Vox Populi*, or *Elephant Smith* turn'd *Pedagogue*, and teaching the People to spell the Horn-book of *Sedition*, *Treason* and *Rebellion*.
> *Earn.* That same Smith is continuously hammering and forging, and like the rest of the Trade, he has an unquenchable spark of *Sedition* in his throat, and a world of Irons in the fire.
> *Jest.* But if this does not burn his fingers, or his hand, he must have better luck than honester men; I know of nothing but hanging that can save him.[25]

On 17 March 1681 Smith replied with a dialogue paper of his own, *Democritus Ridens; or, Comus and Momus*, and then on 13 April 1681 Roger L'Estrange joined in the fray by publishing a strongly pro-Tory dialogue paper, the *Observator* (1681–87), a title first used by Marchamont Nedham for one of his publications in 1654.

Without the Printing Act to assist him, the king tried to regain control of the press by issuing a Proclamation for Suppressing the Printing and Publishing of Unlicensed News-Books. But with political passions at boiling point over the Popish Plot, the Exclusion Crisis and a suspicion of the king's pro-France, pro-Catholic stance (fears of Popery and Wooden Shoes), he had little chance of immediate success. However, the state had other weapons at its disposal, notably the laws of seditious libel, aimed at the Whig presses. After the tide had turned against the Whigs following the discovery of the Rye House Plot, one by one the Whig presses, already weakened by the discrediting of the Popish Plot, were forced to close down. The Tory papers soon voluntarily followed suit. Elephant Smith fled to Amsterdam to avoid prosecution, and Benjamin Harris was fined £500 and sentenced to the pillory for advocating the claims of the Duke of Monmouth over those of James as successor to Charles II. Unable to pay his fine, Harris spent two years in the King's Bench Prison until, in desperation, he turned informer. Harris later fled to America, where he produced the first American newspaper, *Publick Occurrences, Foreign and Domestick* on 25 September 1690, 'designed, that the Countrey shall be furnished once a moneth (or, if any Glut of Occurrences happen, oftener) with an Account of such considerable things as have arrived unto our Notice'.

The colonial governor suppressed it after one issue. This was because it called the Indians 'barbarous' and 'miserable Savages, in whom we have too much confided', at a time when the British were trying to win the friendship of the Indians in the war in America against the French. Harris later returned to England and started the *London Post* (1699–1705).

**Freedom of the Press**

From the accession of James II there was another dark period in the history of the newspaper. The Printing Act was reinstated and the *London Gazette* once again enjoyed its state monopoly. The Glorious Revolution of 1688 changed nothing. There was a brief flurry of unofficial press activity, but this was soon quashed. The Bill of Rights guaranteed freedom of speech within Parliament, but did nothing to advance the freedom of the press. The new regime owed much to the power of the press to influence public opinion in the intervals of freedom during the Exclusion Crisis and the winter of 1688–89. But Parliament recognized that power could potentially turn against the new regime. It wanted a period of stability and so renewed the Licensing Act. As for L'Estrange, he had identified himself too strongly with the Stuart cause and was replaced by a new licenser who allowed certain serial publications provided they did not contain news.

About the only printed news publication that was tolerated, other than *The London Gazette*, was the monthly pamphlet, *The Present State of Europe; or, the Historical and Political Monthly Mercury*, which was started in July 1690 and reprinted in Edinburgh and Dublin. Like the old corantos, it was a translation of a Dutch original with the English news taken out. Six pages of the issue for August 1692, under the heading 'Advices from Rome and Italy', were given over entirely to a text of a Papal Bull printed in Latin, with a further six pages taken up by the English translation, 'for the satisfaction of the Curious'.

However, the continental campaigns of William III created such a hunger for news that the existing controls became increasingly untenable. In 1695 the predominantly Whig House of Commons attempted to redraft the Printing Act, but, largely due to party squabbling, there were so many objections on matters of mere detail that they ran out of parliamentary time and the Act simply failed to be renewed, much to the dismay of the Stationers' Company. The freedom of the press was thus obtained, not by some conscious act of principle, but by default.

The importance of 1695, which Macaulay claimed 'did more for liberty and civilisation than the Great Charter or the Bill of Rights', was that anyone could set up a printing press and issue publications without permission. Prison and the pillory would replace hanging and mutilation for those whose words offended the government.

The experience of journalism before the watershed of 1695 shows that, even in a rigidly controlled, autocratic regime, political crises create a 'thirst after News', encouraging journalistic enterprise and weakening the authority of the state. But when political calm is restored, the demand for news reduces, driving the less adaptable journalists out of business, and allowing the state to regain control of the press.

The years up to 1695 were marked by a predominantly authoritarian press regime, deriving its authority from the absolute power of the monarch or the state. After 1695 this would be replaced by a predominantly libertarian regime, deriving its authority from its ability to meet the needs of its readers. Ownership would change from those with a Royal Patent or similar authority to those with the money to buy a press or to pay for the printing. No longer constrained by external censorship or the self-censorship of the Stationers' Company, the press after 1695 would be constrained only by market forces and the laws of libel. And instead of the newspaper being used as an instrument for effecting government policy or passively avoiding all political controversy, it would become an instrument for acting as a check on government and informing and entertaining its readers.

The nature of journalism would also undergo tremendous change. The relations of the sixteenth century and the corantos of the early seventeenth century dealt purely with facts, exaggerated facts maybe, but facts nevertheless. Similarly, the Civil War newsbooks dealt mainly with facts, albeit unreliable facts, biased in favour of King or Parliament. Their successors, *Mercurius Politicus* and the *London Gazette*, gave the official presentation of facts as filtered by government. But the consequences of the defeat of the divine right of kings in the Glorious Revolution and the break in the hereditary succession would be that the fate of kings and their governments would depend on their ability to command opinion, and opinion could only be sustained by persuasion. Freed from the constraints of licensing, the newspaper would expand beyond its narrow remit of reporting mere facts. It would also replace the pamphlet as the main vehicle for persuasion, disseminating political opinion in support of one faction against another. The nature of news itself would change. News would no longer be restricted to the information governments decided the public could be allowed to know. It would embrace a much wider selection of material – material that journalists thought the public should have the right to know and would also enjoy reading.

## Notes

1. Steinberg, S. H. (1955), *Five Hundred Years of Printing*, Harmondsworth: Penguin.
2. Cressy, David (1980), *Literature and the Social Order, Reading and Writing in Tudor and Stuart England*, Cambridge: Cambridge University Press.
3. Hill, Christopher (1968), *Puritanism and Revolution*, London: Panther; (1969), *Society and Puritanism in Pre-Revolutionary England*, London: Panther.
4. Star Chamber Decree of 23 June 1586.
5. London Gazette, 3 to 6 May 1680.
6. Braitwait, Richard (1631), *Whimzies: or a new cast of Characters*.
7. Dahl, Folke (1938), 'Short-Title Catalogue of English Corantos and Newsbooks, 1620–1642', *The Library*, Vol. XIX, No. 1.

8. Frearson, Michael (1993), 'The Distribution and Readership of the London Corantos', in Myers, Robin and Harris, Michael (eds), *Serials and their Readers, 1620–1914*, Winchester: St Paul's Bibliographies; New Castle, DE: Oak Knoll Press, pp. 1–25.
9. *A Fresh Whip to all Scandalous Lyers; or A True Description of the Two Eminent Pamphliteers, or Squibtellers of this Kingdome*, 1647.
10. Nelson, Carolyn and Seccombe, Matthew (1986), *Periodical Publications 1641–1700: A Survey with illustrations*, London: Bibliographical Society.
11. Seaver, Paul (1985), *Wallington's World: A Puritan Artisan in Seventeenth Century London*, London: Methuen.
12. *Mercurius Aulicus*, for example. See Thomas, P. W. (1969), *Sir John Birkenhead 1617–1679. A Royalist Career in Politics and Polemics*, Oxford: Clarendon Press.
13. *The character of Mercurius Politicus*, 1651.
14. *Mercurius Britanicus*, 27 January to 3 February 1645.
15. Ibid., 28 July to 4 August 1645.
16. *Mercurius Fumigosus*, 22 to 30 November, and 6 to 13 December 1654.
17. *A true Diurnall of the Passages in Parliament*, 7 to 14 March 1642.
18. *Areopagitica: a Speech of Mr John Milton For the Liberty of Unlicenc'd Printing, To the Parlament of England*, 1644.
19. For Muddiman, see Muddiman, J. G. (1923), *The King's Journalist*, London: John Lane.
20. *Parliamentary Intelligencer*, started 19 to 26 December 1659, continued as *Kingdomes Intelligencer* from 1 to 7 January 1661.
21. The first issue of the *Intelligencer* was dated 31 August 1663 and that of the *Newes*, 3 September 1663. They both ran until January 1666.
22. *Diary*, 22 November 1665. By folly, Pepys meant editorial comment.
23. *Currant Intelligence*, 14 May 1681.
24. Whiting, C. E. (1931), *Studies in English Puritanism from the Restoration to the Revolution, 1660–1688*, London: SPCK.
25. *Heraclitus Ridens*, 4 April 1681.

Chapter 3

# The Developing Newspaper, 1695–1750

Can statutes keep the British press in awe,
When what sells best, that's most against the Law?
James Branston, 'The Man of Taste', 1733

As soon as the Licensing Act lapsed, the London newspaper presses started up again. In the space of the single month seven new titles hit the streets.[1] The next half-century saw an impressive growth in the number of different types of newspaper and other news-carrying publications, ranging from daily newspapers through to annual newsbooks, to meet the demand for news. Demand was stimulated by the social and economic conditions of those years: an expanding middle class; an increasingly literate artisan class; a developing party system needing an active press to further the battles between Whigs and Tories; and a thriving club and coffee-house culture whose participants prided themselves on being well informed.

These friendly circumstances to the developing newspaper were further encouraged by an atmosphere of intellectual curiosity and the emergence of a worldview based on reason and economic and scientific progress – the beginnings of the Age of Enlightenment. That England was at war for most of this period was another favourable circumstance. Newspapers were essential if one was to follow the progress of campaigns in foreign lands – hot news of battles by land and sea.

Even when England was not at war, its position as the paramount trading nation whose ships carried goods from all over the known world ensured a keen interest in foreign news. The huge coverage of foreign news reflected the economic interests of whole groups of the upper and middling ranks in society, who undoubtedly formed the bulk of the newspaper-reading classes – merchants, investors, bankers, tradesmen and shopkeepers – and prompted a wider debate about the conduct of foreign policy.

In addition, England had many commercial interests within continental Europe. British businessmen were based in Stockholm, Danzig, Gothenburg, Riga, Archangel and other major European centres of trade. The Deputy Governor of the British Baltic Company was permanently stationed in Hamburg. Many city merchants had money and credit in Amsterdam – the financial capital of Europe. In the days when it was quicker and easier for a Londoner to travel to Amsterdam than to Exeter or York, it is hardly surprising that foreign news dominated the newspaper for at least the first two decades of the eighteenth century.

### Tri-weekly Posts

Apart from the official *London Gazette*, whose circulation was inflated by its free distribution to a captive audience of public servants, ambassadors, justices of the peace and municipal officers, the most successful newspapers of the immediate post-1695 period were Abel Boyer's *Post Boy*, George Ridpath's *Flying-Post; or, the Post-Master* (Figure 3.1), and Jean de Fonvive's *Post-Man*. These papers are known as tri-weekly morning posts because they were published on Tuesdays, Thursdays and Saturdays, the three nights when the post-horses left London to deliver mail to the major towns.

Such was the importance of the provincial market that the *Post-Man* and the *Post Boy* averaged sales of between 3,000 and 4,000 copies per issue, whereas *The Daily Courant* and other papers which had a mainly London circulation sold less than 1,000. The emergence of the tri-weekly evening posts ended the dominance of the tri-weekly morning posts. Unlike their morning predecessors, the evening posts were published late enough to cover the important news of the day, yet still be in time to catch the country posts. For those living outside London, evening posts became the most important source of news:

> But the sale of the usual papers set up under King William of immortal memory, namely the Post-man, the Flying-post, the Post-boy, and more lately the Daily Courant, has been visibly diminish'd by these Evening Posts … for whereas before people us'd to send all or most of the four papers aforesaid to their friends and correspondents in the country every post-night, now the sale of them is almost confin'd to this town. Nay the vent of them is much lessen'd here, many persons contenting themselves to read over the same evening posts, which they send to their friends at night; as containing the substance of all the rest, with some fresher passages, commonly made up of scandal and sedition.[2]

By the 1720s, the *Flying-Post* was in such a sorry state that its author and proprietor, Stephen Whatley, had to translate the continental papers for other newspapers in order to make a living until he managed to secure a bribe of £50 per year for keeping the *Flying-Post* loyal to the Ministry.

The tri-weekly *Evening Post* (1709–40), published at 'Six at Night', was the first such paper to use the word 'evening' in its title. Other, longer-lasting, evening posts followed, notably the *St. James's Evening Post* (1715–60), the *Whitehall Evening-Post* (1718–1801), the *London Evening-Post* (1727–1806) and the *General Evening Post* (1733–1813).

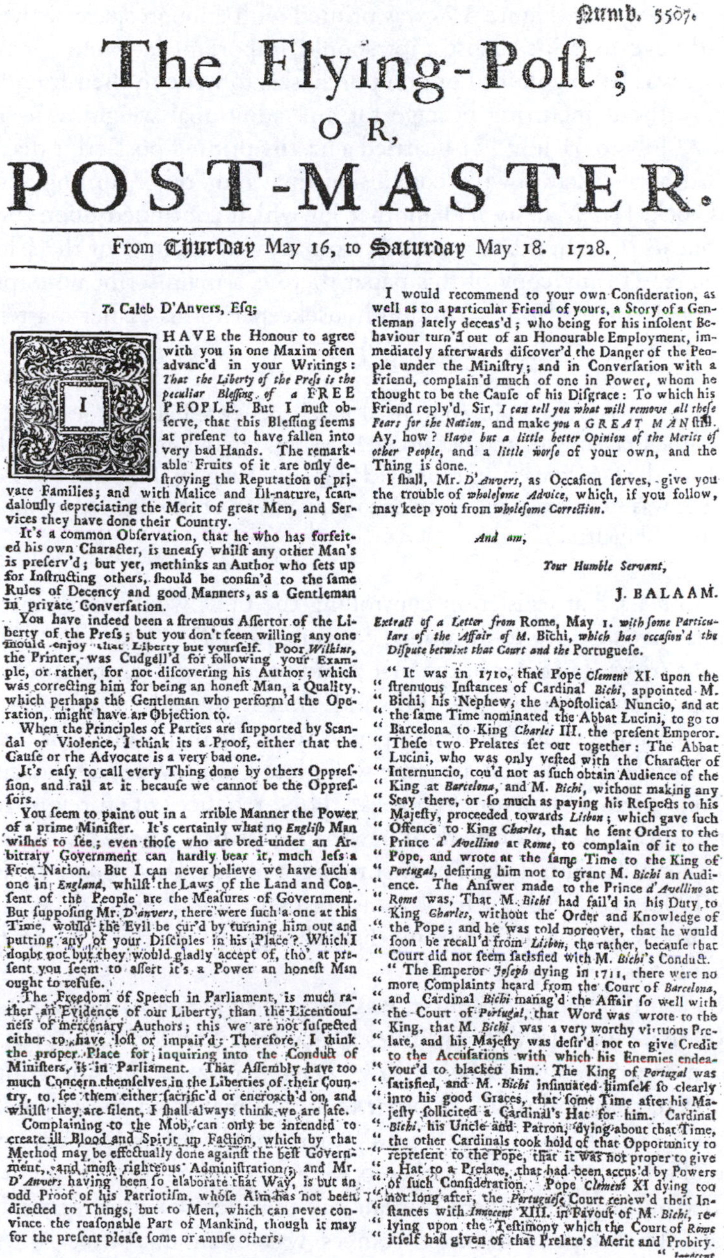

Numb. 5507.

# The Flying-Poſt ; OR, POST-MASTER.

From Thurſday May 16, to Saturday May 18. 1728.

*To* Caleb D'Anvers, Eſq;

I HAVE the Honour to agree with you in one Maxim often advanc'd in your Writings: *That the Liberty of the Preſs is the peculiar Bleſſing of a* FREE PEOPLE. But I muſt obſerve, that this Bleſſing ſeems at preſent to have fallen into very bad Hands. The remarkable Fruits of it are only deſtroying the Reputation of private Families; and with Malice and Ill-nature, ſcandalouſly depreciating the Merit of great Men, and Services they have done their Country.

It's a common Obſervation, that he who has forfeited his own Character, is uneaſy whilſt any other Man's is preſerv'd; but yet, methinks an Author who ſets up for Inſtructing others, ſhould be confin'd to the ſame Rules of Decency and good Manners, as a Gentleman in private Converſation.

You have indeed been a ſtrenuous Aſſertor of the Liberty of the Preſs; but you don't ſeem willing any one ſhould enjoy that Liberty but yourſelf. Poor *Wilkins*, the Printer, was Cudgell'd for following your Example, or rather, for not diſcovering his Author; which was correcting him for being an honeſt Man, a Quality, which perhaps the Gentleman who perform'd the Operation, might have an Objection to.

When the Principles of Parties are ſupported by Scandal or Violence, I think its a Proof, either that the Cauſe or the Advocate is a very bad one.

It's eaſy to call every Thing done by others Oppreſſion, and rail at it becauſe we cannot be the Oppreſſors.

You ſeem to paint out in a terrible Manner the Power of a prime Miniſter. It's certainly what no *Engliſh* Man wiſhes to ſee; even thoſe who are bred under an Arbitrary Government can hardly bear it, much leſs a Free Nation. But I can never believe we have ſuch a one in *England*, whilſt the Laws of the Land and Conſent of the People are the Meaſures of Government. But ſuppoſing Mr. *D'anvers*, there were ſuch a one at this Time, would the Evil be cur'd by turning him out and putting any of your Diſciples in his Place? Which I doubt not but they would gladly accept of, tho' at preſent you ſeem to aſſert it's a Power an honeſt Man ought to refuſe.

The Freedom of Speech in Parliament, is much rather an Evidence of our Liberty, than the Licentiouſneſs of mercenary Authors; this we are not ſuſpected either to have loſt or impair'd: Therefore, I think the proper Place for inquiring into the Conduct of Miniſters, is in Parliament. That Aſſembly have too much Concern themſelves in the Liberties of their Country, to ſee them either ſacrific'd or encroach'd on, and whilſt they are ſilent, I ſhall always think we are ſafe.

Complaining to the Mob, can only be intended to create ill Blood and Spirit up Faction, which by that Method may be effectually done againſt the beſt Government, and moſt righteous Adminiſtration; and Mr. *D'Anvers* having been ſo elaborate that Way, is but an odd Proof of his Patriotiſm, whoſe Aim has not been directed to Things, but to Men, which can never convince the reaſonable Part of Mankind, though it may for the preſent pleaſe ſome or amuſe others.

I would recommend to your own Conſideration, as well as to a particular Friend of yours, a Story of a Gentleman lately deceas'd; who being for his inſolent Behaviour turn'd out of an Honourable Employment, immediately afterwards diſcover'd the Danger of the People under the Miniſtry; and in Converſation with a Friend, complain'd much of one in Power, whom he thought to be the Cauſe of his Diſgrace: To which his Friend reply'd, Sir, *I can tell you what will remove all theſe Fears for the Nation*, and make *you* a GREAT MAN ſtill. Ay, how? *Have but a little better Opinion of the Merits of other People*, and a *little worſe* of your own, and the Thing is done.

I ſhall, Mr. *D'Anvers*, as Occaſion ſerves, give you the trouble of *wholeſome Advice*, which, if you follow, may keep you from *wholeſome Correction*.

*And am,*

*Your Humble Servant,*

J. BALAAM.

*Extract of a Letter from* Rome, May 1. *with ſome Particulars of the Affair of M.* Bichi, *which has occaſion'd the Diſpute betwixt that Court and the* Portugueſe.

"It was in 1710, that Pope *Clement* XI. upon the "ſtrenuous Inſtances of Cardinal *Bichi*, appointed M. "Bichi, his Nephew, the Apoſtolical Nuncio, and at "the ſame Time nominated the Abbat Lucini, to go to "Barcelona to King *Charles* III. the preſent Emperor. "Theſe two Prelates ſet out together: The Abbat "Lucini, who was only veſted with the Character of "Internuncio, cou'd not as ſuch obtain Audience of the "King at *Barcelona*, and M. *Bichi*, without making any "Stay there, or ſo much as paying his Reſpects to his "Majeſty, proceeded towards *Lisbon*; which gave ſuch "Offence to King *Charles*, that he ſent Orders to the "Prince *d'Avellino* at *Rome*, to complain of it to the "Pope, and wrote at the ſame Time to the King of "*Portugal*, deſiring him not to grant M. *Bichi* an Audi-"ence. The Anſwer made to the Prince *d'Avellino* at "*Rome* was, That M. *Bichi* had fail'd in his Duty to "King *Charles*, without the Order and Knowledge of "the Pope; and he was told moreover, that he would "ſoon be recall'd from *Lisbon*, the rather, becauſe that "Court did not ſeem ſatisfied with M. *Bichi*'s Conduct.

"The Emperor *Joſeph* dying in 1711, there were no "more Complaints heard from the Court of *Barcelona*, "and Cardinal *Bichi* manag'd the Affair ſo well with "the Court of *Portugal*, that Word was wrote to the "King, that M. *Bichi*, was a very worthy virtuous Pre-"late, and his Majeſty was deſir'd not to give Credit "to the Accuſations with which his Enemies endea-"vour'd to blacken him. The King of *Portugal* was "ſatisfied, and M. *Bichi* inſinuated himſelf ſo clearly "into his good Graces, that ſome Time after his Ma-"jeſty ſollicited a Cardinal's Hat for him. Cardinal "*Bichi*, his Uncle and Patron, dying about that Time, "the other Cardinals took hold of that Opportunity to "repreſent to the Pope, that it was not proper to give "a Hat to a Prelate, that had been accus'd by Powers "of ſuch Conſideration. Pope *Clement* XI dying too "not long after, the *Portugueſe* Court renew'd their In-"ſtances with *Innocent* XIII. in Favour of M. *Bichi*, re-"lying upon the Teſtimony which the Court of *Rome* "itſelf had given of that Prelate's Merit and Probity.

"*Innocent*

**3.1** *The Flying-Post*, 16 May to 18 May 1728

*The Evening Post* (Figure 3.2) was printed with enough space at the foot of the third page to print a postscript should important late news arrive. The back page was left blank for London purchasers to write to their friends in the country without incurring postage for any additional weight. *The Evening Post* for 29 July to 31 July 1714 carried a hastily printed postscript that Queen Anne had been taken ill with 'convulsion Fits' and, 'this Morning about Ten of the Clock, Her Majesty had another Fit which continued upon Her some Time, but in the Afternoon recover'd from it, and about 3 of the Clock was much better'. In my copy of this paper there is a manuscript note, probably written on 1 August from a London housekeeper to his or her master on his country estate:

> Sr The above is trew & she continwed much Better tell aboute Seven a Clock to day & then taken with another fitt & Died this afternoon about too a Clock was proclaimed ye Electtyer of Brunswick George King of England. Sr I hard ye Postidge was stopt made me sent this to Aquant you of this now. My Umble Sarvis to you & your Ladey.

Due to fears that legislation controlling the press would be re-introduced (attempts were made to re-introduce licensing in 1697, 1698, 1702, 1704 and 1712), the tri-weekly posts of the first decade of the eighteenth century played very safe. Their content was dull and almost devoid of domestic news. Translated reports from the foreign papers were the main source of their news columns. Boyer and de Fonvive were well placed to provide translations, both being bilingual Huguenot refugees. This reliance of foreign material continued in the next landmark of newspaper history, *The Daily Courant*, the first successful English daily. The first number of *The Daily Courant*, dated 11 March 1702, consisted solely of translations of one French paper and two Dutch papers. It was as if nothing had changed since the days of Bourne, Butter and Archer.

The main difference, of course, was that no single paper had a monopoly. By 1709 there were 18 different titles available in London each week. But as the main sources of information, *The London Gazette* and the continental papers, were common to all, in order to steal a march on the others and get an exclusive story, newspapers became increasingly dependent on unofficial sources of information. News gatherers were despatched into the night to seek out coffee-house gossip, tavern rumour and the tales of soldiers returned from the wars. The veracity of these sources was often doubtful. As Addison remarked:

> The Ingenious Fraternity of which I have the Honour to be an unworthy Member: I mean the *News-Writers* of Great Britain, whether *Post-Men* or *Post-Boys* … is, I think, more hard than that of the Soldiers, considering that they have taken more

# The Evening Post.

Numb. 792.

From Thursday September 2. to Saturday September 4 1714.

*From the Supplement to the Amsterdam Gazette, Sept. 7.*

*Genoa, Aug. 23.*

WE have receiv'd Advice from Catalonia, that the Barcelonians have repuls'd the French in three Attacks, and repair'd the grand Breach with Chains, Pallisado's and other Things proper for that Use. 'Tis added, that 2000 Miquelets having descended into the Plain of Barcelona, surpris'd 800 Horses belonging to the French and Spaniards, and enter'd with them into Montjouich.

*Extract of a Letter from Paris the 31st of Aug.*

The King has receiv'd two Expresses from Marshal de Berwick, the Contents whereof are kept very secret, notwithstanding which, we learn, that the Marshal signifies to his Majesty, that his Troops are so discourag'd and diminish'd by the three successive Storms they have made, that it will not be possible for him to take Barcelona without a Reinforcement.

*From the Hague Courant, Sept. 7.*

*Baden, Aug.* 29. Some of the Elector of Bavaria's Domestick Servants being arriv'd here from France, and having receiv'd Passports from the Emperor's Ministers, prosecuted their Journey to Munich, from whence we are advis'd, that the Imperial Commissaries, in Bavaria, have order'd the Taxes there, to be paid no longer than the last Day of September; and begin to use the Inhabitants, that are in Arrears, with great Moderation. The good Understanding between the Emperor's Plenipotentiaries and Baron Malknegh, the Bavarian Minister, encreases daily; and they are frequently together, without admitting any other Ministers to their Conferences, which Proceedings have given great Umbrage to Count St. Luc, Plenipotentiary of France.

*Paris, Aug.* 31. With the King's Will, which was deliver'd to the Parliament the 28th past, a Letter from his Majesty was given in, importing, that his Majesty, having consider'd his own far-advanc'd Age and the Dauphin's tender Years, judg'd it necessary to make his Will, for preventing the Troubles which might arise upon his Death, in the Minority of the Dauphin, and for securing the Tranquility of his Kingdom: That he had thought it proper to send his Will seal'd up to the Parliament of this City, and to commit it to their Keeping, with an Injunction to open it immediately after his Decease, in the Presence of all the Princes of the Blood and Peers of the Kingdom, and that authentick Copies of it should then be sent to all the other Parliaments, that it may be registred and have due Effect according to the Tenour thereof.

*Lisbon*, Aug. 22.

The French Ambassador is to make his publick Entry the 24th Inst. and on the 27th to stand Proxy for the King his Master, at the Baptism of our young Prince, his most Christian Majesty being his Godfather.

The aforesaid Minister has begun his Embassy, with a Demand, with which our Court has not been well pleas'd; neither did they approve the Manner of the said Demand, nor the Stile he made Use of. The Occasion was as follows.

A Majorcan Sattee being arriv'd here with Letters, as 'tis thought, for our Court, a Catalan Merchant, to whom that Ship was consign'd, bought a Frigat of 30 Guns, in our River, and put on Board great Quantities of Sugar, Tobacco and other Provisions, which he design'd as a Present to the Barcelonians. He mann'd that Frigat with the Crew of the Sattee and other Sailors, and to conceal his Design, gave out that she was bound for Majorca, and arm'd for her Defence against the Rovers of Barbary. The French Minister suspecting the Merchant's Design, presented a Memorial, complaining, that his Master's Enemies had not only Protection given them in our Habours, but were also suffer'd to make warlike Preparations and equip Ships to take Merchantmen. Several Councils of State were held on this Affair, and the Merchant was examin'd, and at last the Catalans were permitted to sail with their Ship and Cargo; but before the Frigat could receive all her Lading, the Ambassador presented another Memorial, insisting, that the Ship should be detain'd till further Order. This occasion'd new Councils, wherein, notwithstanding the Ambassador's Protestation and the Interest of his Friends, the former Resolution was confirm'd, and the Catalans, to avoid new Oppositions, weighing Anchor, the Frigat fell down below the Tower of Betlem, and will certainly put to Sea, this Day, for the Streights.

*Brigstock in Northamptonshire, Aug. 29.*

On Sunday the 22d Instant, the High Sheriff of this County, sent to this Town, to let them know, that on Tuesday the 24th, he would come and proclaim the King. About 11 a Clock, all the Men in the Town mounted on Horseback, and drew up before the Door of Matthew Barton, Esq; Lieutenant of the Forest. He immediately mounted, and march'd them round the Town in very great Order, from thence to Brigstock-Park, the Place appointed to meet the Sheriff; here the neighbouring Gentlemen came in to shew their Loyalty to their new King; there was Sir James Robinson from Cranford, Major Creed from Oundle, 'Squire Spinks from Aldwinkle, Mr. Warner and Mr. Walls from Gedington and Hemington, with a great Number of the Duke of Montague's Tenants; about half an Hour after these had all put themselves in Order, the High Sheriff with his Under Sheriff join'd them, and then, with Trumpet sounding, Drums beating, and Colours flying, they march'd in good Order towards the Town. At the Entrance of the Town, all the Boys march'd before with white Wands and Streamers at the Ends of 'em; then all the Maids in white, with Aprons full of Flowers and Greens, strowing the Streets as they went along, then the great Cavalcade, where they proclaim'd the King at the three

**3.2** *The Evening Post*, 2 September to 4 September 1714

> Towns and fought more Battels. They have been upon Parties and Skirmishes when our Armies have lain still; and given the General Assault to many a Place, when the Besiegers were quiet in their Trenches. They have made us Masters of several strong Towns many Weeks before our Generals could do it; and compleated Victories, when our greatest Captains have been content to come off with a drawn Battle. Where Prince *Eugene* has slain his Thousands, *Boyer* has slain his Ten Thousands.[3]

## The *Tatler* and the *Spectator*

By Queen Anne's time, most of the ingredients of the modern newspaper were already in place, but they were served in individual dishes. News, social and literary essays, problem pages and political commentaries each appeared in separate publications.

The social and literary essay came to prominence with Richard Steele's *Tatler* (1709–11) and Joseph Addison's *Spectator* (1711–12).[4] These were single-sheet papers printed in a similar format to *The London Gazette*. Apart from a few news items in the early issues of the *Tatler*, they were essay papers only, albeit produced under journalistic disciplines of size and frequency. The *Tatler* and the *Spectator* dealt in a light and urbane manner with the condition of man as self and social being, covering a wide range of subject matter – London life, manners, religion and morals, ghosts and witchcraft, and literary and theatrical criticism. A number of fictitious characters found fame in their pages, including Sir Roger de Coverley, Sir Andrew Freeport and the other members of the Spectator Club, and the Political Upholsterer who was so addicted to reading newspapers that he neglected his trade and his family and, confused by the conjectures and contradictions in the reports of the continental wars, ended up in Bedlam.[5]

The *Spectator* was not the first periodical to use the Club motif. Earlier examples included Ned Ward's *Weekly Comedy* which ran for ten numbers in 1699 featuring Snarl, a disbanded Captain; Scribble, a News-Writer; Squabble, a Lawyer, among others; and the Scandal Club in Defoe's *Review*. The use of the Club motif introduced a cast of characters readers could recognize and whose opinions they could perhaps identify with. While the *Post Boy* and *The Daily Courant* and the other newspapers of the day presented the news raw and left the readers to devise their own private opinion, albeit one that may be tested and turned into public opinion in coffee-house discussions, the Club, along with the dialogue papers, presented the reader with a ready-made form of public opinion on recent events.

In his introductory notice in the first issue of the *Tatler*, Steele articulated that function of journalism:

> *Tho' the other Papers which are published for the Use of the good People of* England *have certainly very wholesom Effects, and are laudable in their particular Kinds, they do not seem to come up to the main Design of such Narratives, which I humbly presume, should be principally intended for the Use of Politick Persons, who are so publick-spirited as to neglect their own Affairs to look into Transactions of State. Now these Gentlemen for the most Part, being Persons of strong Zeal and weak Intellects, it is both a Charitable and Necessary Work to offer something, whereby such worthy and well-affected Members of the Commonwealth may be instructed, after their Reading,* what to think: *Which shall be the End and Purpose of this my Paper.*[6]

Despite their short lives, the popularity and influence of the *Tatler* and the *Spectator* ensured that the essay or leading article, instructing people 'what to think', would be a prominent feature in most types of newspaper that followed. Newspapers became the medium through which the nation tells itself about itself.

## Problem Pages

John Dunton, who along with Ned Ward and Tom Brown was one of the great characters of Grub Street at the turn of the seventeenth and eighteenth centuries, experimented with different types of periodical literature, notably *Pegasus* (1696), a tri-weekly newspaper, and a monthly publication entitled *The Night Walker: or, Evening Rambles in search after lewd Women* (1696–97). *The Night Walker* was a throwback to John Garfield's periodical, *The Wandring Whore* (1660), a guide to London prostitutes, including the unfortunate Mal. Savery: 'You may know her by her Cullinder face, resembling a turd full of Cherry-stones, a shoemaker's punching-block, or an Islington-Cake with the plumms pickt out, and an unsavory stinking breath to boot.'[7]

Dunton is perhaps best remembered for inventing the problem page. His *Athenian Mercury* (1690–97) printed answers to readers' questions, a technique that was lampooned by Tom Brown's *Lacedomonian Mercury*:

> Query: About fifteen months ago I married a tripe-woman's daughter in Wapping, and within a fortnight after was pressed to sea … When I came home, I was told that my wife was just brought to bed of a child. With that, upstairs I ran, and asked her, You strumpet you, who is the father of this brat? Why, you sauce-box says she, who but you? How can that be, says I, I have been out of the Kingdom above these fourteen months … And then she told me it was customary in Wapping for a woman to go fourteen months with child, and sometimes seventeen, and sometimes twenty … Nay, she told me of a neighbour of hers that went four years and upwards with child; and the reason of it was, because living by the cold waterside, a child would not ripen in their bellies, so soon as it would in other

places. I would fain believe poor Kate if I could; so she desired me to send to your Society … And now, what is your opinion of the matter?

Answ. We can tell you for a certain truth, that although the vulgarly-received opinion has it fixed at nine months, yet every day's observation shows that rule to be uncertain … Several women, and those of no mean quality, at the other end of town have been delivered at four or five months after matrimony; nay, we have heard of some that had need of a midwife after two … We'd advise you to believe her.

## Political Commentaries

Political commentaries were initially published in dialogue form in periodicals modelled on L'Estrange's *Observator*, notably John Tutchin's Whig *Observator* (1702–12) and its Tory opponent, Charles Leslie's *Rehearsal* (1704–09). Not surprisingly, in view of its stilted convention, the dialogue format did not last long. It was superseded by political essay papers such as Daniel Defoe's *Weekly Review* (1704–13), founded 'to prevent the various uncertain Accounts, and the Partial Reflections of our Street-Scriblers',[8] and Jonathan Swift's *Examiner* (1710–14).

Despite 1695, journalism was still a dangerous profession. The risk of prosecution was high. Conviction could result in imprisonment with no hope of release until a change of government or the death of a monarch. The Whig George Ridpath, 'a seditious Person, and a notorious Inventor and Framer of Libels', Tutchin's successor on the *Observator*, and author of the *Flying-Post*, fled the country when he was found guilty of libelling Queen Anne. The High Tory, Charles Leslie, was also forced to flee the country. Dennis de Coetlogan, a hack writer who received 16 shillings per week for writing for William Rayner's piratical *Original Craftsman*, was committed to Newgate for six months without trial where he lost an eye. There was the ever-present threat of physical violence from private quarters. Tutchin wrote that his political opponents were forever threatening to beat him up and eventually they did just that, to the extent that he died of his injuries in 1707. The Tory Swift felt that, as the writer of the *Examiner*, it was safer for him not to walk at night, and Daniel Defoe received anonymous letters threatening to murder him or to arrange to have his house pulled down by the mob.

## Daniel Defoe

Nowadays, most of us only remember Daniel Defoe as the author of *Robinson Crusoe* and *Moll Flanders*. His career as a journalist is almost entirely forgotten.[9] He started his career in journalism by writing pamphlets loyal to the Whig cause, which was in favour under William III. His writings made him many enemies, especially among the High Tories, but while the Whigs were in power and the king was on the throne, he was relatively safe.

With the accession of Queen Anne the political atmosphere changed. The Tories were back in power and Defoe no longer had friends in high places to protect him. When he published *The Shortest Way with the Dissenters*, a satire against the High Tories, he was found guilty of seditious libel and sentenced to the pillory and an indefinite spell in Newgate. Robert Harley, a moderate Tory, was one of the first government ministers to recognize how the influence of the post-1695 press could be harnessed in the government's favour. Harley saw that Defoe's pen might be just as useful to the Tories as it was to the Whigs. Harley also saw that he could take advantage of Defoe's low state by tempting him with the prospect of release on his terms.

Harley arranged for the Treasury to pay Defoe's fine and for Defoe to be released from jail. Bound by a debt of gratitude to Harley, and enticed by a steady stream of payments from the Treasury's secret service funds, Defoe threw himself wholeheartedly into his new roles as an *agent provocateur*, maintaining his Whig credentials by attacking the High Tories in the pages of the *Review*, yet acting as a Whiggish defender of Harley's brand of moderate Toryism; and as a government spy whose reprehensible duties included compiling lists of the names of those who were financing the Whig papers. It is estimated that Defoe received around £400 per year from secret service funds between 1707 and 1714.

It is perhaps Defoe's greatest achievement that he was able to provide his printer with 12 pages of copy each week for nine years for the *Review* at the same time as producing innumerable political pamphlets and other material – including one of the earliest ghost stories, *A True Relation of the Apparition of one Mrs. Veal, the next Day after her Death* – as well as travelling the length and breadth of Great Britain over the foul and rutted roads, making new acquaintances in inns, asking questions, taking notes, setting up a network of informers and reporting the private views of the men of power and influence in the country so his Tory masters could tell who would be useful to them and who would be dangerous.

When Harley fell from power and the Whigs took office, Defoe changed sides yet again. He became outwardly a Tory, writing for the Tory press, but at the same time using his influence to try to dilute the more damaging attacks on his paymasters in the Whig government. In his role as a government spy, he spent a great deal of his time in Edinburgh where, as well as arranging for a Scottish edition of the *Review*, he controlled the *Edinburgh Courant* and the *Scots Postman*. Defoe also edited the *London Post* for Benjamin Harris in 1704–05 and the *Mercator; or, Commerce Retrieved* in 1713–14. In 1714 he produced a *Flying Post* as a rival to George Ridpath's paper of the same name.

He revived Marchamont Nedham's old title, *Mercurius Politicus*, as a monthly from 1716 to 1720. He also wrote for the manuscript publication *Dormer's News Letter* at about the same time. He was the first editor of the *Whitehall Evening-Post* in 1718 and the *Daily Post* in 1719, and he wrote for both Mist's and Applebee's *Weekly Journals* in the 1720s.

Defoe's position of writing Whig propaganda for the *Whitehall Evening-Post* while on the staff of the Tory, Nathaniel Mist's *Weekly Journal*, attracted comment. In both capacities he was in the pay of the Treasury. Defoe offered his services to Mist 'in the disguise of a translator of the foreign news'. His role was to try to tone down the attacks on the government, but he was so ineffectual that he was recalled from that activity. Read's *Weekly Journal* observed:

> As rats do run from falling houses,
> So Dan another cause espouses;
> Leaves poor Nat sinking in the mire,
> Writes Whitehall Evening Post for hire.[10]

Lord Haversham summed up the position by describing Defoe as 'a mean and mercenary prostitute'.

Yet Defoe's boundless energy and the variety of uses to which he put his pen earn him an honourable place in the history of journalism. Defoe was probably the first crime reporter. He knew many of the underworld characters, including Jonathan Wild and Moll King, the model for *Moll Flanders*. He produced paragraphs of crime reports for Nathaniel Mist's *Weekly Journal* and John Applebee's *Weekly Journal*. Defoe interviewed Jack Sheppard in the condemned cell and wrote the account of his escapes in the first person as if narrated by Sheppard himself. It was sold as a cheap pamphlet on 16 November 1724, the day Sheppard was executed. Parts were reprinted in the issue of the *Political State of Great Britain* for that month. It was said that Defoe 'stood on the scaffold to collect the dying words of convicts' which found their way into Applebee's sixpenny pamphlets of the 'Lives and Last Dying Speeches' of recently executed criminals.

## Taxes on Knowledge

One of the most cited examples of the pen being mightier than the sword is the effect Swift's pamphlet, the *Conduct of the Allies*, had in overthrowing the Whig government and bringing to an end the War of the Spanish Succession. This characterized the situation of the years up to around 1715: while the newspapers were safe and bland, the battle to influence public opinion was being fought in the pamphlets. The wounding attacks by the Whig pamphleteers on what they regarded as a damaging attempt to secure a dishonourable peace with France led Lord Bolingbroke to introduce the Stamp Act of 1712 partly as an attempt to silence his critics, but, more importantly, as a means of raising revenue when land tax was high and unpopular.

Under the Act, every copy of a news-carrying publication printed on a half-sheet of paper became liable to a duty of a halfpenny per copy, or, if printed on a full sheet, to a penny. A duty of one shilling was placed on every advertisement. Pamphlets were charged at two shillings a sheet for each edition, and, as a police measure, all periodicals had to include the printer's name and address.

Although the government's intention was to wipe out printed dissent, whose main vehicle was the pamphlet, it had a more damaging effect on the economics of the infant newspaper. Many writers feared that the Stamp Act would put an end to the printed newspaper. Forewarned of the provisions of the Act by his political contacts, Swift wrote to Stella, 'They are here intending to tax all printed penny papers a half-penny every half-sheet, which will completely ruin Grub-street.' Addison wrote in the *Spectator*, 'I am afraid that few of our Weekly Historians, who are Men that above all others delight in War, will be able to subsist under the Weight of a Stamp, and an approaching Peace … A Facetious friend of mine, who loves a Punn, calls the present Mortality among Authors, *The Fall of the Leaf*,[11] and in August 1712, when the Act was passed, Swift declared, 'all Grub-street is dead and gone last Week. No more Ghosts or Murders now for Love nor Money' – not that there was much evidence of ghosts and murders in the newspapers of the day.

Some newspapers did close down immediately. London victims of the Stamp Act included the *Medley*, the *Supplement*, the *Observator* and the *Plain Dealer*. Outside London, where circulations were smaller, at least seven papers went out of business. But for the most part the obituaries were premature, especially as no one foresaw the effects of a loophole in the drafting of the Act. While papers of a half-sheet or a whole sheet were subject to a tax on every single copy, papers of a half-sheet *and* a whole sheet – six pages – were only charged at the pamphlet rate. So a six-page newspaper would only have to pay a single flat-rate charge of two shillings per sheet no matter how many copies were printed.

It seems surprising that most of the existing daily and tri-weekly papers did not increase their size to six pages. However, in a period of relative calm with Britain no longer at war, and foreign news being costly in translation fees, there was little news to report. They simply increased their prices and bore the red tax stamp, the first in a series of taxes on knowledge.

## Weekly Journals

The first paper to exploit the loophole in the Act was a tri-weekly, *The British-Mercury* (1710–16; Figure 3.3), published by the 'Company of the Sun Fire Office in Threadneedle-street, behind the Royal Exchange'.[12] Virtually as soon as the Act was passed, *The British-Mercury* trebled its size from a single sheet to six pages by introducing extraneous matter. For 74 issues from 11 February 1713 to 7 July 1714 a serialization of *A Brief Historical and Chronological Account of all the Empires … of the World … from the Creation, to this present time* almost filled the whole paper. *The British-Mercury* contained very little news, most of which was news of mercantile interest only – diplomatic intelligence from the European capitals, the prices of South Sea and other stocks, the prices of corn and other commodities at Bear-Key, the Course of the Exchange, a schedule of moneys lent and paid off at the Exchequer, and shipping news listing the arrivals and departures at the ports with their cargoes ('Wool and Iron from Bilboa, Wine and Fruit from Lisbon and Elephant's Teeth from Guinea'[13]).

With a whole week's news to report, the weekly journals had more scope to exploit the loophole in the Act. Even so, the printers found it difficult to fill six pages with news. One solution was to copy *The British-Mercury* and pad out the paper with material in serial form in the hope that readers would become hooked and want to buy the next instalment. *The Voyages of Sinbad the Sailor* was serialized in the *Churchman's Last Shift, or, the Loyalist's Weekly Journal* in 1715, and *Robinson Crusoe* was serialized in *Heathcote's London Post* in 1719. James Read's *Weekly Journal, or, British Gazetteer* (Figure 3.4) showed real desperation in 1720 when it decided to serialize *The Lives of the Archbishops of Canterbury*.

The other solution, which was increasingly used after about 1720, was to build on the success of the pamphleteers and lead with a political essay. By that time this was considered relatively safe. Fears that the government would destroy the press by re-introducing the Printing Act had all but disappeared: the government had become dependent on the Stamp Act as a means of raising revenue; and politicians were beginning to realize that newspapers were here to stay and could be used for their own ends.

No other medium was distributed more widely or was more regularly read by the politically aware. Unlike the political pamphlet, the newspapers were periodical, which allowed the writers to develop their arguments over successive weeks, to respond quickly to political events and to use repetition, one of the most effective weapons in the propagandist's armoury; and so the newspaper began to overtake the pamphlet as the main vehicle for political comment.

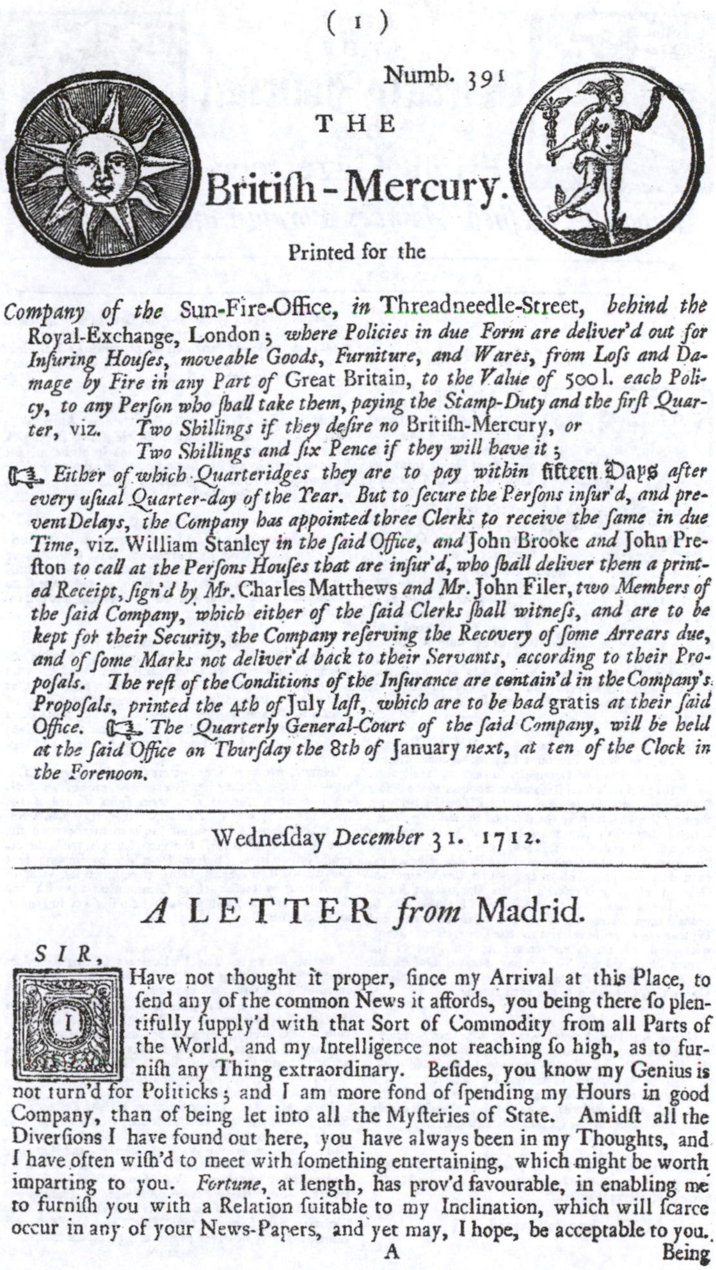

( 1 )

Numb. 391

THE

# Britiſh-Mercury.

Printed for the

*Company of the* Sun-Fire-Office, *in* Threadneedle-Street, *behind the* Royal-Exchange, London; *where Policies in due Form are deliver'd out for Inſuring Houſes, moveable Goods, Furniture, and Wares, from Loſs and Damage by Fire in any Part of* Great Britain, *to the Value of* 500 l. *each Policy, to any Perſon who ſhall take them, paying the Stamp-Duty and the firſt Quarter,* viz. *Two Shillings if they deſire no* Britiſh-Mercury, *or Two Shillings and ſix Pence if they will have it;*
☞ *Either of which Quarteridges they are to pay within* fifteen Days *after every uſual Quarter-day of the Year. But to ſecure the Perſons inſur'd, and prevent Delays, the Company has appointed three Clerks to receive the ſame in due Time,* viz. William Stanley *in the ſaid Office, and* John Brooke *and* John Preſton *to call at the Perſons Houſes that are inſur'd, who ſhall deliver them a printed Receipt, ſign'd by Mr.* Charles Matthews *and Mr.* John Filer, *two Members of the ſaid Company, which either of the ſaid Clerks ſhall witneſs, and are to be kept for their Security, the Company reſerving the Recovery of ſome Arrears due, and of ſome Marks not deliver'd back to their Servants, according to their Propoſals. The reſt of the Conditions of the Inſurance are contain'd in the Company's Propoſals, printed the 4th of* July *laſt, which are to be had* gratis *at their ſaid Office.* ☞ *The Quarterly General-Court of the ſaid Company, will be held at the ſaid Office on Thurſday the* 8th *of* January *next, at ten of the Clock in the Forenoon.*

Wedneſday *December* 31. 1712.

## *A* LETTER *from* Madrid.

*SIR,*

I Have not thought it proper, ſince my Arrival at this Place, to ſend any of the common News it affords, you being there ſo plentifully ſupply'd with that Sort of Commodity from all Parts of the World, and my Intelligence not reaching ſo high, as to furniſh any Thing extraordinary. Beſides, you know my Genius is not turn'd for Politicks; and I am more fond of ſpending my Hours in good Company, than of being let into all the Myſteries of State. Amidſt all the Diverſions I have found out here, you have always been in my Thoughts, and I have often wiſh'd to meet with ſomething entertaining, which might be worth imparting to you. *Fortune*, at length, has prov'd favourable, in enabling me to furniſh you with a Relation ſuitable to my Inclination, which will ſcarce occur in any of your News-Papers, and yet may, I hope, be acceptable to you.

A Being

**3.3** *The British-Mercury,* 31 December 1712

( 1601 )

THE
**Weekly Journal**
OR,
British Gazetteer.

*Being the freſheſt Advices Foreign and Domeſtick.*

SATURDAY, MAY 14, 1720.

### SPAIN.

Coruuna, April 7.

AN the 1ſt Inſtant, a Ceſſation of Arms by Sea, and free Commerce with Great Britain, was Proclaimed here. At the ſame time arriv'd an Order from the King of Spain, diſpatch'd by M. Schaub, for Conſul Parker's being ſet at Liberty, and reſtor'd to the Exerciſe of his Office of Conſul.

Madrid, April 22. Yeſterday the Queen, after having been Complimented by the Foreign Miniſters, as alſo the late Duke of Ormond, performed her Devotions in the Church of Atocha. The 19th, Don Seguera, who is to reſide at the Hague, ſet out for Holland. M. Schaub has not yet appear'd at Court, but he confers frequently with the principal Miniſters. Orders are diſpatch'd for the Evacuation of Sicily and Sardinia; ſo that General Maulevrier is ſhortly expected here from France, and Colonel Stanhope from London.

### SWEDEN.

Stockholm, May 1. Yeſterday the Men of War and Galleys put to Sea. The ſame Day M. Grundel arrived here from the King of Denmark, ſo that we ſhall ſoon know that Prince's final Reſolution about a Peace. The Preliminaries are, That all the former Treaties between the two Crowns ſhall be the Baſis of the enſuing Pacification; there ſhall be a general Amneſty; Denmark is to reſtore to Sweden in ſix Weeks, the Iſland of Rugen, Stralſund, &c. Sweden renounces the Right of being exempted from paying Toll in the Sound; the Affair of the Duke of Holſtein is referr'd to the Congreſs at Brunſwick. In the mean time the Dutchy of Holſtein is to be reſtor'd immediately. The Affairs of Mahrſtrand and Wiſmar are likewiſe referr'd to the Congreſs of Brunſwick, and the Danes to remain in Poſſeſſion of the former Place, till the Swedes pay 200000 Dollars for the Reſtitution of Pomerania and Rugen. The King's Coronation is deferr'd to the 13th Inſtant.

### ITALY.

Genoa, April 25. Yeſterday the Spaniſh Envoy receiv'd an Expreſs from Madrid, with the neceſſary Orders for the Evacuation of Sicily and Sardinia, ſo 'tis hop'd a Battle will be prevented in Sicily; for according to our laſt Letters, the Imperial Army is advanced to Alcamo, to attack the Spaniards, who having abandon'd their Poſts, retired under the Cannon of Palermo.

### GERMANY.

Hanover, May 10. Prince Frederick being perfectly recovered of his late Indiſpoſition, diverts himſelf frequently at Herrenhauſen.

[Price Three Half-pence.]

Vienna, May 1. Yeſterday the Earl of Cadogan had a long Audience of the Emperor; his Excellency has made ſuch moderate Propoſals for preventing a Religious War in the Empire, that all the Grievances on both Sides will be amicably adjuſted.

### SWITZERLAND.

Schafhouſen, May 5 'Tis ſaid Cardinal Alberoni is in the Dominions of Venice ſolliciting that Republick to intercede with the Court of Vienna in his behalf for leave to ſettle in a Place belonging to the Emperor. The King of Spain threatens Repriſals upon the Republick of Genoa for conniving at the Cardinals Eſcape.

### DENMARK.

Copenhagen, May 7. Admiral Norris with the Britiſh Fleet, is arrived in the Sound. Tis ſaid, that 27 Muſcovite Men of War and 377 Gallies beſides Tranſports are ſailed from Revel to Finland and have ſince attempted to land near Calmar in Sweden but this report is not Credited.

### HOLLAND.

Hague, May 18. This Day Count de Morville had a long Conference with the Spaniſh Ambaſſador, who has received Advice by an Expreſs from Madrid, that Orders have been diſpatched for evacuating Sicily and Sardinia, without farther Heſitation. They write from Copenhagen, that the whole Britiſh Squadron is arrived in the Sound, and was ſaluted by the Artillery at Elſignore

Hague, May 17, Our Letters from Leghorn and Genoa tell us, that they hourly expect Advice of an Action in Sicily. And as they write from Vienna of the 4th Inſtant, by way of Poſtſcript, that they had a Report, that there has been an Engagement between the two Armies. We expect the next Letters with the utmoſt Impatience. Letters from France import, that the Spaniards in Sicily being ſtreightned for want of Proviſions, by reaſon their Communication with the Sea is cut off, they will probably be oblig'd to ſurrender at Diſcretion.

### FRANCE.

Paris, May 18. The Parliaments of this Kingdom being ſtill unwilling to Regiſter the Edict formerly mention'd, the ſame will be declared formal aſſoon as the inferiour Courts have Regiſter'd it. The Spaniſh Ship of 60 Guns, which was lately brought to Port Lewis, is called the Gloceſter, which the Spaniards formerly bought in England. The Cardinal de Noailles ſeldom appears abroad upon a Pretence of Illneſs. 'Tis ſaid the Card. de Bois is to carry to Rome the Project of Accommodation about the Conſtitution.

Paris, May 13. This Afternoon arrived Letters from Sicily, dated the 27th of laſt Month, which adviſe, that the Spaniſh Army commanded by the Marquiſs de Lede, had retreated under the Walls of Palermo, and that Gen. Mercy, with the Imperialiſts, was incamped within Cannon-Shot of them. The Marquis de Lede had intrench'd himſelf, and drawn 36 Pieces of Cannon out of Palermo, for defending his Intrenchments. His Situation was between two Hills, and judg'd ſtrong. General Mercy however determin'd to attack him.

11 N A Con-

**3.4** Read's *Weekly Journal*, 14 May 1720

### Mist's *Weekly Journal*

Nathaniel Mist's *Weekly Journal, or, Saturday's Post* was the first weekly journal to take the risk of publishing strongly anti-ministerial essays. Almost from the start Mist courted trouble. The first issue of his *Weekly Journal* appeared from Mist's printing house in Great Carter Lane near St Paul's Cathedral on 15 December 1716. Shortly afterwards, in April 1717, Mist was arrested for printing libels against the government, and in November of the same year the *Weekly Journal* was presented by the Grand Jury for Middlesex as 'a false, seditious, scandalous and profane libel'. In 1721 Mist was sentenced to stand in the pillory at Charing Cross and the Royal Exchange and to pay a fine of £50 for articles 'scandalously reflecting on the King'. Unable to pay the fine, he spent the best part of 1721 in jail. On 8 June 1723 he printed another libel on the government for which he was sentenced to pay a fine of £100 and suffer a year's imprisonment. The young Benjamin Franklin, who was working in London as a printer at the time, recorded that 'Mist's treasonable papers are being sold for half a guinea' as a result of the prosecution. In 1727 Mist was tried at the Court of King's Bench for a libel on the king. He was sentenced to pay a fine of £100, to give security for good behaviour during life and to be imprisoned until the sentence was fulfilled.

The crunch came on 24 August 1728, when Mist published the 'Persian Letter' which purported to describe recent events in Persia, but was in fact an obvious allegory of the state of Britain as seen from Mist's Jacobite perspective. It referred to 'the miseries that Usurpation had introduced to that unfortunate Empire' and praised the Pretender in its description of the rightful heir, the Sophi, as having 'the greatest Character that ever Eastern Monarch bore'. The Grand Jury for Middlesex found it to be

> a false, infamous, scandalous, seditious and treasonable Libel … in which Paper are also contained … the most false, malicious and scurrilous Reflections, tending to scandalize and vilify His most Excellent Majesty's sacred Person, Family and Government, to poison the Minds of his loyal and faithful Subjects with Jealousies and Distrust, concerning his wise and gentle Administration, and to alienate from his Majesty the Allegience and Affections of his People.[14]

Within days over 20 people were arrested, including Elizabeth Nutt and her daughter Catherine, who together controlled a network of Mercury Women, all of Mist's printing staff, his housekeeper and even 'Robt Combstock – Mist's nephew, a little boy'. When the case came to court, the pressman and the compositor were both sentenced to be pilloried and imprisoned for six months, the printer's apprentice was sentenced to walk round the four courts in Westminster Hall with a paper on his forehead denoting his offence and to be imprisoned for one month, and Amy Walker,

Mist's maid, was sentenced to six months' hard labour 'and to be stript down to her Waist, and receive the Correction of the House'.[15] Mist fled to France, where he continued to run the paper by remote control under its new title, *Fog's Weekly Journal*, which continued until his death in 1737.

Anti-ministerial papers like Mist's were commonly harassed by the authorities. Papers were stopped by the Post Office, and their printers lived under the ever-present threat of the law of seditious libel, general warrants and sudden arrest. Seditious libel covered a wide area, which if taken to its logical conclusion, would have prevented virtually all political comment in the press. Sedition was defined as anything that was likely to incite disaffection against the king and his heirs, the government, the Houses of Parliament or the administration of justice, even where the comment was based on the truth. The responsibility for determining whether an article was seditious lay entirely with the judge. The jury's function was limited to deciding whether the accused bore some responsibility for the article's publication.

The general warrant was the principal weapon used to intimidate the press. Between 1715 and 1759 the Secretaries of State issued over 70 such warrants against newspapers. They were called general warrants because they specified the offence but not the offender. They were used to hold in custody large numbers of people who had only the remotest connection with the alleged offence. The warrants were enforced by the King's Messengers, a gang of hired thugs, who had the power to arrest anybody they wanted, to seize their property and destroy their printing equipment.

The unfairness of these prosecutions was emphasized in the essay in the *Craftsman* for 3 September 1737 after its printers were seized under general warrant for printing the satire on the Stage Licensing Act in the issue for 2 July 1737:

> The *Compositors* themselves, whose Business it is to put the Letters together, which they pick out of different Cases, one by one, have often the Copy deliver'd to them by Piecemeal, and in disjointed Fragments, without any Coherence or Connection, one Part of it being given to one Compositor, and another to another, for the Sake of Expedition; especially in periodical Writings; so that they have seldom any Opportunity to read or judge of what they are composing. The *Press-Men* are still more in the Dark; for as soon as they receive the Forms ready set from the *Compositors*, they have nothing to do but to work them off as fast as they can, at so much a Thousand; and the *Devil*, as he is call'd, is only the Servant of the rest, whom they hire to run upon Errands, and do all their Drudgery. Many of *these poor Creatures* cannot so much as read; or if they can, is it to be suppos'd that they are able to judge what is strictly speaking a *Libel*, or not a *Libel*, which is so far from an easy Point to determine, that it often puzzles the *nicest Splitters of Cases?*

In a business relying heavily on a network of credit and debt, imprisonment, or even the threat of it, was a particularly savage blow as it could panic creditors into calling in their debts. Nonetheless, because the anti-ministerial papers trod dangerously and were generally more fun, they enjoyed far higher sales than those papers that were simply dull apologists for the government, reacting to the agenda set by the opposition papers.

Due to the availability of newspapers in coffee-houses (in 1739 there were 551 coffee-houses in London alone[16]), barbershops and alehouses, it is estimated that a single copy of a weekly paper could reach as many as 40 people.[17] Those who could not read could have the newspaper read to them by the light of the tavern fireplace or on street corners. Charles Leslie remarked in 1708, referring to 'Tutchin, De Foe, and the rest of the Scandalous Clubb':

> *Their* Books *and* Pamphlets *have been solidly and seriously Answer'd. But their* Papers *have been neglected, that is their* weekly penny Papers, *which go through the Nation like* News-Papers. A*nd have done much more* Mischief *than the others. For the greatest Part of the* People *do not Read* Books, *Most of them cannot* Read *at all. But they will Gather together about one that can* Read, *and listen to an* Observator *or* Review *(as I have seen them on the Streets); where all the* Principles *of* Rebellion *are Instill'd into them … which they suck in Greedily, and are Prejudic'd past Expression.*[18]

Yet the type of news in *The London Gazette* and *The Daily Courant* – foreign affairs and official announcements – were only of interest to a small élite. So there began a gradual shift towards home news that would attract a wider, semi-literate audience.

Mist's *Weekly Journal* was remarkable for its coverage of home news, which was far more extensive than that of any of its predecessors. Recognizing that certain aspects of the news could be exploited for their entertainment value, Mist was said to have

> an agent scraping the Jails in Middlesex and Surrey of their Commitments; another has a warrant for scouring the Ale-houses and Gin-shops for such as dye of excessive Drinking; a Person is posted at the Savoy to take up Deserters and another in the Park to watch the Motions of the Guards.[19]

Charles Delafaye, an Under Secretary and a former editor of the *London Gazette*, complaining about the popularity of Mist's, attributed this to the fact that it was 'being wrote *ad captum* for the common people'. The *Weekly Medley* described Mist's as being 'mightily spread about among the vulgar'.[20]

Before Mist's, the social geography of newspaper content was firmly located in the upper and middle reaches of society – the political and trading classes – despite the fact that newspapers penetrated below those levels; hence the focus on political debate and, for the trading community, the heavy emphasis on foreign news and price information. Mist widened the appeal of the newspaper to cover the interests and preoccupations of a lower class. A number of foreign visitors to England in the eighteenth century reported with amazement that people of all classes, even workmen, could be seen in the streets reading newspapers.

The characters who appear in the pages of Mist's *Weekly Journal* read like the cast list of the *Beggar's Opera*: highwaymen, prostitutes, receivers and thief-takers, including the model for Peachum himself, Jonathan Wild. Here is how the *Weekly Journal* described Wild closing down the Spiggot gang who refused to join Wild's organization of thieves and receivers:

> About a Month since the Monmouth Waggon being robbed to a great Value, near Butcher's-Grove on Hounslow-Heath; the Master made Application to Jonathan Wild, who being under a disposition, gave Orders to his Gentlemen of Horse to be very diligent in the Discovery of the Thieves; and accordingly, last Monday, he got Intelligence of the Persons he suspected, viz Wm. Spiggot, Thomas Phillips, alias Cross, and Joseph Lindsey, that they were then at Finsbury, near Moorfields; Whereupon one Mr Merritt, a Friend of the Master Waggoner's, went along with Mr Wild's Agent in Quest of them; but being gone from thence some Minutes before, they pursued 'em, unknown, to Westminster, where they found them in the Black Horse Inn, in the Broad Way: A Constable and others being got, they went into the House to seize 'em, when the Rogues took to their Pistols, and Spiggot offered to fire his close against the Breast of the Master of the Inn, but it flash'd in the Pan; the others attempted to fire, but were prevented. There was seized with them a Porter, who plied at the upper Watch-House in High Holborn, who used to set the Waggons and Passengers out of Town for them, hire their Horses for them, and receive their Plunder. They were all carried before a Justice of the Peace, and committed to the Gate-House; but upon a Representation of Mr Wild, that that Prison was not strong enough for such notorious Offenders, they were removed to Newgate last Wednesday Night. It appears by the Confession of Thomas Phillips, that these were the same Men that committed the following Robberies, as formerly mentioned in this Paper, viz. on several Countrymen about two Months ago, on Hounslow-Heath; on the five Waggons near Tyburn; on a Chapman near Uxbridge, from whom they took one hundred and fifty Pounds worth of Buttons and Mohair, which goods they sold to – Hogg, living at one Ball's, a Brandy-Shop, the Sign of the two Pewter Flaggons, in Newtners-Lane, who used to take off the Goods they brought him, notwithstanding he knew how they came by them. The said Thomas Phillips further confesses, that on the eighth of this Instant, he, with the other two, robbed several Waggons on a Heath near Clare-Mount, in their Way from London to Portsmouth; and, that at the time they were Apprehended, they were setting out for Hertford Road, with Intent to rob the Waggons and Carriers passing that Way.[21]

## The *Craftsman*

After Mist fled to France, the *Country Journal; or, the Craftsman* became the most influential anti-ministerial weekly representing the uneasy coalition of Tories and disaffected Whigs in opposition to Walpole. It started life in 1726 as an essay sheet, but was soon transformed into a four-page weekly journal to win a wider audience by adding a news section. The *London Journal* for 2 January 1731 accused the *Craftsman* of making the people '*ripe for Seditions*, by Ten Thousand *seditious Papers* scatter'd among 'em every Week, for three or four Years together'. At the height of its success when the opposition campaign was in full swing, it was said to have achieved sales of 13,000 copies per week.[22]

The huge sales of the *Craftsman* made it an attractive advertising medium. Half of its production costs were covered by advertising revenue,[23] mainly from quack doctors who made block bookings advertising their Quintessence of Vipers and other aphrodisiacs, and 'True and Certain Cures for the Clap'.

The *Craftsman* was conducted on behalf of the Tory Lord Bolingbroke and the opposition Whig William Pulteney by Nicholas Amherst, an Oxford scholar turned hack, best known by his pen name, 'Caleb D'Anvers, Esq; of Gray's Inn', which was actually a pseudonym for Amherst, Bolingbroke, Pulteney and other anonymous contributors, possibly including Henry Fielding.[24] Amherst was a good man who was shabbily treated. When the printer of the *Craftsman* was arrested by a warrant from the Secretary of State for libel, Amherst surrendered himself in his stead and was imprisoned. Despite this punishment and years of risk-taking, when Pulteney and his friends made their peace with the government, they had no further use for Amherst. He ended his days in poverty and died in 1742 'of a broken heart' at the early age of 45. He would have suffered a pauper's funeral had his former printer not paid for his tomb.[25]

The leading articles of the *Craftsman* attacked the corruption and abuse of power of Walpole's administration. They accused Walpole of placing self-interest above the national interest to the detriment of the middling orders the *Craftsman* claimed to represent. Many of the essays were devoted to the freedom of the press, emphasizing that the liberty of the press bore a direct relationship to the liberty of the individual.

Although the government and the ministerial supporters tended to yoke *Fog's Weekly Journal* and the *Craftsman* together as ploughing exactly the same furrow, there were vast differences between them. Mist's and *Fog's* were out and out Jacobite Tory papers. They had no time for the opposition Whigs who paid homage to the House of Hanover. The *Craftsman* sought to woo the Tories away from the Jacobite influence and into alliance with the opposition Whigs to form a Country party. Moreover, the papers had completely different styles and appealed to different audiences. Mist's papers were more popularist, whereas the *Craftsman*, especially in its leading articles, was more earnest and intellectual, written for an educated élite who could understand its classical and historical allusions and who had a good understanding of domestic politics and international affairs.

Despite the *Craftsman*'s high sales, it would be difficult to claim that it had any major effect on government policy or the outcome of history. The failure of the Excise Bill against which the *Craftsman* campaigned so vociferously in 1733 was due to Walpole's small parliamentary majority at the time. Walpole's eventual downfall was caused by other factors and not by the arguments of the *Craftsman*. Like most newspapers with a strong line in polemic, it was bought by readers to have their prejudices confirmed. Many people in the country shared the same views as the *Craftsman*. Its high circulation probably means nothing more than that it was preaching to the converted. Perhaps the most that can be said for the *Craftsman* is that, in giving the false impression that the Tories and the dissident Whigs were one united party, it frightened Walpole into spending so much money on ministerial papers just to counter the threat of a single paper. Without the *Craftsman*, Walpole would not have spent so much money, and without the money the ministerial papers would not have survived for as long as they did.

## Bribery and Corruption

Political sponsorship became a major factor in newspaper finance. Newspapers and individual writers received backhanders from government and opposition groups in an attempt to influence public opinion. According to the Secret Committee investigating Walpole's financial management, Walpole's corrupt ministry was reported to have spent a total of £50,077 18s. of Treasury funds between 1731 and 1741 on bribes to newspapers[26] – around £5 million at today's prices.

This is likely to be an underestimate. According to the *Craftsman* (31 July 1731), Walpole was spending £20,000 *per year* in subsidizing the ministerial press. William Arnall, author of the *Free Briton*, alone was receiving £6,000 per year from the Treasury for supporting the ministry – at a time when a labourer in regular employment was lucky to earn £20 per year. In addition, the *Free Briton*, *The Daily Courant* and the rest of the ministerial press were sent free through the posts, were given away to coffee-house proprietors, and were favoured with the placing of official advertisements. In 1735 Walpole decided to put all his eggs in one basket by closing down the *Free Briton*, *The Daily Courant*, the *Corn-Cutter's Journal* and other ministerial papers and amalgamating them in a new paper, the *Daily Gazetteer*.

As we have seen from the career of Daniel Defoe, in an age characterized by bribery and corruption it was not unknown for newspapers or their writers to change allegiances by threats on the one hand and bribes on the other. The *London Journal* is a good example of this. The *London Journal* attained some brief notoriety in 1720 by publishing the letters from 'Cato' attacking the South Sea scheme and attempts to reintroduce press censorship:

> Without Freedom of Thought, there can be no such Thing as Wisdom; and no such Thing as Publick Liberty … Guilt only dreads Liberty of Speech, which drags it out of its lurking Holes, and exposes its Deformity and Horrour to Day-light … Freedom of Speech is the great Bulwark of Liberty; they prosper and die together: and it is the Terror of *Traytors* and *Oppressors*, and a Barrier against them … All Ministries, therefore, who were *Oppressors*, or intending to be *Oppressors*, have been loud in their Complaints against Freedom of Speech and the License of the Press.[27]

The letters of Cato increasingly irritated the government. So it decided to open negotiations to buy up the paper. The final terms are not known, but a document survives written by the proprietor estimating that, as an opposition paper, its sales of 15,000 copies produced a profit of £960 a year, but if it turned into a ministerial paper, sales would fall to 8,000 at the most, advertising revenue would be halved, and the profit would drop to £124.[28]

After the paper was turned, the main writers, John Trenchard and Thomas Gordon, left and the letters of Cato began to appear in a new paper, the *British Journal* (1722–31). On Trenchard's death, Thomas Gordon was bribed into supporting the government by the offer of the post of Commissioner of the Wine Licences with a salary of £300 per year, and the *British Journal* became a ministerial paper, edited by William Arnall and Matthew Concanen, who also wrote for *The Daily Courant.* Walpole later rewarded Concanen by giving him the post of Attorney General in the West Indies.

In the 1730s the *London Journal* was written by James Pitt under the pseudonym Francis Osborne, lampooned by his detractors as 'Mother Osborne' for his nannyish style, scolding the opposition press. Pitt, like Concanen, received lucrative sinecures in return for his support for Walpole. In 1729 he was given a place in the Customs, which he sold for £1,100,[29] and was later given the post of Surveyor of Tobacco.

William Guthrie, who had been arrested for writing against the government in *Common Sense* and *Old England*, was turned by an annual pension of £200 from secret service funds. James Ralph, who co-founded *Old England* with Guthrie and had made a career out of attacking the government, received a pension of £300 under similar conditions. As the *Grub-street Journal* explained:

> The Province, or rather the States, of Grub-street, like those of Switzerland, never

> enter into any alliance offensive and defensive with any one contending power, against another; but wisely keep themselves in an exact neutrality. At the same time, their private members are ready to engage on either side for good pay, without ever inquiring into the merits of the cause.[30]

It is debatable how many wrote from political conviction or how many adopted a political stance from necessity. If a regular income from government patronage was not forthcoming, writing against the Ministry with its potentially higher rewards (because more people read the anti-ministerial press) and its attendant risks was the only option. Nicholas Amherst unsuccessfully sought employment writing for the government before starting his career with the *Craftsman*. Moving the other way, Ralph Courteville is thought to have written for the *Craftsman* before becoming the principal writer for the *Daily Gazetteer*.

## Leading Articles

Despite the political provocation from the six-page weekly journals and their avoidance of stamp duties, the government did not act until 1725, when it passed another Stamp Act that finally closed the loophole in the law. The weekly journals reduced their pages from six to four, increased the size of their pages and reduced the size of their mastheads to leave more room for editorial matter, which was expanded to three columns per page by using smaller type. Prices increased from three-halfpence to twopence.

After the 1725 Act, the four-page weekly journal with its three distinct parts – an essay or leading article on page one, news on pages two and three, and advertisements on page four – became a popular and well-established format.

The popularity of Mist's *Weekly Journal* and the *Craftsman* led to a new wave of weekly journals providing employment for the scribes of Grub Street. Major new titles included the *Universal Spectator* in 1728, the *Grub-street Journal* in 1730, the staunchly Anglican *Weekly Miscellany* in 1732, which was answered by the dissenting *Old Whig* in 1735, *Common Sense* in 1737, the *Westminster Journal* in 1741 and *Old England* in 1743.

Henry Baker, Defoe's son-in-law, started the *Universal Spectator* as an attempt to emulate the social and literary essays that characterized the *Spectator*. Defoe wrote the introduction to the first paper: 'If this paper was not intended to be what no paper at present is, we should never attempt to crowd in among such a throng of public writers as at this time oppress the town.'[31] Because its leading articles eschewed politics and concentrated for the most part on social commentary, they were some of the most entertaining of the 1730s, as in the essay on modesty in the issue for 23 September 1732:

> As the immodest Man never sets Bounds to his Conduct, so when this Vice is improv'd by a corrupted Fancy and Imagination, it sallies out into all the Excesses of Lewdness and Obscenity: the *Pen* drops *Smut*, and the *Tongue* is the Drain and Common Sewer of all the Filth that is in the Heart. Obscene Conversation is so much worse than Action, as it is capable of being so much oftener repeated; and obscene Writing is still worse than obscene Conversation, because it is Poison gilded over, and prepar'd by Art, capable of doing Mischief when the Author of it is no more; and able to infect thousands, and to extend its pernicious Contagion to, perhaps, many Generations … The thin Gloss and Laquering that gilds and encompasses the filthy Dose, and is falsely call'd *Wit*, soon wears away when the Tinsel Crust is once broken, and is lost and overwhelm'd by the breaking up of the Mud and Slime that were under it. Such Wit generally consists of *Pun* and *double Entendre* … To be always dabbling in Dirt and Nastiness, what is it but the Life of a most contemptible Animal? What is it but a more ignominious Office than that of the *Night Man*, who professes to do his Duty with Decency, and carefully conceals the Filth, which the obscene Man is so careful to spread abroad under the Nostrils of all about him? To be always roving in quest of Carrion or a Dung-heap, what is that but the Life of a *Grub*, or of a Fly and Reptile, of the lowest and most infamous Species? … *Obscene Conversation* has its Rise from a defective or a very loose and corrupt Education. Some Families of Note are not without here and there an ill Example of this Sort; and the Youth of such Families are suffer'd to converse too often and too freely with pamper'd impudent *Menials*, or to make Excursions among the Vulgar; and amidst the Amusements and Diversions of low Life, to glean up many Impurities which the Rabble, the sole and original Authors of them, ought wholly to appropriate to themselves. From the luscious Caresses and flatteries of a Chambermaid, and the courser Conversation of a Page or a Footman, they are brought on to a smutty *Health* or *Toast*, a *Tale* or a *Jest*, a new obscene *Phrase*, or *Term of Art*, an immodest *Picture* or *Figure*, a *Song*, a *Novel*, or a *Play*; 'till at last they are introduc'd to some accomplish'd Rake, and by him to the Brothel.

A standard technique employed by the opposition journals was to use a notorious figure as a means of launching a coded attack on Walpole. The most famous example was the essay in *Common Sense* for 30 July 1737 on 'the infamous Turpin … known to be a Thief by the Whole Kingdom', which probably seemed sharply satirical at the time:

> Must not a Foreigner laugh to hear the whole Nation exclaiming every Day in the publick News Papers against the Depredations of one pitiful Fellow, one of very mean Rank and Qualifications, every Way contemptible? – What must they think of a Nation who quietly permits such a Wretch as this to carry on a successful Series of impudent Robberies, which every one knows, every one exclaims against, and yet every one submits to.

While the leading articles of the new wave of weekly journals included a smattering of social essays and literary criticism, they dealt mainly with the political and religious controversies of the day, sometimes seriously, sometimes satirically, and usually from a partisan viewpoint. The *Craftsman* dropped its serious stance in its leading article on 30 April 1737 by proposing a tax on urine:

> *Such a Tax* will best serve our Turn. It will pay off our *Debts*, even supposing there are within this Island but *8 Millions of Souls;* and should every Soul upon an Average, vent but a *Quart* a Day; (which, at a *Farthing* a *Quart*, would be *7s. 2d. Farthing* a Year) yet this trifling Tax would produce above *3 Millions* a Year.

Ten years later, in December 1747, the *Westminster Journal*, having pointed out the drawbacks to the proposed new taxes on plate, servants and malt, suggested taxing turds as they were

> something necessary to all people, of all ranks and sexes: Something that's secure against frauds in individuals, and which the collectors would not chuse to *secrete* any part of for themselves … From the duke down to the beggar, he must *pay his due*, and would not do otherwise for any pecuniary consideration.[32]

On 9 December 1745, when the Jacobite rebels under Bonnie Prince Charlie had taken Derby and were thought to be marching on London, the *Westminster Journal* offered its advice on military strategy:

> The rebels, we are told, are particularly fond of *exercising their parts* on the female sex; and being fellows of *pretty keen appetites*, commonly take up with whatever falls in their way: Wherefore methinks it would be no wrong policy to serve them up a *dish*, which, for taking its *name* and *origin* from their good friends the *French*, must therefore be the more acceptable to them. This may be done by providing as many ladies as we can *conveniently spare* from the hundreds of *Drury*, and other parts of the great metropolis, and see them safe convey'd to the places that are likeliest to be visited by the *Highlanders*; who, pleased with such fine ladies in silk gowns and large hoop petticoats, will take every one of them to be a *Laird's daughter*, and think it no little honour to storm such illustrious forts; whereby they'll contract a *disease* which will effectually stop their progress, and afford his majesty's forces an easy and cheap-bought conquest.

## The *Grub-street Journal*

Of all the non-political weekly journals of the eighteenth century, the *Grub-street Journal*, the eighteenth-century equivalent of *Private Eye*, 'Sold at the Pegasus (vulgarly called the Flying-Horse) in Grub-street', was the most notorious for its propensity for starting quarrels with other writers and generally stirring up trouble.

It started life as a literary journal, renowned for the vigorous way in which it conducted its literary vendettas and the ferocity of its personal attacks on individual writers. It is thought that the *Grub-street Journal* was founded as a vehicle for Pope to attack his many enemies – a continuation of the Dunciad by other means. The full extent of Pope's involvement with the journal is not known. He contributed numerous verses to the early issues, and the editors, Richard Russel and John Martyn, went out of their way to pick a fight with anybody Pope did not like.

Gradually Pope's influence, or interest, in the paper began to decline and the paper began to develop its own character, expanding the range of its satire beyond the confines of Pope's literary squabbles to cover a much wider range of material, including medicine, theology, the theatre, the administration of justice and other social issues. It attracted a large number of correspondents who used the paper to carry out their squabbles in public while the editors sat back and enjoyed the spectacle, prodding the antagonists into action where necessary. Whenever one controversy looked like running out of steam, the journal would invent a new one to keep up the excitement.

Journalism was one of its main targets. The preface to the collected essays of the *Grub-street Journal* explained:

> To furnish materials for the Daily Papers, Collectors are sent all over the City, suburbs and surrounding villages, to pick up articles of News; who being payed according to the length and number of them, it is no wonder that so few of them are true … as to the Foreign, there is good reason to think the case worse: so that the chief, if not the only articles, upon the truth of which we can safely depend, are those inserted in direct contradiction to some published before … All News-papers, as to their historical parts, may be justly looked upon as the productions of Grub-street; and even as to those which are moral, political or literary, they are frequently seen to come from the same place … We profess ourselves Members of the Society of Grub-street in general, but we have formed ourselves into a select company, in order to restrain the enormities of our brethren.[33]

As a means of attempting to restrain the enormities of its brethren, the *Grub-street Journal* printed contradictory accounts of the same event taken from the preceding week's newspapers, with sarcastic remarks on their discrepancies and inaccuracies. The carelessness in reporting deaths attracted this comment:

> There is no privilege in which the authors of our daily and weekly papers may more justly glory than that of the power of life and death. Whom they will they send to the grave, and whom that they will they restore to life again … The Archbishop of Canterbury, who, God be thanked, is still living, has often with pleasure and surprise read in these papers the account of his own death.[34]

## The *Old Whig*

The news columns of the daily and tri-weekly papers catered for the man of business. There was a strong emphasis on foreign news, politics and trade. The news values of the weekly journals were more downmarket, following the trend set by Mist's and Applebee's *Weekly Journals*. The *Old Whig* is representative of the weekly journals of the 1730s. Drawing on a week's newspapers to furnish its columns, it invariably selected human-interest stories that were simply and entertainingly reported to appeal to all classes.

Take the issue for 24 June 1736, for example. Apart from accounts of a running race, the meeting of 'The Commissioners appointed by Act of Parliament to build a Bridge from Westminster to Lambeth', a suicide, and the usual list of those who died in the preceding week, including one who 'Complain'd of being out of Order, and went to the necessary-House, where he was found dead', most of the remaining domestic news items are either crime stories or accounts of fatal accidents.

The crime reports include the obligatory highwayman story, a murder, the seizure of smuggled goods from a Sussex barn, two cases of body-snatching (one committed by the 'Grave-Digger of Stepney Parish, who took up four Dead Bodies out of the Church-yard and sold them to a Surgeon' and the other a gangland rescue of 'the Body of one of the Malefactors who was executed from the Beadles of the Barbers and Surgeons Company'), a number of burglary cases including one where the guilty party was 'the Turnkey at Newcastle Newgate', and two macabre accounts which show that crime does not always pay:

> We hear that the Officers of Newgate, in searching the Sewer to find Daniel Maldon, who lately made his Escape from Newgate, have found the Bodies of two of the four Prisoners who made their Escape from Newgate about two Months ago: It is supposed that they were smothered in the Sewer.
>
> Early Yesterday Morning, as a Chimney-Sweeper was sweeping a Chimney at Mr. Boyd's the Woolpack at Paddington, about half way the Boy met an Obstruction, and putting his Hand up to feel what stopt him, took hold of the Leg of a Man, which frighted him so much, that he came down immediately, and could scarce be kept from going into Fits; immediately after the Body of a Man quiet smoak-dry'd tumbled down; by the Appearance it made it must have been there several Months, and is thought to have been some Thief that endeavoured to come down the Chimney to rob the House.

The fatal accidents include deaths by drowning, a woman crushed to death by a wagon, a brewery employee who 'fell into a Copper of boiling Liquor, and was scalded to death', and the case of one who 'had been at Dinner at the Cock at Holloway … where 'tis suppos'd he drank too freely, wou'd clime up a very high Tree to shew his Agility, which he accordingly did' and accordingly 'fell to the Ground and died immediately'. Perhaps the most painful of all was the accident that befell

> one Wood, Master of the Chatham Coach, as he was driving some Company to Maidstone, the Rein slipp'd out of his Hand as he was going down a Hill, by which Accident he fell on the Splinter-Bar, and bruised himself in such a Manner, that he died next Day. He never spoke from the Time he was hurt, except upon being asked how they should get the Coach home, when he reply'd, *How do they think, but with the Horses.*

History does not relate whether those famous last words were spoken in a high-pitched voice.

The leading article in the *Old Whig* for 16 March 1738 provides an early example of what can only be described as campaigning journalism ahead of its time, arguing the case for the abolition of slavery:

> But what Right have those *Europeans*, who carry the Trade upon *Negroes*, thus to degrade human Nature, and treat them in the same Matter as they treat the *Brutes that perish*? Are not those unhappy *Africans* in the same Rank of Beings with those that enslave them? Or, do they weakly imagine, that the Tincture of the Skin makes an Essential Difference between the Blacks and other Men? If the Tables were turned, and the *Africans* could play the same Game with the *Europeans*, as some of *them* do with the *Blacks*: if they should come upon the *English* Coast to steal Slaves, or, which is altogether as bad, should offer to *purchase Slaves*, and thereby excite some *Barbarians* among us to do as is done among other Savages abroad, to make War upon others for the Sake of having to Captives to sell, (which Offer would certainly prevail even in *England* with many) I suppose we should then hear loud Cries of *Injustice* and *Cruelty* against such *Traders*. And yet have not the Negroes as much Right (if it were in their Power) to invade *England*, and carry away, by Force, Men, Women, and Children, and make them Slaves in a foreign Country, or to come and purchase Slaves here, as any of the *English* have thus to deal with them?
>
> I presume all, who have not quite thrown off *Humanity*, are shocked at the Thought of making *innocent* Creatures among *Mankind Slaves*; excepting only those, who upon account of the *Gain* they find from this *Trade*, have persuaded themselves into a Belief in the Lawfulness of it.
>
> And if *Trading* in Slaves cannot be justified, much less can any Thing be offered sufficient to excuse the *buying* or *accepting* of *Slaves* as *Presents*, merely for *Grandeur* or *Pleasure*. And is not a little surprising, to find some *English Ladies* valuing themselves above their Neighbours, on their having a *Black*, when others have only a *White* Footman.
>
> The great *Indignities* offered *human Nature* in the Manner of *buying* and *selling Slaves*, and the *Handling* them like *Cattle* in the *publick* Markets; the Obliging some of the Men Slaves to wear *Collars* about their Necks, like *Dogs*, made of

> *Metal*, with the *Names* of their *Masters* graven upon them; and the many other Hardships and Miseries that those poor Creatures often endure from their cruel Masters, who are by far greater *Savages* than their suffering *Slaves, is too moving a Subject.*

Although leading articles tried to mobilize public opinion – telling their readers what to think – any claim for the power of the newspaper press in the early eighteenth century conflicts with the fact that, at times of relative political calm, policy was not visibly determined by words in newspapers. This article appears to have had no effect whatsoever. Britain's involvement with the slave trade grew to the extent that, by the 1780s, some ninety British ships were carrying about 35,000 African slaves each year across the Atlantic. It was not for another 50 years after the article was written that any organized abolitionist movement began.

Although the power of the eighteenth-century press to shape public opinion to the extent of effecting real changes was generally very limited, it is possible that newspapers made some difference at times of political crisis. In those instances newspapers were simply articulating and amplifying the mood of significant sections of the country, so the contribution of the press is difficult to quantify. Walpole's position was weakened by criticism of the 1739 treaty with Spain at a time when the majority of the press was clamouring for war, and by the abortive attack on Cuba in 1741, which the press blamed on the government's failure to provide Admiral Vernon with sufficient support. The anti-Semitic hysteria unleashed by several newspapers during the introduction of the Jewish Naturalization Bill in 1753 led the Pelham Ministry to repeal the Act shortly after it was passed, and the newspaper reaction to the loss of Minorca in 1756, caused by 'the Treachery, Negligence, or Incapacity of those entrusted with Power' contributed to the replacement of the Newcastle Ministry with that of William Pitt.

### The *Gentleman's Magazine*

The 1730s also saw the birth of the magazine. The *Gentleman's Magazine* was the first of its kind. It was started by Edward Cave (Figure 3.5) in 1731 from his office at St John's Gate, a short walk from Grub Street. Cave was the son of a Warwickshire cobbler. He became apprenticed to a London printer and at the age of 22 he was sent to Norwich to manage the *Norwich Courant*, which was started in opposition to the *Norwich Gazette*. He returned to London where he was employed on various kinds of literary hackwork, including a spell on Mist's *Weekly Journal*. About the same time he got a job with the Post Office, where he exploited his position by supplying provincial papers with London news, and London papers with paragraphs of country

Edvardus Cave, ob. 10 Jan. 1754. Ætatis 62.

**3.5** Edward Cave

news from the provincial papers. According to John Nichols, Cave sold material from the country newspapers to a London journalist for a guinea a week.[35] Eventually he saved up enough money to buy a printing press and set up office in St John's Gate, where he produced a number of Grub Street pamphlets including *A General History of Executions for the Year 1730* and *The Benefits of Farting.*

Cave announced that the *Gentleman's Magazine* would be a 'Monthly Collection, to treasure up, as in a Magazine, the most remarkable Pieces … on various Subjects for Entertainment and … Matters of Publick concern'. The word 'magazine' originally meant 'a Storehouse for Arms and Ammunition of War'.[36] Due to the success of the *Gentleman's Magazine*, the word soon took on a new meaning – 'Of late this word has signified a miscellaneous pamphlet, from a periodical miscellany named the *Gentleman's Magazine* by *Edward Cave*'[37] – and Cave is therefore credited with founding the first magazine. There were, however, earlier monthly miscellanies that are contenders for the title, such as the *Gentleman's Journal; or, the Monthly Miscellany* (1692–94), Abel Boyer's *Political State of Great Britain* (1711–40) and the *Monthly Chronicle* (1728–32).

The success of the *Gentleman's Magazine* compared to its predecessors was largely due to the bulk distribution of copies to Cave's network of bookseller contacts in the provinces. For only sixpence a month the *Gentleman's Magazine* gave the country reader access to digests of a dozen or so essays from the twopenny weeklies, the debates in Parliament, as well as a summary of news. Such was the effect of the *Gentleman's Magazine* outside London that Johnson told Boswell that when he first visited London and saw St John's Gate, he 'beheld it with reverence'.

In its early issues, the *Gentleman's Magazine* was simply a digest of the social, political and literary essays taken from the weekly journals, to which was added a 'Monthly Intelligencer' (continued after 1735 as the 'Historical Chronicle'), a summary of news culled from the previous month's papers,

> to give Monthly a View of all the Pieces of Wit, Humour, or Intelligence, daily offer'd to the Publick in the News-Papers, (which of late are so multiply'd as to render it impossible, unless a Man makes it a business, to consult them all) … upon calculating the Number of News-Papers, 'tis found that … no less than 200 Half-sheets per Month are thrown from the Press only in London, and about as many printed elsewhere in the Three Kingdoms.[38]

The plagiarism of the *Gentleman's Magazine* (Figure 3.6) reflected the normal newspaper practice of the first half of the eighteenth century when the main source of news was the news reports in other newspapers. Cave stole his material from the weekly journals, which, in turn, stole their news columns from the tri-weekly papers that had already plundered the dailies. As Samuel

# The Gentleman's Magazine:

Lond Gazette
Read's Journ
Craftsman:
D. Advertiser
St James's Evening Post
London Evening Post
General Evening Post
London Gazetteer
Public Advertiser
Westminster Journal
Whitehall Evening Post
Monitor
Adventurer
World

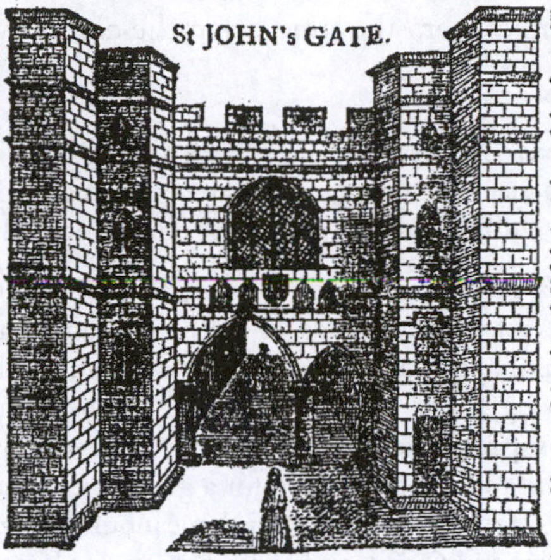


York 2 News
Dublin 3
Edinburgh
Bristol 2
Norwich 2
Exeter
Worcester
Northampto
Gloucester
Stamford
Nottingham
Chester
Derby
Ipswich
Reading
Leeds
Newcastle 2
Canterbury
Sherborn
Birmingham
Manchester
Bath Oxford
Cambridge
Glasgow

## For SEPTEMBER 1753.

CONTAINING,

More in Quantity and greater Variety than any Book of the Kind and Price.

I. Account of the marriage act.
II. To make pot ashes.
III. Weather and reigning diseases.
IV. M. *de Reaumur* on digestion.
V. Bleeding bad in apoplexies.
VI. Dr *Hallet*'s bolus.
VII. Picturesque history of *Britain*.
VIII. Bridges of *Trajan* and *Cæsar*.
IX. Ancient bridges of *Pozzuoli*, &c.
X. An offer to the literati.
XI. Of the peopling of *America*.
XII. *Asia* and *America* joined.
XIII. Critics on *Virgil* mistaken.
XIV. Burials, *&c.* in *Boston, N. England*.
XV. Observations on inoculation.
XVI. To obtain flowers in winter.
XVII. On preserving fruit.
XVIII. A sweaty hand, not to cure.
XIX. Knife swallowed and extracted.
XX. MS on free masonry, by K. *Hen.* 6.
XXI. Notes and glossary, by Mr *Locke*.
XXII. *Adventurer*, N° 90, On Criticism.
XXIII. Conference with the *Indians*.
XXIV. Case of oaths to *Jews*.
XXV. *Jewish* phrases in prayer censur'd.
XXVI. Considerations on pendulums.
XXVII. Electricity, different effects of.
XXVIII. Account of *Maria Cunitia*.
XXIX. Meazles in hogs, cure for.
XXX. Difficulty in the *Hebr*. language.
XXXI. Turnpike tolls payable in *Surry*.
XXXII. Bite of the tarantula cured.
XXXIII. The wonder working tune.
XXXIV. POETRY.—Whimsical Wealthy's will.—Vanity of Life.—*Bolingbroke*'s epitaph.—*Anti Lucretius*, B. I.—Translations required.
XXXV. HISTORICAL CHRONICLE. *Edinburgh* exchange, foundation stone of, laid; fires; riots; trials; benefactions; collections, *&c.*
XXXVI. Lists of births, deaths, &c.
XXXVII. New books and pamphlets.
XXXVIII. Foreign History.

Illustrated with the draughts of three antient bridges; St *Thomas*'s chapel on *London* bridge, and a coloured chart of the different governments in the *British* islands, engraved on copper. Also cuts, of a knife that had been swallowed, of the solar eclipse, and a song set to musick.

By *SYLVANUS URBAN*, Gent.

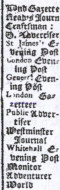

*LONDON*: Printed by E. CAVE, at *St John's Gate*.

**3.6** *The Gentleman's Magazine*, September 1753

Johnson observed, 'the tale of the morning paper is told in the evening, and the narratives of the evening are brought out again in the morning'.[39]

To give a flavour of the kind of news reported in the *Gentleman's Magazine*, here are some examples from the time when the castrati were the toast of the Italian Opera:

> *Newport, Shropshire.* On the 17th ult. a man taking his wife with her gallant, a shopkeeper of this place, in a barn, criminally concerned, with assistance qualify'd him for the opera, and the patient is in great danger of his life.[40]

> Henry Timbrell, a petty farmer near Malmesbury in Wilts, was committed to Salisbury gaol for castrating two lads whom he had undertaken to breed up for a small sum. These unhappy youths the barbarous villain had before endeavoured to destroy, by throwing them in the way of small-pox; but not succeeding, his rapacity at length suggested to him this operation, by which he thought to qualify them as singers, and to dispose of them for a good price. For this fact he was tried at Salisbury assizes, found guilty of a misdemeanour, his sentence was four years imprisonment, a fine of 26s. 8d. and to find surety for his good behaviour during life. This sentence was thought so unequal to his crime, that it was with the utmost difficulty he was preserved from the rage of the populace.[41]

The validity of the *Grub-street Journal*'s scepticism about the truth of the news stories in the papers can be judged from the following items which, taken separately, appear plausible, but taken together, seem suspiciously like the recycling of an eighteenth-century urban myth:

> A stocking-maker near *Nottingham* having brought home a loin of veal, desired his wife to dress it by twelve o'clock; but not coming home at the time, the wife, being ill, put it by. When he came home about four, he brought some beef-stakes for his own dinner, and desired that they might be fried; on eating them, he was suddenly taken ill, and being told, that the stakes were fried in the dripping of the veal, *Then*, said he, *I'm a dead man*; and after confessing that he had rubb'd a large quantity of arsenic into the veal to poison his wife, he instantly expir'd. The veal was examined by a surgeon, who pronounced, that it would have poison'd a hundred persons if so many persons had eat of it.
>
> *Gentleman's Magazine*, May 1762

> A remarkable instance of the hand of providential justice was exhibited last Monday at Hoxton. On the Saturday previous to that day, a man took the diabolical resolution of destroying his wife and children; to perpetrate which, he bought a leg of mutton, and rubbed it over with a considerable quantity of arsenic; so done, he took it home, and told his wife to dress the mutton on Sunday, and as he did not expect to be at home, he desired that she and the children might eat it, without waiting for him. On Sunday the mutton was dressed; but he not coming home, his wife, not wishing to eat it without his being at dinner, made some yeast dumplings for herself and children, and left the mutton uneaten. He did not

return that evening, and still the leg of mutton remained whole; but on Monday he came home, and brought with him a few flat fish (as supposed to save appearance of guilt, expecting his family to have been poisoned). On seeing his wife, he, somewhat agitated, asked her if she and the children were in health; and being answered that they were very well, he asked whether they had eaten the mutton? The wife told him that it had been dressed, but he not coming home, they had made their dinner on dumplings, and the mutton they had not touched. At that answer he appeared much vexed, and surlily ordered his wife to dress him some of the flat fish. She immediately dressed him three, and he sat down and eat them. Directly afterwards, in great confusion, he asked his wife in what had she fried the fish; and being told, in the dripping from the mutton which had been dressed on Sunday, he exclaimed, 'Then I am a dead man.' – He then made a full confession of his wicked intention, and in two hours afterwards he expired in great agonies.

*Edinburgh Evening Courant*, 21 May 1787

The *Grub-street Journal* gave Cave the accolade of 'Chief Engineer of Grub-street'. Cave gave employment to an assorted collection of Grub Street characters including his brother-in-law, David Henry, who also ran *Henry's Reading Journal* and *Henry's Winchester Journal*; Samuel Boyse; Moses Browne, a pen-cutter and minor poet who held court in a Clerkenwell ale-house; Richard Savage, the reprieved murderer and drunken rake, who died a debtor in a Bristol gaol (Savage claimed to be the bastard son of Earl Rivers and the Countess of Macclesfield, much to the Countess's annoyance); William Guthrie who would write anything for money; and an unsuccessful playwright from Lichfield named Samuel Johnson.[42]

From the late 1730s onward, the *Gentleman's Magazine* printed the words and music of the latest popular songs. The words and music of the National Anthem were first published in the *Gentleman's Magazine* for October 1745 under the heading, '*A Song for two Voices, As sung at both Playhouses*'.

Johnson said that Cave scarcely looked out of the window but with a view to improving the magazine. During the 1740s Cave expanded the scope of the magazine beyond reporting the news and reprinting commentaries on current affairs to include items on science, mathematics, astronomy, economics, history, literature and the lives of famous men.

Cave also made increasing use of letters from private contributors, which was a cheap way of filling his pages. Many of his correspondents offer an insight into contemporary attitudes to social issues. One correspondent in the December 1750 issue considered that hanging was an insufficient deterrent against crime:

At the parade at Tyburn, where even a love of fame may raise a brutal hardiness above all sense of ignominy, or future distress; whilst the mob secretly rejoices at the intrepid conduct of their hero, with wishes, that they might imitate a conduct

> so glorious, if their villainies should qualify them to act the same part, in this kind of publick entertainment … [concluding that 'intemperate lust is the cause of crimes', instead of hanging or imprisonment, offenders should be castrated, and] … should a capital C be marked on each cheek, their contemptible infamous circumstance would be known to every one they meet: Yet they would still be capable of labour, and in a condition of benefiting society both by it and by example.

A letter in the July 1755 issue suggested that instead of giving the bodies of felons to the surgeons for dissection after they had been executed, they should be dissected while still alive as medical research would benefit from those 'experiments as can only be made upon a living subject'.

Suicides were similarly regarded with a lack of compassion. One letter to the editor in October 1751 recommended that the bodies of suicides should be hung upside down in the most public place in their town. Next month, someone wrote in to complain that this was too lenient. Their bodies should be

> delivered to some surgeon, who should be obliged (under penalty for non-compliance) publickly to dissect all such bodies upon a stage erected for that purpose, in the market-place: and that the bones of each should be formed into a *skeleton,* to be fixed up in some public room of the said town, for the use and benefit for all surgeons thereof.

The success of the *Gentleman's Magazine* inspired a number of imitators, notably the *London Magazine* (1732–85; Figure 3.7). The *London Magazine* was founded by a consortium of booksellers who were previously involved with the *Monthly Chronicle.* In the 1730s, when the main body of the magazines consisted of condensed versions of the leading articles of the weekly journals, the *London Magazine* tended to produce fewer, but longer, extracts than the *Gentleman's Magazine.* In all other respects, the *London Magazine* was so closely modelled on the *Gentleman's Magazine*, especially when Richard Savage employed his usual practice of selling the same poem to both magazines, that without the front covers it is difficult to tell them apart.

Other imitators included the *Bee* (1733–35), a weekly magazine written by Eustace Budgell who committed suicide when it looked certain that he would be convicted of forging a will in his own favour;[43] the *Universal Magazine* (1747–1815); the *Town and Country Magazine* (1769–96) and the *Lady's Magazine* (1770–1847).

However, from the *Spiritual Magazine* (1761–84) to the *Sporting Magazine* (1792–1870) most magazines founded after 1750 tended to be geared towards a specialist audience. In order to retain a market share, even the *Gentleman's Magazine* under David Henry in the 1750s, and more especially under John Nichols after 1778, began to specialize in antiquarian subjects.

# The LONDON MAGAZINE:

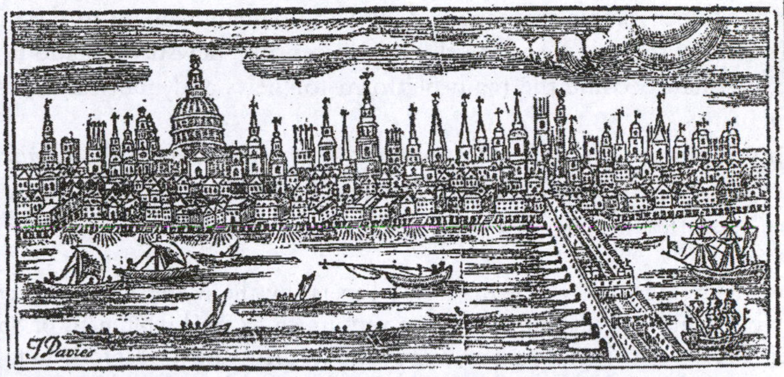


## Or, GENTLEMAN's *Monthly Intelligencer.*

For JULY, 1747.

To be Continued. (Price Six-Pence each Month.)

Containing, *(Greater Variety, and more in Quantity, than any* Monthly Book *of the ſame Price.)*

I. Memorial of Meſſieurs *Raudot* concerning *Cape Breton,* with the *French* Opinion of the Importance of that Settlement.
II. A particular Account of the late Battle in *Flanders,* as publiſhed by Authority.
III. *Eaſt-India* Company's Advices from the Governor and Council of *Bombay.*
IV. A further Account of the Action in *Nova Scotia.*
V. Articles of the Charge againſt the late Lord Provoſt of *Edinburgh.*
VI. A true Copy of Dean *Swift*'s Will.
VII. Improvement of the new Electrical Machine, with a Draught of it, and its Uſes.
VIII. Curious Obſervations on *May-Flies.*
IX. Victory over the *French* near *Exilles.*
X. Relation of a brave Action in *America.*
XI. Deſcription of *Bergen-op-Zoom* and *Maeſtricht.*
XII. Deſcription of the *Catholick Provinces* in the *Low Countries.*
XIII. Reply concerning *Scotch* Hereditary Juriſdictions.
XIV. Eſſay on Moral Poetry,
XV. Addreſs of Thanks to Sir *William Pepperrell.*
XVI. *St. Domingo* Ships taken by our Men of War, with a Liſt of them, and their Lading.
XVII. City Election, with the Speeches of Sir *William Calvert* and *Steph. Theod. Janſſen,* Eſq;
XVIII. Promotion of Flag Officers.
XIX. Memorial of the *Dutch* Miniſter to the Diet of *Ratiſbon.*
XX. POETRY: To Miſs *M—a B—ſd—n* at *B—h* Aſſembly; to Miſs *C——k* at *York*; *Wallis's Wall*; Specimen of Moral Poetry; to the Memory of Capt. *Grenville*; the Fair Muſician; Song by a young Lady; Song ſet to Muſick, and ſung by Mr. *Lowe*, *&c.*
XXI. The MONTHLY CHRONOLOGER: Seſſions at the *Old Baily,* Malefactors executed, *&c. &c.*
XXII. Promotions, Marriages and Births, Deaths, Bankrupts.
XXIII. Prices of Stocks for each Day, *&c.*
XXIV. Monthly Bill of Mortality.
XXV. FOREIGN AFFAIRS.
XXVI. Catalogue of Books.

With a MAP of the Iſland of CAPE BRETON, and a PLAN of MAESTRICHT, Curiouſly Engraved on COPPER.

*MULTUM IN PARVO.*

*LONDON:* Printed for R. BALDWIN, jun. at the *Roſe* in *Pater-Noſter-Row.*

Of whom may be had, compleat Sets from the Beginning to this Time, neatly Bound, or Stitch'd, or any ſingle Month to complete Sets.

**3.7** *The London Magazine*, July 1747

In the meantime, annual sales of newspapers had increased from 2.5 million copies in 1713 to 7.3 million in 1750 and 10.7 million in 1756. The increased circulation of newspapers, particularly in the provinces, the wider range of subject matter they covered, and the demand for up-to-date news, meant that, by the middle of the eighteenth century, newspapers, and not the magazines, had become the main platform for news and political and social commentary.

Samuel Johnson, in his Preface to the collected numbers of the *Gentleman's Magazine* for 1740, celebrated 'the Use and Amusement resulting from these diurnal Histories':

> Every-body must allow that our News-Papers, by the Materials they afford for Discourse and Speculation, contribute very much to the Emolument of Society; their Cheapness brings them into universal Use; their Variety adapts them to every one's Taste: The Scholar instructs himself with Advice from the literary World; the Soldier makes a Campaign in safety, and censures the Conduct of Generals without Fear of being punished for Mutiny; the Politician, inspired by the Fumes of the Coffee-pot, unravels the knotty Intrigues of Ministers; the industrious Merchant observes the Course of Trade and Navigation; and the honest Shop-keeper nods over the Account of a Robbery and the Prices of Goods, till his Pipe is out.

This demonstrates not only the variety to be found in the mid-century newspaper, but also the social diversity of its readers.

## Notes

1. *London Newsletter*, 29 April; *An Historical Account of the Publick Transactions in Christendom*, 4 May; *Post Boy*, 14 May; *Intelligence Domestick and Foreign*, 14 May; *Flying-Post; or, the Post-Master*, 17 May; *English Courant*, 28 May; *Harlem's Courant*, 28 May.
2. Toland, John (1717), *Proposal for Regulating ye Newspapers.*
3. *Tatler*, 21 May 1709.
4. Useful background on the *Tatler* and the *Spectator* can be found in Ross, Angus (ed.) (1982), *Selections from the Tatler and the Spectator*, Harmondsworth: Penguin. See also Bond, R. P. (1971), *The Tatler, the Making of a Literary Journal*, New York and Oxford: Oxford University Press.
5. *Tatler*, 6 April, 18 April and 30 May 1710.
6. Ibid., 12 April 1709.
7. *The Wandring Whore*, No, 4, poss. 28 December 1660.
8. *Weekly Review*, 19 February 1704.
9. For further details on Defoe's career as a journalist, see Lee, W. (1869), *Daniel Defoe, his Life and Recently Discovered Writings*; Sutherland, James (1937), *Defoe*, London: Methuen; and Novak, Maximillian E. (2001), *Daniel Defoe: Master of Fictions*, New York and Oxford: Oxford University Press.
10. Read's *Weekly Journal; or, British Gazetteer*, 6 December 1718.
11. *Spectator*, 31 July 1712.

12. Dickson, P. G. M. (1960), *The Sun Insurance Office*, Oxford: Oxford University Press.
13. *The British-Mercury*, 31 December 1712.
14. *Political State of Great Britain*, August 1728.
15. *London Evening-Post*, 20 May 1729.
16. Maitland, William (1756), *The History and Survey of London.*
17. *The D'Anverian History of the Affairs of Europe, for the memorable Year 1731.*
18. Preface to *A View of the Times* (1708), the collected edition of the *Rehearsal.*
19. Read's *Weekly Journal*, 12 September 1724
20. *Weekly Medley*, 3 October 1719.
21. Mist's *Weekly Journal*, 24 December 1720.
22. *D'Anverian History.*
23. Ibid.
24. See Battestin, Martin C. (1989), *New Essays by Henry Fielding: His Contributions to the Craftsman and Other Early Journalism*, Charlottesville, VA: University Press of Virginia.
25. *Dictionary of National Biography.*
26. *Gentleman's Magazine*, July 1742.
27. *London Journal*, 4 February 1720.
28. Reprinted in Hanson, Lawrence (1936), *Government and the Press 1695–1763*, Oxford: Clarendon Press.
29. *Craftsman*, 25 September 1731.
30. *Grub-street Journal*, 21 August 1731.
31. *Universal Spectator*, 12 October 1728.
32. *Westminster Journal*, 5 December 1747.
33. *The Memoirs of the Society of Grub-street*, 2 vols, 1737.
34. *Grub-street Journal*, 19 December 1734.
35. *The Rise and Progress of the Gentleman's Magazine*, 1821.
36. Bailey's *Dictionary*, 1726 edn.
37. Johnson's *Dictionary*, 1792 edn.
38. *Gentleman's Magazine*, January 1731.
39. *Idler*, No. 7 for *Payne's Universal Weekly Chronicle*, reprinted in the *London Chronicle*, 1 June 1758.
40. *Gentleman's Magazine*, April 1751.
41. Ibid., March 1764.
42. For Johnson and the *Gentleman's Magazine*, see Clifford, James L. (1955), *Young Samuel Johnson*, London: Heinemann; and Kaminski, Thomas (1987), *The Early Career of Samuel Johnson*, New York and Oxford: Oxford University Press.
43. For a full account of Budgell, see Herd, Harold (1955), *Seven Editors*, Ch. 1, London: George Allen and Unwin.

## Chapter 4

# The Mature Eighteenth-century Newspaper, 1750–1800

> I sing of News, and all those vapid sheets
> The rattling hawker vends through gaping streets;
> Whate'er their name, whate'er the time they fly,
> Damp from the press, to charm the reader's eye:
> For, soon as morning dawns with roseate hue,
> The Herald of the morn arises too;
> Post after Post succeeds, and, all day long,
> Gazettes and Ledgers swarm, a noisy throng.
> When evening comes, she comes with all her train
> Of Ledgers, Chronicles and Posts again,
> Like bats, appearing when the sun goes down,
> From holes obscure and corners of the town.
>
> George Crabbe, *The Newspaper*, 1785

The growth of advertising and the rise in newspaper sales from 45,000 a week in 1710 to 210,000 a week in 1756 meant that, instead of just being a printer's sideline, ancillary to his other interests, the newspaper had become a business in its own right. Consequently, printer–publishers like Nathaniel Mist and John Applebee were gradually being replaced by groups of shareholders, mainly bookseller–publishers, who provided the capital to meet the costs associated with larger and more frequent print runs. The printer was relegated to the position of a contractor employed by the shareholders.

In return for their investment, the booksellers expected to benefit from the profits from sales and advertising revenue, which, unlike the fluctuating and uncertain profits from the sale of books, had the potential to provide a regular and possibly long-term income. Another advantage was the ability to advertise their own publications for free or at least at cut-price rates. Some booksellers became shareholders in a number of titles in order to block advertisements from their rivals. Through their involvement with the distribution network, they were also able to make contact with provincial booksellers who were fast becoming established to meet the demand for books, a demand which was stimulated by the lists of new publications appearing in the *Gentleman's* and other magazines.

By the 1740s the position of the weekly journal had begun to wane. Being largely dependent on sales outside London, it was vulnerable to the challenge from the rapidly increasing numbers of provincial newspapers, from the *Gentleman's* and *London Magazines* and from the tri-weekly evening posts. Also, after the downfall of Walpole in 1742 and the swing in public opinion behind the government in the face of the Jacobite threat in 1745, the political essay had lost its attraction.

Edward Cave, who kept his finger firmly on the pulse of the public mood, sensed the declining interest in politics. After 1744, the parliamentary debates published in the *Gentleman's Magazine* got shorter and less frequent until they disappeared altogether. The Preface to the volume for 1747 explained:

> Such is the Plan of our Magazine, that it must necessarily bear the stamp of the times, and the political, historical and miscellaneous parts, dilate or contract in proportion to the zeal of parties, the number and importance of events, and the reigning taste for literary entertainment.
>
> While a determin'd spirit of opposition in the national assemblies communicated itself to almost every individual, multiplied and invigorated periodical papers, and render'd politics the chief, if not the only object of curiosity, we acted a secure and easy part … which … had a ready and extensive reception. But as a fondness for politicks, tho' general, was never universal, we happily substituted other subjects … so that … we have experienced an increasing sale.

In the Preface to the volume for 1749, Cave added:

> Politics, which some years ago, took up a large field, is now reduced to a small compass; this topic having … failed to engage attention: a change, though very sensibly felt by those who still pursue this subject to their loss, not at all to be regretted by the public, if Literature and Science, raised up from their great depression in the reign of Politics, shall again flourish with proportionable vigour.

Commercial groups replaced political groups as the main source of capital for newspapers. And commercial groups were less inclined to print controversial essays for which there was now little demand and risk losing sales as a result of prosecutions or stoppages in the post. Without the political essay, the weekly journal with its stale and derivative news lacked the immediacy of the tri-weekly posts or the daily papers that began to grow in importance in the period after 1750.

**Chronicles**

The sales of the monthly magazines showed there was an audience for journals providing miscellaneous material as well as news. To cater for the public interest in the arts, scientific discoveries, new inventions and social issues, a new kind of newspaper was born, the 'chronicle', which combined up-to-date news with the type of feature articles that were appearing in the magazines. Using the same amount of paper as their four-page competitors, the chronicles were small-format eight-page papers printed with smaller type in three columns. This allowed them to include much more material for the same price.

*The London Chronicle* (Figure 4.1) was the first of its kind. Like the evening posts, *The London Chronicle* was published on Tuesday, Thursday and Saturday evenings. Issue number one, dated Saturday, 1 January 1757, led with a manifesto for the paper, a piece of literary hackwork by Samuel Johnson for which he was paid a guinea. The manifesto declared the paper would provide 'an accurate Account of foreign Transactions and domestick Incidents' free from political bias. It would be distinguished from all others by a 'Literary Journal, or Account of the Labours and Productions of the Learned' and would be a repository for 'Entertainment and Instruction'.

As was usually the case, whenever a new formula was invented, others would soon copy it. The first imitator was *Lloyd's Evening Post*, another eight-page tri-weekly, started in July 1757. The following year two new Saturday papers were started using the chronicle format: the *Universal Chronicle*, which also had its manifesto written by Johnson and which featured Johnson's *Idler* essays; and *Owen's Weekly Chronicle*.

Some of the material in the chronicles is of interest to the social historian: 'The Grievous effects of the Press Gang',[1] 'Mr Dingley's Proposals for establishing a Public Place of Reception for Penitent Prostitutes',[2] 'The Histories of some of the Penitents in the Magdalen-House' ('The second who told her story was about three-and-twenty, tall and genteel: her complexion brown, but her features good; and her countenance animated with a pair of the finest black eyes imaginable'[3]), and a 'History of the London Brewery from the Year 1688'.[4]

The front page of *Lloyd's Evening Post* for 22 December 1769, headed 'A faithful Account of the INNS, in a TOUR of the NORTH, by ARTHUR YOUNG, Esq.', provides a consumer's guide to the 89 inns he stayed at. Among them were:

> Stamford. George. Exceeding good, and reasonable; but wretched waiting.
> Newark. Saracen's Head. Disagreeable and dear.
> Rotherham. Crown. Very disagreeable and dirty; but very cheap. Hashed venison, potted mackarel, cold ham, tarts, cheese, and a melon, at 1s. a head.
> Leeds. Old King's Arms. Dirty and disagreeable. Veal cutlets, tarts and cheese for supper, at 8d. a head without malt liquor being charged.
> Driffield. Nag's Head. Very civil, and cheap. Mutton steaks, ducks, tarts, and cheese, mushrooms, capers, walnuts, gurkins, and other pickles, 2s.

# The London Chronicle: N° 75.

OR,

# UNIVERSAL EVENING POST.

From TUESDAY, JUNE 21, to THURSDAY, JUNE 23, 1757.

WEDNESDAY, JUNE 22.

COUNTRY NEWS.

*Dorchester, in Oxfordshire, June* 18.

THERE has been great Rioting with us, particularly at Abingdon, six Miles from us. It began on Monday last, by the Mob taking away Wheat and Flour, and connued till Thursday, when the Military Power was obliged to be called in to suppress the Rioters. And on Wednesday it began at the City of Oxford, and continued till last Night, the Mob breaking open Granaries, and carrying away the Corn in Triumph, notwithstanding the Magistrates appeared, and endeavoured to prevent them.

*Marlborough, June* 18. Last Thursday a Waggon Load of Wheat, belonging to Farmer Stroud of Baydon, was taken from him coming thro' Swindon, and sold by a Sample to a Baker, which so intimidated the Farmers, that two Waggon Loads of Corn coming to the same Place put back.

*Taunton, June* 18. On Wednesday Evening the Wife of one William Porter, Serge-Weaver of this Town, was delivered of four Children.

LONDON.

Yesterday the Right Hon. Lord Anson kissed his Majesty's Hand at Kensington, on being appointed First Lord of the Admiralty. *Daily Advertiser.*

The King has been pleased to recommend Dr. Richard Terrick, one of his Majesty's Chaplains, and Canon Residentiary of St. Paul's, to be elected Bishop of Peterborough. *London Gazette.*

The King has been pleased to present Stanhope Ellison, B. A. to the united Rectories of St. Benedict and St. Peter Paul's Wharf, void by the Translation of Dr. Thomas, late Bishop of Peterborough, to the See of Salisbury. *Ibid.*

Yesterday Henry Fane, Esq; elected last Week for Lyme in Dorsetshire, took his Seat in the House of Commons.

His Majesty's Ships the Lancaster and Dunkirk arrived at Plymouth the 18th inst. and by a Letter from Capt. Edgcumbe to the Admiralty Board it appears that they have taken in their Cruize the under-mentioned Privateers and Vessel, viz.

Le Comte de Gramont, of 36 Guns, and 370 Men.

Le Nouveau Saxon, of 16 Guns, and 150 Men.

And a Schooner from Bourdeaux, bound to Quebeck, with Wine and Brandy. *London Gazette.*

Capt. Duff, of the Rochester, at Sea, also gives an Account of his having taken the Jean Baptist Privateer of St. Maloes, of 8 Guns, and 41 Men.

Three Privateers were taken among the Leeward Islands, by the Blandford and Saltash Men of War, and are carried into Antigua.

The St. Anthony, Costa, and the Virgin of Cadro, Valiant, both from Marseilles for Turky; la Vierge de Grace, Latty, from Salonica for Tripoly; and the St. Antonio, Vittal, from Constantinople for Marseilles; are taken and carried into Malta by the Hawke, Wilson, an English Letter of Marque.

A French Polacca was drove ashore near Salonica, by the Lilly, Ross, Letter of Marque, from Dundee for Alexandria, out of which they took to the Value of 20,000 Dollars.

The Prince Royal, a Neapolitan, from Civita Vecchia for London, had an Engagement with a Tunis Privateer on the 4th of May, for three Hours, and is put into Cagliari to refit.

It is the Lion, ——, from St. Domingo for Bourdeaux, that is brought into Bristol by the Dreadnought Privateer, Capt. Leisman, who, about a Fortnight since, fell in with the Tartar and Hawke Privateers of Bristol, and the Black Prince and Tartar ditto of London, but does not mention the Latitude, all well.

The Danish Ship, from London for Fieume, formerly mentioned as carried into Tetuan, is the Old Simon.

The Vulcan Privateer, from Weymouth, is taken by the French.

The Happy Return, Lejett, from Sunderland for Jersey, is taken and ransomed for 310 l.

Admiral Pawlet's Flag is shifted from the Princess Royal to the Charlotte Yacht at Sheerness.

There are several Letters in Town from Gibraltar, which confirm the safe Arrival of the Leghorn Fleet there, and that they were to be joined by another Man of War, and then proceed to England. By some of the same Letters we are informed, that several rich Prizes have lately been brought in there by Admiral Saunders's Cruizers.

Commodore Moore was expected at Portsmouth last Monday, to take on him the Command of the Fleet for the West-Indies, which will consist of the following Ships; the Cambridge (the Commodore's Ship) of 80 Guns; Buckingham, Trident, Devonshire, and Prince Frederick, of 70 Guns; the Norwich of 50; the Amazon of 20; and the Weazle Sloop of 16 Guns. The Buckingham and Norwich were not yet arrived at Spithead when the last Letters came away, which will impede the Sailing of this Squadron some Days.

Yesterday several loaded Waggons belonging to his Grace the Duke of Marlborough, Master of the Ordnance, went to the Camp at Chatham.

On Thursday last Capt. Hill, late Commander of his Majesty's Ship the Dover, was married to Miss Eall of Carey-Street.

Saturday was married William Trantur, Esq; of Hampstead, to Miss Betsy Lorder, of Finchley.

On Monday was married, at Putney, John Hook, Esq; of Oxfordshire, to Miss Sally Hutchinson.

Yesterday was married Dr. Morris, Physician, to Miss Ballard, Daughter of Mr. Ballard, Wholesale Druggist and Chemist, in Leadenhall-Street.

A few Days ago died, at his House near Muswell Hill, Mr. William Cowell, an eminent Soap-boiler in Thames-Street.

On Saturday last died, at Hammersmith, Mr. Peter Maynard, formerly an eminent Distiller in Thames-Street.

On Sunday died Mrs. Wilkins Mistress of the Windmill Inn at Salt-Hill.

On Monday died, at his House in St. James's Square, William Wollaston, Esq; He represented Ipswich in the 7th and 8th Parliaments of Great Britain; that is, from January 1729, to April 1741.

Monday died, at his Lodging in Conduit-Street, James Balford, Esq; of Herefordshire.

Yesterday died, at Richmond, Mr. Alexander Phillips, Dry-Salter and Hop Merchant in the Borough.

Last Saturday a Man in Liquor riding a Horse a Gallop by Stockwell, was flung off, and killed on the Spot.

On Saturday last Mr. Mason, a Farmer at Sydenham-Court, near Salt-Hill in Bucks, returning from Windsor Market in the Evening, was stopt by two Footpads, who robbed him of 25 Guineas, and one of them stabbed him in the Belly, of which Wound he languished till Monday Morning, and then died.

Last Sunday Evening two Gentlemen were stopped on Barnes-Common, by a single Footpad, whom they seized. Upon Enquiry, he proved to be a poor hard-working Man near that Place, and had a Wife and six Children, who were starving for Want of Bread. The Gentlemen gave him two Guineas, and discharged him.

Monday Night last Lucy Roberts was committed to Newgate by Justice Welch, for keeping a House of ill Fame in Exeter Street, Covent Garden; also Ann Simpson, for robbing Mr. Stuart, of five Guineas, and a Thirty-six Shilling Piece, in the said House.

MIDLAND CIRCUIT.

Lord Chief Baron Parker, and the Hon. Baron Legge.

Northamptonsh. Tuesday July 19, at Northampton.
Rutlandshire, Friday 22, at Okeham.
Lincolnshire, Monday 25, at Lincoln Castle.
City of Lincoln, the same Day, at that City.
Nottinghamshire, Thursday 28, at Nottingham.
Town of Nottingham, Friday 29, at that Town.
Derbyshire, Saturday 30, at Derby.
Leicestershire, Wednesday Aug. 3, at the Castle.
Borough of Leicester, Thursday 4, at that Bor.
City of Coventry, Saturday 6, at that City.
Warwickshire, same Day, at Warwick.

NORTHERN CIRCUIT.

Mr. Justice Bathurst, and Mr. Justice Noel.

City of York, Saturday July 23, at the Guildhall.
Yorkshire, same Day, at the Castle of York.
Durham, Tuesday Aug. 2, at the Castle.
Newcastle upon Tyne, Monday 8, at the Guildhall.
Northumb. same Day, at the Castle of Newcastle.
Cumberland, Saturday 13, at Carlisle.
Westmoreland, Friday 19, at Appulby.
Lancashire, Wednesday 24, at Lancaster Castle.

[ Price Two-Pence. ]

**4.1** *The London Chronicle*, 21 June to 23 June 1757

Scarborough. New Inn. Very cheap, but very dirty. Cold ham, chicken, lobster, tarts, anchoveys, and cheese, 1s.4d. Coffee or tea, 6d. a head.
Castle Howard. New Inn. An excellent house, but dear, and a saucy landlady.
Richmond. King's Head. Good. Brace of partridges, leash of trout, and cheese, 1s. a head.
Cambo. White Hart. Where you will find a haughty landlady, who lays it down as a maxim of conduct, never to come near her customers, send as often as you please.
Choloford Bridge. George. Very civil, and to a degree cheap. Mutton chops, pickles, potatoes, tarts and cheese, 6d. a head.
Carlisle. Bush. Good. A broiled chicken, with mushroom sauce, a plover, a plate of sturgeon, tarts, mince-pies, and jellies, 1s.6d. a head.
Kendal. King's Arms. A good house, very civil, and remarkably cheap. A brace of woodcocks, veal cutlets and cheese, 1s. a head, dinner. A boiled fowl and sauce, a roast partridge, potted charr, cold ham, tart, and three or four sorts of foreign sweetmeats, 8d. a head. Tea or coffee, 6d. a head. Other things proportionally cheap.
Preston. Black Bull. Indifferent, and dear; bad bed-chambers, and beds.
Liverpool. Talbot. Cheap; a very bad house.
Oxford. Angel. Very dirty; and not obliging.

Apart from some original poetry written expressly for the chronicles, most of the material in their literary pages was second-hand. Early issues of *The London Chronicle* copied whole sections from new books, papers on husbandry, medical and scientific papers from the Royal Society, extracts from Johnson's *Idler* filched from the *Universal Chronicle*, and essays taken from other papers.

However, by the end of the eighteenth century, book reviews had become a regular feature of most newspapers. Here is the review of Boswell's *Life of Johnson* in the *Oracle* for 23 June 1791:

This long promised book is at length before the Public. The Biographer has got out of the attendant BARK with which he ventured to the Hebrides, and has equipped two bulky vessels, *Second* Rates, to honour the Sage's voyage through life – In plain language, 2 volumes Quarto, price Two Guineas.
To use one of Mr BOSWELL's favourite expressions, we must borrow GARRAGANTUA's mouth to speak of the contents of this Publication – The Index itself in inconceibably diverting – Under the letter *P*, we have the following arrangement:

Philosophy,
Pig, the learned,
Piozzi, Mrs.

The general complexion of the work is, to us, infinitely too minute. If, as Mr BOSWELL seems to imagine, every thing is to be told, what may perhaps be gained in the knowledge of MAN, will be lost in the subduction of our reverence for an INDIVIDUAL. Many of his Anecdotes are surely frivolous, and contribute not a particle to the development of either opinion or character. Such for instance as JOHNSON's clearing rubbish with a pole, and told *Bozzy* (we beg pardon, we mean Mr BOSWELL) to labour in his turn; and *how* Mr B *did* labour; and *how*, being a *fresh man*, he succeeded in supplanting a dead cat from her situation, and fairly threw her down the River!

All this had surely have been better unnoted … The sample has many equivalents. We think, upon a deliberate perusal of much of these volumes, that the character of JOHNSON stands nearly as it previously stood – that, as he conversed frequently for victory, his conversation was no certain *chart* of his opinions – that his Biographer's zeal has been blind and undistinguishing.

Mr MALONE revised the first Volume, but both are scandalously incorrect, and paged abominably.

### Daily papers

The second half of the eighteenth century saw the dominance of the daily paper. The circulation of daily papers in the first half of the century was mainly restricted to London. By the middle of the century investment by booksellers and shareholders that provided the capital to print newspapers on a continuous basis, the introduction of daily posts by Ralph Allen in the 1740s and the growing appetite for news, stimulated by the weekly and tri-weekly papers, encouraged the growth of the daily press. An earlier example is *The Daily Post* (Figure 4.2).

Walpole's former tool, the *Daily Gazetteer*, fell into the hands of the booksellers and underwent a number of name changes to emerge as the *Gazetteer* and become a successful and independent newspaper, without benefit of political subsidy. While the *Daily Gazetteer* of Walpole's day was a double-sided single sheet of six columns in all comprising a lengthy political essay, often extending well into the second page, scarcely two columns of news and a couple of advertisements, its more commercial successor provided much more.

The *Gazetteer* for Monday, 26 April 1762 offered its readers four pages of four columns each. The first two columns of the front page carry advertisements from quack doctors and booksellers, including one from Tom Davies in whose bookshop the famous first meeting of Boswell and Johnson took place. The other two front-page columns contain four letters addressed 'To the PRINTER'. The first letter compares Pitt's administration favourably to that of the present age. The second decries the impertinence of the Society of Sign Painters for daring to hold an exhibition of their paintings at the same time as the exhibition of the Society for the Encouragement of Arts. The third advises the Manager of Vauxhall Gardens to sack the singer as 'his voice is not

Numb. 3430

# The Daily Post.

WEDNESDAY, September 16, 1730.

713

*Berlin, Sept.* 12.

ON Sunday the King received the Sacrament at Potsdam, where he has had a Fit of the Gout, of which he is perfectly recover'd, and is expected here To-morrow, to go and take the Diversion of Hunting about Wusterhausen. The Prince Scherbato, who has been in Spain on the Part of the Empress of Russia, is to come hither to relieve Prince Demetrius Galiczin, who by Reason of his Indispositions, has desir'd and obtain'd his Revocation.

*Cologn, Sept.* 16. The Deputies of the States of this Electorate, who have been assembled here some Days, have finish'd their Deliberations. Most of the Recruits that have been raised here, and in the other Imperial Towns, are design'd for the Troops that are in the Austrian Netherlands. We hear from Mentz, that Orders have been issu'd in that Electorate, to raise 1100 Foot, and three Squadrons of Horse The Prussian Officers have again begun to raise new Levies.

*Yesterday arrived the Mail from* France.

*Rome, Sept.* 1.

ON the 27th of last Month the Pope consecrated the Linnen for the Dauphin of France: The Abbot Lanti, who is appointed to carry it to him, will set out forthwith: The Chevalier de la Motte has receiv'd Orders to get two Galleys ready to carry that Prelate into France, where he is to stay some Months 'till the Arrival of a new Nuncio. On the 30th was held a Consistorial Congregation, which made us conjecture, that the Pope would hold a Consistory that Week. The 28th, Cardinal Caraccioli received the extreme Unction, and his Holiness's Benediction (*in articulo mortis*) at the Point of Death. The Pope has recall'd M. Cerbelloni, Inquisitor of Malta, on Account of some Differences he has had with the Great Master. Several Persons of Distinction are come from Sicily, and have brought all their Effects, for fear of an approaching War in that Kingdom. The Abbot Bentivoglio, Nephew to the Cardinal of that Name, has quitted the Holy Orders, and is about to marry a rich Heiress of Brescia. All the Cardinals who came hither to assist in the Conclave, are gone away to return to their Dioceses.

*Paris, Sept.* 20. The 16th the General Assembly of the Clergy ended their Session, and on the 18th their Deputies went to Versailles to return Thanks to the King. The Bishop of Nismes made the Speech to his Majesty.

The Pope's Nuncio is to set out this Week to return to Rome, and it is believ'd that in the first Consistory he will be created a Cardinal.

The Lady Sophia Bulkeley, Mother-in-law to the Duke of Berwick, dy'd at St. Germain en Laye the 6th of this Month, aged 84 Years. She was Daughter of Charles Lenos, Duke of Richmond, who dy'd Embassador in Denmark in the Year 1672. She was Widow of Henry Bulkeley, Esq; younger Brother of Robert Lord Viscount Bulkeley of Cashel in the Kingdom of Ireland.

The last Letters from Turin import, that the King of Sardinia, after his Abdication, took the Name of Count de Teude, and that he had declared his Marriage with Madam de St. Sebastian, Lady of Honour to the Princess of Piemont, and who is fifty Years of Age.

The last Letters from Cadiz import, that on the 20th of last Month the Azorgues, or Quicksilver Ships, three in Number, commanded by the Commodore Don Roderigo de la Torre, sailed from thence for New Spain.

*Upon a Lady's Challenge, Spickspan.*

*At the* ORATORY,

THE Corner of *Lincoln's-Inn-Fields*, near Clare-market, this Evening, being Wednesday, at Seven o' Clock, will be a new Oration on

No FOOLS, like WITS; Or, EVERY BODY MISTAKEN.

A Fool is known by much laughing; you are mistaken; the Mind is better than the Body; you are out; a Coward is not a Hero; wrong again: Nature the best Guide; I deny it; all Things would preserve themselves; worse and worse; Women should not pout; they ought to pout; they should not be inconstant; they should be inconstant; Things encrease by Concord; that's a Fib: There is more Evil than Good in the World; that's a wonder; we like best what is most for our Opinion; that's false; it is pleasant to be out of Danger; no: There are Cuckolds in the World; no such Thing; Content is Happiness; not at all; better to wear a Crown than to beg; I say, nay; burning is Pain; Nonsense; better to walk than be lame; by no Means; our Enemies are not our Friends; yes, they are; a true Wife is honest; ridiculous; the Dunciad is Slander; not Guilty, my Lord E—— and B—— and O—— and B—— in short, that Desire is Enjoyment, that Men are brought to Bed, that Dr. —— is an Ass, &c. will be shewn at large; a PLEASANT PICTURE.

II. My LORD's Knack of knowing my LADY: or, the Lad's Lesson for the Lasses.

III. A BLACK PATCH for the TIMES; Comment on Mr. D'Anvers; and Mr. Fog; Answer to an Answer to at Paris; two Ostenders taken; the Fair at Portobel in October, before the S. S. Company's Ship: The Oxford Holly-bush; a Military Road; Qu——n's Contination of Processions; K. of S's Schodula, no Good from it: The Windsor Painter robb'd, why.

NO. 158. The Wife of a certain Tradesman, formerly dwelling in the Borough in Southwark, was violently afflicted with the Stone and Cholick, and finding no Relief in other Remedies, she sent for

*Mr.* JOHN MOORE, *Apothecary,*

*At the Pestle and Mortar in Laurence Pountney's-Lane, the first Great Gates on the Left-Hand from Cannon-street.*

And by taking some of his Medicines she voided a very large Stone, and above fifty small ones, none of them less than a Pepper Corn; since the coming away of which she has continued very easy: Any Person that desires further Satisfaction will be directed to the Gentlewoman herself, though she is now in the Country.

N. B. The said JOHN MOORE's Worm Medicines and Green Sickness Powder, are sold at the following Places, viz. Mrs. Leader's at the Three Tobacco Pipes, a Chandler's Shop in Hungerford-Market; Mr. James Abree't and Mr. William Aylett's Printing-Office in Canterbury; Mr. Benjamin Smithurst's, Bookseller, in Plymouth; and at Mr. Peter Brown's, at the Plough in St. Thomas's-street, Bristol; with plain Directions by his Order sealed with his Coat of Arms, being a Cross, with the Words, *John Moore's Worm-Powders*, &c. inscribed round it. And if any are sold at any Place, except at his own House, without that Seal and Inscription, they are Counterfeits.

Note, His WORM-POWDER is sold in most Market Towns in England.

LONDON.

The King has been pleased to promote Dr. Edward Tennison, one of his Majesty's Chaplains in Ordinary, to the Bishoprick of Ossory in the Kingdom of Ireland, vacant by the Death of Sir Thomas Vesey, Bart. late Bishop thereof.

His Majesty has been pleased to appoint Major Francis Leighton, of Brigadier-General Barrell's Regiment of Foot, to be Major to Col. Handasyd's Regiment of Foot, and a Captain of a Company in the same, in the Room of Major Sleigh, deceas'd: And also to appoint William Hook, Esq; to be Major to Brigadier General Barrell's Regiment of Foot, and Captain of a Company in the same, in the Room of the said Francis Leighton, Esq;

We hear that Sir Charles Hotham, Bart. will soon be sent again to the Court of Prussia. And that

A Solemn Embassy will also be sent to the Court of Spain.

Abraham Stanyan, Esq; his Majesty's late Ambassador at the Ottoman Porte, is expected here the Beginning of the next Month from Constantinople.

Col. Montagu, Brother to the Earl of Hallifax, Representative in Parliament for the Town of Northampton, and Colonel of a Regiment of Foot, arrived here on Sunday last from the Island of Minorca, along with Capt. Levitt, an Officer in his Regiment: He went the next Day to Windsor to wait on their Majesties, and met with a most gracious Reception: He hath taken the House in Golden Square that Gen. Wills lately lived in.

On Saturday last the new Church at Limehouse was consecrated by the Bishop of London. Mr. Laelybourne, who preach'd the Sermon, is to be Rector of the said Church; and the Rev. Mr. Ridley, Minister of Popler, who read Prayers, is to be Lecturer.

This Day Sir William Ogborne, and the rest of the Gentlemen that were Stewards of the Stepney-Feast, will give an Entertainment at Pontack's to Thomas Revell, Esq; one of the Commissioners of the Victualling-Office, and the rest of the Gentlemen, Stewards of the said Feast for the Year ensuing; and we hear the Hon. Sir Charles Wager will favour them with his Company.

The Rev. Mr. Grant, mention'd in our former to have been presented to the Rectory of Lesnet in the County of Cornwall, is Son-in-Law to the Right Rev. Dr. Weston, Bishop of Exeter, and one of the Prebendaries of that Cathedral.

Last Week died the Rev. Mr. Wright, who succeeded the late Mr. Kinnersley (who was Minister of the Minories) in his Living in Suffolk of 300 l. per Annum.

Yesterday died at his House in Charter-House Square, Dr. Charles Beal, Fellow of the Royal College of Physicians, Physician to the Charter-House, and Fellow of the Royal Society.

On Monday Morning the Corpse of the Lady Viscountess Tyrconnel, who lately died in Arlington-street, is to be carry'd out of Town, to be interr'd at Belton in Lincolnshire, and is to lie in State at several Places on the Road, and afterwards to be bury'd there at the Burial Place of the Family in a most splendid Manner.

On Monday Morning last the Corpse of Mrs. Broughton of Hatton Garden, was carry'd out of Town in great State, to be interr'd near Reading in Berkshire.

They write from Bristol, that Sir Thomas Jones, Knt. was given over by his Physicians.

On Monday Night last Isabella Eaton, alias Gwinn, who keeps the Crown Tavern in Sherrard-street, St. James's (Sister to the noted Mary Philips, alias Sincleer, alias Harvey, alias Mackeig, so often mentioned in the publick Prints) was committed to Newgate by Sir John Gonson, Justice Railton, Justice Young, and six more of his Majesty's Justices of the Peace, and charged upon Oath to be Accessary to a Felony committed by one Mary Sullivan (a notorious Pickpocket) in privately stealing from Matthias Knigge, a German, a Pair of Diamond Ear-rings, Value 25 l. and for receiving, harbouring and concealing the said Sullivan, knowing her to have committed the said Felony, which is made a Capital Offence by an Act of the 5th Year of the late Queen Anne.

One Hearn, an Irishman, taken at the said Eaton's, alias Gwinn's House, reputed to be her chief Bully, or Captain, and not being able to give any good Account of his Way of Living, but appearing to be a dangerous Fellow, was by the said Justices committed to Tothillfields Bridewel to beat Hemp.

Yesterday Sir John Gonson and the Committee of Justices met at Covent Garden Vestry, and examin'd several idle and disorderly Persons apprehended late the Night before on Search Warrants at the Night-Houses in and near Drury-Lane, and some of them being known to be old Offenders, were committed to Bridewell to hard Labour, and the rest were discharged; and one Robert Camel and Henry Fairbank were also committed to Bridewell, they belonging to a Gang of idle and disorderly Fellows, who nightly infest the Streets about Covent Garden, and under Pretence of going about with rugged Musick, frequently assault, knock down and rob People in the Streets, and are a great Terror and Disturbance to the Neighbourhood. One John Pavier, a Soldier of the Foot Guards, was also committed for threatning to kill the Constables when they were on Monday Night on their Duty in executing a Search-Warrant.

On Monday Night last one James Rogers was committed to Newgate for a Street Robbery, in snatching away from a Man in Bishopsgate-street his Hat, and taking from him 12 Shillings in Money.

Yesterday South Sea Stock was 103 to 1 8th. South Sea Annuity 108 1 8th. to 1 qr. Bank 145 1 qr. for the Opening. Bank Circulation 5 l. Premium. India 186 to 1 qr. Three per Cent. Annuity 96 5 8ths. Royal Exchange Assurance 91 1 half. London Assurance 12 1 qr. York Buildings 26 1 half. African 44. English Copper 3 l. 8 s. Welch ditto 2 l. 13 s. South Sea Bonds 5 l. 10 s. Premium. India ditto 5 l. 17 s. ditto.

General Post-Office, Aug. 31, 1730.

*WHereas the Post-Boy, in bringing the Bristol Mail to London, was set upon and robb'd by a single Person on Foot, about Nine o' Clock last Night, half a Mile before he came to Maidenhead, the* Post-Master-General *thinks proper to make it publickly known, that whoever shall apprehend the Person who committed this Robbery, will upon his Conviction be entitled to a Reward of Two Hundred Pounds, besides the Reward by Act of Parliament for apprehending of Highwaymen: Or if any one Accomplice in the said Robbery shall make a Discovery of the Person who committed the Fact, such Accomplice will be entitled to the said Reward of Two Hundred Pounds, and also have the King's most Gracious Pardon.*

*The Person who committed this Robbery, is described to be a lusty Man; he carried off the following Bags, viz.*

| | | |
|---|---|---|
| Bristol, | Hungerford, | Bruton, |
| Bath, | Great-Bedwin, | Tinehead, |
| Frome, | Netherhaven, | Bradford, |
| Calne, | Uphaven, | Warminster, |
| Marlborough, | Aimsbury, | Shipton-Mallet, |
| Ramsbury, | Lavington, | Pusey, |
| Newbury, | Westbury, | Wells. |
| Reading, | Trowbridge, | |

*By His Majesty's Company of Comedians,*

AT the Theatre Royal in Drury-lane, To-morrow, being Thursday, the 17th Day of September, will be presented a Comedy, call'd

The OLD BATCHELOR.

Written by the late Mr. CONGREVE.

The Part of Fondlewife by Mr. Cibber: Laetitia, Mrs. Thurmond; Bellmour; Mr. Wilks; Sharper, Mr. Mills; Heartwell, Mr. Harper; Vainlove, Mr. Watson; Sir Joseph Wittol, Mr. Cibber, Jun. Capt. Bluff, Mr. Johnson; Setter, Mr. Oates; Belinda, Mrs. Horton; Araminta, Mrs. Butler; Silvia, Mrs. Cibber; Lucy, Mrs. Mills.

With select Pieces of Musick between the Acts, and Entertainments of Dancing.

*By the Company of Comedians,*

AT the New Theatre in Goodman's-Fields, this present Wednesday, being the 16th Day of September, will be presented a Comedy, call'd,

LOVE makes a MAN:

OR,

The FOP's FORTUNE.

The Part of Carlos by Mr. Giffard; Don Cholerick Snapshorto de Teste, Mr. Penkethman; Clodio, Mr. W. Bullock; Don Antonio, Mr. W. Williams; Don Charino, Mr. Collet; Governor, Mr. W. Giffard; Don Duart, Mr. Smith; Don Manuel, Mr. Bardin; Sancho, Mr. R. Williams; Louisa, Mrs. Woodward, being the first Time of her appearing on this Stage; Angelina, Mrs. Giffard; Elvira, Mrs. Houghton; Honoria, Mrs. Thomas.

With several Entertainments of Singing and Dancing.

*Charitable Corporation House, London, Sept.* 15, 1730.

NOTICE is hereby given, that the Transfer-Books of the said Corporation will be shut from and after Friday the 25th Instant, and open'd again upon Friday the 9th of October next; and that a General Court of the said Corporation will be held at their House in Spring-Garden on Thursday the 1st of October next, at Eleven in the Morning, to consider of a Dividend for the half Year ending the 29th Instant, the same being also a Quarterly General Court.

LOST on Friday last, a large white Dog of the Pointing Kind, his Head and Ears very much mottled, with a small Patch on his Left Side; belonging to Capt. Dilkes. Whoever brings him to the Grass-hopper, the Corner of Suffolk-street near the Hay-market, shall receive a Guinea Reward and no Questions ask'd.

To be SOLD,

DOUBLE Russia Matts, by JOHN NICHOLSON, Jun. at the Iron Gate near the Tower in St. Catherine's, at Sixteen Pounds Ten Shillings per 1000.

**4.2** *The Daily Post*, 16 September 1730

so good as it was ten years ago'. The last letter suggests that the new theatre to replace the 'Drury-lane play-house' should be built on Lincoln's Inn Fields:

> The place is near equally distant from the best parts of London and Westminster. The houses round the square being occupied by nobility or gentlemen of the law, the theatre would be secured from the usual indecencies of a playhouse-neighbourhood. The gentle votaries of Venus might keep their present quarters, which would be no way ill-situated, and would prevent a fall in rents.

The second page is full of news, starting with half a column headed '*Yesterday arrived a Mail from* Flanders', with paragraphs of news datelined Genoa, Vienna, Lubeck, Paris, Versailles and Hague, followed by a quarter column of extracts of foreign and shipping news from the *London Gazette*. The next section is headed 'PLANTATION NEWS', with two paragraphs datelined Charles Town, Feb. 28 and Charles Town, March 6 expressing fears that the peace with the Cherokees will be of little duration. The main section of two columns, headed 'LONDON', contains 42 short paragraphs of foreign, naval and domestic news. The domestic news is the usual mixture of crimes, accidents, marriages and deaths. The final column, headed 'Articles of intelligence from the other daily papers of Saturday', leads with the contents of a '*Letter from Corke, dated April* 12' about the rebellion of the White Boys in Ireland.

The third page comprises 29 advertisements, including nine from ships' brokers advertising sales by the candle of recently imported goods to be held in coffee-houses, two advertisements from dancing masters ('LADIES and GENTLEMEN taught to dance Country Dances, in Six Hours, the whole Expense at One Guinea and a Half each Person … A Minuet may be attained in two or three Weeks'), and an advertisement offering five guineas reward from Sir John Fielding for the capture of Henrietta Reinholdt:

> She is of Stature rather under the middle Size, a fair Complexion, very hoarse Voice, about 30 Years of Age, frequently dresses in Man's Cloaths, and has been used to all the Houses of ill Fame in London, where she is very well known by the Name of Kitty Hawley. She has also gone by the name of Davis, &c, and has lately been at York.

The back page has two more columns of quack doctors' and booksellers' advertisements, a column headed 'The Commercial Register' containing a list of ships entered inwards and cleared outwards, the prices of stocks and goods at the Corn Exchange, the price per ounce of Pieces of Eight and the Weekly Bill of Mortality (19 people died of Teeth that week), and a column of 'Articles of Literature and Entertainment, from the Morning and Evening Papers':

> There is a piece of impertinence practised at the out-side of almost every Church, in the Country especially, which is this. –
>
> As soon as service is over, a set of fellows hurry out of church … and place themselves just at the entrance of the door, in a front line, as regularly as if under military direction, making their observations on the congregation as they pass along. And if any happen to be remarkable either in dress or person, they are sure to undergo their slovenly censure and unmannerly ridicule. But if any unfortunate piece of deformity, (whether male or female it matter not) should happen to present itself, then you are sure of a horse-laugh, accompanied with most shocking reflections on the unhappy object; and the more confusion the person is put into, the more pleasure they receive. Nay, give me leave to assure you, the audaciousness of those gentry is got to such a pitch, that the minister himself can hardly escape their impudent remarks.

Other noteworthy daily papers included the *London Courant* (1745–47), the *London Daily Advertiser and Literary Gazette* (1751–53) and the *Public Ledger* (1760). The short life of the *London Courant* illustrates how the demand for news depends on outside events. The *London Courant* became a daily paper in September 1745 to cash in on the demand for news of Bonnie Prince Charlie and faded away after the last trials and executions of the rebels.

The *London Daily Advertiser* was well known for its daily letter from '*The Inspector*' written by Dr John Hill. Hill was one of the more colourful characters in the history of journalism. He became the most talked-about columnist of his day and was reported to have earned the unprecedented sum of £1,500 per year from journalism.

A fop and a supreme self-publicist, Hill had a spectacular talent for making enemies when he conducted the *British Magazine* from 1746 to 1750. He used his daily column in the *London Daily Advertiser* to make even more. Almost single-handedly Hill revived the battles of Grub Street. Within a short period he attacked David Garrick, Henry Fielding, the poet Christopher Smart and many others that time has now forgotten. Having started a paper war with Fielding, he audaciously suggested that Fielding was continuing the war for the money that was in it.

Not content with vilifying his fellow writers, he proceeded to attack the scientific establishment. Antiquarians were dismissed as mere medal-scrapers, conchologists as cockleshell merchants, and naturalists as compilers of pompous histories of sticklebacks and cockchafers. It is little wonder, therefore, that when he applied to become a Fellow of the Royal Society, he could not get the necessary three signatures of recommendation. After he left journalism, he made a second fortune as a manufacturer of quack medicines.[5]

The *Public Ledger: Or, the DAILY REGISTER of Commerce and Intelligence* was, as its sub-title indicates, a paper of mainly mercantile interest. The early issues adopted the rather eccentric policy of devoting a quarter of the paper to an index of advertisements from 11 London and 32 provincial newspapers:

> By this Index, to our *Wants and Desires*, will be raised such a Fund of Intelligence and useful Knowledge, relating to the Trade, Commerce, Proposals, Schemes and Connections of Mankind, as may not be improperly called the *Bank of Enquiry*, which bringing all Parties together, as it were in a Center, will readily help them to whatever they require, and every Man to see at one View as he sits at Home in his Chair, the various Sollicitudes of the rest, and know where to avail himself of the Wants of others, or to supply those of his own.[6]

Its first editor was Hugh Kelly, who proclaimed that it was 'Open to all parties, and influenced by none', belied by his receiving £100 for keeping the paper favourable to Lord North. Oliver Goldsmith wrote the *Chinese Letters* for the *Public Ledger*, which were later published in two volumes as *The Citizen of the World*.

## Letters to the Printer

The increasing page sizes in the second half of the eighteenth century enabled editors to develop their relationships with their readers by devoting more space to readers' letters. This meant that the printed expression of social and political views was no longer the sole preserve of professional politicians and essayists (although the use of pseudonyms does raise the question of how many letters were written by politicians or their paid hacks).

Letters to the press gave the impression of the newspaper as a national forum, open to all, and so helped the newspaper-reading classes develop a clearer sense of inclusion in national political life, even if they did not have the vote. The newspaper thus became an interactive medium, letting the English public speak for itself, and providing editors with a useful insight into the preoccupations of their readers. Letters were usually addressed to the printer, a sign that the existence of a separate editorial function had yet to be recognized by the public.

Readers' contributions to *The Craftsman; or Say's Weekly Journal* for 11 July 1767 are mainly concerned with political issues, although there is some social commentary and a report of a curious medical case. Here are a couple of extracts:

> When I read in the public papers that playhouses and assembly rooms are set up in every country town, I do not wonder that marriages are so few … [The writer went on to explain that every young woman resorts to those places, yet the men consider such women to be bad matches as they will want to spend their lives in

pleasure, and cause bankruptcies by their expense] ... and indeed, a man cannot have any good notion of a woman, whose delight is in spending her precious time at cards.

To the PRINTER

The following extraordinary case of a lady that died of a tympany, the truth of which may be relied on, is sent for insertion in your paper.

Lady Hastings, daughter of the late Rev Dr Moses Terry, of Lincoln, was, in the prime of life, subject to the dropsy ... Her belly swelled to an enormous size, by the water collected between the skin and the flesh, and which, if struck, sounded like a drum, and was stretched and braced nearly as tight ... During the last year of her life she was swelled so much that she was unable to remove herself, or help herself to any thing ... Her bulk, the time I am now speaking of, was bigger than a large sugar hogshead ... One day, as she was sitting in company, she felt herself on a sudden so much lighter, that she could not help signifying it by her countenance to those she was with, which she had hardly done, before the cause of it was plainly discovered, by a prodigious quantity of water running upon the floor in a plentiful stream. She was delighted beyond expression at the discharge of her load, and looked upon it as a favourable symptom that would provide a cure – But neither she, nor her friends, who gladly took part in her joy, obtained their wishes, for the flesh mortified, and she died the fourth day after this happened, a shocking spectacle indeed. Her belly, after the rupture, was as black as ink, and the skin hung down over her knees, upon the floor. Such an instance of magnitude had not been known by any body then living: and how she could carry upwards of forty gallons of water within her, will be amazing, no doubt, to those who never before heard of her case; but this astonishing quantity absolutely came from her when she burst.

## Wilkes and Liberty

The 1760s saw a peak of activity in the struggle to secure the freedom of the press. In 1762 John Wilkes started the *North Briton*, an anti-ministerial essay sheet in response to Tobias Smollet's pro-Bute *Briton*. In an echo of the Letters of Cato from 40 years before, the first issue declared:

> The Liberty of the Press is the birthright of a Briton, and is justly esteemed the firmest bulwark of the liberties of this country. It has been the terror of all bad Ministers; for their dark and dangerous designs, or their weakness, inability, and duplicity, have thus been detected.[7]

The *North Briton* kept up a relentless attack on the government. It exposed the system of government corruption, describing the official responsible for distributing the bribes as 'a most treacherous, base, selfish, mean, abject, low-lived and dirty figure that ever wriggled himself into a Secretaryship' and insinuated that Bute and the Queen Mother were lovers.

On 23 April 1763, Wilkes used number 45 of the *North Briton* to produce a long and damaging article attacking the King's Speech:

> The *King's Speech* has always been considered by the legislature, and by the public at large, as the *Speech of the Minister* … *This* week has given the public the most abandoned instance of Ministerial effrontery ever attempted to be imposed on mankind … Every friend of this country must lament that a prince of so many great and amiable qualities, whom England truly reveres, can be brought to give the sanction of his sacred name to the most odious measures … I wish as much as any man in the kingdom to see the *honour of the crown* maintained in a manner truly becoming *Royalty*. I lament to see it sunk even to prostitution.

Declaring number 45 to be 'an infamous and seditious libel, tending to inflame the minds and alienate the affections of the people from his Majesty, and to excite them to traitorous insurrections against his Government, and therefore punishable as a misdemeanour of the highest nature', the government issued a general warrant authorizing the arrest of the writers, printers and publishers of number 45. Wilkes and 48 others, including printers, proofreaders and news hawkers, were arrested. Wilkes was sent to the Tower of London.

When the case came to court, Wilkes, as MP for Aylesbury, a privilege for which he had paid £7,000, successfully pleaded parliamentary immunity. He sued for wrongful arrest and encouraged the other 48 to do likewise. In his speech before Lord Justice Pratt, Wilkes declared that the liberty not only of all peers and gentlemen was at stake, but also that of all 'the middling and inferior set of people who stand in most need of protection'. In a rare display of judicial independence, Pratt declared that the issue of a general warrant was illegal. A sum of £100,000 in damages for false imprisonment was awarded against the government.

The government tried to claw back what it could by pushing through a motion that parliamentary privilege did not extend to writing or publishing seditious libels. Wilkes was expelled from Parliament. Number 45 was ordered to be burnt by the common hangman at the Royal Exchange. But the crowd chased the sheriffs away and, so legend has it, rescued number 45 from the flames by pissing on the fire.[8]

Encouraged by the decision on the illegality of general warrants and the favourable mood of the country towards the liberty of the press, other trials of strength between the press and an increasingly defensive government began to take place. In particular, the fiercely anti-ministerial Letters of Junius began to appear in the *Public Advertiser*. They increased its sales from 2,800 to a little under 5,000 copies almost overnight and quickly became the talking point of London.

*The Public Advertiser* (Figure 4.3)was the most important daily paper of the

The Public Advertiser.

NUMB. 10002[illegible]

MONDAY, DECEMBER 22, 1766.

[Price Two-pence Halfpenny.

HAY-MARKET.
The LAST Time of performing till after the Holidays.
AT THE
KING's Theatre in the Haymarket,
To-morrow will be performed a new comic Opera call'd
La BUONA FIGLIUOLA.

DRURY-LANE.
By His MAJESTY's Company.
For the AUTHOR.
The SIXTH DAY.
AT THE
Theatre Royal in Drury Lane,
This Day will be presented a new Tragedy call'd
The EARL of WARWICK.

HIGH LIFE Below STAIRS.

COVENT-GARDEN.
For the AUTHOR.
The SIXTH DAY.
AT THE
Theatre Royal, Covent Garden,
This Day will be presented
The ACCOMPLISHED MAID.

COVENT GARDEN THEATRE.
THE Performers of this Theatre

AT the Little Theatre in the Haymarket, This Day, Signor PLACIDO's Company will exhibit
Variety of new PERFORMANCES.

From the POLICE.
THE extensive Sale of the PUBLIC ADVERTISER, (joined to the *Variety* of Channels thro' which it passes) has always been the Means of *detecting of many* ROBBERIES, and of *apprehending so many* OFFENDERS, that it may be proper to give THIS PUBLIC NOTICE, That, for the Future, all Informations of this Kind, sent to BOW-STREET, will be *constantly inserted in* THIS PAPER: And if SUCH INFORMATIONS are *properly* attended to, by PAWNBROKERS, JEWELLERS, SILVERSMITHS, STABLE-KEEPERS, BUYERS OF SECOND-HAND CLOATHS, &c. *few Robberies will escape Detection*; especially if ALL PERSONS ROBBED *make use of* THIS PAPER *to advertise their Losses in*.
J. FIELDING

Mrs. CORNELYS begs leave to acquaint
THE NOBILITY and GENTRY,
SUBSCRIBERS to
The SOCIETY in Soho-square,

By particular Desire of the Right Honourable and Honourable the GOVERNORS.
For the Benefit of the GENERAL LYING-IN HOSPITAL, Quebec-Street, Oxford Road.
Theatre Royal, Covent Garden,
The INCONSTANT;
Or, The WAY to WIN HIM.

The CITIZEN.

This Day is published,
MEMOIRS of a Magdalen; or, the History of LOUISA MILDMAY.

This Day is published,
A SPEECH in Defence of the Constitution, against the Suspending and Dispensing Prerogative, &c.

This Day is publish'd,
LETTERS from ITALY;

TINCTURE of CENTAURY;
IT strengthens a weak Stomach,

Thursday Jan 15 will be published,
In Two VOLUMES in OCTAVO,
COMEDIES of PLAUTUS,
Translated into familiar BLANK VERSE.
By BONNELL THORNTON, M.A.

To be SOLD,
THE Manor of Lympsfield in the County of Surry

This Day is published,
MR. POSTLETHWAYT's Universal Dictionary of TRADE and COMMERCE.

An Entire NEW WORK.
THE HISTORY of ENGLAND

DAUME DE VIE.
THE most excellent Remedy ever yet discovered

In the Press, and very soon will be published,
MILITARY INSTITUTIONS of VEGETIUS.
Translated from the Original Latin.
By an OFFICER.

For the Public Advertiser.
An EPISTLE to whomsoever it may concern.
THE Anniversary Day is not far distant whereon it pleased the Almighty and Universal Creator,

PUBLICUS.

REFLEXIONS on the partial Distribution of Ministerial Favours,

**4.3** *The Public Advertiser*, 22 December 1766

1760s. Originally the *London Daily Post and General Advertiser*, subsequently the *General Advertiser*, it was little more than a purely advertising paper, with very little news, until it was taken over by its printer, Henry Woodfall. Woodfall renamed it the *Public Advertiser*, increased its news content and circulation before handing it over to his 19-year-old son, Henry Sampson Woodfall, in 1758.

Junius, thought to be Sir Philip Francis, and Henry Sampson Woodfall, who never disclosed Junius's identity, provide an outstanding example of the partnership between a bold master of invective and a brave publisher prepared to stand by him. The authorities were goaded into action by the letter addressed to George III on 17 December 1769. It began:

> It is the misfortune of your life, and originally the cause of every reproach and distress which has attended your government, that you should never have been acquainted with the language of truth, until you have heard it in the complaints of the people.

The letter was instantly reprinted by most of the other anti-ministerial papers. Prosecutions were started against Woodfall, John Almon of the *London Museum*, Henry Baldwin of the *St. James's Chronicle*, John Miller of the *London Evening Post* and Charles Say of the *Gazetteer*. Because Almon fell under the jurisdiction of Westminster, where juries were more amenable to the government's wishes, he was the first to be tried and, as expected, he was found guilty.

Having established this precedent, the government placed Woodfall, Baldwin and Miller on trial at the Guildhall. Despite a firm direction by Chief Justice Mansfield to convict on the grounds that the judge alone had the power to determine whether a publication was a seditious libel and all the jury had to do was decide whether the defendant had published the letter, the jury acquitted Baldwin and Miller. Their ambiguous verdict in Woodfall's case, 'guilty of printing and publishing only', was such that he too was acquitted. This case established the right of juries to decide whether the article complained of was a libel and not simply whether it was published by the accused. Fox's Libel Act of 1792 later enshrined this principle in law.

Junius described the significance of this verdict as follows:

> The liberty of the press is the palladium of all the civil, political and religious rights of an Englishman, and that the rights of juries to give a general verdict, in all cases whatsoever, is an essential part of our constitution, not to be controuled or limited by the judges, nor in any shape questionable by the legislature. The power of Kings, Lords and Commons is not an arbitrary power. They are the Trustees, not the owners of the estate.[9]

**Parliamentary Reporting**

Having established the illegality of the general warrant and determined the independence of juries and their right to disregard judges' directions in cases of seditious libel, the final hurdle to clear was the ban on reporting parliamentary debates.

The right to report parliamentary proceedings has a chequered history. From the *Perfect Diurnal* in 1642, parliamentary reports were a major feature of the Civil War newsbook. However, less than a month after Charles II entered London, the Commons passed a resolution banning the printing of 'any votes or proceedings of the House'. The manuscript newsletters carried on reporting the debates without too much harassment. This was probably because newsletters were a lot less visible than the printed newspaper and their clientele were mainly country gentry and not L'Estrange's 'meddling Multitude'. None the less, Dyer, the manuscript newswriter, was summoned to the bar of the House of Commons in December 1694 and reprimanded for reporting the proceedings of Parliament.

While the early London newspapers were forced to stay silent, a number of provincial newspapers took advantage of their distance from London to print extracts of the debates copied from the manuscript newsletters. Occasionally there was a clampdown. In 1718 and 1719 George Bishop of the *Exeter Mercury*, Jos. Bliss of the *Protestant Mercury* (formerly the *Exeter Post-Boy*), and Andrew Brice of the (Exeter) *Post-Master* were brought before Parliament and taken into custody for publishing the debates. The same fate befell Robert Raikes of the *Gloucester Journal* in 1728, along with Edward Cave who supplied Raikes with the copies of the debates. In 1745 and 1746 it was the turn of two newspaper printers from York.

It was generally considered, however, that the ban only applied when Parliament was actually sitting. Out-of-date reports of debates were a regular feature in the *Political State of Great Britain*, the quarterly *Historical Register* and, later, in the *Gentleman's* and *London Magazines*. In 1738 Parliament resolved that it was also a breach of privilege to print accounts of the debates in the recess. The *London Magazine* was the first to circumvent the ban in May 1738 by giving the speakers the names of eminent Greeks or Romans. The next month the *Gentleman's Magazine* introduced the 'Debates in the Senate of Great Lilliput' in which the speakers' names were thinly disguised by anagrams, Walelop for Walpole, and Haxilaf for Halifax, for example.

The Lilliput debates were originally written by William Guthrie with the assistance of Samuel Johnson. In July 1741 Johnson replaced Guthrie and continued the debates single-handedly until 1744. The debates were almost entirely the invention of Johnson, whose only source material was the names of the speakers and the part they had played in the debate which Cave had managed to obtain from the doorkeeper of the House of Commons.

There is no evidence that Johnson or any other writers for the magazines actually attended Parliament to report the debates directly. When Thomas Astley of the *London Magazine* and Edward Cave appeared before the House of Lords in 1747 for reporting the trial of Lord Lovat, Astley said he received his information about the parliamentary debates from correspondents, including Clark, an attorney, who hid behind the throne in the House of Lords, taking notes.

Many years later, when Johnson had made his reputation as a writer under his own name, he attended a dinner party where politics and oratory were the main topics of conversation. Someone remarked that Pitt's speech at the vote of no confidence in the Walpole Administration was the finest he had ever read. Others agreed and began quoting whole passages from memory. Johnson waited for a lull in the conversation before astonishing the whole company by telling them, 'That speech I wrote in a garret in Exeter Street.'

In the 1760s, perhaps feeling that their increased circulation meant that newspapers had won a respectable place in society, a number of papers took the chance of printing extracts of parliamentary proceedings: the *London Chronicle*, the *Daily Advertiser*, the *Public Advertiser* and the *Gazetteer* in 1760; and the *St. James's Chronicle* and the *Public Advertiser* and the *Gazetteer* again, in 1765. But in both instances the printers were called to the bar of the House of Commons where they were ordered to kneel before the Speaker before being confined to Newgate until they had each paid a fine of £100. Parliament was as intent as ever on denying the people the right to know what their representatives were debating and deciding on their behalf.

The breakthrough came in 1771 when a number of printers were summoned to appear before the House of Commons for printing the debates in contravention of the 1738 resolution. John Wheble, the printer of the pro-Wilkes *Middlesex Journal*, Roger Thompson of the *Gazetteer* and John Miller of the *London Evening Post* ignored the summons, so a Royal Proclamation was issued for their arrest. Wilkes, who had become a City Alderman, arranged for Wheble to be arrested by E. T. Carpenter, a journeyman printer, and for Wheble to appear at the Guildhall on a day when Wilkes was acting as a magistrate. Wilkes promptly dismissed the case on the grounds that Wheble had not been arrested for any legal offence, but under a proclamation that violated the rights of an Englishman. Similar arrangements were made for Thompson, who appeared before Alderman Richard Oliver, one of Wilkes's cronies.

The best was yet to come. Next day John Miller allowed himself to be arrested by a House of Commons messenger within the City's jurisdiction. The messenger himself was immediately arrested and charged by a City constable with assault and false imprisonment. The messenger was brought before Wilkes, Oliver and Brass Crosby, the Lord Mayor, who ruled that the Speaker's warrant was illegal, as it was not backed by an order from the City's magistrates.

The scene was now set for a direct confrontation between Parliament and the City, with the City in the role of the protector of English liberties against the arbitrary powers of a corrupt and authoritarian Parliament. The government, regarding its honour and dignity to be at stake, summoned Crosby and Oliver, as Members of Parliament, to answer for their breach of privilege. Crosby and Oliver refused to apologize and were committed to the Tower, whereupon the London mob came out into the streets and threw mud and stones at ministers and their supporters. They dragged Lord North, the Prime Minister, from his carriage, seized his hat which they tore into fragments and sold for sixpence a piece, and destroyed his carriage.

Crosby and Oliver were released at the end of the parliamentary session. They were given a hero's welcome with a twenty-one-gun salute and escorted to the Mansion House by over fifty carriages. Having perceived the strength of feeling over this issue, and not willing to risk another bruising encounter with the City, the government made no further attempts to prevent the publication of reports of parliamentary proceedings. Note-taking was still forbidden and it was not until 1972 that Parliament formally renounced the resolution against reporting its debates.

The reporting of Parliament reinforced the public nature of British politics and confirmed the newspaper's role as a progressive force that opened up political culture to a wider class of people who had hitherto been excluded from political debate, and so helped forge a sense of national identity. By providing universal access to information, reason and argument, and now to the deliberations of Parliament itself, the newspaper helped to form public opinion, which, in turn, influenced a Parliament that could no longer ignore the expressed requirements of the propertied public.

However, the reporting of Parliament led to occasional complaints that speeches had been misquoted. This was not surprising as the atmosphere in the Commons was not conducive to accuracy. The gallery where the parliamentary reporters sat was notorious for hard drinking. William Hazlitt, parliamentary reporter for the *Morning Chronicle* in 1813–14, damaged his health by drinking there.

## The *Middlesex Journal*

The *Middlesex Journal; or, Chronicle of Liberty* (Figure 4.4), which had played such an active part in the struggle to secure the right to report the proceedings

# MIDDLESEX JOURNAL:
## Or, CHRONICLE OF LIBERTY.

Price Two Pence Half-Penny.] From TUESDAY, April 28, to THURSDAY, April 30, 1772. [No 481.

WEDNESDAY, April 29.

FOREIGN INTELLIGENCE.

*Extract of a letter from Stockholm, April 9.*

THE following are the contents of the Act of Bond or Obligation which his Swedish Majesty signed the 28th of February last.

In the beginning of it his Majesty obliges himself to an uninterrupted Reign. This expression was brought in well considered, and means that the King shall not, after the example of the late King in 1768, lay down the Government.

"Art. I. The King obliges himself during his whole life to remain in and maintain the Lutheran Religion, according to the Augsburg Confession, with his whole family, and all his subjects. II. He shall not allow any *person whatsoever*, who does not profess the said religion, to hold or enjoy any place under the Government; in particular such persons as are known to be Freethinkers, irreligious, impious, and wicked persons. III. Contains the repetition of the foregoing article concerning the established religion; and that all officers, both military and civil shall strictly be bound to observe that it is firmly kept and adhered to. IV. His Majesty obliges himself to refrain from buying, or endeavouring to get to himself or his family, any Principality, Province, Castle, or Hotel, &c. which belong to any of his Majesty's subjects, and who have regularly paid the revenue to the Crown, without the consent of the States. V. The King declares before God, that he will hold principally and preferably the Administration of the Kingdom; maintain the rights of the States, the liberty and security of the subjects; and reign with mildness and justice according to the form instituted in this Kingdom, *Anno 1720*; in the Bond or Obligation Act. VI. The King condemns and despises all such persons as traitors to the Kingdom, according to the declaration of the States, who openly or secretly do bring, or intend to bring, into this Kingdom any Sovereignity; for which purpose every subject is to take an oath of allegiance before he or they can hold any place under the Crown. VII. Concerns the Cabinet and the States; that the King shall not do any thing concerning the Crown unless a plurality of voices of the States have been previously given, and never without their approbation, and against their Counsel to reign. VIII. The King promises further never to intermeddle with the election of the Depoties of the Diet, the Marshals, and the speakers, and not suffer any other person to do it. IX. Concerns the election of the Councellors of the States, and the posts which the King gives in the presence of the States, and not in the Cabinet; that is, from Field Marshals to Colonels, both inclusive. X. No person in this service shall be cashiered before he is first condemned, nor put into any other employment against his will. XI. No privilege shall be given to any of the States without the consent of all the Four Orders, nor any thing altered without the consent of the whole four. XII. The Revenues of the Crown to be disposed of according to the Conventions of the States. XIII. No foreigner shall be naturalized of what condition soever, without the consent of the States; nor shall any foreigner be admitted to a place in that Senate, nor at Court. XIV. The King is not permitted to go out of the Kingdom, except in defence of the Crown; the same restriction is likewise laid on the Prince, unless required so to do by matters of importance. XV. In absence of the King, or in case of sickness, the Privy Council shall sign all dispatches. XVI. The Sense of the Convention of the States, from the 23d of June 1743, concerning the heirdom to the Crown of Sweden, and the heirs mentioned therein, to remain unaltered. XVII. The King shall not commence war, nor make new laws, nor alter the old ones; but if the frontiers of the kingdom should be attacked by an enemy, he shall defend them; and with the consent of the Senate, levy the necessary supplies till the Diet can meet.

"The remainder of the articles shall be transmitted to you by the next post."

*From the* LONDON GAZETTE.

*War-Office, April 27.* PROMOTIONS.

1st. Troop of Horse Guards, Thomas Otger is appointed Sub-Brigadier and Cornet.

1st Troop of Horse Grenadier Guards, John Beckford, Adjutant and Sub-Lieutenant.

15th Reg. Dragoons, the Hon. Henry Fitzroy Stanhope, Cornet.

1st Reg. Foot Guards, Charles Frederick, Lieutenant. Charles Whitworth, Ensign.

Coldstream Reg. Foot Guards, Richard Grenville, Captain. Justice Willis, junior, Sollicitor.

3d Reg. Foot Guards, Arnoldius Jones Skelton, Ensign.

1st Battalion Royal Reg. Foot, Robert Corsane, Ensign.

S H I P  N E W S.

*Deal, April 27.* Sailed to the westward, his Majesty's ship Seaford; and the Mary-Ann, Hoddart, for the Baltick. Remain in the Downs, his Majesty's ship Glory; and the Antigua Frigate, Butler, for Lisbon. Wind N. E.

The Hen and Chickens, Riordan, from Dunkirk, is arrived at Cork; Two sisters, Clibbert, from Portsmouth, at ditto; Dependant, Christian, from London, at Embden; Neptune, Ferguson, from London at Dublin; Monder Lass, Reed, from Bourdeaux, at ditto; Grabes, Strindman, from Stockholm, at ditto; Jonathan and Hannah, Blair, from Newcastle, at ditto; and Gurney, Wilkins, from Liverpool, at Waterford.

L O N D O N.

Yesterday morning Mr. King, one of his Majesty's Messengers, arrived at the Earl of Rochford's Office, with an express from Copenhagen.

They write from the Hague, of the 14th inst. that a considerable loan was just on the point of being negociated there, for the service of his Danish Majesty.

A treaty is just negociated at the Hague between the States-General, London, Petersburgh and the Court of Turin.

Certain advice is received, that a squadron of great force is now fitting out at the Sea Port of Halem in Holland, said to be intended *for a secret expedition*.

His Royal Highness the Duke of Gloucester has ordered a complete set of new accoutrements to be prepared for the first regiment of Foot Guards against the review. This is the third regiment that his Royal Highness has completely accoutred at his own expence.

It is said that a Chapter of the Most Noble Order of the Garter will be held on Monday next at St. James's, in order to invest Lord North with the dignity.

A Bill was *yesterday* ordered into the House of Commons to encourage the subjects of foreign States to lend money upon security of freehold and leasehold estates, &c. in the British Colonies; on a division 20 against 19.

Yesterday Sir Watkin Williams Wynne, Bart. elected Member for Salop, in the room of the late Sir John Astley, Bart. took his seat in the House of Commons.

Yesterday two printed papers, one intitled, "Reasons against some parts of the Quakers Title-Bill;" and the other, "Reasons for altering that part of the bill for the better observation of the Lord's day, which allows Chandlers to sell on that day," were delivered to the Members going into the House.

The King of Poland has lately done the Chevalier D'Eon the honour to write to him a letter under his own hand, which was sent directed to him in London, and received by the General Post, conceived in the most friendly and polite terms, in answer to a letter of felicitation that the Chevalier had addressed to his Majesty on the imminent danger he was lately in, and from which he escaped but by a kind miracle. That Monarch, whose goodness is his glory, and whose love of truth and humanity renders him equal to a Socrates and a Titus, and who from his youth was acquainted with the Chevalier at the Imperial Court of Russia, assures him of the continuation of his esteem, and offers his protection if he will go to Poland.

*Extract of a Letter from Gibraltar, dated Feb. 26.*

"Our Barbary Consul, Mr. Sampson, arrived here some weeks ago, having narrowly escaped the pursuit of some Moors, who were supposed to have had some intention to detain him, upon account of some misunderstanding between him and the Emperor. The story is long—but upon the whole it appears to us, that he has been most shamefully and ignominiously used there by the Emperor; and all this owing to ourselves, in not having supported him properly, when invested with such a character. On every occasion he has been neglected; presents, when sent from England for the Emperor, were not suffered to go through his hands, as they certainly ought, in order to make him of consequence; but, instead of

By a gentleman just arrived from Paris we are informed, that the Pretender, from his being so many years devoted to his bottle, had no great devotion to the deed of matrimony; but was egged on by the French Court to preserve the breed of Stuart, as a future convenience to their machinations. It is likewise said, that the French King has added considerably to the Princess's fortune.

The Lord Chancellor has appointed the remainder of this week to hear the petitions which stood adjourned on account of his Lordship's indisposition.

It is said there are near one hundred and fifty petitions in causes, lunaticks and bankrupts, set down for hearing.

A company of foot intended for the youngest son of Lord Holland, who is at present a Cornet of horse, was among the commissions from Ireland that were rejected by the King, and sent back unsigned.

A correspondent informs us, that the private accounts from Ireland are filled with relations of the national discontents, and real miseries of the people of that kingdom.

We hear from Ireland, that for several months past they have had a large importation of wheat from America; great part of which is expected to be landed in Britain, as soon as the present corn bill is passed.

C Fox has been so lucky at last Newmarket races, that it is said he won very near 16,000l. the greater part of which he got by betting against the celebrated Pincher, who lost the match by one half a neck. The odds at starting were six to four, and two to one, in favour of the losing horse. The Duke of Cumberland and Sir C. Bunbury have likewise been considerable gainers.

Thursday last being St. George's day, the anniversary of the Society of Antiquaries, the following Members were chosen the President, Council, and Officers of the Society for the year ensuing, viz.

| | |
|---|---|
| Rev. Dr. Milles Dean of Exeter, Pres. | Jam. West, Esq. V. P. |
| Sir Jos. Ayloffe, V. P. | Daniel Wray, Esq. |
| Hon. Daines Barrington, V. P. | * Gust. Brander, Esq. |
| Owen Salusb. Brereton, Esq V. P. | * Matt. Duane, Esq. |
| Sir J. Colebroke, Tr. | * Sir Wm. Hamilton. |
| R. Gough, Esq. Dir. | * W. Heberden, M.D. |
| T. Morell, D. D. Sec. | * Ld. Visc. Nuneham. |
| W. Norris, A. M. Sec. | * Tho. Percy, D. D. |
| Thom. Pownall, Esq. | * Char. Rogers, Esq. |
| | * H. Stebbing, D. D. |
| | * Sam. Wegg, Esq. |
| | * Sir J. Eard. Wilmot. |

N. B. Those marked thus * were not of the former Council.

The Society then proceeded to the Mitre tavern in Fleet-street, where an elegant entertainment was provided for them.

Captain Wilkinson, of his Majesty's ship Fowey, is appointed to the command of the Winchelsea, at Portsmouth.

They write from Portsmouth, that the Regiment quartered at Gosport, has received orders to hold themselves in readiness to embark for Gibraltar.

His Majesty has ordered an annuity of 20l. per ann. to be paid to the widow of the journeyman Slater, who was killed a few days ago by falling from Kew House, where he was at work.

His Majesty has likewise been pleased to order (on account of the dearness of provisions) 1s. per week to be added to the pay of each of the labouring men now employed at Richmond and Kew; and also a quart of strong beer every day to each of them.

Last week the workmen began making the road from the New Bridge through Battersea-fields to Wandsworth.

No Court of Aldermen was held yesterday at Guildhall; bread is continued at the same price as last week.

Yesterday came on the election for an Organist to St. Mary, Islington, when Miss Crooke (a pupil of Mr. Selby, Organist of Allhallows, Bread-street, and St. Sepulchre's, Snow-hill) was chosen: The numbers being, before six o'clock,—For Miss Crooke 212—Mr. Davis 12—Mr. Davis begged leave to decline the poll.

*Extract of a letter from Gosport, April 23.*

"The Centaur and Egmont, two of the ships that were ordered out, are compleated for sea, and will go out of the harbour the first fair wind.

"The foremast men and petty officers of the four ships that were ordered for sea are not suffered to go on shore, as they expect to receive their sailing orders every hour.

"It is now certain they will go no further than cruising the channel for exercise.

"The Britannia, a first rate now in dock, notwithstanding she was never at sea, is so

On Monday morning several smugglers, bringing tea through Mitcham in Surry, were attacked by a party of Custom house officers and overcome. It is said that one of the officers and three smugglers were killed. The tea was conveyed to the Custom-house.

Friday a young woman went to a Pawnbroker's in High Holborn, in order to purchase a pair of stays, and desired leave to fit them on in one of the slips in the shop; but while the master was busy in serving his customers, she stole off with the stays, and, tho' pursued, got clear off.

On Sunday night the servant maid of Lady Ann Cecil, sister to the Earl of Exeter, was found hanging in her own apartment.

A person who robbed his uncle about six months since, and was tried at Hertford Assizes and acquitted, yesterday morning robbed his aunt of 150l. and was committed to New Prison.

Thursday Mr. Little, of Ashton-Ingham, in Herefordshire, a Farmer of considerable fortune, whilst he was overlooking some workmen repairing a barn, had the misfortune to be crushed to death by the fall of a beam.

Friday was committed to Maidstone goal, by John Russell and John Moneypenny, Esqrs. James Riley and Alexander Buchanan, for stealing old rope out of the ships at Deptford.

The same day was convicted before John Russell, Esq. a Baker, for selling bread short of weight, and paid the penalty of one pound five shillings.

Monday at the general quarter session of the Peace for the Liberty of his Majesty's Tower of London, held at the Court-house in Well-close-square, John Mason was convicted of petit larceny, in stealing two bushels of coals, value 10d. and was sentenced to be transported.

Ann Harley, committed some time since to the Poultry Compter for stealing goods the property of Abraham Slade, died yesterday in Newgate, where she was removed to take her trial.

Yesterday Lady Dering was safely delivered of a daughter at Sir Edward's house in Savile-Row.

MARRIED.] On Saturday, by a special licence, at Knowsley, the seat of the Earl of Derby, in Lancashire, Jeffery Hornby, jun. Esq of Preston, in the said county, to the Hon. Miss Stanley, second daughter of Lord Strange. Sunday, Robert Kendall, Esq. of King-street, Bloomsbury, to Miss Amelia Newland, of Henrietta street, Cavendish square. Yesterday, Mr. Mich. Cope Hopton, of Bucklersbury, to Miss Jones, of Croydon. Yesterday, Mr. James Bedford, of the General Post-office, to Miss Susanna Nash, of Tunbridge, in Kent. Same day, Mr. Thomas Bolus, of Fenchurch-buildings, to Mrs. Henrietta Gilbert, relict of the late Thomas Gilbert, Esq. of Kingsland. Thursday, at the Cathedral church of Exeter, Francis Colman, Esq. of Hillersdon, in Devonshire, to Miss Jemima Serle. Thursday, at Greenwich, Mr. Cunningham, of Limehouse, to Miss Salter, of the same place.

DIED.] Lately, at Amsterdam, after a few days illness, Mr. Dirk Cloes Lurkeman, formerly a Merchant, and partner in the house of Messrs John and Wolfert Van Hemert here. Yesterday, at Clapham, William Gibbs, Esq. formerly a wealthy Clothier. Same day, the wife of Mr. Lavington, Linnen-draper, of Bond-street. Yesterday, Mr. Slater, Pawnbroker, in Shoe-lane. Monday, at North Nibley, in Gloucestershire, George Smith, Esq.

B A N K R U P T S.

James Woolley, of Bromsgrove in Worcestershire, Hop Merchant, to surrender May 19, 20, June 9, at the house of John Meredith, Innholder, in Birmingham.

*Dividends to be made.*

May 19. William Dresser, of Scackleton, in Yorkshire, Flax-Dresser, at Harry's Coffee-house, in Kingston upon Hull.

June 26. Thomas Dunn, of Bedale, otherwise Bedal, in Yorkshire, Shopkeeper, at Guildhall, London.

May 26. Samuel Pye, of Snow-hill, London, Grocer and Tea-dealer, at Guildhall.

May 22. Francis Greaves, of Guildford, Surry, Brewer and Innholder, at Guildhall.

CATCHES and GLEES.

*This Day was published,*

Price 3s. handsomely bound and well printed.

THE NEW MERRY COMPANION; or, COMPLETE MODERN SONGSTER: Being a select Collection of the most celebrated Songs, lately sung at the Theatres, Vauxhall, Ranelagh, &c. Few of which ever were printed in

**4.4** The *Middlesex Journal*, 28 April to 30 April 1772

of Parliament, was started in 1769 by William Beckford, the then Lord Mayor of London, and other supporters of Wilkes,

> to vindicate the cause of suppressed liberty by exhibiting in full view to the people every measure that has already been taken, and every attempt that may further be made, upon that great charter of our laws, that palladium of English liberty, which, purchased by the best blood, has been maintained by the warmest zeal of the wisest and best men this nation has ever produced.[10]

The *Middlesex Journal* is an example of how far the victories of Wilkes and Junius had damaged the government's nerve. It is unlikely that it would otherwise have got away with paragraphs such as these from the issue for 30 April 1772:

> His Majesty, we are told, intends to make the tour of England. Weak as he is, he has got more wisdom. He knows too well the contempt or detestation in which he is held in all parts of the Kingdom, to expose himself to the neglect or insults he would every where meet with. Instead of travelling through England, he will bury himself at Kew.
>
> An amiable personage, expected soon from abroad, will shew how incapable he was of contaminating his Royal blood by an unsuitable marriage, by his resentment against a near relation. This will confute the malice of those who pretended to believe the grandson of G——— the Second would make the daughter of a w——— any thing but a w———. The subscribers to the masked ball at Mrs. Cornelys's have given orders for their said ball being deferred until Tuesday fortnight. This is an error of the press. It ought to run thus: Sir John Fielding has given orders for Mrs. Cornelys's masked ball being deferred till the *Greek Calends.*
>
> The only argument that has ever been used in favour of masquerades is, that they promote trade. So did the bawdy-houses about Covent-Garden promote Mrs. Philip's trade in ———.
>
> Every thing is estimated by comparison. A man does not think himself poor because he has little, but because he sees every body about him have a great deal. The sufferings of the poor from their real wants are infinitely aggravated by those scenes of riot, luxury, and dissipation, which they see every where around them. What must a man think who is starving for want of bread when he beholds such a riot of nobility and gentry as in this night at the Pantheon? – Query, Would not the money expended there this night be sufficient to maintain all the City of London for at least one day?
>
> I am, says a Correspondent, no friend to mobs. But if the people were never to be guilty of any greater crime, than to meet this evening, enter the Pantheon, and unmask all the knaves and fools that are assembled, they would not, in my opinion, commit a very venial trespass.

Contemporaries would have recognized the reference to 'Mrs. Philip's trade' as referring to Mrs Constantia Philipps, who was the eighteenth-century equivalent of the London Rubber Company. She had a virtual monopoly in the sale of condoms.

## Morning Papers

The next fashion in newspapers was the morning paper. William Woodfall, the younger brother of Henry Sampson Woodfall, founded the *Morning Chronicle* (1769–1862). Woodfall, nicknamed 'Memory' Woodfall, was famous for his powers of recollection which enabled him to sit in the public gallery of the House of Commons for up to twelve hours at a time and then return to his printing-house where, by candlelight, he would write up to sixteen columns of speeches from memory for the following morning's paper. For nourishment, and to keep his bowels under control during the twelve-hour sittings, Woodfall used to smuggle a supply of hard-boiled eggs into the chamber inside his hat.

The *Morning Chronicle* became the leading political daily on the strength of Woodfall's parliamentary reporting. However, being reliant solely on one man, Woodfall's method had its disadvantages:

> The two Houses of Parliament having more than once sat 'till after midnight, and very frequently 'till past nine at night, we have often been unavoidably driven to the necessity of delaying the publication of our paper an hour or two later than usual; many of the newsmen have taken abundant advantage of this circumstance, they have foisted other prints upon our customers, and they have, in a variety of instances, grossly exaggerated the true state of the case, and with a most impudent confidence of assertion, declared that we did not publish 'till past nine in the morning. Not content with this, they have committed outrages at the Printer's dwelling-house, and, by their riotous behaviour, became a nuisance to his neighbours. In order to check their lawless proceedings in the last instance, he has directed his Attorney to commence prosecutions against those Newsmen most forward in disturbing his neighbours, and destroying his premises; and in order to prevent the Publick from being any longer disappointed, he has established such regulations as will in future render the publication of his paper much earlier.[11]

James Perry, the editor of the *Gazetteer*, introduced a new method of reporting parliamentary debates. This involved employing relays of young 'impecunious barristers' keen to practise their powers of recall by acting as parliamentary reporters. They took turns to listen to the debates for short periods and then rush back to the printing office to write out their reports while their memories were still fresh; another person took their place. By this means, the whole day's proceedings could be covered without any gaps.

Perry was thus able to produce a fuller, faster and more accurate report than any of his competitors, including Woodfall, at a time of great public interest in parliamentary affairs in the furore surrounding the loss of the American colonies, the rise of Pitt the Younger and the impeachment and trial of Warren Hastings. Sales of the *Gazetteer* rose at the expense of the *Morning Chronicle*, yet Woodfall refused to change his methods. Woodfall quarrelled with his partners over this issue and left to start a new daily newspaper, the *Diary; or, Woodfall's Register* (1789–93).

When the *Chronicle*, fallen in sales and prestige, came on the market in 1789, Perry borrowed enough money to buy it, and, as a proprietor in his own right, was now free to adopt his own organizational and editorial policy. He turned the *Chronicle* into the leading Whig newspaper, selling 4,000 copies a day. He achieved this by a combination of using the same methods of parliamentary reporting he had employed at the *Gazetteer* and attracting a first-class team of writers to work for the paper, including Sheridan, Coleridge, Lamb, Thomas Moore and, as theatre critic, William Hazlitt.

The *Morning Post* (1772–1937; Figure 4.5) was founded by a group of twelve shareholders, including Christie the auctioneer, Tattersall the horse dealer, John Bell the bookseller and printer, and the Rev. Henry Bate, 'The Fighting Parson'. It began as a cheap advertising pamphlet of eight small pages, but within a fortnight it became a conventional four-page newspaper, little different in appearance from the *Morning Chronicle*. Under Bate's editorship, for which he was paid four guineas a week and whatever he could get from Treasury bribes, the paper's support for the government was so blatant that it was nicknamed *Lord Sandwich's Post*. In 1780 Bate published a reckless libel alleging that the Duke of Richmond had treasonably provided the French with a map of the Sussex coast at a time when it was believed that the French were preparing to invade England. Richmond sued and won, and the disgraced Bate left the *Post* to start the *Morning Herald* (1780–1869) which, surprisingly in view of Bate's past record, was a serious newspaper, second only to the *Morning Chronicle* in its coverage of political news.

After Bate left the *Morning Post*, the *Post* continued its downward path and became little more than a society gossip paper read by a small circle only. In 1795, when its circulation had sunk to just 350 copies per day, it was sold to its printer, Daniel Stuart, for £600. Stuart transformed the *Post*'s fortunes by widening its content to include serious political comment, literary contributions from Wordsworth and Southey among others, and entertainment. He increased the readership by incorporating the *Gazetteer* and another daily paper, the *Telegraph* (1794–97) and expanded the advertising side.

When Stuart sold the *Morning Post* for £25,000 in 1803, its regular circulation was 4,500 copies per day.[12] The rise in the capital value of the *Morning Post* was almost entirely due to profits from advertising. It was

**The Morning Post and Fashionable World.**

No. 7135. SATURDAY, December 13, 1794. Price Fourpence Halfpenny.

KING'S THEATRE.
THIS Present EVENING, SATURDAY, December 13, 1794, will be performed for the Third Time, a New Comic Opera, called
L'AMORE CONTRASTATO,
Or, LA MOLINARELLA.
The Music entirely by PAESIELLO.
End of the first Act,
A DIVERTISEMENT,
End of the second Act,
A Grand Heroic Pantomime Ballet, called
GIUSTINO I.
IMPERADORE DE ROMANI;
Or,
IL TRIONFO DELL'AMORE, E DELL'AMICIZIA.
A NEW SERIOUS OPERA, (never performed at this Theatre) called,
ZENOBIA IN PALMIRA,

THEATRE ROYAL, DRURY-LANE.
THIS PRESENT EVENING, His MAJESTY's SERVANTS will act the Tragedy of
JANE SHORE.
THE DRUMMER.

THEATRE ROYAL, COVENT-GARDEN.
THIS PRESENT EVENING, will be presented
THE RAGE!
HERCULES AND OMPHALE.

GRANTHAM CANAL NAVIGATION.

SANS SOUCI.
THIS EVENING, SATURDAY, Dec. 13, 1794, will be presented, at SANS SOUCI, in the Strand, an Entertainment entirely Original, replete with uncommon Novelty, called,
GREAT NEWS;
Or, A TRIP TO THE ANTIPODES.
Mr. DIBDIN.

ROYAL ACADEMY, SOMERSET-PLACE.
JOHN SHELDON, Esq. PROFESSOR in ANATOMY, will give his SIXTH, and LAST LECTURE, for this Season, on MONDAY next, December 15, at Eight o'Clock.
JOHN RICHARDS, R. A. Sec.

CHEAP SATTINS, BLACK MODE CLOAKS, MUFFS TIPPETS, &c. &c.
CHAPMAN, IRVING, and EDWARDS

PEACE AND WAR.
MR. ORMES's GALLERY of PAINTINGS, No. 14, Old Bond-street, is now open.

MONEY NEGOCIATIONS.
THE Nobility, Gentry, Ladies (married or single) and the Public, are respectfully acquainted,
JERVOISE BIDDULPH, Superintendant.

LITERARY PRODUCTIONS.
THE OFFSPRING OF RUSSELL, Castle of Zettau, a German Tale, by C. R. in 3 vols price 9s. sewed.

WM. PARK, Brandy Merchant, No. 125, Leadenhall-street,

GRAND EXHIBITION,
FOR THIS NIGHT ONLY,
In the GREAT EXHIBITION ROOM, No. 28, HAY-MARKET,
THIS PRESENT EVENING, SATURDAY, Dec. 13,
THE SIEUR COMUS will add to his various other amazing Performances the following particulars:
THE GRAND MAGICAL HOUSE,
Admittance HALF-A-CROWN each Person.

A VARIETY OF NEW PERFORMANCES THIS WEEK.
HANDY's NEW CIRCUS, LYCEUM, STRAND,
THIS PRESENT SATURDAY, Dec. 13, 1794,
LOVER'S TRIAL.
Or, The LOYAL VILLAGERS.
LA FORCE D'HERCULE,
TRAMPOLINE TRICKS,
THE COUNTRY RECRUIT;
Or, DOLLY IN THE DUMPS.
POLANDERS PERFORMANCES,
HORSEMANSHIP,
UNRIVALLED,
TIGHT ROPE DANCING,
TUMBLING,
VAULTING on the SLACK ROPE,
The Taylor Riding to Brentford.

AT a General Meeting of the Commissioners to execute the Act for granting an additional Duty on Inhabited Houses, held at the Commissioners' Rooms, Guildhall-yard, the 10th of December, 1794.
By Order of the Commissioners,
CORNELIUS BELL.

To all PARTS of ENGLAND, from one Centre.
The SARACEN's HEAD INN, SNOW-HILL, LONDON.
BURY NEW POST COACH,

PAREGORIC LOZENGES.
THESE, LOZENGES are a safe and effectual remedy in Colds, Coughs, Hoarseness, Soreness of the Throat and Breast, and Asthmatic, and Consumptive Complaints;

**4.5** *The Morning Post*, 13 December 1794

receiving between £40 and £50 per day from closely packed advertisements. Stuart described his philosophy thus:

> I encouraged the small and miscellaneous advertisements in the front page, preferring them to any others, upon the rule that the more numerous the customers, the more permanent and independent the custom. Besides, numerous and various advertisements attract numerous and varied readers, looking for employment, servants, sales, and purchasers etc. etc. Advertisements act and react. They attract readers, promote circulation, and circulation attracts advertisements.[13]

Despite the taxes on newspaper advertisements (1s. per advertisement in 1712, rising to 2s. in 1757, 2s. 6d. in 1776, 3s. in 1789, and 3s. 6d. in 1794), there was a steady growth in the volume of advertising. This is reflected in the increases in the revenue from advertising duty:

| | **London papers** £ | **Provincial papers** £ | **Total** £ |
|---|---|---|---|
| 1715 | 931 | 92 | 1,023 |
| 1720 | 1,319 | 136 | 1,455 |
| 1730 | 1,882 | 436 | 2,318 |
| 1740 | 2,969 | 814 | 3,783 |
| 1750 | 4,951 | 1,248 | 6,199 |
| 1760 | 11,239 | 4,567 | 15,806 |
| 1770 | 15,642 | 9,505 | 25,147 |
| 1780 | 20,796 | 15,748 | 36,544 |
| 1790 | 36,660 | 18,230 | 54,890[14] |

Income from advertisements became an increasingly significant factor in the commercial success of newspapers. In the 1770s the leading daily newspapers with sales of around 3,000 could each expect to carry some 23,000 advertisements per year and make profits of over £2,000. The *Public Advertiser*, with an average daily sale of 3,133 copies, carried 23,612 advertisements in 1770 and made an advertising profit of £2,223.9s. By 1819, the *Morning Chronicle* carried 41,067 advertisements and made an advertising profit of £12,421 18s. 6d.

Without the profits from advertising, even the best-selling newspapers would have made a loss. The *Public Advertiser* would have lost £800 on a respectable average daily sale of 2,228 in 1766 were it not for advertising profits of £1,750, giving a net profit of £950. The less successful *Gazetteer* actually made a net loss of £850 in 1796, despite advertising profits of £960.

The newspaper changed from being just a subsidiary part of a printer's or bookseller's business, a means of using up spare printing capacity or a means to advertise a bookseller's publications, a plaything to be dropped if the printer was unable to attract political subsidy or if the booksellers' management by committee stifled innovation and led to stagnation. Profits from advertising meant that a newspaper could become a lucrative business venture in its own right, attracting full-time proprietors like Perry and Stuart. The profits enabled newspapers to maintain and enlarge their editorial staffs: paid editors, parliamentary reporters and theatre critics. By the 1770s, the proprietors of the *Gazetteer* were employing an editor and 14 paid correspondents to provide Guildhall and Bow Street intelligence, ship news, feature articles and news paragraphs. The fortunes to be made by successful proprietors and the growth of professionalism amongst editorial staff raised the social standing of journalism.

The physical make-up of newspapers changed: bigger pages, smaller print and an increase in the number of columns were used to accommodate the growing number of advertisements. Advertisers were encouraged to keep their messages short to guarantee inclusion, and small advertisements could be highly profitable because, even if they were only four or five lines long, they still had to pay the minimum charge applicable for up to ten or a dozen lines. Proprietors discovered they could charge premium rates for advertisements on the front page. The *Morning Chronicle* charged a minimum of 6s. for the front page and 4s. 6d. for the back. This led to the practice of covering the whole of the front page with advertisements.

## Evening Papers

Not long after the daily morning papers began to dominate the scene, a new category of paper began to emerge – the daily evening paper. For the birth of the daily evening paper we have John Palmer, inventor of the mail coach, partly to thank. In 1785 he opened an office for the distribution of newspapers. Provided the newspapers reached his agents by six o'clock in the evening, his coaches would deliver them to various parts of London and beyond. Evening papers, issued on a daily basis, thus became feasible.

Daniel Stuart's brother, Peter, was the first to take advantage of this service by starting an evening paper called the *Star* in 1788. Daniel Stuart was also involved in the pioneer days of the daily evening paper. In 1796 he purchased the second oldest evening paper, the *Courier*, which was founded in 1792, and increased its sales from 1,500 to 7,000. During Stuart's ownership it became the first evening paper to issue a second edition.

The *Courier* was started by a 24-member consortium sympathetic to the ideas of the French Revolution. This not only prompted the loyalist press to mount paper attacks on the *Courier*, but 'Church and King' mobs mounted physical attacks on anyone connected with the *Courier* and other newspapers suspected of domestic Jacobinism. In 1794, a drunken mob singing 'God Save the King' demolished the house of the local agent of the *Courier* in Bath.

## John Bell

John Bell, another giant of late-eighteenth-century journalism, was involved in a number of titles and different kinds of newspaper. His chief contribution to the development of the newspaper was to set new standards for newspaper design.[15]

His daily paper, the *World* (1787–94), was vastly superior in type and layout than anything that had gone before. By leaving gaps between paragraphs, Bell showed an imaginative and pleasing use of white on a page. Bell is also credited with being the first printer to abandon the long 's' as he found that it was often confused with the letter 'f', and the *World* was the first newspaper to do so.

In a word, the *World* was elegant, and this was reflected in its contents. Bell's editor, Captain Edward Topham, used the paper as a vehicle for promoting the career of his mistress, Mrs Wells the Drury Lane actress, who returned the compliment by bearing him four children. But the *World* was much more than this. Light-hearted, sophisticated and fashionable, it soon became *the* authority on taste and fashion.

Here is an example of Topham's journalism taken from the *World* for 18 August 1790:

HOT LOBSTERS

---

A FAT CIT in the West of England, who had been several years married to a beautiful woman, often complained of his unhappy lot in not having a son to enjoy his inheritance; and this complaint being most affectingly renewed on his arrival in the Isle of Wight, a wag, who often kept him company, desired him to eat Hot Lobsters, as a food which had an uncommon effect in giving a manly tone to the constitution.

A fine young fellow, an intimate acquaintance of our wag's, on being acquainted with the circumstance, paid great attention to the Lady, while the husband made his excursions of some miles to eat Hot Lobsters; and in nine months the good man had the happiness to find his wife had given him a son and heir.

Overjoyed at the circumstance, he continued to devour Hot Lobsters at times ever since, with a ravenous appetite, and has had an addition to his family of two fine *twin girls*. All this was wonderful happiness; but his ardour for eating Lobsters has been a little *damped* within these few days, in consequence of his having discovered the Lady playing with the young gallant, on his unexpected return one evening from his favourite gratification, which is the more embittered, because it has occasioned him to be provokingly called, 'the Hot Lobster'.

After Bell left to start another daily, the *Oracle*, in 1789, Topham turned the *World* into a vehicle for blackmail. His most famous exploit was to threaten to expose the Prince of Wales's marriage to Mrs Fitzherbert. The Prince offered to buy the paper outright for a down payment of £4,000 plus an annuity for Topham of £400. Topham refused, but accepted a subsidy from the Prince instead. This was on top of a Treasury bribe of £600 per year.

The *World* was not the only paper receiving Treasury bribes. During the regime of Pitt the Younger the government was making the following payments to the ministerial papers:

£600 each to the *Morning Herald* and the *World*
£400 to *Woodfall's Diary*
£300 to *The Times*
£200 each to the *London Evening Post, St. James's Chronicle, Whitehall Evening Post* and the *Oracle*
£100 to the *Public Ledger*.

The government also controlled three new titles which were started to promote anti-Jacobin propaganda: the *True Briton* and the *Sun*, both founded in 1792; and the *Anti-Jacobin*, started by George Canning in 1797 to counter what he considered the pro-revolutionary views of the *Morning Post*, the *Morning Chronicle* and the *Courier*.

Pitt's attempts at controlling public opinion by Walpole's old tactic of bribing the press were not only expensive, but were also of doubtful value – despite the Treasury bribe, the *Morning Herald* continued to support Fox. Once it became known that a paper was 'bought', its opinions were discounted and it became an object of ridicule, 'a ministerial paper, a lackey of the government'. Unlike the situation with certain titles in Walpole's time, newspapers were now entirely commercial enterprises dependent on sales; and sales attracted advertisers. Thanks to advertising receipts, the level of subsidy offered by the government was not enough to seriously affect the finances of a successful paper. Realizing this, the government changed tactics and threatened to withdraw its advertising from papers which criticized the government. In 1803 Cobbett lost his Post Office advertising, and the following year, after an attack on the First Lord of the Admiralty, government advertising was withheld from *The Times*. However, by that time, each copy of *The Times* contained over 100 advertisements, so the loss of income from government advertising was a mere fleabite.

Apart from the Treasury subsidy, papers were making money from suppression fees (advising the subject that a damaging paragraph was in type, but could be taken out if a certain fee was paid), and contradiction fees (when the subject had responded too late and the paragraph had been printed, a fee could be paid to have the paragraph contradicted in the next day's paper). An example of this practice concerns Mrs Wells, Topham's former mistress. Her second husband found *The Times*'s interest in her to be too intrusive and visited William Finey, the 'editorial conductor', to put a stop to this. Pulling out a wad of notes, he asked Finey, 'Will this be enough?' Finey is reported to have replied, 'Give me a few more, and by St Patrick I'll knock the brains out of anyone who dare ever *whisper* her name.'

With the arrival of the morning daily paper the newspaper had come of age. Having won the battles with Parliament and the courts, it had become an accepted force in the land. Within the passage of the century the small-format weekly or tri-weekly single sheet had been replaced by a closely printed four-column daily paper with four pages about the size of a modern tabloid. The injection of capital from shareholders and the profits from advertisements led to the emergence of the paid editor and professional reporters.

The growth of the press during the eighteenth century was partly the result of the entrepreneurial innovations of successive printers, proprietors and journalists, who made their papers attractive to a wider class of readers and who sometimes took great risks to make their papers more relevant to the needs of the political nation. It was also the economic expansion that led to the growing affluence and influence of a serious-minded middle class, whose pursuit of genteel status and acquisition of polite manners had a significant effect on the content of the late-eighteenth-century newspaper.

Despite the practice of taking bribes and suppression and contradiction fees, newspapers, like society, had become more gentle and respectable. The increasing reliance on parliamentary reports to fill their pages and their reflection of the commercial interests of their new middle-class owners meant that the tone of the papers at the end of the eighteenth century was much more polite than their predecessors of 50 or 80 years before. But it also meant that, in marked contrast to the low-life stories in *Mist's Weekly Journal*, the cynicism and crude vitality of the *Grub-street Journal* and the explicit advertisements for aphrodisiacs and cures for venereal disease in the *Craftsman*, their contents were a great deal duller. Newspapers were no longer composed in taverns. The journey from Grub Street to Fleet Street was well under way.

## Notes

1. *The London Chronicle*, 11 April 1758.
2. Ibid., 13 April 1758.
3. Ibid., 15 December 1758.

4. Ibid., 2 June 1759.
5. For further information about Hill, see Herd, Harold (1955), *Seven Editors*, Ch. 2, London: George Allen and Unwin.
6. *Public Ledger*, 12 January 1760.
7. *North Briton*, 5 June 1762.
8. For further information see Rude, G. (1962), *Wilkes and Liberty*, Oxford: Clarendon Press.
9. 'A Dedication to the English Nation', in the *Collected Works of Junius, Printed for Henry Sampson Woodfall*, 1772.
10. *Middlesex Journal*, 4 April 1769.
11. *Morning Chronicle*, 2 April 1779.
12. Hindle, W. (1937), *The Morning Post, 1772–1937*, London: Routledge.
13. Stuart, Daniel, 'Anecdotes of Coleridge and of London Newspapers', in *Gentleman's Magazine*, July 1838.
14. Adapted from Bruttini, A. (1975), 'Advertising and the Industrial Revolution', *Economic Notes*, vol. 4, nos 2 and 3.
15. For further information about Bell and his publications, see Morison, Stanley (1930), *John Bell, 1745–1831*, Cambridge: Cambridge University Press.

## Chapter 5

# Provincial Newspapers, 1700–1899

> Almost every large town has its weekly historian, who regularly circulates his periodical intelligence, and fills the villages of his district with conjectures on the events of the war, and with debates on the true interests of Europe.
>
> Samuel Johnson, *The Idler*, 11 November 1758

Of all the different types of newspaper the eighteenth century produced, provincial papers provided the best value – a round-up of the week's news from the London papers with the boring bits taken out, a few paragraphs of local news, and columns of advertisements displaying the wares of the shopkeepers, innkeepers and tradesmen from the local market towns. Unschooled printers produced these papers. They selected stories appealing to their own taste – human interest stories, the adventures of highwaymen and other light-hearted fare to keep their readers entertained.

In the country in the seventeenth century, the wealthy got their news by subscribing to the manuscript newsletters and the *London Gazette*. The less well-off got their news by word of mouth – announcements from the town crier and the pulpit, market gossip, tavern rumour and the eavesdropping of servants in country houses. By the eighteenth century these meagre sources were no longer considered adequate. The growth in trade and commerce brought with it a new class of literate clerks and skilled artisans and other products of the growing number of charity schools. A new reading public was rapidly coming into existence.

The failure to renew the Printing Act in 1695 meant that printing presses could now be set up anywhere in the country. As the vast majority of trained printers were in London, the London printing trade soon became overcrowded. Many printers left London to seek their fortunes in other towns where there was less likelihood of competition. At the same time, the proliferation of London newspapers created a taste for newspaper reading. But, as Addison pointed out,

> They … [newspapers] … all of them receive the same advices from abroad, and very often in the same words; but their way of cooking it is so different, that there is no citizen, who has an eye to the public good, that can leave the coffee-house with peace of mind, before he has given every one of them a reading.[1]

This was possible in London where all the papers could be read for the price of a cup of coffee. But in the country there were few coffee-houses, and the increasing number of London papers meant that it was too expensive for all but the very rich to have them all sent into the country.

It did not take much imagination on the part of the newly arrived country printers to recognize the gap in the market that could be filled by starting a newspaper. The only additional capital required was the cost of subscribing to the London newspapers and the manuscript newsletters, and perhaps buying a new case of type.

## The Eighteenth Century

The earliest copy of a provincial newspaper still surviving is the *Bristol Post-Boy* for 21 August 1704.[2] But it is almost certain that the first provincial paper was the *Norwich Post*, which was probably founded in 1701.[3] Important provincial papers started in the first half of the eighteenth century, many of which have survived to this day, include the *Worcester Post-Man* (later *Berrow's Worcester Journal*; Figure 5.2) (1709), *Newcastle Courant* (1711), *Stamford Mercury* (1713), *Norwich Mercury* (1713), *Ipswich Journal* (1720), *Gloucester Journal* (1722), *Reading Mercury* (1723), *York Courant* (1725), *Salisbury Journal* (1729), *Aris's Birmingham Gazette* (1741), *Cambridge Chronicle* (1744) and the *Sussex Weekly Advertiser* (1746).

The early provincial newspapers were essentially scissors-and-paste affairs put together by the local jobbing printer and published once a week for sale to the farmers and others who thronged to the town on market days. The printer would select those items from the London papers that they thought would appeal to their readers. Perhaps in order to distance themselves from the material they were printing, in case it was false or libellous, many of the early papers showed the source of their news paragraphs. The *Leeds Mercury* (Figure 5.1) in the early 1730s headed its news columns 'From the London Evening Post' and 'From Wye's Letter'. When its printer, John Hirst, died in 1733, his successor, James Lister, substituted the *Evening-Post* for the *London Evening-Post* as the printed source of his London news. However, both printers regularly reprinted essays from the *Weekly Miscellany* and the *Universal Spectator* to keep their readers in touch with metropolitan opinion.

Because printing in those days was such a time-consuming, laborious business, country newspapers were usually printed in stages when the post boy delivered a fresh consignment of London papers. It is quite common to find the final day's post printed in a different size of type from that used in the rest of the paper where the printer had misjudged the amount of space needed for that day's news. Printing the week's news in the order it was received meant

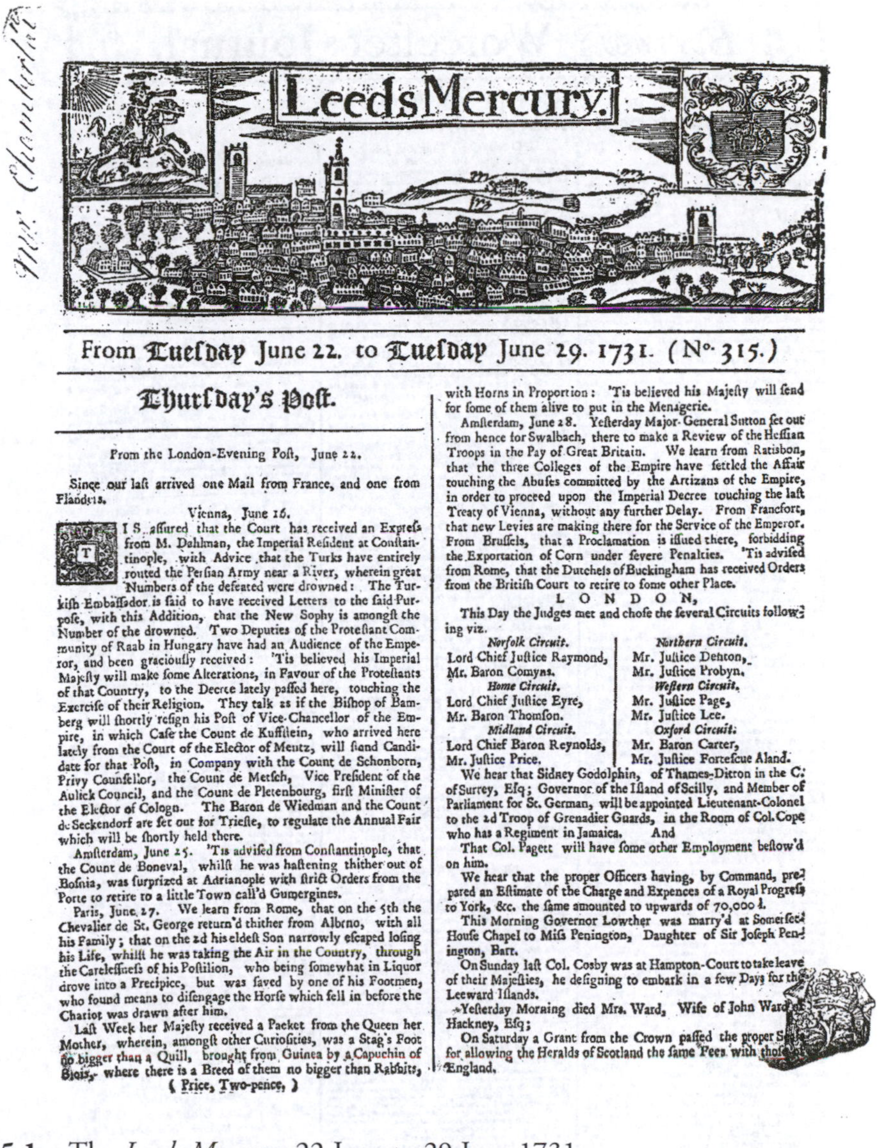

Leeds Mercury.

From Tueſday June 22. to Tueſday June 29. 1731. (No. 315.)

Thurſday's Poſt.

From the London-Evening Poſt, June 22.

Since our laſt arrived one Mail from France, and one from Flanders.

Vienna, June 16.

T IS aſſured that the Court has received an Expreſs from M. Dahlman, the Imperial Reſident at Conſtantinople, with Advice that the Turks have entirely routed the Perſian Army near a River, wherein great Numbers of the defeated were drowned: The Turkiſh Embaſſador is ſaid to have received Letters to the ſaid Purpoſe, with this Addition, that the New Sophy is amongſt the Number of the drowned. Two Deputies of the Proteſtant Community of Raab in Hungary have had an Audience of the Emperor, and been graciouſly received: 'Tis believed his Imperial Majeſty will make ſome Alterations, in Favour of the Proteſtants of that Country, to the Decree lately paſſed here, touching the Exerciſe of their Religion. They talk as if the Biſhop of Bamberg will ſhortly reſign his Poſt of Vice-Chancellor of the Empire, in which Caſe the Count de Kuffſtein, who arrived here lately from the Court of the Elector of Mentz, will ſtand Candidate for that Poſt, in Company with the Count de Schonborn, Privy Counſellor, the Count de Metſch, Vice Preſident of the Aulick Council, and the Count de Pletenbourg, firſt Miniſter of the Elector of Cologn. The Baron de Wiedman and the Count de Seckendorf are ſet out for Trieſte, to regulate the Annual Fair which will be ſhortly held there.

Amſterdam, June 25. 'Tis adviſed from Conſtantinople, that the Count de Boneval, whilſt he was haſtening thither out of Boſnia, was ſurprized at Adrianople with ſtrict Orders from the Porte to retire to a little Town call'd Gumergines.

Paris, June 27. We learn from Rome, that on the 5th the Chevalier de St. George return'd thither from Albeno, with all his Family; that on the 2d his eldeſt Son narrowly eſcaped loſing his Life, whilſt he was taking the Air in the Country, through the Careleſſneſs of his Poſtilion, who being ſomewhat in Liquor drove into a Precipice, but was ſaved by one of his Footmen, who found means to diſengage the Horſe which fell in before the Chariot was drawn after him.

Laſt Week her Majeſty received a Packet from the Queen her Mother, wherein, amongſt other Curioſities, was a Stag's Foot no bigger than a Quill, brought from Guinea by a Capuchin of Blois, where there is a Breed of them no bigger than Rabbits, with Horns in Proportion: 'Tis believed his Majeſty will ſend for ſome of them alive to put in the Menagerie.

Amſterdam, June 28. Yeſterday Major-General Sutton ſet out from hence for Swalbach, there to make a Review of the Heſſian Troops in the Pay of Great Britain. We learn from Ratisbon, that the three Colleges of the Empire have ſettled the Affair touching the Abuſes committed by the Artizans of the Empire, in order to proceed upon the Imperial Decree touching the laſt Treaty of Vienna, without any further Delay. From Francfort, that new Levies are making there for the Service of the Emperor. From Bruſſels, that a Proclamation is iſſued there, forbidding the Exportation of Corn under ſevere Penalties. 'Tis adviſed from Rome, that the Dutcheſs of Buckingham has received Orders from the Britiſh Court to retire to ſome other Place.

L O N D O N,

This Day the Judges met and choſe the ſeveral Circuits following viz.

| | |
|---|---|
| *Norfolk Circuit.* | *Northern Circuit.* |
| Lord Chief Juſtice Raymond, | Mr. Juſtice Denton, |
| Mr. Baron Comyns. | Mr. Juſtice Probyn. |
| *Home Circuit.* | *Weſtern Circuit.* |
| Lord Chief Juſtice Eyre, | Mr. Juſtice Page, |
| Mr. Baron Thomſon. | Mr. Juſtice Lee. |
| *Midland Circuit.* | *Oxford Circuit.* |
| Lord Chief Baron Reynolds, | Mr. Baron Carter, |
| Mr. Juſtice Price. | Mr. Juſtice Forteſcue Aland. |

We hear that Sidney Godolphin, of Thames-Ditton in the C. of Surrey, Eſq; Governor of the Iſland of Scilly, and Member of Parliament for St. German, will be appointed Lieutenant-Colonel to the 2d Troop of Grenadier Guards, in the Room of Col. Cope who has a Regiment in Jamaica. And

That Col. Pagett will have ſome other Employment beſtow'd on him.

We hear that the proper Officers having, by Command, prepared an Eſtimate of the Charge and Expences of a Royal Progreſs to York, &c. the ſame amounted to upwards of 70,000 l.

This Morning Governor Lowther was marry'd at Somerſet-Houſe Chapel to Miſs Penington, Daughter of Sir Joſeph Penington, Bart.

On Sunday laſt Col. Coſby was at Hampton-Court to take leave of their Majeſties, he deſigning to embark in a few Days for the Leeward Iſlands.

Yeſterday Morning died Mrs. Ward, Wife of John Ward of Hackney, Eſq;

On Saturday a Grant from the Crown paſſed the proper Seals for allowing the Heralds of Scotland the ſame Fees with thoſe of England.

( Price, Two-pence. )

**5.1** The *Leeds Mercury*, 22 June to 29 June 1731

that key items of news often got buried in the inside pages. It is not until you turn to the inside pages of the *Gloucester Journal* for 20 June 1727 that you see on page two, under the heading 'Saturday's Post', the news that

> Yesterday, about Four in the Afternoon Mr. Crew, one of his Majesty's Messengers, arrived here … [London] … being dispatch'd by the Lord Viscount Townshend

# Berrow's Worcester Journal.

Price *Two-pence Halfpenny.* THURSDAY, JULY 16, 1767. 3020 { Weeks this JOURNAL has been publish'd.

## SATURDAY's POST.

*Arrived a Mail from Flanders.*

NAPLES, *June* 9.

We no longer have any Talk here concerning the Jesuits. Every Thing is absolutely silent on that Head. Cardinal Orsini, who set out the Day before Yesterday, from this Capital, for Rome, has obtained Permission of the King to converse with the General of the Order, and even to afford him Subsistance.

*A* LETTER *from Leiden, dated July* 3.

"We have Advices from the Frontiers of Spain, which speak of some Marks of Discontent that appear there on Account of what has passed with Regard to the Jesuits. The Governors, Commanders, and Justiciaries, have the most precise Ord rs, each in his Department, to watch over the Maintenance of the publick Tranquillity; to prevent all Sorts of tumultuous Assemblies, and to cause all such Persons to be arrested, as either by Word of Mouth or Deed, shall shew themselves inclined to oppose the King's Intentions; and, in order to secure the State against all Surprise, as there are in the whole Kingdom but Eighty Thousand regular Troops, and Twenty-five Thousand Militia, his Catholick Majesty has entreated the King of France to re-enforce his Troops in the Garrisons on the Side of Spain, in order to be able to assist the Spanish Forces, in Case there should be Need of them, to suppress this Spirit of Sedition."

### AMERICA.

CHARLES-TOWN *(South Carolina) May* 19. In a Letter from Carthagena, *Via* Jamaica, Captain Henderson, of the Sloop Fanny, bound from thence to the Bay, gives a dismal Account of the Loss of the said Sloop, on the 31st of October last, off Cape Gracious à Dois; with many other Circumstances that befell the Crew (eleven in Number) who all, except three, died through Fatigue and the Want of Subsistance; those who survived being obliged to eat the Flesh of their deceased Shipmates for Food, and drink their own Urine to quench their Thirst; and to make their Case still more dismal, the brutish Spaniards refused them Subsistence, as Men saved from Shipwreck; alledging, that they were not bound to the Bay, and therefore must take up their Abode in the common Goal, amongst Thieves, Negroes, and Murderers!

### IRELAND.

DUBLIN, *June* 30. At a Meeting of several Gentlemen of the County of Galway, in Dublin, on the 25th of June, 1767, it was resolved, that a Bill for Limitation of Parliaments for seven Years would be of the greatest Utility to this Kingdom, and that an Address should be presented to their Representatives, to use their utmost Endeavours to promote it.

### COUNTRY NEWS.

SALISBURY, *July* 6. On the 28th ult. at the River Side, near Alderbury, about two Miles from this City, a Boy being placed with a Fowling Piece to keep the Birds from a Plot of Ground sown for Turneps, two Journeymen Shoemakers came down to wash themselves in the mean Time, when one of them took up the Gun, which happened to be charged, to look at it, and inconsiderately pointing the Muzzle towards his Companion, who was sitting close by on the Ground, it went off, and killed him on the Spot.

BATH, *July* 6. On Thursday last, by a Mandate from the Bishop of Bath and Wells, the Rev. John Taylor was instituted into the Rectory of Bath, vacant by the Death of the Rev. Mr. Duel Taylor.

YORK, *July* 7. Last Week were imported at Liverpool, 2750 Quarters of Wheat, 250 ditto of Rye, ditto of Beans, from Rotterdam; 500 Quarters of Wheat, and 14 ditto of Beans, from Newport; 425 Quarters of Beans, 18 ditto of Pease, and 16 ditto of Wheat, from Ostend; 73 Barrels and 54 half ditto of Rice, from South Carolina; 223 Quarters of Oats, 212 ditto of Rye, and 12 ditto of Barley, from Apenrade: Also 136 Tierces of Beef, and 145 Casks and 108 Firkins of Butter, from Ireland.

Within these three Weeks 500 Quarters of Wheat, a Quantity of Wheat Flour, and 370 Quarters of Rye, have been imported at Whitby, where the best Wheat now sells at 5s. 8d. and Rye at 3s 6d. the Bushel.

Last Week one Mr Jordan, of Bridlington (a Man possessed of a large Fortune) being at Work in a Well which he had dug a great Depth, the Earth and Stones fell in upon him and a Labourer he had with him, and crushed them in such a Degree, that almost every Bone in their Bodies was broke.

LEEDS, *July* 7. We learn from Carlisle, that last Week nine Couple passed through there from the South, for Gratna-Green, in order to be married.

On Sunday Night we had the most violent Storm of Wind and Rain ever known at this Season of the Year in the Memory of the oldest Man living: Great Numbers of People were so terrified, that they could not continue in their Bed, but got up, and went into the Streets, expecting every Moment their Houses would have tumbled about their Ears; providentially, however, it ceased about Four o'Clock the next Morning, without having done any considerable Damage, except blowing down a few Trees, and a Windmill in the Neighbourhood, belonging to John Batley of Seacroft.

We hear from Berwick upon-Tweed, that Black Cattle has lately fallen there in Price upwards of Twenty per Cent. and all Kinds of Butchers Meat in Proportion.

## LONDON, Thursday, July 9.

Letters from Spain, dated June 26, say, "We learn from Spain, that in a Dungeon belonging to the Imperial College of the Jesuits at Madrid, they found Father Fresneda, a Jesuit Missionary, who had been confined there 14 Years upon Bread and Water, for altering the Will of a Lady, who would have left a considerable Sum to the Jesuits. Father Fresneda told her, that the Company was in no Want of Money, and that she would make a better Disposal of it if she would leave it to portion poor Orphans, and the Lady followed his Advice. His Brethren gave out he was dead."

*In the Course of last Sessions of Parliament* two hundred and nine Bills received the Royal Assent, viz. ninety five publick, and one hundred and fourteen private, which is the greatest Number that have received the Royal Assent in one Sessions for several Years.

His Majesty's Post-Master General has been pleased to order the West India Packet-Boats, for the future, to stop two Days at the Island of Dominica.

We are informed that the fine House and Gardens of the late Lord Melcombe will be purchased for the Summer Residence of his Royal Highness the Duke of Cumberland

We hear that most of the Royal Forests in England are to be survey'd this Summer, in order to their being laid out into Farms.

We hear that Mr. Alderman Beckford will set out next Week for the South of France, for the Recovery of his Health.

It is reported that two Aldermen of this City will resign their Gowns shortly, on Account of their ill State of Health.

The Dean and Chapter of Rochester have presented the Rev. Samuel Deane, M. A. to the Vicarages of Darent and Welmington, in Kent; and the Rev. Chardin Musgrave, D. D. (Provost of Oriel College, Oxford, and Prebendary of Rochester) to the Vicarage of Lamberhurst in the same County.

The Right Hon. the Lord Chancellor has appointed the following Seals to be held at Lincoln's-Inn-Hall, before Michaelmas Term, viz. July 13, First Seal, ditto 17 and 14, August 1, Fourth and Last General Seal.

Yesterday the Purser of the Glatton East Indiaman, Captain Doveton, came to the India-House with an Account of the above Ship being safe arrived off Portland from China. She sailed from the Downs on her Voyage the 26th of December 1765.

The Hawk East Indiaman, Capt. Cotton, on the 3d of September last, by a sudden Gale of Wind, in the Chinese Sea, lost all her Masts, and was in Danger of sinking, but happily weather'd it out, and arrived at Wampoa in China on the 6th of October last, from whence she was expected to sail for England the latter End of January last.

Tuesday Morning a Tradesman and his Wife, in the Parish of St. Martin in the Fields, having some Words, she asked him for only the trifling Sum of Sixpence to purchase some Provisions; he gave her the Money, but advised her to buy some Arsenick, which the poor Woman, by a false Spirit of Resentment, put into Execution, took the same, and expired soon after in great Agonies.

On Saturday last the Compting-House of Mr. Inman, Merchant, on Tower-Hill, was broke open, and from his Desk were stolen three Bank Notes, one of 300l. Value, and two of 100l. each, two Gold Watches, three Brilliants, and a Purse of Money.

The Clerk of the Bank, confined in the Poultry Compter for filing of Guineas, continues so bad of the Wounds he gave himself, as to be unfit for Examination. The filed Guineas were deficient in Weight from 8d. to 14d. It is said the above Person has a Thousand Pounds in the Stocks, and not long ago had a Thousand Pounds Portion with his Wife.

### WINE LICENCE OFFICE,

Lincoln's Inn, London, June 27, 1767.

HIS *Majesty's Commissioners for managing the Duties arising from Wine Licences, give Notice, That there will be Attendance every Day, at the Office, from Nine till One o'Clock, (Holidays excepted) for granting such Licences: And whereas the said Commissioners have received certain Information of divers Persons who presume to retail Wine without Licence;* NOTICE IS HEREBY GIVEN, *That unless such Persons speedily apply for Licences, by themselves or Agents, they will be prosecuted as the Act of Parliament directs.*

NOTE, *Every Person selling Ale and Spirituous Liquors, is to produce those Licences when he applies for his Wine Licence.*

### To be LETT,

*And Enter'd upon at* CANDLEMAS *next,*

SHIPEND HOUSE FARM, in the Parish of Mathon, in the Counties of Worcester and Hereford; consisting of a commodious Dwelling-House, one large Barn, two Stables, Beast-Houses and Sheds for Cattle, two Cyder Mills, and other convenient Out-Buildings, all in good Repair, with three hundred and thirty-one Statute Acres of Meadow, Pasture, Orcharding, Arable Land, and some Hop Ground. The Orchards are well stocked with the best Sort of Fruit Trees for Cyder, now in their Prime; and the whole Estate inclosed, lying together, with a very extensive Sheep Walk, and Right of Common on Malvern Hills.——The above Farm is situate within four Miles of the Market Town of Ledbury, in the County of Hereford, and about ten measured Miles from the City of Worcester. The Dwelling-House, Meadow, and Pasture Lands, are well supplied with Water, and may, in the greatest Drought, be watered by a Stream that directs its Course through the whole Estate.

For further Particulars apply to Robert Cliffe, Esq; upon the Premisses; or to Mr. Samuel Collet, Attorney at Law, in Worcester.

*N. B.* There is a very considerable Stock of Milking Cows and young Cattle, upon the Estate, which are to be sold, with an Ox Team, Horses, Waggons, and many Implements in the Husbandry Business.

### To be Lett, or Sold,

*And may be Enter'd upon at Michaelmas next, or sooner if requir'd,*

THE WATER-WORKS of the City of Worcester, holden under the Corporation of the [illegible] the Remainder of a Term of Five Hundred Years, commencing the 25th of February, 1689, at a Chief-Rent of Forty Shillings, [illegible] and a Couple of Capons; with a good Dwelling House, Garden, and a large Out-building adjoining thereto, containing three Lofts, and a good new Room backward, wherein a Snuff-Mill lately stood: Together with a good Corn-Mill, and a Blade-Mill, all entirely new, and may be converted to various other beneficial and advantageous Uses required in a Water-Wheel. The Works are in good Condition, are capable of great Improvement, and may be conducted by a Person on the Spot, well skilled therein, if the Purchaser chooses; being conveniently situated on the River Severn, for any Branch of Business that requires Land or Water Carriage.—— That Part of the Water-Works alone, for the Service of the City (exclusive of the Corn-Mill and Blade-Mill) brings in upwards of 120l. per Annum.

Enquire of Mr. Parker, Attorney, in Worcester.

### To be Sold by Auction,

*On Friday the 24th Day of July Instant, at Mr. Joseph Chatten's, at the Star and Garter, in Droitwich, in the County of Worcester, between the Hours of Three and Six in the Afternoon, according to the Conditions of Sale to be then produced,*

A Modern well-built MESSUAGE or TENEMENT, sashed in Front, with the Garden and Premisses thereto belonging, in good Repair, and now in the Occupation of Mr. Bre[illegible], Salt Officer, as Tenant thereof, being situated in a pleasant Part of the Town of Droitwich.

Particulars in the mean Time may be had by applying to Mr. William Jones, Attorney at Law, at his House in Droitwich; on a Tuesday at his Chambers at the Dog, in Bromsgrove; and on a Saturday at his Chambers at the Star and Garter, in Worcester; of whom MONEY may at any Time be had, on reasonable Terms.

### To be SOLD by Private Contract,

A Freehold FARM, called MORTON HALL, in the Parish of Inkberrow, in the County of Worcester, late in the Occupation of William Griffin, deceased, consisting of a good Dwelling-House, Barns, and other convenient Out-Buildings, with one hundred and eight Statute Acres of Meadow, Pasture, and Arable Land, the Whole of which (except four Acres of Meadow, and seven Acres of Arable) are inclosed, lying together near the Dwelling-House, within Half a Mile of the Turnpike Road, leading from the Market-Town of Droitwich, in the County of Worcester, to Alcester, in the County of Warwick. ——On the above Farm are three Hundred and ninety Oak and Ash Trees, sixty Elms, and a small Rabbit Warren.—— The present Tenant will quit the Estate at Michaelmas or Lady-Day next.

ALSO,

A Freehold FARM, called NORRIS's, situate and being at Morton Underhill, in the Parish of Inkberrow, late in the Tenure of Mrs. Laugher, Widow, consisting of a good Barn, and thirty-five Acres of Meadow, Pasture, and Arable Land, with an extensive Right of Common in the four Common Fields of Inkberrow aforesaid. —— Part of this Estate is adjoining to the Lands belonging to the Farm called Morton-Hall, and lies so contiguous thereto that the Whole may be thrown together to make one compleat Farm.

For further Particulars enquire of Mr. Samuel Collet, Attorney at Law, in Worcester.

### LUDLOW RACES, 1767.

ON Tuesday the 25th of August, will be Run for, on the Old Field near Ludlow, in Shropshire, a PURSE of FIFTY POUNDS, by any Horse, Mare, or Gelding, Aged, or six Years old, that never won a King's Plate; Aged carrying 9st. 7lb. six Years old 9st. Bridle and Saddle included; the best of three Four-mile Heats. ——To be entered (with proper Certificates of being duly qualified) at the Market House in Ludlow, on Tuesday the 18th of August, between the Hours of Twelve and Nine, and to pay Three Guineas for Entrance if a Non-Subscriber, but if a Subscriber One Guinea only; which Entrance-Money is for the Benefit of the second best Horse, &c. Certificates of the Ages of such Horses, &c. as are six Years old, must be produced at the Time of Entrance for the above Plate, under the Hands of the Breeders.

On Wednesday the 26th, will be Run for, on the said Course, a PURSE of FIFTY POUNDS, by any Horse, Mare, or Gelding, five or four Years old. The five Years old to carry 9st. four Years old 8st. Bridle and Saddle included; the best of three Heats, each Heat being two Miles. ——To be entered (with proper Certificates of the Age of each of them) at the Hours and Place abovementioned, on Wednesday the 19th of August; and to pay Three Guineas for Entrance if a Non-subscriber, but if a Subscriber One Guinea only; which Entrance-Money is for the Benefit of the second best Horse, &c. ——Fillies to carry 3lb. less than Colts of the same Year.——Any Horse, &c. that shall start for this Plate, and has won a Plate of Fifty Pounds, shall carry 4lb. more than such Horses, &c. that have never won any Thing. And such Horses, &c. as have won more than one Plate of Fifty Pounds, shall carry 6lb. more than Maiden Horses, &c.

*Every Horse, &c. that shall start for either of the aforesaid Plates, must be kept at the Town of Ludlow from the Time of Entering to the Time of Running, and at such Houses only as subscribe Ten Shillings to either of the said Plates. No Horse, &c. to enter in a Subscriber's Name, for either of the said Plates, that is not actually his own: But any Horse, &c. not entered on the Days of Entrance as above, may run, after paying double Entrance at the Starting Post: But not less than two Horses, &c. to start for either of the said Plates; and if only one Horse, &c. is entered, he shall not start, but shall have Ten Guineas.*

N. B. There will be a CONCERT of MUSICK on Wednesday Morning, for the Benefit of Mr. HARRIS, the Organist.

CHARLES BALDWYN, AND THOMAS KNIGHT, } Esqrs. STEWARDS.

### SUNDAY's and MONDAY's POSTS.

*Arrived the Mails from France and Holland.*

VERSAILLES, *July* 1.

THE Sieur Ame de la Laune, Standard-Bearer to the Admiral, arrived here the 26th of last Month, having been despatched from Morocco by the Sieur Breugnon, the King's Ambassador there, to bring his Majesty the News of the Conclusion of a Peace with the Emperor Muley Mohamed. The Treaty was signed on the 30th of Ma[illegible] all the French Slaves, without Exception, were [illegible]

**5.2** *Berrow's Worcester Journal*, 16 July 1767

with an Account that his Majesty King George departed this Life at Two a clock last Sunday Morning, of a Fit of Apoplexy, at Osnaburg (a City of Germany) on his Way to Hannover … And this Day his Majesty King George the Second was proclaimed with the greatest Pomp and Magnificence that ever was known on the like Occasion; nor were ever the Acclamations of the People more universal, or any Prince ascended the Throne with greater Applause than his present Majesty, whose great Wisdom and Impartiality from the Time of his Arrival in this Kingdom is a sure Foretaste of the Happiness we shall enjoy under his Administration.

Often the news printed under the heading of the final day's post directly contradicts an item in the same issue that had been printed several days earlier:

[Page 1] The following melancholy accident, we are informed, happened on Friday last, at a principal Inn on the road to Reading, viz. As a Gentleman was going up stairs he met the Landlady coming down, when he insisted upon a kiss, which she complied with; but the Gentleman not content with that, attempted to put his hand into her bosom, which she resented, and pushing him from her, he unfortunately fell down the stairs, broke his neck, and expired soon after.

[Page 3] The story propagated about town (and which is inserted in the former part of this paper) of a Gentleman attempting too great a freedom with the Landlady of a great Inn on the road to Reading, and that she pushed him down stairs, whereby he was killed, is without any sort of foundation, no such circumstances having happened or been attempted; but is supposed to arise from envy, on account of the great resort of genteel company to the said Inn.[4]

The early provincial papers were local papers only in the sense that they were printed locally and contained local advertisements. There was no systematic attempt to cover local news. In a close-knit community local news would already have circulated by word of mouth before the weekly publication date, and in the next decades when provincial papers began to be circulated over long distances, local insularity meant that the news of one town was of little or no interest to those living in another town.

Most early provincial papers had scarcely any local news at all. The *Norwich Gazette* (Figure 5.3) for 4 March 1727 contained only two items of local news: announcing two forthcoming charity sermons in Norwich churches; and the news that 'Here were Baptiz'd the last Week in this City 15, and Bury'd 22.'

The *Chester Weekly-Journal, With the most material Advices FOREIGN and DOMESTICK* for 6 October 1731 did a little better, managing three paragraphs of local news, and one of these was a paid insertion:

*Chester, Oct. 2.* This Day as a Country-Man and his Wife were going Home, the Man being somewhat Disorder'd, rid on Horseback with his Child before Him; it

Volume 21. THE Num. 1665.

# Norwich Gazette.

From Saturday February 25, to Saturday March 4, 1727.

MONDAY, February 27, *Laſt Saturday arrived a Mail from Holland, and another from Flanders.*

Conſtantinople, January 4.

THE Particulars of the Defeat of our Army in Perſia, are variouſly reported: Some ſay we had about 25000 ſlain, 8000 wounded, and 14000 taken Priſoners; others, that we loſt but 4000 in all: Whatever there may be in it, the Grand Seignior has order'd thither a conſiderable Body of Troops from Babylon, to reinforce our Army, and preſerve our Conqueſts.

Bologna, February 6. Some Days ago a Hanoverian Gentleman, who obſerv'd all the Motions of the Pretender, and carried on a Correſpondence with ſome Perſons of his Court, was arreſted in the Suburb of St. Peter by the Captain of the Shirry, aſſiſted by 20 Men well arm'd; who cauſed the Door of the Houſe where he was to be broke open, and carried him to Jail: All his Papers were ſeiz'd, and are to be examin'd by the Auditor Criminal, aſſiſted by Mr. Attorney General and Mr. Solicitor General to the Pretender, who continues to dance Engliſh Country-Dances at all Balls.

Madrid, February 10. The Duke of Liria has receiv'd 4000 Piſtoles, with Orders at the ſame Time to repair to Petersburg with all poſſible Speed; whereupon he went Yeſterday to the Pardo, and took his Leave of their Majeſties. Money has alſo been ſent to the Army before Gibraltar, for paying the Troops. The late Duke of Ormond has receiv'd 1000 Piſtoles. Preparations for the Siege of Gibraltar go forward, and we daily expect to hear of the opening of the Trenches: The laſt Courier from thence brought Advice, That the Army is advanc'd near that Place as far as the Houſe the Marſhal de Teſſe was quarter'd at, when the united Forces of France and Spain beſieg'd it. On the 4th Inſtant Engineer Montogon was ſent away Poſt to our Army, where many Facines have been brought by Sea; and the Veſſels which tranſported them were ſent back for more, and alſo for Timber: Eight Pieces of Cannon have been ſent for from Ceuta.

Vienna, February 19. The vigorous Reſolution of the Parliament of Great Britain, and the Probability of the Acceſſion of the Kings of Sweden, Denmark, and Sardinia, to the Treaty of Hanover, make it be conjectur'd that the Emperor will ſacrifice Something for preventing a War; nay, ſome pretend to aſſure, That His Imperial Majeſty has already tranſmitted to the Court of France, by the Interpoſition of the Pope's Nuncio, freſh Propoſals concerning the Oſtend Company, which is the main Obſtacle to the Preſervation of Peace: But this wants Confirmation.

Paris, March 1. The laſt Letters from Madrid ſay, That no Trenches were open'd before Gibraltar. The Pope's Nuncio does ſtill work all he can to accommodate Matters, and to prevent if poſſible a War, eſpecially between France and Spain.

London, February 25. By Letters from Vice-Admiral Hoſier, Commander in Chief of His Majeſty's Squadron in the Weſt-Indies, dated from Jamaica the 14th of December laſt, we have an Account, That by Reaſon of the great Mortality and Sickneſs on Board the Ships, they had been oblig'd to repair to that Iſland, where 600 ſick Men had been put on Shoar; but by the Vigilance and Care of the Vice-Admiral, ſeconded by the hearty and zealous Aſſiſtance of the Preſident and Council, the Squadron was ſo far recruited, that he would put to Sea again with the greateſt Part of it in 6 or 7 Days: So that it was thought the Spaniards could not poſſibly take any Advantage of his Abſence, to get Home their Galleons.

There is Advice by the Severne from Gibraltar, who left that Place the 28th of January Old Stile, That a few Days before ſhe came thence, the Marquis of Mont-Real from the Spaniſh Camp came to pay a Viſit to Governor Kane, attended by 2 Perſons in Troopers Habits, whom he would have had with him in the Town; but they were order'd to ſtay without, and walk their Horſes till the Marquis return'd: Soon after which it was diſcover'd, that one of the Troopers was the Conde las Torres the Spaniſh General, and the other their Chief Engineer.

WYE's Letter to Day has the 6 following Paragraphs, viz. Letters from Petersburg of the 8th Inſtant ſay, That the King of Spain has notified to that Court by his Secretary there, his Reſolution of ſending thither the Duke of Liria in Quality of his Ambaſſador, for eſtabliſhing the good Harmony between the 2 Courts; and that His Catholick Majeſty was diſpos'd to grant the Ruſſian Merchants trading to Spain, the ſame Privileges and Advantages which the Engliſh, French, and Dutch, have hitherto enjoy'd: They add, That the Ruſſian Fleet will act upon the Offenſive next Spring, and in the mean-time they were fortifying the Iſland of Nargen. There is yet no Account of the Swedes Acceſſion to the Treaty of Hanover: The Czarina has declar'd to them, That if they do not accept of her Propoſals, ſhe will do herſelf Juſtice. 'Tis pretended amongſt the reſt, that ſhe can land Forces in Sweden, by Means of her Gallies, even after the Britiſh Fleet ſhall be there.

By the Advices from Madrid, we find the King of Spain perſiſts in his Reſolution of undertaking the Siege of Gibraltar at all Hazards; accordingly all Preparations poſſible are carrying on at Cadix, where on the 29th paſt they were lading 50 Veſſels with Iron Cannon and other Ammunitions of War: But ſhould they after all dare to open their Trenches, their Hoſtilities will be return'd in ſuch a Manner, as will ſhew how vain and ridiculous it was for them to proceed on ſuch an Enterprize; and conſequently oblige the King of Spain and his new Allies to truckle to Peace, though at preſent they ſeem to be ſtrengthening themſelves for War.

'Tis believ'd that Sir Charles Wager, who is arriv'd with his Squadron and Land-Forces at Gibraltar, has Orders to continue there: And Admiral Hopſon with 5 Men of War to ſail thence, and join Admiral Hoſier in the Weſt Indies; for whoſe Squadron the Commiſſioners for Victualling have contracted Yeſterday with Capt. Trahee, an eminent Commander in the Jamaica Trade, to take in Freight to ſupply with Proviſions and other Neceſſaries. We hear from the Freke-Galley, who left Jamaica the 20th of December laſt, That Admiral Hoſier, on his Arrival at that Iſland, had put 600 of his Men ſick Aſhoar at Port Royal: That they had Advice from Porto Bello, That the Spaniards, believing they ſhould ſee the Engliſh no more, were going to fit out their Galleons on their Voyage Home; but 5 of the Ships of the aforeſaid Admiral were ſo well mann'd, that he would put to Sea by the 24th or 25th of the ſaid Month, and that the reſt would ſail as ſoon as recruited.

Laſt Night the Committee of Elections ſat on that for Petersfield in Hampſhire, between Mr. Serjeant Miller Petitioner, and Joſeph Taylor, Eſq; ſitting Member: And after ſome Debate in relation to the Conduct therein of ſplitting and admitting of Votes, which increas'd the Number almoſt double, the Queſtion was put and carried by about 30 Votes, That the Right of Electing was only in the Freeholders, and ſuch Tenements as are built on antient Foundations in the Borough; and that Mr. Gibſon, the Lord of the Manour, has no Right by his Quit-Rents to multiply Votes: And the Committee is to proceed on Monday, to qualifie or diſqualifie accordingly.

'Tis believ'd that if the Affairs require, His Majeſty will go this Y[...] to his Dominions in Germany, and command the Army in Perſo[...] whom, we are told, a fine Tent is making at Hanover.

We hear from Ireland, That Dr. Nicholſon, Biſhop of London[...] fell down dead ſuddenly in his Cloſet: He was advanc'd not above [...] Days before his Death to the Archbiſhoprick of Caſſell.

We hear, That Two Sergeants, Two Corporals, and Five M[...] to be taken out of the old Troops, and added to each of the new [...] to inform and inſtruct the raw and unexperienc'd Men.

633

**5.3** *The Norwich Gazette*, 25 February to 4 March 1727

happenn'd 2 unluckly Boys each on Horseback, riding a Race, the poor Woman being afraid of her Husband and Child, stept out of the way to bid the Boys keep off; they rid over her, and she is trampled by the Horses in a miserable manner, her Tongue being bit off that she cannot speak, and the rest of her Body so Bruis'd 'tis tho't she cannot live.

*Nantwich, Oct. 4.* Last Friday a very unhappy Accident happen'd here, two Butchers scalding a Swine, the one in a Jesting manner threw a little Water at the other and so provk'd him, that he said, *If he did not give over he would fling his Knife at him*, which being repeated again exasperated him so that he Darted his Knife at him and it went between his Ribs, who said no more words than these, *Thou has done my Business now*, he pluck'd out the Knife himself, and the Blood gush'd forth in such a manner that he died immediately.

*Chester, October 6.* We have had further Accounts from Edinburgh which inform us, that the Deaf and Blind People continue to resort in great Numbers from many distant as well as the adjacent Parts to Mr. Taylor, and they add, that it appears to the personal Knowledge of many Persons of Distinction in that City, that there has not a Day pass'd since he has been amongst them but he has effectually reliev'd several Persons from the most deplorable Species of those Disorders. Agreeable to what has been often intimated, we thought proper to inform our Readers, that this Gentleman will certainly be in this City on his Progress for London on Friday the 29th of this Instant October, and continue at the White Talbot Inn till the Monday Evening following, and the next Morning proceed for London.

## The *Weekly Worcester Journal*

The *Weekly Worcester Journal with the most Material Occurrences Foreign and Domestick* for Friday, 15 September 1738 is typical example of an early provincial newspaper. Comprising four pages of three columns each, the front page and the first column of the second page are devoted to the contents of Saturday's post. As was the usual convention with the newspapers of the period, it begins with foreign news. Under the heading, '*By the Foreign Mails we have the following Advices*', the first column has news from Warsaw, Frankfurt and Paris. The second column, headed '*Home* AFFAIRS', begins with three items datelined '*Reading, Sept. 4.*', probably taken from a Reading paper: the results of the Reading collection for the relief of the sufferers from the fire at Wellingborough; an account of a fire in Reading, 'discover'd by the Watchman of St. Mary's Parish, who ran through the Town, crying out *Fire, Fire!* which alarm'd a great Number of People'; and this paragraph:

On Tuesday last in the Afternoon, a surprizing Noise was heard in the Air, which astonished every Body that heard it: It happened when the Air was serene and clear, and the Crack was very sudden and very violent, was succeeded by a

> rumbling Noise that lasted for a Space of a Minute. It was heard 15 Miles round but nobody can account for it, and no one ever heard the like.

This is followed by the rest of the day's post, headed 'LONDON', containing, among other stories, an extract from a letter from County Down about the good progress of a Protestant Working School; news from Hanover about the precautions against the plague spreading from Hungary; a fiery meteor seen above 'Cranborne in Dorsetshire' ('What this portends we must leave the Learned in such Affairs to determine'); an account of the death of a miser in Hampshire; a report of a 'Gardener at Southgate' whose 'black Sow litter'd 23 Pigs, the 13th of which was roasted last Sunday'; convictions for 'retailing Spiritious Liquors contrary to Law'; the effects of the 'late Convention settled between Us and Spain', including orders not to impress any more seamen, merchants fitting out ships again for the Guinea trade and the laying up of a number of men-of-war; a summary of the meeting of the Directors of the East India Company who were receiving complaints from ship owners, 'on account of the high Wages the Seamen require at present, which is 35s. per Month, when in time of profound Tranquillity the Company can man their Ships at 23s. per Month for each able Sailor'; and the following:

> We hear from Christchurch in Hampshire, that on the 24th of August a Man aged 90 was married to a Girl of 15; his former Wife having been dead but ten Days; he is very hearty, and says, He doubts not but in a Year he shall invite his Neighbours to a Christening.

Monday's post fills the next five columns, starting with news from Dresden, 'Petersburgh', Vienna, Amsterdam, Mannheim and a letter from Bordeaux with the proposals of the Royal Academy of Belles Lettres, Sciences and Arts in that city for issuing prizes for the best pieces on scientific topics set for the year. Then 'COUNTRY NEWS' – two brief stories from Bath, followed by the London news of robberies, trials at the Old Bailey and Hick's Hall, deaths and accidents:

> On Thursday as they were carrying along Cheapside a Caravan with a Collection of wild Beasts for Southwark Fair, unluckily one of the Wheels broke down, which so alarm'd the Neighbourhood that they were about to shut up their Shops, though at Noon Day, for fear of the Creatures; but after some time the Master proving to them that the Beasts were securely chain'd down, their Fears were dispers'd, a new Wheel fix'd, and the Caravan convey'd safely to Southwark

and a copy of a letter '*To the Author of the* White-hall Evening-Post' about the relative merits of the *Gentleman's Magazine* and the *London Magazine.*

Hidden in the news columns, underneath an account of the funeral of the Bishop of Llandaff, is the comment:

> As it is hop'd we never shall have any more Italian Operas, it is also to be wish'd that the Persons who gave such large Sums to the Encouragement of that Diversion, and Strolers from Italy, may employ their Largesses and Contributions for the future towards the Establishment of an Hospital for Foundlings and for the Encouragement of useful Learning, by enabling the Royal Society to distribute Prizes every Year, like les Academes des Sciences, Arts et Belles Lettres in France.

Thursday's post takes up just over one column of the back page and includes the details of the nine people sentenced to death at the Old Bailey, the skirmishes between a 'Custom-House Sloop' and a 'Man of War's Lieutenant in a Long Boat' and a 'Smugling [*sic*] Vessel' off the coast of Weymouth. The Lieutenant and the Captain of the custom-house sloop boarded the smuggling vessel and, while they were searching below decks, 'the Master of the Smuggler, taking advantage, he shut down his Hatches, set Sail, and carried clear off ('tis supposed to travel)' with the Lieutenant and the Captain as his prisoners.

Thursday's post also carries a report datelined Edinburgh about a grand Conventicle of Erskinites whose preaching was interrupted by a Quaker

> that was mov'd to think he had as good a Call to preach them, gave way to the Motions of the Light within, and began to cant and harangue the Congregation: But he had a too dangerous Rival in the Tent, who, with an authoritative Air commanded Silence; he still proceeded, without any Regard for his Brother's Exhortation; who, upon that became full of Holy Zeal, and address'd himself to the People, telling them, That the Devil was in the Man, and he was a Messenger of Satan sent to buffet him. The Congregation believ'd, and thought it not convenient to have an infernal Agent so near, they began a loud Murmur, and at last were like to tear the poor Quaker to Pieces: He patiently bore the Assault, but had certainly fallen a Sacrifice to their Rage, had not some Gentlemen timely interposed and rescued him.

It is only in the last one and a half columns that the local nature of the paper comes to light. There is only one item of local news: a paragraph on the amount of hops sold and the prices they reached at Worcester Fair. This is followed by 15 local advertisements, mainly for property to be let or sold, but also including a Wolverhampton undertaker's advertisement ('A Good Hearse and Mourning-Coach, for any Part of England, may be had at very reasonable Rates'), the announcement of a concert at Worcester Town Hall of the Oratorio of *Esther* 'Compos'd by Mr Handell', and a reward of five guineas for the discovery of a chicken thief ('Whereas there was lately stolen from Pendleston's Mills in Bridgenorth, a spotted breasted Red shitten wing'd

Cock-Chicken, having a Rose Comb, light-blue Legs, dun Nails, and slit both right').

The paper ends with the signature, 'Worcester: Printed by Stephen Bryan.'

All in all, Mr Bryan produced a lively epitome of the London papers for that week, selecting sufficient extracts for the connoisseur of foreign affairs to be able to trace the movements of the Turkish and Russian armies, a piece of moralizing to show that even the despised French can teach us a thing or two about where our priorities should lie, and plenty of entertaining matter for all classes to enjoy.

## Distribution

It is reckoned that the average sale of a provincial newspaper in the early eighteenth century was in the region of 200 copies per week. Almost all of these were sold within the immediate vicinity. By around 1750, the larger papers were enjoying sales of around 2,000 copies per week and more than 100 provincial newspapers had been started. Some had very short lives, like the *Cirencester Post* (1718–23) and the *Ludlow Post-Man* (1719–20), so that there were generally no more than about thirty-five titles in circulation at any one time. But these thirty-five or so titles accounted for about 20 per cent of all newspaper sales. By the 1780s, the circulation of the *Salisbury and Winchester Journal*, and doubtless other successful country newspapers, had risen to 4,000.[5]

Paradoxically, the rise in circulation was partly due to increases in newspaper taxation. The Stamp Acts of 1757 and 1776 made it increasingly uneconomic for the country reader to continue to subscribe to the London papers, while at the same time they were anxious to read the latest hot news of the progress of the Seven Years War and, later, the American War of Independence. After 1757, you would have had to pay £2 2s. 6d. for a year's subscription to just one of the London *Evening Posts*. Yet you could get the same news in the country paper for just twopence-halfpenny a week – less than 11 shillings a year.

However, the main reason for the increased sales of provincial newspapers was the development of distribution systems outside the newspapers' town of origin. Newsmen carried the newspapers by foot and horseback to agents in the towns and populous villages, delivering the paper to individual subscribers on the way. The newsagent was responsible for the local distribution of newspapers within his/her immediate area. He, and quite often she, sometimes employed newsmen of their own. The newsagent often acted as a local reporter, sending 'articles of intelligence' to the printer to be published the following week. Advertisements could be placed through the agents, who also took orders for books and patent medicines sold by the printer. Copies of the newspapers were also sent to London coffee-houses, which also acted as agents for the sale of advertising space.

The extent of the area covered by the early provincial papers can be gauged from the list of agents printed on the back page of most papers. *Aris's Birmingham Gazette* in 1761 listed agents in London, Shrewsbury, Wolverhampton, Worcester, Bridgnorth, Newcastle (Staffs), Lichfield, Stafford, Dudley, Walsall and Stratford-upon-Avon. The *Reading Mercury* in 1765 had agents in London, Oxford, Bath, Bristol, Portsmouth, Southampton, Windsor, Guildford, Farnham, Oakingham (Wokingham) and Winchester. In 1769, the *Northampton Mercury* boasted:

> This PAPER, for more than forty-eight years, hath, and continues to be, circulated in all the Market-Towns and populous Villages in the following Counties, Viz. Northampton, Leicester, Nottingham, Rutland, Lincoln, Huntingdon, Cambridge and the Isle of Ely, Bedford, Essex, Hertford, Buckingham, Berks, Oxford, Warwick to Birmingham, and Stafford &c. and by the Post to greater distances.[6]

Although the provincial papers were in competition with each other where they covered the same area, where they were sufficiently distant to pose no threat, a degree of mutual assistance could be seen. The list of agents for the *Bristol Journal*[7] in 1775 included J. Gore of *Gore's Liverpool General Advertiser*, Robert Goadby at Sherborne (*Western Flying Post*) and Robert Raikes at Gloucester (*Gloucester Journal*).

The distribution system was augmented by other means, as can be seen from the announcement at the head of the *Cambridge Chronicle and Journal* in 1773:

> This PAPER is dispatched Northwards every Friday Night, by the Caxton Post, as far as York, Newcastle and Carlisle; through the Counties of Cambridge, Huntingdon, Bedford, Buckingham, Rutland, Leicester, Nottingham, Lincoln, Northampton, Norfolk, Hertford, Essex and the Isle of Ely, by the Newsmen; to London the next Morning, by the Coach and Fly; and to several Parts of Suffolk, &c. by other Conveyances. – *Persons living at a Distance from such Places as the Newsmen go through, may have the Paper left where they shall please to appoint.*[8]

The provincial newspaper and its distribution system helped to open up the country and break down the old isolation and parochialism. In some remote villages the newsmen and their newspapers provided the first regular communication with the outside world. Until the increases in Stamp Duty towards the end of the eighteenth century and in the early nineteenth century, newspapers were the cheapest form of literature that was readily available. They helped to stimulate the growth of literacy in the countryside.

As the century wore on, more provincial newspapers were established. The thirty-five or so provincial titles in the middle of the eighteenth century grew to fifty by 1780, to 150 by 1832 and to over 250 by 1851. This was despite the increased circulation in the provinces of the London newspapers. In 1764 the Post Office sent 1.09 million papers into the country. This had increased to 4.65 million by 1790. With more towns having their own newspaper, the area of distribution of each newspaper contracted to just one or two counties, but with no loss in circulation due to the increase in literacy.

Although there are no reliable statistics for the level of literacy in the eighteenth century, it is generally accepted that the numbers of those in the countryside who could read and write increased, despite a reduction of literacy in the industrial towns towards the end of the century. In addition to private educational establishments – there were 400 advertisements for such institutions before 1770 in the *Salisbury Journal* – Church of England charity schools were established in 1699 to teach the children of the poor to read and write. According to John Chamberlayne, *The Present State of Great Britain*, 1737 edn, 'in the Year 1721, there were 1491 Charity-Schools, wherein above thirty-two thousand poor Children of both Sexes were taught to read, write, and say the Catechism'. By the middle of the century most villages had at least a dame school. These were augmented from 1780 by the Sunday School movement, which also taught reading and writing. The London bookseller James Lackington may not have been exaggerating when he wrote in 1791:

> The sale of books in general has increased prodigiously within the last twenty years. The poorer sort of farmers, and even the poor country people in general who before that period spent their winter evenings in relating stories of witches, ghosts, hobgoblins, etc. now shorten the winter nights by hearing their sons and daughters read tales, romances, etc., and on entering their houses you may see *Tom Jones, Roderick Random* and other entertaining books, stuck up in their bacon-racks etc. If John goes to town with a load of hay, he is charged to be sure not to forget to bring home *Peregrine Pickle's Adventures*, and when Dolly is sent to market to sell her eggs, she is commissioned to purchase *The History of Joseph Andrews.* In short, all ranks and degrees now read.

And, perhaps the most common thing they read was their local newspaper. By the end of the eighteenth century local news became a more important feature of the provincial newspaper. As well as providing news of the outside world, newspapers were becoming a mouthpiece for local news and local views.

**Finance**

The financial position of the early provincial papers was precarious; hence the large number of titles which folded after a relatively short life. Unlike the London papers, there were no political paymasters. The printer had to pay for his stamped paper in advance and arrange for it to be sent from London. He had to give discounts on the sale of papers to his newsmen and agents. Most advertisements were placed on credit because the agent or newsman who took the advertisement could not predict the eventual printed size of the advertisement. Subscriptions were also on credit, although some newspapers did offer discounts for cash. The printer had to pay for his news sources, initially by subscribing to the London papers, and, later in the eighteenth century, by paying agents and correspondents to send him news.

By the 1740s *Aris's Birmingham Gazette* and the *York Courant* and possibly other provincial papers had established correspondents in London and in the larger towns within the paper's distribution area. The *Ipswich Journal* for 25 February 1764 contains paragraphs of news datelined Ipswich, Ely and Much Clackton. It is not clear how much of the news from independent sources was paid for or received for free. Throughout the 1760s the *Reading Mercury* asked 'Our Correspondents in all parts … to transmit no Articles of news but what they know to be true, and all Intelligence that is genuine will be thankfully received.' This indicates that some of their stringers had other motives than financial gain. *Jackson's Oxford Journal* had a similar notice: 'Our Correspondents are particularly requested to communicate nothing but facts.' These warnings had some justification. It is common to see the sentence, 'The article printed in our last paper … [that so-and-so had happened] … was false.'

On the plus side, running a provincial newspaper was a part-time activity undertaken to use up spare printing capacity. The benefits were the income from cover sales and advertising, and the ability to advertise the printer's own goods and services over a wide area at no additional cost. As early as 1706, the *Norwich Post* was said to have been making a profit of 50s. per week from sales and advertising.[9]

As the century progressed, the importance of the provincial newspaper as an advertising medium increased. The number of advertisements in *Aris's Birmingham Gazette* increased from 9 in 1742 (20 December 1742), to 43 in 1761 (11 May 1761), 99 in 1771 (22 April 1771) and 110 in 1781 (19 November 1781). Common subjects included nationally advertised products such as books, magazines, patent medicines and lottery tickets, and local advertisements for day schools and boarding schools, houses for sale or rent, local entertainments, the letting of turnpike tolls, stagecoach services, rewards for the return of runaway horses and absconded apprentices, situations vacant and, towards the end of the eighteenth century, notices placed by local Associations for the Prosecution of Felons.

As far as consumer goods were concerned, there were not many advertisements for everyday purchases. Local people knew where their shops were and advertisements only appeared when shops were changing hands or starting up. Generally it was only luxury items that might attract purchasers from further afield that were advertised, such as London fashions and coffee and tea.

From the 1730s, the nationwide popularity of the *Gentleman's Magazine*, which printed a list of new publications issued that month, increased the demand for books in the country. As the provincial printers were in regular contact with London as the only source of stamped paper, they developed links with the London book trade and other businesses that needed access to provincial markets. Quite a few provincial printers became booksellers and retailers of patent medicines. The signature at the foot of the last page of the *Glocester* [*sic*] *Journal* in 1761 announced:

> At the said Printing Office are sold Dr. *Bateman*'s Pectoral Drops; *Ratcliffe*'s, *Stoughton*'s, and *Daffy*'s Elixirs; *Betton*'s British Oil, *Hooper*'s, *Boerhave*'s and *Scotch* Pills; Liquid Shell; Hypo-Drops; Dr. *Eaton*'s Styptick; *Greenough*'s Tincture for the Gums and Tooth-Ach; Dr *Rayment*'s Powder; Mr *Goodrick*'s Powder; *Hungary* Water; Opodeldock; Golden and Plain Spirits of Scurvy Grass; *Berrow*'s Tincture of Bark; *Taylor*'s Cholick Cordial; *Dalby*'s Carminative Mixture; *Friar*'s Balsam of Health; Dr. *James*'s Fever-Powder; *Clinton*'s Snuff and Oil; *Story*'s Cakes for destroying Worms; *Lord*'s Corn-Salve; *British* Tooth Powder; the Volatile Essence called *Eau de Luce*; Royal Flour of Mustard Seed; Water for the Itch; *Sexton*'s Powder for curing the Small-Pox and Fever; and the Powder for Cattle.[10]

The signature of the *Reading Mercury* in 1774 also gives a glimpse of the enterprising nature of the country newspaper printer:

> Printed by J CARNAN and CO. in the Market-Place, READING; of whom may be had, all Sorts of Books and Stationery Wares, Printed Warrants, Summonses, Certificates, Orders of Removal, etc., etc., as cheap as in London: and by whom PRINTING in general is performed, in the most correct manner, on reasonable Terms. Advertisements for this Paper are taken in at the Place above-mentioned, also by … [a list of agents in the London coffee-houses and towns in Berkshire and neighbouring counties] … and by the men who distribute it. Of whom may be had all the BOOKS, MEDICINES, etc. advertised herein.[11]

A number of printers went a step beyond simply being agents for the sale of quack medicines to becoming part owners. William Dicey of the *Northampton Mercury* and Robert Raikes of the *Gloucester Journal* became partners in 1730 to market Dr Bateman's Pectoral Drops. John Newbery of the *Reading Mercury* bought a quarter share in Dr Hooper's Female Pills, and in 1746 he purchased a half share with sole right of sale in Dr James's Fever Powders.

John Newbery graduated to become a prominent member of the London book trade, famous for his successful series of children's books. Benjamin Collins, printer–proprietor of the *Salisbury Journal*, used his London contacts to buy shares in a number of copyrights, including Richardson's *Pamela*, Smollett's *Humphrey Clinker* and Goldsmith's *Vicar of Wakefield*. He also helped start the *London Chronicle* and the *Public Ledger*.

Another source of income came from exploiting their homemade distribution systems to operate unofficial letter- and parcel-carrying services. Initially, the Post Office declared these services illegal and tried to take action against the newsmen. But by the middle of the eighteenth century the Post Office realized the extent of the demand and introduced its own system of cross-country posts.

Some of the provincial papers showed remarkable examples of enterprise. The *Northampton Mercury* hired special couriers and was able to scoop the London papers by being the first to report the retreat of Bonnie Prince Charlie from Derby. It also employed a rider to rush the London papers to the *Mercury's* office in relays of four horses stationed on the road between London and Northampton. A messenger from *Aris's Birmingham Gazette* met the London post at Daventry and the *York Chronicle* met the post at Grantham. The *Reading Mercury* and the *Salisbury Journal* hired express riders to fetch the latest newspapers from London in advance of the posts. The *Hampshire Chronicle*, which was owned by the proprietor of the *Salisbury Journal*, paid H. Morley of Basingstoke 5s. per week to intercept the Salisbury express rider to bring extra copies of the papers to its printer in Winchester. This allowed those papers to start printing much earlier.

## News for the Berkshire Farmer

The character of the eighteenth-century provincial newspaper was markedly different from the London papers. As well as the cost of the tax stamp, the price of paper acted as a constraint on the amount of material a newspaper could carry. Before wood-pulp and esparto grass replaced expensive linen and cotton waste as the raw materials for paper, a sheet of paper cost about a halfpenny, which was a considerable proportion of the pre-tax price of a newspaper. The pressure on space from local news and local advertisements meant that the printer had to be more selective over what he included from the London papers. An editorial function thus developed. Taking into account the wider social groups that had access to provincial newspapers, from the county magnate to the literate craftsman, most printers tried to appeal to all classes and tastes. As we have seen from the *Weekly Worcester Journal*, their purpose was to entertain as well as to inform. The editor selected what he considered to be the most significant items of political and diplomatic news, lists of deaths, promotions and preferments and stock and commodity prices for the gentry, the clergy and the merchants within his distribution area; and crimes and accidents, items about freaks of nature; strange signs seen in the heavens; and humorous stories for the yeoman and tradesman.

The *Reading Mercury* of the 1760s ran paragraphs like these to be read aloud by Berkshire farmers in the hearth of the village inn:

> They write from Denbighshire in North-Wales, that about three weeks ago, a cow belonging to Mr. William Vaughan, Butcher, of Bettws Abergeley, dropt a calf which had two heads, four eyes, four ears, two mouths, two tongues, and two necks; the body and legs as usual. It lived for several days seemingly in good health, and was observed at different times to suck with each mouth.[12]

> A few days since, the following affair happened at a parish somewhat south-east of London-bridge. A corpse was brought, by appointment, at six o'clock, to be interred, but the Minister was not to be found, so that the company were obliged to wait near an hour, when he came from Black-heath, in a chaise, but so sadly *fatigued*, that, in attempting to alight, he tumbled out of the chaise, and notwithstanding every effort was tried to recover his speech and legs, yet all were ineffectual. And had it not been for a clergyman accidentally passing by, the company must have departed without the ceremony being performed.[13]

> Last Tuesday night, at about nine a most extraordinary phaenomenon appeared in the air over the City of London: at first, a strong light was seen on the gravel and paved walks of the Temple, bright enough to pick up a pin; which surprise was increased on the beholders looking upwards, when a globe of ruddy fire was seen descending from a great altitude over Temple-Bar; as large as the full moon a little after her rising; and taking its course obliquely towards the River Thames, as if it would have fallen therein; but coming low and over the same, it shot itself into a sheet of fire, with one edge turned towards the water, in the form of a boy's kite, with head, wings and tail, appearing half as long, and in one part half as broad, as Fleet-street. It fell or vanished on the Southwark side of the water, in a yellow fire.[14]

> PARIS, (the capital town or city of France) Oct. 21. A letter from Avianches of the 12th of this month gives the following information: A woman had been long ill of vapours and convulsions, which turning to a palsy, she was bled by order of the physician, and in his presence. The blood after running a little while stopt on a sudden, and a white matter appeared at the orifice, which being drawn out by the head with a pin, was found to be a living worm, with bright eyes and a muzzle coated with small hairs like that of a cat. It is preserved in spirits of wine.[15]

> However incredible the following particular may appear, you may be assured of the veracity of it: About a year since an old man of this place, aged 94 years, was

married to a woman of 83, by whom he had a child born on the 29th of last month, which is likely to live, as the mother went her full time.[16]

*Jackson's Oxford Journal* for 24 October 1778 contained two items which would make a couple of wonderful ten-minute films:

Last Sunday, as the Congregation at New-College were quitting the Chapel after Evening Service, a Lady's Head, in the present *Ton*, unhappily took Fire, by accidentally coming in Contact with one of the Lights; and the Composition of this Paraphernalia, according to Custom, being composed of combustible Matter, the Conflagration appeared dreadfully alarming; but a Lady in Company having Presence of Mind to push off the whole Pile at once, the Flames were fortunately extinguished without communicating to the Heads of any other of the Ladies; and this sudden Alarm, which seemed pregnant with the most fatal Consequences, terminated in Jocularity, and was productive of many Witticisms at the unfortunate Lady's Expence.

South-Brent (Somersetshire). Yesterday, during Divine Service, two Gentlemen came to the Fox-and-Goose in this Parish, and called for a Dram, and on their riding off the Landlord told one of them his Horse had lost a shoe; on which he asked for a Smith; and on being informed he was at Church, (being Clerk of the Parish) he immediately dismounted, went up to the Church, and on entering, enquired for the Clerk; when being directed to the Singing-Gallery he enquired him out, and addressed him as follows: 'Sir, I am sorry to be the Messenger of bad News, but your House is on Fire and nearly consumed to the Ground, and for God's Sake make Haste.' On which the Singers ran out of the Gallery crying Fire, and all the Congregation followed for near three Quarters of a Mile, till they arrived at the Clerk's House, where nothing was the Matter but the Gentleman's Horse tied up in the Hovel waiting to be shoed; on which the Company were so exasperated, that they gave him a very severe Ducking in the Pond near the House. – There were but four Persons left in the Church, viz, a Man with a Wooden-Leg, a blind Woman, the Sexton, (who is very lame) and the Clergyman, who is much troubled with the Gout.

## Politics

Most provincial papers in the eighteenth century were politically neutral. They were intended for profit, not propaganda. With such a limited circulation, there was no point in adopting a party-political stance as this was likely to alienate half the potential readers and advertisers, and encourage a rival printer to start up a newspaper in the opposite interest. If a printer decided to start a rival paper, the established paper generally saw off the interloper, using ridicule, as was the case when the short-lived *Northampton Journal* was set up in opposition to the *Northampton Mercury* in 1722. The

Mercury referred to this upstart as 'a Sheet and a Half of Waste Paper … a Parcel of Bum-Fodder … to carry away the Excrements of those young Boys, who, barely prompted by Nature, attain to more knowledge than [the author of the *Journal*'s] doting Brain could ever fathom'.[17]

However, in the larger towns that could support two or more newspapers, there were rival newspapers at a very early stage. The *Norwich Post*, *The Norwich Gazette*, and the *Norwich Post-Man* competed for the same market from 1706 to about 1712. Where this happened, the newspapers tended to take opposing political views. Even as early as 1716, Philip Bishop, printer of the *Exeter Mercury*, became the provincial newspaper's first press martyr. He died in gaol in 1716 awaiting trial for printing *Nero the Second*, a seditious ballad attacking George I. His competitor, Joseph Bliss, printer of the loyalist *(Exeter) Protestant Mercury*, reported that Bishop's punishment would have been to 'stand in the Pillory three several times, and to have his Ears (if not his Hands also) cut off and nail'd to the same; To be whipp'd at the Cart's Tail three several Market Days round this City; And to be imprison'd during Life', which Bliss considered would have been 'a sentence too mild for his inexorable Villainy'.[18] Exeter yielded up another press martyr in 1729 when Edward Farley, the printer of *Farley's Exeter Journal*, died in gaol, 'loaded with irons', for reprinting the 'Persian Letter' from *Mist's Weekly Journal*.

The provincial newspapers were an important factor in the transition from the system of parliamentary government following the Glorious Revolution of 1688 to the emerging parliamentary democracy of 1832. As even the neutral papers copied political news and views from the London papers, they acted as an intermediary between Parliament and the provinces. The traffic was not all one-way. Provincial papers began to report local political speeches and addresses, and to include letters from local MPs and others commenting on national and local issues which, due to the distribution of provincial papers to London coffee-houses, were intended to influence a political audience in London as well as the local readership.

The skill of a successful provincial editor lay in determining the content of the newspaper that would reflect the majority interests and opinions of the locality. If the paper could attract readers and keep them coming back for more, this would attract advertisers. Increased sales and advertising meant increased profits. So, even among those papers that professed themselves to be politically neutral as far as national politics were concerned, they would quite happily campaign on local issues, criticizing local oligarchies and promoting local concerns, either directly or through the letter columns, if that was the popular thing to do.

The growing influence of the provincial newspaper meant that all classes of society were becoming politically aware. During the American War of Independence, many provincial papers began to take sides. The *Cambridge*

*Chronicle*, *Kentish Gazette*, *Leeds Mercury*, *Norfolk Chronicle* and *Newcastle Chronicle* supported the Americans, while the *Hampshire Chronicle*, *Manchester Mercury*, *Nottingham Journal* and *Newcastle Courant* were for the Ministry. The polarization of opinion over the French and Industrial Revolutions led to the emergence of opposition newspapers. In 1792 Richard Phillips started the radical *Leicester Herald*. He was later sentenced to 18 months' imprisonment for selling Tom Paine's *Rights of Man*. The following year the monopoly of the Tory *Cambridge Chronicle*[19] was broken by Benjamin Flower's radical *Cambridge Intelligencer*.[20]

Some inkling of the *Cambridge Intelligencer*'s radicalism can be seen from an article that appeared in the issue for 4 February 1797 under the heading, 'Effects of the Present War':

> Two or three millions of men have been killed in attempting to settle disputes, which they did not understand, and which are, after all, to be determined by four or five men who never saw a gun fired. One eighth of our forces have been employed to keep the enemy in check abroad, and the other seven eighths to keep the people quiet at home.
>
> The supporters of the war refuse their aid unless they are well paid for it, and our volunteers are obliged to be hand-cuffed.
>
> Several worthy men have been alarmed into places of great trust and emolument.
>
> The Constitution has been personified in eight or ten men who know not what it means and who have altered it so that scarcely any person can know it.
>
> Great Generals have become so expert in the art of retreating, as, in most cases, to save themselves!
>
> The emoluments of the Church are mistaken for religion, and the income of a pensioner is called property.

After more in similar vein, the writer produced a large list of new taxes that had been introduced to help finance the war, followed by:

> CALCULATIONS OF THE QUANTUM OF HUMAN MISERY
> OCCASIONED BY THE WAR

| | | | | |
|---|---|---|---|---|
| Died by sickness and the sword | | | – | 2,000,000!! |
| Each of these unhappy persons had, upon a moderate calculation, four persons relative to him, and either dependant [*sic*] on him for support, or deriving comfort and consolation from him. The number of human beings rendered miserable by those two millions will amount to | | | – | 8,000,000!! |
| Of the two millions we may fairly suppose that one in four had a wife and a child; there will therefore have been left | | | | |
| orphans | – | – | – | 500,000!! |
| and widows | – | – | – | 500,000!! |

> Nor is this all: upon those who have lost neither relative or friend by the war, the load of misery imposed will not be found to be small. – We will confine our remarks to England alone … We have added by the war 100 millions to our debt, and five millions a year to our taxes. The necessities of life are at least increased one third; for example, a poor man, with his wife and five children, who earns fifteen shillings a week, can now purchase about as much as he could for 10s. before the war. Thus he is forced to maintain seven persons at one shilling and five-pence per week! We purposely leave out of our calculation the manner in which our liberties have suffered and been curtailed during the war, though we are not unmindful that every particle that is taken from our liberties is so much taken from the dignity as well as the happiness of man.

Flower was fined £100 and sentenced to six months in Newgate for breach of privilege in 1799. His defence costs amounted to £400, but his paper was so popular with radicals all over the country that the people of Liverpool alone subscribed £90 towards his costs.

Despite this, most provincial papers in the 1790s either remained politically neutral or turned fervently loyalist. The few editorial comments the printers allowed themselves usually supported the government and the loyalist associations that sprang up in the wake of the patriotic and conservative reaction to events in France and the imagined threat of Jacobinism at home:

> The Proclamation issued against inflammatory writings, and seditious combinations, is acceptable to all true friends of this country; for it comes forward at a period when the basest arts are put in practice to delude the judgement of the lower classes of the people, debauch the soldiery, and finally to overthrow a Constitution which has been the boast of ages, and, if properly maintained, will always be the glory and safeguard of Britain.[21]

> The meeting of Parliament has shown how great a majority of the nation are determined to support the war. We all know how far preferable peace is to war; but if ever war was necessary, it is under the existing circumstances: Upon the issue of it depends the possession of every thing that is dear and valuable to us: Our enemy is vigilant and active; and if we, who have more at stake, do not oppose him with equal exertion, we shall not merit the blessings which we are fighting to preserve.[22]

After reporting the latest news of the Mutiny at the Nore, the *Northampton Mercury* for 20 June 1797 commented:

> The present awful crisis may serve to teach those who are earnest in asserting the *Rights of Man*, and forgetful in enforcing his *Duties*, of how much greater importance to the peace and happiness of Society the latter are than the former. If this consideration had universally governed the conduct of Englishmen for the last five years, we should not now have seen the crews of more than twenty ships of war in open rebellion.

The importance of the eighteenth century provincial newspapers cannot be overestimated. Although each title had its own individual voice, to reflect the character of the communities from which they sprang, they opened up a national consciousness by providing readers (and listeners) with a digest of up-to-date news and opinion. They also performed an economic service by providing access to a range of books, periodicals, medicines and other goods and services.

## The Nineteenth Century

In the first decades of the nineteenth century there was a steady growth in the provinces in the numbers of reform and radical papers, which was matched by an increasing political awareness in the conservative press. In 1801 eleven wool merchants and dissenters lent Edward Baines £1,000 so that he could purchase the *Leeds Mercury* and turn it into a reform newspaper in opposition to the Tory *Leeds Intelligencer*. The reformist *West Briton* was started in 1810 in opposition to the Tory *Royal Cornwall Gazette*. Thirty-two Tory gentlemen of Kendal subscribed £1,675 to start the reactionary *Westmoreland Gazette* in 1818 in opposition to the *Westmoreland Advertiser and Kendal Chronicle*, 'one of the most furiously Jacobinical in the Kingdom'; and in 1821 eleven middle-class reformers subscribed £1,050 to start the *Manchester Guardian* (Figure 5.4).

With two or more newspapers operating in the same limited area of circulation, they were not only fighting their political corner, they were fighting for their very existence. The fight became bitter, and an entertaining degree of mutual invective was poured on each other. The exchange of insults between the *Eatanswill Gazette* and the *Eatanswill Independent* in the *Pickwick Papers* was no exaggerated figment of Dickens's imagination. The Whig *Aylesbury News* carried a piece on 21 September 1839 that began:

> We perceive that the Brill district Conservative dinner is fixed for 26th inst. His Grace the Duke of Buckingham will be the turn of the day, attended by about eight of his clerical providers, and his scribe, Henry Thomas Ryde, the gemman wot does the Bucks Herald … The Marquis will declare his determination of following the path of his predecessors (viz. pocketing the people's cash – a trick the Grenvilles have been prone to.) Lacquey Ryde will declare Buckinghamshire eminently Conservative.

The reform papers were essentially middle class. The two most successful papers, the *Leeds Mercury* with sales of 5,500 per week in 1833 and the *Manchester Guardian* with sales of 4,000 per week in 1834, were for moderate reform only. Edward Baines turned the *Leeds Mercury* into a vehicle for his

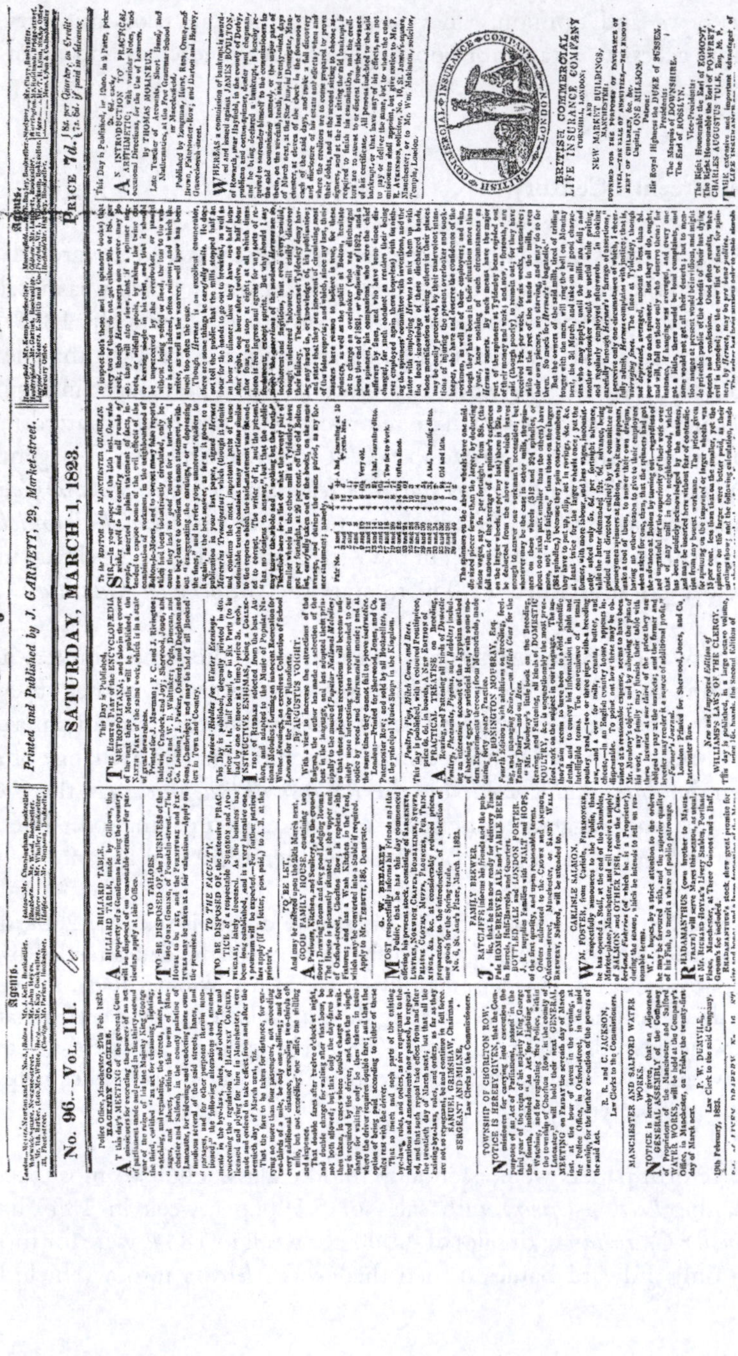

The Manchester Guardian.

No. 96.—Vol. III.

Printed and Published by J. GARNETT, 29, Market-street.

SATURDAY, MARCH 1, 1823.

PRICE 7d.

5.4 *The Manchester Guardian*, 1 March 1823

own political views, views that reflected influential opinion in the industrial North. The *Leeds Mercury* under Baines showed that, as long as his views commanded popular support, a politically committed editor could be a positive advantage to a newspaper. The *Leeds Mercury* supported the peace movement in 1812 on the grounds that the war had brought economic hardship to merchants, manufacturers and tradesmen and contributed to the rise of Luddism. Baines supported municipal and parliamentary reform, both in the pages of the *Leeds Mercury* and as a speaker at numerous reform meetings in Yorkshire. He led a successful campaign to elect the reformer, Henry Broughton, MP for Yorkshire in 1830, and Baines himself became Liberal MP for Leeds in 1833. The *Leeds Mercury* was vocal in its support for the abolition of the slave trade, but was not averse to slavery at home. It supported the manufacturers against factory reform, opposing moves to reduce the working hours of women and children in factories from 12 to 10 per day. In April 1832, some two hundred factory workers marched on the offices of the *Leeds Mercury* and burned an effigy of Edward Baines.

The *Manchester Guardian* was also a firm advocate of electoral, educational and municipal reforms. It was a leading supporter of the Anti-Corn Law League. But, as the organ of the Northern cotton manufacturers, it was the voice of hard-faced Manchester economic liberalism: supporting the New Poor Law; campaigning against the 10 hour day on the grounds that the most industry could afford was an $11\frac{1}{2}$-hour day ('to yield to the senseless and popular outcry for a reduction to ten hours would be an act of suicidal madness'); and siding with the bosses against striking workers. In the opposite corner stood conservative papers, such as the Tory *Leeds Intelligencer*, and the unstamped radical press, who formed a curious alliance in support of factory reform.

Almost overnight the sales of the reform papers were eclipsed by the radical *Northern Star*, founded by Feargus O'Connor, the 'Physical Force' Chartist, in Leeds in November 1837. Within four months of its birth it was selling more copies than the *Leeds Mercury* and the *Manchester Guardian* combined. But as a single-issue paper, its fortunes were firmly hitched to the Chartist bandwagon. At the peak of Chartist activity in the early 1840s it was selling over 50,000 copies per week. The failure of Chartism brought an end to the fortunes of the *Northern Star* and by 1844 its sales had slumped to 7,000 copies. This was still a respectable figure, but it was an indication that the future of the political paper lay in supporting one of the two mainstream political parties.

It also became clear that there was money to be made from a successful provincial paper. A paper selling 1,000 copies per week could make around £1,000 per year. By the 1840s the *Manchester Guardian* was making over £6,000 per year.[23] During the third quarter of the nineteenth century, improvements in communications, particularly the spread of the railways and the introduction of the electric telegraph, the abolition of newspaper taxes, the increase in literacy, the extension of the franchise, and the flood of new money coming into newspapers from the beneficiaries of industrialization led to an explosion in the numbers of new, mainly party-political, provincial papers.

Provincial papers were also changing their character by extending the range of local issues they covered. Instead of simply providing a resumé of the London papers, with a bit of local news thrown in for good measure, they were becoming the noticeboard for the community covered by their hinterland. Arguments over the benefits and disbenefits of proposed routes for canals and the trade they would bring to one community and take away from another filled many columns of the provincial papers from the 1760s onwards, only to be replaced by similar arguments over railway building.

The growth of the provincial press and improved communications reduced the reliance on the London press as the sole source of external news items. The *Reading Mercury* for 16 May 1806 copied a story from the *Hull Advertiser* about the 'considerable sensation experienced amongst the merchants of Manchester by the sudden disappearance of some Jews, who had purchased goods to an extensive amount, and shipped them to the Continent'. The *Kentish Gazette* for 27 November 1818 quoted the *Gloucester Herald* as the source of its account of the visit of two emissaries from the King of Persia to Gloucester that took in the 'Pin Manufactory of Messers Dumford and Co. The making of pins seemed to afford them high satisfaction.' The *Liverpool Mercury* for 20 December 1817 treated its readers to this example of rustic ingenuity taken from the *Kentish Chronicle*:

> *Summary Justice.* A trial of a novel description, of a countryman, for attempting to seduce a servant girl from the paths of virtue, took place at a public house in Up-street, a few days since, before an impartial jury of villagers: where, after a most patient investigation of the case, the countryman was found guilty, and sentenced to be hung by the heels, to the beam of the room for the space of twenty minutes, and to drink four pints of strong onion broth – two pints previous to, and the remaining two during the time of suspension.

Improvement was the watchword, with the pages of the provincial papers taking on a public service role as correspondents offered advice from curing the bite of a mad dog to improving municipal arrangements, educational facilities and the agricultural practices of the locality. *Aris's Birmingham Gazette* for 21 January 1828 tried to address the perennial problem of juvenile delinquency:

> As nearly one-half of the convictions for felony in the County of Warwick are of offenders under 21 years of age, many of whom are scarcely above the age of

childhood; and as it seldom happens that boys of tender age are guilty of those excesses, or convicted of those offences, which lead older offenders to commit crimes of greater magnitude; it appears that there must be some other cause, besides those affecting the general class of offenders, which peculiarly affect them, and lead them into the paths of vice and criminality.

That one of the chief causes of the increase of crime throughout the kingdom is the treating of the boy of tender age for a first offence, and that of a trifling nature, in the same manner as the most hardened offender for offences of greater turpitude; and by thus making no distinction between the two, all hope of amendment is cut off in the juvenile delinquent, by deadening at the earliest age all those feelings of shame and compunction which are the best groundworks of reform and amendment.

That if some plan could be adopted by which juvenile offenders could for their first offence be proceeded against in a summary manner, without undergoing injurious imprisonment and the disgrace of a public trial, the chance of reform would be more probable, and an opportunity held out to them of relinquishing the yet unbeaten path of criminality.

## Regional Dailies

With the abolition of the stamp duty in 1855, many of the established weekly papers became dailies, for example the *Manchester Guardian*, the *Leeds Mercury*, the *Yorkshire Post* (formerly the *Leeds Intelligencer*) and the *Nottingham Journal*. New morning papers were started, notably the *Sheffield Daily Telegraph*, the *Western Morning News*, the *Birmingham Daily Post*, the *Liverpool Daily Post* which in 1855 was the first regional morning paper to run an evening edition, and the *Northern Echo* (founded in 1870), the first halfpenny morning paper outside London.

The *South Shields Daily Gazette* was the first provincial halfpenny evening paper in 1864. It was followed by a flood of cheap evening sporting papers that became a feature of most large towns, cashing in on the development of organized sport, particularly football and cricket, and the interest in new types of sport, particularly cycling. The 1880s saw the creation of Saturday night football specials such as the Birmingham-based *Saturday Night* (1882) and the Bolton-based *Football Field and Sports Telegram* (1884) and the Saturday night editions of the *Blackburn Times* (1883) and the *Wolverhampton Express and Star* (1884).

By 1900 there were 1,947 different titles, of which 1,475 were provincial newspapers, including 171 regional dailies.[24] An editorial in the *Yorkshire Post* in 1866 described the influence of the major regional newspapers:

When we consider that the population of two such counties as Lancashire and Yorkshire, to say nothing of the North of England in general, now draws its

> political opinions quite as much as from the Press of Manchester, Liverpool and Leeds as from the Press of London, we shall understand at once the whole extent of the power which for good or evil may be wielded by provincial journalism.[25]

Their success lay in being able to receive national and international news from London by electric telegraph so that news could be printed and on the streets hours before the London papers arrived. Apart from the inclusion of news from their own region and local advertisements, the regional dailies were little different in character from the London dailies, or indeed from each other. Most subscribed to the Press Association, which supplied a weekly summary of general news for an annual payment of £7 5s. Digests of Reuter's telegrams were available for a subscription of £1 per week. The Central Press supplied speeches of Conservative Members of Parliament and the National Press Agency did the same for Liberal Members, so that readers could keep tabs on their local MP.

## Local Papers

While the powerful and influential regional dailies stood at one end of the provincial spectrum, the small local newspapers with no claims to great power and influence stood at the other end. During the second half of the nineteenth century, local newspapers covering very limited geographical areas were established in more and more locations so that, by the end of the century, there was scarcely any small market town that did not have its own newspaper (Figure 5.5).

Some places seemed to be saturated with newspapers. The Isle of Wight, which did not have a single newspaper in the eighteenth century, produced ten different titles in 1878 to serve a population, including children, of only 66,000.[26] According to the 1893 edition of the *Newspaper Press Directory*, Melton Mowbray, with a population of 6,392, was served by the *Melton Mowbray Mercury*, *Melton Mowbray Journal* and the *Melton Mowbray Times*. In addition it had access to three Leicester dailies (*Leicester Daily Express*, *Leicester Daily Mercury* and *Leicester Daily Post*). Nine different titles were produced each week in Croydon alone.

Many local papers were supplied by material from the news agencies. The agencies could provide national and international news, parliamentary reports and sketches, law reports, City and commodity prices, football and racing results, London letters and gossip, serialized stories and even leading articles for the newspapers. The only extra work a local proprietor needed to do was to collect the local news, receive advertisements, print the product and arrange distribution.

Like the first provincial papers 150 years earlier, local papers were mostly

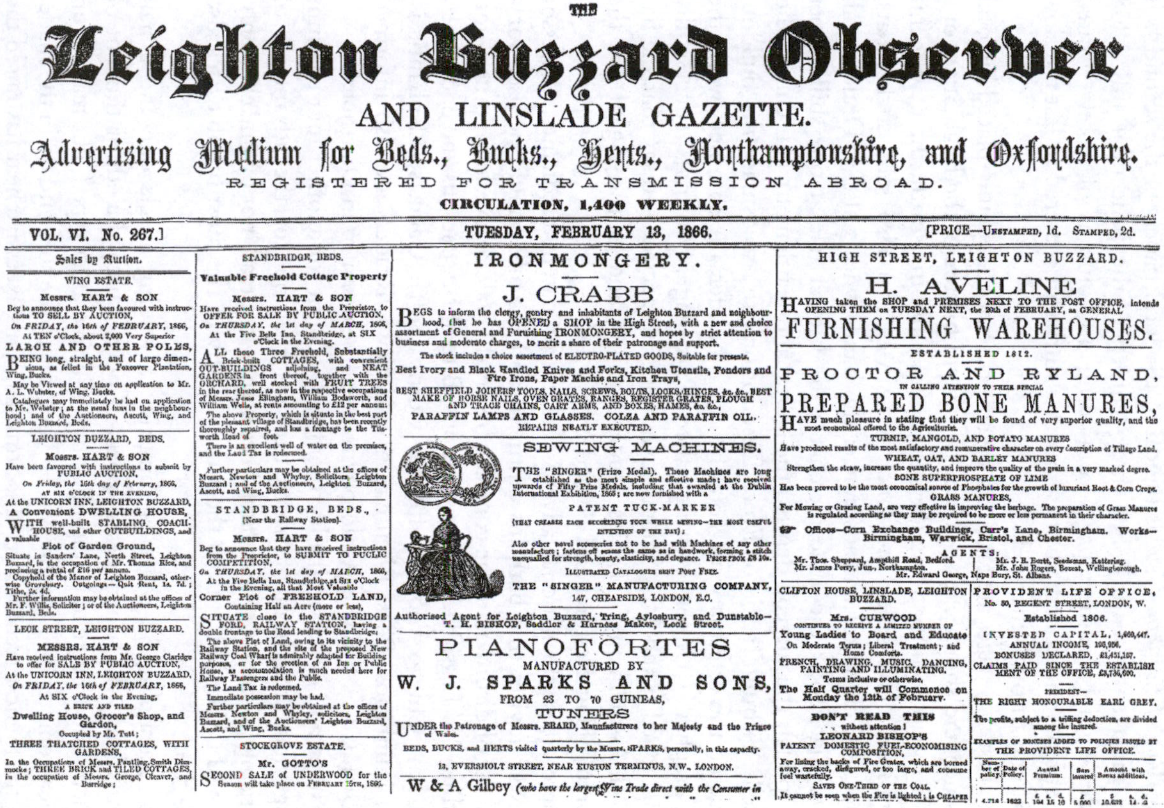
THE

# Leighton Buzzard Observer

AND LINSLADE GAZETTE.

Advertising Medium for Beds., Bucks., Herts., Northamptonshire, and Oxfordshire.

REGISTERED FOR TRANSMISSION ABROAD.

CIRCULATION, 1,400 WEEKLY.

VOL. VI. No. 267.] TUESDAY, FEBRUARY 13, 1866. [PRICE—Unstamped, 1d. Stamped, 2d.

Sales by Auction.

WING ESTATE.

Messrs. HART & SON

Beg to announce that they been favoured with instructions TO SELL BY AUCTION,

On FRIDAY, the 16th of FEBRUARY, 1866,

At TEN o'Clock, about 2,000 Very Superior

LARCH AND OTHER POLES,

BEING long, straight, and of large dimensions, as felled in the Foxcover Plantation, Wing, Bucks.

May be Viewed at any time on application to Mr. A. L. Webster, of Wing, Bucks.

Catalogues may immediately be had on application to Mr. Webster; at the usual Inns in the neighbourhood; and of the Auctioneers, Ascott, Wing, and Leighton Buzzard, Beds.

LEIGHTON BUZZARD, BEDS.

Messrs. HART & SON

Have been favoured with instructions to submit by PUBLIC AUCTION,

On Friday, the 16th day of February, 1866,

AT SIX O'CLOCK IN THE EVENING,

At the UNICORN INN, LEIGHTON BUZZARD,

A Convenient DWELLING HOUSE,

WITH well-built STABLING, COACH-HOUSE, and other OUTBUILDINGS, and a valuable

Plot of Garden Ground,

Situate in Sanders' Lane, North Street, Leighton Buzzard, in the occupation of Mr. Thomas Rice, and producing a rental of £16 per annum.

Copyhold of the Manor of Leighton Buzzard, otherwise Grovebury. Outgoings—Quit Rent, 1s. 7d.; Tithe, 2s. 4d.

Further information may be obtained at the offices of Mr. F. Willis, Solicitor; or of the Auctioneers, Leighton Buzzard, Beds.

LECK STREET, LEIGHTON BUZZARD.

MESSRS. HART & SON

Have received instructions from Mr. George Claridge to offer for SALE BY PUBLIC AUCTION,

At the UNICORN INN, LEIGHTON BUZZARD,

On FRIDAY, the 16th of FEBRUARY, 1866,

At SIX o'Clock in the Evening,

A BRICK AND TILED

Dwelling House, Grocer's Shop, and Garden,

Occupied by Mr. Tutt;

THREE THATCHED COTTAGES, WITH GARDENS,

In the Occupations of Messrs. Pantling, Smith Dimmocke; THREE BRICK and TILED COTTAGES, in the occupation of Messrs. George, Cleaver, and Burridge;

STANDBRIDGE, BEDS.

Valuable Freehold Cottage Property

Messrs. HART & SON

Have received instructions from the Proprietor, to OFFER FOR SALE BY PUBLIC AUCTION,

On THURSDAY, the 1st day of MARCH, 1866,

At the Five Bells Inn, Standbridge, at SIX o'Clock in the Evening.

ALL those Three Freehold, Substantially Brick-built COTTAGES, with convenient OUT-BUILDINGS adjoining, and NEAT GARDENS in front thereof, together with the ORCHARD, well stocked with FRUIT TREES in the rear thereof, as now in the respective occupations of Messrs. Jesse Ellingham, William Bodsworth, and William Wells, at rents amounting to £12 per annum:

The above Property, which is situate in the best part of the pleasant village of Standbridge, has been recently thoroughly repaired, and has a frontage to the Tilsworth Road of feet.

There is an excellent well of water on the premises, and the Land Tax is redeemed.

Further particulars may be obtained at the offices of Messrs. Newton and Whyley, Solicitors, Leighton Buzzard; and of the Auctioneers, Leighton Buzzard, Ascott, and Wing, Bucks.

STANDBRIDGE, BEDS.,

(Near the Railway Station).

Messrs. HART & SON

Beg to announce that they have received instructions from the Proprietor, to SUBMIT TO PUCLIC COMPETITION,

On THURSDAY, the 1st day of MARCH, 1866,

At the Five Bells Inn, Standbridge, at Six o'Clock in the Evening, all that Most Valuable

Corner Plot of FREEHOLD LAND,

Containing Half an Acre (more or less),

SITUATE close to the STANDBRIDGE FORD, RAILWAY STATION, having a double frontage to the Road leading to Standbridge;

The above Plot of Land, owing to its vicinity to the Railway Station, and the site of the proposed New Railway Coal Wharf is admirably adapted for Building purposes, or for the erection of an Inn or Public House, as accommodation is much needed here for Railway Passengers and the Public.

The Land Tax is redeemed.

Immediate possession may be had.

Further particulars may be obtained at the offices of Messrs. Newton and Whyley, solicitors, Leighton Buzzard, and of the Auctioneers' Leighton Buzzard, Ascott, and Wing, Bucks.

STOCKGROVE ESTATE.

Mr. GOTTO'S

SECOND SALE of UNDERWOOD for the Season will take place on February 15th, 1866.

IRONMONGERY.

J. CRABB

BEGS to inform the clergy, gentry and inhabitants of Leighton Buzzard and neighbourhood, that he has OPENED a SHOP in the High Street, with a new and choice assortment of General and Furnishing IRONMONGERY, and hopes by strict attention to business and moderate charges, to merit a share of their patronage and support.

The stock includes a choice assortment of ELECTRO-PLATED GOODS, Suitable for presents.

Best Ivory and Black Handled Knives and Forks, Kitchen Utensils, Fenders and Fire Irons, Paper Machie and Iron Trays,

BEST SHEFFIELD JOINERS' TOOLS, NAILS, SCREWS, BOLTS, LOCKS, HINGES, &c. &c., BEST MAKE OF HORSE NAILS, OVEN GRATES, RANGES, REGISTER GRATES, PLOUGH AND TRACE CHAINS, CART ARMS, AND BOXES, HAMES, &c. &c.,

PARAFFIN LAMPS AND GLASSES. COLZA AND PARAFFIN OIL.

REPAIRS NEATLY EXECUTED.

SEWING MACHINES.

THE "SINGER" (Prize Medal). These Machines are long established as the most simple and effective made; have received upwards of Fifty Prize Medals, including that awarded at the Dublin International Exhibition, 1865; are now furnished with a

PATENT TUCK-MARKER

(THAT CREASES EACH SUCCEEDING TUCK WHILE SEWING—THE MOST USEFUL INVENTION OF THE DAY);

Also other novel accessories not to be had with Machines of any other manufacture; fastens off seams the same as in handwork, forming a stitch unequalled for strength, beauty, elasticity, and elegance. PRICE FROM £8 10s.

ILLUSTRATED CATALOGUES SENT POST FREE.

THE "SINGER" MANUFACTURING COMPANY,

147, CHEAPSIDE, LONDON, E.C.

Authorised Agent for Leighton Buzzard, Tring, Aylesbury, and Dunstable—T. H. BISHOP, Saddler & Harness Maker, Lock Street.

PIANOFORTES

MANUFACTURED BY

W. J. SPARKS AND SONS,

FROM 23 TO 70 GUINEAS,

TUNERS

UNDER the Patronage of Messrs. ERARD, Manufacturers to her Majesty and the Prince of Wales.

BEDS, BUCKS, and HERTS visited quarterly by the Messrs. SPARKS, personally, in this capacity.

13, EVERSHOLT STREET, NEAR EUSTON TERMINUS, N.W., LONDON.

W & A Gilbey (who have the largest Wine Trade direct with the Consumer in

HIGH STREET, LEIGHTON BUZZARD.

H. AVELINE

HAVING taken the SHOP and PREMISES NEXT TO THE POST OFFICE, intends OPENING THEM on TUESDAY NEXT, the 20th of FEBRUARY, as GENERAL

FURNISHING WAREHOUSES.

ESTABLISHED 1812.

PROCTOR AND RYLAND,

IN CALLING ATTENTION TO THEIR SPECIAL

PREPARED BONE MANURES,

HAVE much pleasure in stating that they will be found of very superior quality, and the most economical offered to the Agriculturist.

TURNIP, MANGOLD, AND POTATO MANURES

Have produced results of the most satisfactory and remunerative character on every description of Tillage Land.

WHEAT, OAT, AND BARLEY MANURES

Strengthen the straw, increase the quantity, and improve the quality of the grain in a very marked degree.

BONE SUPERPHOSPHATE OF LIME

Has been proved to be the most economical source of Phosphates for the growth of luxuriant Root & Corn Crops.

GRASS MANURES,

For Mowing or Grazing Land, are very effective in improving the herbage. The preparation of Grass Manures is regulated according as they may be required to be more or less permanent in their character.

Offices—Corn Exchange Buildings, Carr's Lane, Birmingham. Works—Birmingham, Warwick, Bristol, and Chester.

AGENTS:

Mr. Thos. Sheppard, Ampthill Road, Bedford.
Mr. James Perry, Jun., Northampton.
Mr. J. B. Bortt, Seedsman, Kettering.
Mr. John Rogers, Bozeat, Wellingborough.
Mr. Edward George, Naps Bury, St. Albans.

CLIFTON HOUSE, LINSLADE, LEIGHTON BUZZARD.

Mrs. CURWOOD

CONTINUES TO RECEIVE A LIMITED NUMBER OF

Young Ladies to Board and Educate

On Moderate Terms; Liberal Treatment; and Home Comforts.

FRENCH, DRAWING, MUSIC, DANCING, PAINTING AND ILLUMINATING.

Terms inclusive or otherwise.

The Half Quarter will Commence on Monday the 12th of February.

DON'T READ THIS

without attention!

LEONARD BISHOP'S

PATENT DOMESTIC FUEL-ECONOMISING COMPOSITION,

For lining the backs of Fire Grates, which are burned away, cracked, disfigured, or too large, and consume fuel wastefully.

SAVES ONE-THIRD OF THE COAL.

It cannot be seen when the Fire is lighted; is CHEAPER

PROVIDENT LIFE OFFICE,

No. 50, REGENT STREET, LONDON, W.

Established 1806.

INVESTED CAPITAL, 1,660,447.

ANNUAL INCOME, 193,956.

BONUSES DECLARED, £1,451,157.

CLAIMS PAID SINCE THE ESTABLISHMENT OF THE OFFICE, £3,736,600.

PRESIDENT—

THE RIGHT HONOURABLE EARL GREY.

The profits, subject to a trifling deduction, are divided among the insured.

EXAMPLES OF BONUSES ADDED TO POLICIES ISSUED BY THE PROVIDENT LIFE OFFICE.

| Number of policy. | Date of Policy. | Annual Premium. | Sum insured. | Amount with Bonus additions. |
|---|---|---|---|---|
| 4,718 | 1822 | £ s. d. 104 15 10 | £ 5,000 | £ s. d. [illegible] |

**5.5** *The Leighton Buzzard Observer*: an example of a small-circulation local paper, 13 February 1866

started by local jobbing printers as a profitable sideline to their other business interests. They provided the local community with a synopsis of national and international news, a record of local events, a general advertiser and a package of fireside entertainment for all the family.

The *Vale of Evesham News* is typical of the local papers in the second half of the nineteenth century. For three halfpence, the issue of 4 July 1868 provides eight broadsheet pages containing 48 columns of closely printed news, entertainment and advertisements – sufficient material to last the slow reader right through the week.

The first two pages are taken up by advertisements, mainly placed by local tradesmen and shopkeepers. These give a vivid picture of the High Street of a mid-Victorian country town: the shoeing and jobbing smith; the newsagent; the stationer, bookseller and fancy repository that also sells cricket bats, croquet sets, china tea and insurance; the baker who is also a 'Dealer in all kind of Pig Food'; the wine merchant; the brewer (ale at one shilling per dozen pints); the surgeon dentist; the ladies' and gentlemen's hair cutter who also sells 'Fishing Tackle of Every Description'; the seedsman; the building contractor; the veterinary surgeon; the coach builder; the chimney sweep; the photographer ('Under Distinguished Patronage. Animals successfully photographed'); and Miss Sprague, who 'begs respectfully to say that she has a Good Assortment of Ladies Underclothing' and is the 'Agent for the Celebrated Hair Restorer and Pomade'.

There are some national advertisements for patent medicines. Professor Holloway advises that both his ointment and his pills should be used for a whole list of disorders, some contractable in the Vale of Evesham, others not, including Bad Legs, Bad Breasts, Bunions, Bite of Meschetous and Sand-Flies, Coco Bay, Chiego Foot, Chilblains, Corns (Soft), Cancers, Elephantiasis, Gout, Lumbagos, Piles, Rheumatism and Yaws. Readers are also informed that Dr J. Collis Browne's Chlorodyne 'acts like a charm in Diarrhoea'.

Personal and other small advertisements account for another four columns of page four, the head of which explains that one of the advantages of advertising in the *Vale of Evesham News* is that it is read 'not by one class only, but by ALL CLASSES, from the most wealthy to the most humble'; see also Figure 5.6.

The remaining 32 columns comprise: a leading article one and a half columns long which includes snippets of news which the editor thought of sufficient importance to be dignified by a slightly larger type ('The reading on the thermometer on Saturday was 157 degrees in the sun, and 88 in the shade, being the highest recorded yet this Summer. This excessive heat has raised the weekly mortality of London considerably and last week 18 deaths from cholera and 171 from diarrhoea were recorded'); three columns of national and international news; one and a half columns of parliamentary news; two

THE
THAME GAZETTE,
AND OXFORDSHIRE AND BUCKS ADVERTISER.
No. 541. (Circulation, 800 copies weekly.) TUESDAY, JULY 24, 1866. ONE PENNY.
SALE THIS DAY.
OAKLEY, NEAR CHINNOR, OXON.
VALUABLE
FREEHOLD HOUSES
AND
BUILDING LAND,
MR. HOWLAND
Three Freehold Cottages,
FREEHOLD COTTAGES,
Freehold Building Land.
SALE THIS DAY.
POSTCOMBE.
THE
PROPERTY,
MR. HOWLAND.
DINTON.
Midway between Thame and Aylesbury.
VALUABLE
GROWING CROPS OF CORN
AND
RICKS OF CLOVER HAY,
MR. HOWLAND
WHITCHURCH, BUCKS.
ONE OF THE
VERY BEST FARMS
MR. HOWLAND,
Freehold & small part Copyhold
ESTATE,
MR. HOWLAND'S
PERIODICAL SALES
THAME MARKET.
STOCK
MONEY.
HADDENHAM.
MR. CLARKE,
HOUSEHOLD FURNITURE,
LIVE AND DEAD
FARMING STOCK,
Growing Crops of Corn,
HERBAGE & KEEPING
GIBRALTAR FARM,
HOOK NORTON, OXON.
GROWING CROPS OF CORN,
Three Active Horses,
AGRICULTURAL IMPLEMENTS,
J. A. MUMFORD,
BUCKINGHAMSHIRE.
J. A. MUMFORD
FREEHOLD
TITHE-FREE ESTATE
BRICK YARD,
THOUSANDS NOW USE
Johnson, Johnson & Co's
PURE TEA
EIGHT-PENCE PER POUND.
LOCAL AGENTS.
KAYE'S VEGETABLE PILLS.
CHOLERA! CHOLERA!!
CAN BE IMMEDIATELY CURED BY
BOOTH'S CHOLERA MIXTURE,
Which is a Certain & Safe Medicine for Adults & Children.
Prepared and Sold only by
S. BOOTH,
PHARMACEUTICAL AND DISPENSING CHEMIST,
(QUALIFIED BY EXAMINATION,)
MARKET HILL, THAME.
FOR CHEAP
WATCHES, CLOCKS, JEWELLERY,
Gold and Silver Chains, &c., &c., go to
CHENEY'S,
HIGH STREET, THAME.
CHURCH, TURRET, & ILLUMINATED CLOCKS.
"Purity and Excellence of Quality."
COLMAN'S PRIZE MEDAL MUSTARD.
Bears the Trade Mark, the Bull's Head, on each package.
For Medicinal purposes nothing finer can be produced.
Sold by all Grocers and Druggists.
J. and J. COLMAN, LONDON.
Sets of Croquet complete, from 15s. the Set,
Cricketing Goods, all descriptions, by best Makers,
At C. ELLIS'S Stationery Warehouse, Thame.
HAIL STORMS.
THE ROYAL FARMERS'
INSURANCE COMPANY,
HAIL STORMS
MODERATE RATES.
IMPERIAL WINE COMPANY.
DANIEL ORPEN,
Grocer and Wine Merchant,
SHERRIES.
PORTS.
FRENCH GERMAN & HUNGARIAN WINES
HOME CURED BACON STORES.
Starch Manufacturers
Glenfield Patent Starch
USED IN THE ROYAL LAUNDRY.
Batley's Rat & Mouse Poison.
JOHN I. DEVERELL,
CHEMIST, THAME.
JOHN E. W. FALLOFEILD,
FAMILY & DISPENSING
CHEMIST
CORNMARKET, THAME, OXON,
FALLOFEILD'S
Alterative Condition Powders
FOR HORSES.
FALLOFEILD'S
RHEUMATIC BALSAM.
FALLOFEILD'S
EAST INDIAN SAUCE.
A Certain cure for Corns.
RHEUMATISM.
No more Grey or Red Hair.
COOPER'S
SHEEP DIPPING POWDER,
(SOLUBLE IN COLD WATER.)
JOHN E. W. FALLOFEILD.
Epps' Homœpathic Medicines,
SODA, SELTZER,
AND OTHER
AERATED WATERS.
HORSE AND CATTLE
MEDICINES!

**5.6** The printer of *The Thame Gazette*, 24 July 1866, used his paper as a vehicle for displaying the variety of his fonts

columns headed 'Literary and Scientific' of odd facts attributed to a variety of books and magazines; two columns of sports news and market information; half a column each of births, marriages and deaths, gardening hints and 'Ladies News' mainly about the latest fashions; and one and a half columns of 'Varieties', anecdotes and jokes, mainly of the Christmas cracker type ('Why is my foot like a stable? Because there's a corn bin there'). Local news, mainly court cases and verbatim accounts of political and other meetings, filled the remaining 20 columns.

Each paragraph of news is separated by a headline printed in capitals using minion type:

> FOWL-STEALING AT NORTHFIELD
> STEALING GIN AT KIDDERMINSTER
> STEALING BOOTS AT HILLHAMPTON
> UTTERING COUNTERFEIT COIN AT KING'S NORTON
> STEALING PIGS AT DUDLEY
> ROBBING THE GREAT WESTERN RAILWAY AT TENBURY
> ('stealing a woollen shirt, the property of the Great Western Railway Company')
> UNLAWFULLY LIVING IN AN OUTHOUSE AT DUDLEY.

Anecdotes and jokes were a common feature of many local papers. Here is just one example from the *Halifax Courier* for 5 November 1859:

> At a fashionable city ball, at which low-necked dresses were a prominent feature, Miss B addressed her country cousin: 'Cousin Sam, did you ever see such a glorious sight before?' 'Never since I was weaned,' said Sam, blushing.

As the nineteenth century drew to a close, local weekly newspapers began to abandon their pretensions of being able to compete with the national papers and the regional dailies in providing national and international news. Instead, they concentrated on recording every public aspect of life in their immediate neighbourhood, often inserting long lists of those who had attended charitable and other events, relying on the probability that all those people would buy the paper in order to see their names in print. They chose wisely. Many of the regional dailies fell victim to the circulation wars of the 1930s as readers were bribed to switch to the national dailies with the offer of free gifts, while others succumbed to the pressures of increasing production costs and competition from radio and cinema newsreel as providers of news from the outside world.

## Notes

1. *Spectator*, 8 August 1712.

2. Copy in Bristol Reference Library.
3. *The First Provincial Newspaper: A Brief Survey of the Earliest Norwich Newspapers.* (Norwich Mercury Office, 1924.)
4. *Reading Mercury*, 9 September 1765.
5. Ferdinand, C. Y. (1997), *Benjamin Collins and the Provincial Newspaper Trade in the Eighteenth Century*, Oxford: Clarendon Press.
6. *Northampton Mercury*, 20 February 1769.
7. *Bristol Journal*, 28 October 1775.
8. *Cambridge Chronicle and Journal*, 13 July 1773.
9. Allnutt, W. H. (1896), 'English Provincial Presses', *Bibliographia*, 2.
10. *Glocester Journal*, 16 June 1761.
11. *Reading Mercury*, 18 July 1774.
12. Ibid., 8 July 1765.
13. Ibid., 14 October 1765.
14. Ibid., 14 October 1765.
15. Ibid., 4 November 1765.
16. Ibid., 22 February 1768.
17. *Northampton Mercury*, 9 July 1722.
18. *Protestant Mercury*, 26 December 1716.
19. The *Cambridge Chronicle* was initially bi-partisan. If anything, it leaned towards the left, supporting the Americans during the War of Independence. However, it turned loyalist in response to the French Revolution, creating the opportunity for the *Cambridge Intelligencer* to enter the field, representing the radical viewpoint.
20. Other radical titles included the *Manchester Herald* and the *Sheffield Iris*, both started in 1792.
21. *Leeds Intelligencer*, 28 May 1792
22. *Lincoln, Rutland and Stamford Mercury*, 31 January 1794.
23. Ayerst, David (1971), *The Guardian: Biography of a Newspaper*, London: Collins.
24. *The Newspaper Press Directory and Advertiser's Guide.*
25. *Yorkshire Post*, 2 July 1866.
26. *White's Hampshire* (1878).

# PART TWO
# The Content of the Eighteenth-century Newspaper

# Chapter 6

# Advertisements

> There is a great deal of useful learning sometimes to be met with in Advertisements. I look upon mine to be a kind of Index of all Arts and Sciences, they contain the Advices both from the learned and the unlearned World; Fools and Philosophers may there meet with equal Matter to divert and amuse themselves.
>
> *Mist's Weekly Journal*, 22 May 1725

One of the main delights of any old newspaper is its advertising columns. Here, at a glance, can be seen the necessities and luxuries, and the pains and pleasures of everyday life over two hundred years ago – the contents of the grocer's shop ('Bohea Tea, of the best sort, and finest Flavour, at 14s. a Pound'), the price of clothes, fashionable silks newly imported ('Damasks, Velderovs, Armozeens, Ducapes, Cornelly Tabbies and Paolis … Shaloons, Callimancoes and Ruffels'), a ship's cargo of spices to be auctioned, and innkeepers offering 'the very best Beds which are always kept well aired', 'a stock of the best old Wines' and 'every other Article requisite to accommodate such of the Nobility and Gentry as shall please to honour him with their Company'. Those in search of pleasure could choose between the latest play at Drury Lane or a cockfighting match. The precarious lives of the people and the lack of central services are illustrated by the advertisements for quack medicines, fire insurance, associations for the prosecution of felons and rewards for the recovery of horses 'stolen or stray'd', while husbands warned others not to trust their wives as they would not be responsible for the debts they incurred.

The advertisements provide a glimpse at the social history of childhood:

> *This is to give Notice*
>
> That there is now in the Workhouse belonging to the parishes of St. Margaret and St. John the Evangelist, Westminster, a great Number of Children, both Boys and Girls, from the Age of ten to seventeen Years, fit for Service; therefore all Masters of Ships and Vessels, and all other Persons whatever, that want Apprentices, upon applying themselves to the Churchwardens or Overseers of the Poor of the said Parishes, may have any of the said Children upon Liking.
>
> *Daily Advertiser*, 27 October 1741

The workhouse was one way of getting rid of unwanted progeny. For those with a bit more cash, there were the forerunners of Dotheboys Hall advertised in the *Daily Advertiser* for 4 April 1758: one at Wanless-Hall, near Richmond, Yorks; one at Knaton, near Thirsk; and two at 'Bowes in Yorkshire' where boys are 'cloathed, boarded, educated, and supplied with Books and all Necessaries, for 10l. a Year each'.

The foundation of *The Daily Advertiser* (Figure 6.1) in 1730 was a significant milestone in the history of journalism. It was a formal recognition of the importance of advertising in the economics of the newspaper. This was reflected in the use of the word 'advertiser' in the titles and subtitles of many of the newspapers that followed.

Newspaper advertising was by no means new. The first known advertisement appeared in Nathaniel Butter's coranto for 23 August 1622, albeit advertising his own wares. He let it be known that back issues of his 'Weekely Relations of Newes' were still available and that 'which manner of writing and printing he doth propose to continue weekly by God's assistance, from the best and most certain intelligence'. In September 1624, Butter advertised his intention to publish a map to illustrate the siege of Breda, 'wherein you may with the eye behold the siege, in a manner, as lively as if you were an eye witnesse'.

For the rest of the seventeenth century, most news publications carried some form of advertising. There is the oft-quoted advertisement Charles II placed in *Mercurius Publicus* for 5 July 1660 seeking the return of his lost dog. When it was believed that the royal touch was able to cure diseases, Charles advertised in the *Intelligencer* in 1664 'his Royal Will and purpose to continue the healing of his people for the Evil during the month of May'. Towards the end of the seventeenth century *The London Gazette* was receiving about £6 a week in advertising revenue.

The first attempt at a purely advertising paper was Marchamont Nedham's *Publick Adviser* in 1657, 'weekly communicating unto the whole Nation the several occasions of all persons that are in any way concerned in matters of Buying and Selling or in any kind of Imployment or Dealings whatsoever, according to the intent of the Office of Publick Advice newly set up in several places in and about London and Westminster'. It included an advertisement for a newly discovered drink:

> In Bartholomew Lane, on the back side of Old Exchange, the drink called Coffee, which is a very wholsom and Physical drink, having many excellent virtues, closes the Orifice of the Stomach, fortifies the heat within, helpeth Digestion, quickeneth the Spirits, maketh the heart lightsom, is good against Eyesores, Coughs and Colds, Rhumes, Consumptions, Headach, Dropsie, Gout, Scurvy, King's Evil, and many others, is to be sold both in the morning, and at three of the clock in the afternoon.

# The Daily Advertiser.

Numb. 993.

FRIDAY, April 5, 1734.

*Parma, March 20.*

THE Marshal de Villars has made an Offer to send hither some of his Troops, for the better Security of this City, but the Governor refus'd to receive them, under pretence that he had no Instructions with relation thereto. 'Tis certain that a Jealousy has got head between the Spaniards and Sardinians, and that the former refuse utterly to undertake any Enterprize in Conjunction with the latter. If we are not misinform'd, France has something to do at present to keep Matters within decent Bounds; and what Turn things may take hereafter, is a Pain to pretend to foresee.

*Vienna, March* 27. Every thing is dispos'd for opening early the Campain, both on the Rhine and in Italy, and very extraordinary Preparations are made for that purpose. The Military Chancery set out this Day for the Rhine; Prince Eugene's Equipages go next Week, and his Highness will follow in a few Days. The last Letters from Italy confirm, that the Count de Merci is so well recover'd from his late Illness, that he will be fit for Business in a very short time. 'Tis assured that the Duke of Lorrain's Marriage with the Archdutchess will take Place this Year, and perhaps that may be the Reason why we hear no more of his making a Campaign with the Imperial Army on the Rhine.

*Leipsick, March* 30. The sudden Arrival of King Augustus at Dresden, set all his People in a Surprize; but we are now inform'd that his Majesty, in the Course of his Journey to Polish Prussia, finding himself near the Borders of Silesia, and believing that his Presence in Saxony might be necessary on many Occasions, particularly with regard to the ensuing Assembly of the States of his Electorate, thought proper to take Advantage of the Time his Army will be on their March to Dantzick, and so turn'd off for Dresden, from whence he can still with Ease get to Dantzick before his Troops.

*Hague, April* 9. Our next Advices from Dantzick are expected to bring an Account of the Russians having cut off the Communication of that City with the Sea; but we fancy the Arrival of the Muscovite Artillery thro' the King of Prussia's Dominions will not be so hasty. We hear that some Difficulties are like to arise in the Province of Neuf-Chatel, belonging to his Prussian Majesty, which will make the Friendship of France so necessary to him, that to break with that Court *at this Time*, would be the *Loss* of his Country. By the Hurry France makes on a sudden to embark Troops for Dantzick, it should seem as if the Ministry began to rely less on the Diversion they promis'd themselves on the Part of the Turks, and to despair of the Succours expected from Sweden; at which Court we learn, the Proposals of the British Minister are most attended to.

*Deal, April* 3. Wind S S.W. In the Downs Remain his Majesty's Ships the Namur, the Right Hon. Sir John Norris, Admiral, Princess Carolina, Grafton, Newcastle, Edinburgh, the Right Hon. Admiral Steward, Dreadnought, Sunderland, York, Swallow, Hampton-Court, Orford, Buckingham, Diamond, and Antelope; with the King William, Sanders, for East-India; Knellington, Pitts, for Port-Mahon; John and Mary, Johnson, for Virginia; Peter and Mary, Prince, for Boston; Charles, Brown, for Genoa; Hampshire, Smith, the George, Moon, and Salisbury, Smith, for Lisbon; Evesdon, Thompson, and Two Brothers, Hopson, for Gibraltar; Stretham, Huddy, for Falmouth; Nancy, Paramore, for Madeira; Success, Watts, and Phoenix, Dun, for Dublin. Since Writing his Majesty's Ships the Newcastle, Diamond, and Antelope are under sail for the Westward. Came down, America, Noble, for New-England; Hopwell, Tomson, for Lisbon.

LONDON.

The following Persons are appointed to preach the Lent-Sermons this Day.

Dr. Clarke, before the King.
Dr. Foulkes, at Whitehall-Chapel.
Dr. Clarke, at St. Katherine Cree-Church.
Dr. Hay, at St. Anne Aldersgate.
Dr. Thomas, at St. Dunstan in the West.
Dr. Pearce, at St. Paul Covent-Garden.
Dr. Barton, at St. Saviour's, Southwark.
Bishop of Chester, at St. Katherine by the Tower.
Dr. Mangey, at Clerkenwell.

We hear that his Majesty will review his Horse and Foot Guards soon after the rising of the Parliament; and that there will be a Camp this Summer in Hyde-Park.

Yesterday the Prince of Orange went to see the Earl of Burlington's fine House at Chiswick, after which his Highness, accompany'd by the Princess Royal and the other Princesses, went to view Westminster Abby.

Yesterday the Right Hon. the Lord William Hamilton, Brother to his Grace the Duke of Hamilton and Brandon, arriv'd here with his Lady from Scotland, her Ladyship being very near her time.

Last Saturday died at her Seat at Whitehaven, the Lady Lawson, Mother of Sir Wilfred Lawson, Bart. Member of Parliament for Cockermouth in Cumberland.

Last Night the following Gentlemen were declar'd Directors of the East-India-Company for the Year ensuing, viz.

640 John Cook, *Esq*;
640 Matthew Martin, *Esq*;
638 Abraham Adams, *Esq*;
637 Baltzer Lyell, *Esq*;
636 * *Sir* W. Billers, *Kt. Lord Mayor*,
636 Josias Wordsworth, *sen. Esq*;
635 *Sir* Francis Child, *Kt. and Alderman*,
631 Dodding Braddyl, *Esq*;
631 *Capt.* Robert Hudson,
624 Samuel Feake, *Esq*;
624 *Mr.* William Rous,
624 Josias Wordsworth, *jun. Esq*;
622 *Mr.* John Eccleston,
616 *Dr.* Caleb Cotesworth,
609 John Gould, *jun. Esq*;
608 William Gosselin, *Esq*;
416 *John Salter, *Esq*; *Alderman*,
403 *Charles Boone, *Esq*;
391 *St. Quintin Thompson, *Esq*;
390 * *Mr.* Samuel Hyde,
380 *Jones Raymond, *Esq*;
332 *Charles Colborne, *Esq*;
332 *Capt.* Richard Boulton,
328 Peter Godfrey, *Esq*;

*N. B. Those mark'd with * are new ones.*

Last Monday his Majesty was pleased to make the following Promotions in the Army, viz.

Capt. John Mitchell, Lieut. and Adjutant in his Majesty's first Regiment of Foot-Guards, to be Colonel of a Company in the said Regiment, in the Room of Col. Colston, deceas'd.

Maurice Bockland, Esq; Member of Parliament for Yarmouth, Hants, to be Captain of a Troop in his Majesty's own Royal Regiment of Horse.

Oliver Smith, Esq; Captain-Lieutenant of a Company in a Regiment of Foot in Ireland, to be Captain of a Company in the Hon. Col. Nevil's Regiment of Dragoons on the Irish Establishment.

George Sloper, Esq; Captain of a Company of Invalids in Garrison at Portsmouth, to be Captain of a Company in a Regiment of Foot, commanded by Col. Jasper at Gibraltar.

William Campbell, Esq; to be Captain of a Company in General Grove's Regiment of Foot at Gibraltar.

And Mr. George D'Oyley to be an Ensign in General Wetham's Regiment of Foot.

All Officers who are absent from their respective Posts, are order'd to repair to the same immediately.

On Tuesday last in the Afternoon, Sir John Norris came into the Downs on board his Majesty's Ship the Britannia, a first Rate of 100 Guns, having several other Men of War with him. He was saluted by Admiral Stuart and the rest of the Navy with the usual Honours.

'Tis again confirm'd, that the French Troops are daily gathering upon the Coasts of Calais and Dunkirk; and that they talk of embarking there from 5 to 6000 Men, as 'tis presum'd for Dantzick.

Last Sunday died at Molesey in Surry, Joseph Barker, Esq; one of his Majesty's Justices of the Peace for that County.

Yesterday the Rev. Doctor Williams, Rector of Gascob in Herefordshire, was introduc'd by the Right Hon. the Lord Baltimore to his Royal Highness the Prince of Wales, and had the Honour to kiss his Highness's Hand, on his being appointed one of his Royal Highness's Domestick Chaplains.

On Wednesday Morning the Depositions on the eleventh and twelfth Articles against the Rev. Dr. Bentley (upon which a Consultation was awarded by the House of Lords) were read before the Right Rev. the Lord Bishop of Ely; after which his Lordship adjourn'd the Court to this Morning 9 o'Clock.

Yesterday No. 18009 was drawn a Prize of 2000 l. and No. 5105, 67783, 71730, 81996, 82111, and 90578, 100 l. each.

*Next Sunday two Charity Sermons will be preach'd at the Parish Church of St. Sepulchre's; that in the Morning by the Right Rev. the Lord Bishop of St. David's, and that in the Afternoon by the Rev. Dr. Green, Rector of St. George the Martyr.*

Yesterday Bank Stock was 132. India 135. South-Sea Trading Stock 73 a 1 4th. Annuities 100 a 1 4th. Ditto New Annuities 98 3 4ths a 7 8ths. Three per Cent. Annuity 88. Million Bank 106 1 half. African 23. York-Buildings 3 1 4th. Royal Assurance 90. London-Assurance 11 1 half. New Bank Circulation 5l. Prem. South-Sea Bonds 1s. Prem. India ditto 18s. Prem. Three per Cent. ditto 3s. Prem. English Copper 1l. 15s. Welsh ditto 1l. 13s. Lottery Tickets 3l. 15s.

*THE Gentlemen, Clergy, and Freeholders of the County of* ESSEX, *that are in the Interest of*
Sir ROBERT ABDY, Bart.
AND
THOMAS BRAMSTON, Esq;
*Are desir'd to meet at the Sun Tavern in Holborn, this Day, the 5th Instant, at 6 o' Clock in the Evening.*

High Water at London-Bridge this Day, at 44 Minutes after 12 in the Morning, and 9 after 1 in the Afternoon.

*THE Gentlemen, Clergy and Freeholders of the County of* HERTFORD, *that reside in or near the Cities of London and Westminster, and are in the Interest of*
CHARLES CÆSAR, *Esq*;
*Are desir'd to meet at the Queen's-Arms Tavern in St. Paul's Church-yard, on Tuesday the 9th of this Instant April, at 6 o'Clock.*

*Custom-House, London, 29 March 1734.*
For SALE,
By Order of the Honourable Commissioners of His Majesty's Customs, *&c.*

*ON Friday the 5th of April, at three o'Clock in the Afternoon, will be expos'd to Sale by Inch of Candle, in the Long-Room at the Custom-House, London, a Parcel of Brandy, Rum, Geneva, Spruce-Beer, and Tobacco; (clear of all Duties.) Which are to be seen at the King's Warehouse, on Wednesday the 3d, Thursday the 4th of April, from 8 to 12 in the Forenoon, and from 3 till 5 in the Afternoon, and on Friday Morning before the Sale. Catalogues to be had at the King's Warehouse.*

BY HIS MAJESTY's COMMAND.
AT the King's Theatre in the Hay-Market, Tomorrow, being Saturday, the 6th of April, will be reviv'd
DEBORAH.
*An* ORATORIO, *or* Sacred Drama,
In ENGLISH,
*Compos'd by Mr.* HANDEL.
To be perform'd by a great Number of the best Voices and Instruments.
The House to be fitted up, and illuminated in a particular manner.
Pit and Boxes to be put together, and no Persons to be admitted without Tickets, which will be deliver'd this Day and Tomorrow, at the Office in the Hay-Market, at half a Guinea each. Gallery 5 s.

AT the Theatre Royal in Lincoln's-Inn-Fields, Tomorrow, being the 6th of April, will be reviv'd an OPERA, call'd
ASTARTUS.
*Compos'd by Sig.* BONONCINI.
*The Pit and Boxes are put together at Half a Guinea.*
*First Gallery 4s. Upper Gallery 2s. 6d.*
Tickets will be deliver'd at the Bedford-Head Tavern in Southampton-street, at White's Chocolatehouse in St. James's-street, and at the Office, next Door to the Entrance on the Stage.
*The Pit and Boxes will not be opened till 5, the Galleries at 4.*
No Person whatever to be admitted behind the Scenes.
*It is desir'd that all Persons would be pleased to order their Coaches to wait within the Rails in Lincoln's-Inn-Fields, which will entirely prevent any Stop at the Door of the Theatre.*

*For the Benefit of*
*Mrs.* CELESTINA HEMPSON.
AT the Theatre Royal in Lincoln's-Inn-Fields, on Wednesday the 10th Instant, will be perform'd, a new Oratorio or Sacred Drama, call'd
DAVID.
*Set to Musick by Signor* NICOLA PORPORA.
The Pit and Boxes are put together at Half a Guinea, and also Seats upon the Stage. First Gallery 4 s. Upper Gallery 2 s. 6 d. And the Pit and Boxes, as well as both the Galleries, will be open'd at Three o'Clock.
Tickets will be deliver'd at the Office, next Door to the Entrance on the Stage, and at Mrs. Celestina's Lodgings in the same Theatre, where they may be had at any Hour every Day, (Sunday excepted) she humbly hoping that the Gentlemen Subscribers to the Opera will not make use of their Silver Tickets that Night.

By Command of his ROYAL HIGHNESS.
*For the Benefit of Mr.* CHAPMAN.
AT the Theatre Royal in Covent-Garden, Tomorrow, the 6th of April, will be presented a Comedy, call'd
The 'SQUIRE of ALSATIA.
Sir Edward Belfond, Mr. Quin; the 'Squire Mr. Chapman; Lolpoop, Mr. Hippisley; Teresia, Mrs. Younger; Termagant, Mrs. Kilby, being the first time of her appearing in Boy's Cloaths.
*With Entertainments of Dancing, particularly*
The Scots Dance by Mr. Glover and Mrs. Laguerre.
And the last new Dance, call'd Pigmalion.
To which will be added a new Dramatic Entertainment, call'd
The NUPTIAL MASQUE:
OR,
The Triumphs of CUPID and HYMEN.
*Set to Musick by Mr.* GALLIARD.
Cupid, Miss Norsa, in Boy's Cloaths; Hymen, Mr. Salway; 1st Priest of Hymen, Mr. Leveridge; 2d, Mr. Laguerre; Venus, Mrs. Wright; Britannia, Mrs. Sanderson; Liberty, Mrs. Kilby; Bridal Virgin, Miss Hillyard; Zephyrs, Mons. Malter, Mr. Glover, Mr. [illegible] Mr. Lesac, Mr Delagarde and Mr. Duke; Bridal Swains, Mr. Lesac, Mr. Delagarde and Mr. Duke; Bridal Nymphs, Mrs. Ogden, Miss Rogers and Miss Baston; Un Amour, Mr. Glover; Deities of Pleasure, Mons. Malter and Mr. Houghton; a Bridal Nymph, Mademoiselle Sallé. With new Cloaths, Scenes and other Decorations, proper to the Masque. Being the last Time of the Company's Acting till Easter Holidays. Tickets deliver'd out for Monday the 1st Inst. will be then taken.
*Boxes 5 s. Pit 3 s. Gallery 2 s.*

92

**6.1** *The Daily Advertiser*, 5 April 1734

Other specifically advertising papers included *Publick Advertisements* (Roger L'Estrange, 1666), the *City Mercury; or, Advertisements concerning Trade* (various dates and versions from 1675 to 1693) and the *Generous Advertiser, or Weekly Information of Trade and Business* (1707).

However, the newspaper became the dominant vehicle for advertising. No other medium could offer such wide circulation, instant publication, regular appearance and extensive distribution. The news-carrying magazines were also used as an advertising medium. Samuel Johnson's first appearance in print for a national audience was his advertisement for the school at Edial in the *Gentleman's Magazine* for June 1736.

The seventeenth-century advertisements make curious reading today. On 6 October 1682, James Maddox used the advertising columns of the *London Mercury* to announce his abilities in

> the keeping and securing of any Humane dead Corps, above ground, from any ill scent, smell, or annoyance, for three, six, or twelve Months space, or for as long as shall be desired, without Embowelling, Embalming, or wrapping in Searcloth, (and the Face to be seen all the while if required) … one Rarity he performed was the taking up a Corps at Panswick in Gloucestershire, after it had been Interred thirteen Weeks, which he took out of the Coffin it was buried in, and put into another new Coffin, and so brought it up to London, and after it had remained three days at his House, it was sent into Germany, where it safely arrived without any ill scent or annoyance to any of the Ships Company, or the Persons who desired it, to their great satisfaction. He has likewise an excellent Remedy, which (by God's Blessing) gives great ease (if not total cessation of Pain) to any Person afflicted with the Gout … And you may also be furnished with Coffins of all sizes, of the best and newest Fashion, at reasonable Rates.

In the same paper Lady Huxley advertised for the return of her absconded servant, 'a short thick chubbed Fellow, about 25 years of Age, in a new Mourning Suit, with a light colour'd brown short Periwig, and a Womanish Voice'.

## Quack Doctors

The eighteenth century has been described as the golden age of the quack. One look at the newspaper advertisements will confirm this, especially in the weekly journals where the two advertising pages were full of advertisements for quack medicines describing nauseatingly explicit details of the maladies they purported to cure.

With a strong stomach and an adolescent mind, it is quite entertaining to sit back and watch the quacks trying to outbid each other over the efficacy of their cures. This was particularly so in the case of the worm-doctors whose schoolboy bragging of 'my worm is bigger than your worm' was the main element of their advertising pitch. The worm-doctor, John Moore, specialized in the personal testimonial. Edward Steward told the readers of the *St. James's Evening Post* on 26 June 1718 that for three years he was troubled with 'Convulsion Fits' until he was advised to take

> the Worm Powders of Mr. John Moor's … which Powders brought away from me, Worms of several Sorts, viz. Some like Earth-Worms, others like pieces of White Thread, likewise some of a round knotted Sorts with Joynts; since the coming away of which, my Fits has perfectly left me.

John Moore advertised in other papers, but little changed except the names of the worm-eaten and the shapes and sizes of the worms:

> These are to certify, That I THOMAS REED Dwelling with Mr Hyde, Merchant, in Rude-lane, Was for a considerable Time troubled with the Joint Worm, for the Relief of which I went to
>
> *Mr.* JOHN MOORE, *Apothecary,*
>
> *At the Pestle and Mortar in Lawrence-Pountney's-Lane, the first Great Gates on the Left-hand from Cannon street,*
>
> And by taking a few of his Medicines voided a Worm more than three Yards long and very broad, with 400 Joints, and 20 or 30 small ones: This Worm I have at my Master's House, and will be ready to satisfy any curious person of the Truth of this.
>
> JOHN MUNCK, a Servant to a certain Noble Lord, was troubled with a Pain in his Stomach and Belly; for Relief of which he made use of several Medicines, but all proving ineffectual, he at last applied himself for advice to Mr. JOHN MOORE … Who apprehending his Pains to be caused by Worms, prescribed to him his Worm Medicines, by using of which he voided a very broad Worm, nine Foot six Inches long; after the coming away of which he was freed from his forementioned Pains, and so continued for a considerable time after, till finding himself again to labour under several Disorders, he took more of the said Mr. Moore's Worm Medicines which brought away a Worm about twelve Foot long and a very monstrous one for Thickness; and lately finding himself out of Order again he took more of the said Mr. Moore's Worm powders, and has voided a monstrous jointed Worm, with a Head, flat on the Belly, having a Ridge on the Back, with a forked Tail, and in length about four Foot. All which three Worms can be seen at the said Mr. Moore's House.
>
> *London Journal*, 14 November 1730

This obsession with size continues in this extract from an advertisement for a 'Cure for the Stone and Gravel' in the *Daily Post* for 16 September 1730:

> she had been above twenty Years afflicted with a Stone in the Bladder, and for the last three Years could not stir abroad, nor make any Water but by Drops,

> immediately after taking this Remedy voided between 30 and 40 Stones, the least as big as a Pea, and some as a Kidney-Bean, and one large Stone above three Inches about and more than two Inches long, after the coming away of which she made almost a Gallon of Water.

And in this, from the versatile Sir William Read, 'Her Majesty's Oculist', who claimed in the *Tatler* on 8 December 1709 not only to remove cataracts but

> also to remove Hair-Lips, or Wry Necks, tho' never so deformed; or contracted Limbs; and has lately taken several Wens of a great Bigness; particularly one lately from a Gentleman that weigh'd 26 Pounds.

The quack medicine advertisements must have kept whole armies of Grub Street copywriters occupied. My guess is that they were composed in taverns with the whole company laughing at the next excesses they managed to dream up. An advertisement in *Mist's Weekly Journal* for 11 June 1720 describes the progress of the Asthmatick Julep:

> it penetrates into the inmost Recesses of the Lungs, and there meeting with rough, thick, cold, clammy, slimy Phlegm, so attenuates, divides, moves and works it, that by coughing and spitting, it expectorates and throws up all such Matter with the greatest Ease and Pleasure.

Similar processes were at work with Godbold's Balsam:

> I took the Balsam agreeable to the directions, beginning in the evening, and in twenty-four hours the Temple of Health appeared in view … I soon began to sleep nearly the whole night, although I expectorated at least one gill of thick greenish matter, yet in ten days time I slept the whole night once without spitting, save a little in the morning after I arose.
>
> *Chelmsford Chronicle*, 5 June 1789

Godbold continued to advertise from the grave. His memorial tablet in Godalming Church reads:

Sacred
To the Memory of
Nathaniel Godbold Esq
Inventor and Proprietor
of that Excellent Medicine
The Vegetable Balsam
For the Cure of Consumption and Asthmas
He departed this Life
The 17th Day of Decr 1799
Aged 69 Years

The *Craftsman* for 4 November 1738 and many of the other weekly journals of the period carry advertisements for the 'so-much famed Hypo-Drops', the cure for

> Crudities and flatulent or windy Disorders in the First Passages, sour Belchings, Cholick, Uneasiness in the Bowels, and ill Fumes, which offend the Nerves, and affect the Head, and produce sometimes Giddiness, Dimness of Sight, confused Thoughts, pertinacious Watchings, Frights, groundless Fears, and the deepest Melancholy, with direful Views and terrible Apprehensions, Fits, flushing Heats, Reachings, Faintness, Lowness and Sinking of the Spirits, Palpitation of the Heart, Startings, Tremblings and Twitchings in the Limbs and other Parts, with many convulsive Disorders.

One of the most dramatic testimonials came from the man with the exploding bowels. He describes his condition before taking Doctor Henry's Nervous Medicine:

> For I have great pains in my Head and Ears, with a singing Noise, a bad Digestion, windy griping Pains in my Bowels and Stomach; and about an Hour after eating and drinking those Parts are ready to burst until all is ejected up again; and this is followed with windy Belchings as acid as Vinegar, great Twitchings … and at times somewhat arises in my Throat as big as an Egg; which almost choaks me. Something very frequently seems like live Mice running up and down in my Body; in short my Wind is ready to burst my whole Body to Pieces, my Breast and Bowels swell with the Wind to such a surprising Degree, and rise to my Throat and Head, that I am deprived of all my Senses, and am ready to commit an Act of Violence on myself.
>
> *General Evening Post*, 29 November 1755

According to the advertisement in the *Reading Mercury* for 18 July 1774, Speediman's Stomach Pills 'by the blessing of God dispersed the wind in a very surprising manner'.

A quick glance at the quack advertisements of early-eighteenth-century newspapers could easily lead to the conclusion that theirs was an age obsessed with sex. There is almost a symmetry of cause and effect with the sellers of aphrodisiacs plying their wares next to cures for venereal disease.

The advertisements for aphrodisiacs went to no great lengths to shroud in euphemism the claimed effects of their concoctions. The advertisement for the Cordial Quintessence of Vipers in the *Craftsman* on 12 August 1738, claims that

> A few DROPS of it only, gives such a generous Warmth, and so increaseth the Vital and Animal Spirits, it not only promotes, and prompts the Desire, but also furnishes proper Matter … Nor does it only furnish Matter, and create Desire,

> but also true Power (as it braces up and corroborates the Testes) and gives an elastic Springiness to the Musculi Erectoris Penis, in Men, and corrects, cleanses, and comforts the Uterus, or Womb in Women, the Lankness and Laxity of the former, and the Foulness, Coldness or Obstruction of the latter. Those who but once try it, will so pleasantly experience its nutritive Quickening Properties, in exhilarating the Heart, reviving the Spirits, comforting the Vitals, circulating the Juices, and recreating, and renovating, as it were, the whole Man, that they will never be without it; for it is such a present Help in time of Need, as that on taking then but a Dose or two more of it than ordinary, it will so instantaneously animate the dull inactive Spirits, and rouze up, and activate the sluggish, enfeebled Faculties in both Sexes, as to excite and capacitate, where it could hardly be expected, and at the same Time, seldom fail to render that conjugal Intercourse, Prolifick.

Similar effects are claimed for the Superlative Enlivening Drops, 'to be had only at Mr. Radford's Toy-Shop', advertised in the *Universal Spectator* for 3 March 1733, and Dr Smyth's Restorative Medicine in *Drewry's Derby Mercury* for 20 September 1787:

> If in Cases of this Delicacy it were allowable to publish Names, the Doctor would give the World a long list of Fathers, become so, by the Use of his Medicine; of Mothers rejoycing in the Fruitfulness they never knew before.

So much for the cause, now for the effects. There are more advertisements for cures for venereal disease in the first half of the eighteenth century than for any other ailment. As the advertisement for Dr Smith's Specific Drops in the *Reading Mercury* for 18 June 1774 proclaimed, 'The Venereal Disease is the Ruin of half our Youth'. The following advertisement from the *Westminster Journal* for 27 December 1746 is typical of its kind:

> At the GOLDEN-BALL
>
> In Bow-Church-Yard, Cheapside, London,
>
> Livest G West … who cureth all the various Symptoms of the FRENCH DISTEMPER, whether freshly contracted, or of long Continuance, by a new, speedy, and sure Method, and a RECENT CLAP, in a few Days, without Confinement, Hindrance of Business, or the Knowledge of a Bedfellow, And as for such unfortunate Persons, who by neglect of themselves, or for want of the timely Use of my never-failing Remedies, lie under the miserable Circumstances of virulent Runnings, old Gleets, Heat of Urine, Cordees, Buboes, Shankers, Tumify'd Testicles, Ulcers in the Nose or Throat, daily or nocturnal Pains, or any other filthy Symptoms arising from this Distemper, I cure according to the best approv'd Method now in Practice.
>
> N.B. There is a Back Door into Goose-Alley, A Golden-Ball hanging over it, that leads to my Surgery.

Richard Rock, one of the most famous pox-doctors of his day, spent a small fortune on newspaper advertisements over several decades (Figure 6.2). His copy, which mainly consisted of long lists of symptoms, changed from time to time as he included new horrors with which to frighten his prospective clients. But by the time he advertised in the *Penny London Post* in 1749, signs of tiredness were setting in. Having listed, among others,

> Pustules all over the Body, and in the Mouth, Nose and private Parts; spots like Measles in the Glands, tumified Scrotum, scaly Pustules, Blood slimy and corrupt, broad scaly Scabs, Ulcers of the Jaws, Nose and Palate …

he concluded lamely with, 'and many other bad Symptoms, too tedious to enumerate in this Advertisement'. In his younger days, his enthusiasm for his product inspired him into verse. His advertisement in the *Craftsman* for 24 August 1734 ends with this refrain:

> If Venus's Toys allure your Hearts,
> By which you feel Venereal Smarts,
> And grievous pains endure,
> Tho' Shank'rous Ulcers Rest Annoy,
> And stubborn Gleets your Health destroy,
> In this you'll find a cure.

The advertisers for Willmot's Grand Preservative, 'sold at the sign of the Archimedes and Three Golden Spectacles in the West Passage of the Royal-Exchange, going into Castle Alley', make no attempts to flatter their clientele:

> One Spoonful applied by Way of Injection, within Eighteen Hours after Enjoyment, will assuredly secure any Gentleman from the virulent Infection of the foulest Woman … One Bottle is sufficient to serve any Gentleman for several Years, if he be not very profuse in the Use of it.
>
> *Mist's Weekly Journal*, 29 April 1721

The Specifick Injection, or Lotion, advertised in the *London Evening-Post* for 3 October 1734, 'which in 19 Years private Practice has cured 673 Gonorrheas or Claps', promises to cure 'all the dismal attendants of impure Embraces, as dribbling of Semen at Stool or Urine … nay, even if you piss thro' a Dozen Holes'.

Dr Nelson cautions those readers of the *Craftsman* for 4 November 1738 who 'have only some Relicks of the Disease, or but suspect their Blood has got a snatch of the Taint' that they,

> should never venture to marry if they are single, or meddle with their Wives, if

*At the Hand and Face in Water-Lane, Black-Fryars, near Apothecaries-Hall, liveth* RICHARD ROCK, *Practitioner in Physick and Surgery,*

WHO has a ſafe and ſpeedy Method of Curing the French Diſeaſe in all its various Symptoms, viz. nocturnal and diurnal Pains in the Head, Shoulders, Arms, Hips, Legs, Shin-Bones and Small of the Back, a painful Swelling in the Teſticles and Groin, Buboes, Shankers, Excreſcences of divers Sorts about the Anus, Ulcers in the Privites, Phymoſis, Paraphymoſis, with a Running between the Glands, eating Ulcers in the Mouth Throat, Noſe or Palate; Scabs, large Blotches, Itching, with Heats, Inflammations, Faintneſs, old Gleets, Carbuncles, or fleſhy Excreſcences in the Urethra, cauſed by a Relaxation of the internal Parts from the Corroſiveneſs of the Venereal Running, creating a Difficulty in making Water and running with Streams, I promiſe (under God) to make a perfect Cure in a ſhort Time; thoſe that have lately got a Clap, running of the Reins, Heat, ſcalding of the Urine, I doubt not of curing in a few Days, without Hindrance of Buſineſs or the Knowledge of their Bedfellows, with pleaſant Remedies, and, in ſome Caſes, without Phyſick.

N. B. The Doctor gives his Attendance from Seven in the Morning till Ten at Night: his Medicines may be ſent to any Part of England only on writing the Caſe.

He has likewiſe a ſpeedy Cure for the Itch or Leproſy, and gives his Advice gratis.

**6.2** VD cure, *London Evening Post*, 6 June 1734

> married, till they are sure they are safe, as they most certainly will be, upon their taking only a Pot or two of Dr. Nelson's Most Wonderful Panacea.

Many quack remedies claimed to cure a bewildering range of unrelated ailments. It was as if a blindfolded man, who had been given a medical dictionary, opened the pages at random, and was asked to prick at the entries with a pin. The Famous Italian Bolus advertised in *Mist's* in the early 1720s claims to cure 'Venereal Disease, Scurvy and Rheumatism', which presumably allows the pox-ridden to pretend they are only buying it for their rheumatism. More ambitious is Albinolo's Ointment, which advertised in the *Halifax Guardian* in 1839 that it would cure 'Cancer, Scrofula, Eruptions of the Skin, Cholera, Plague, Contagious Diseases, Wounds of every description, Chilblains and various other Diseases'.

I am not sure how effective these medicines were. The Irish logic in the 1759 advertisement for a cure for venereal disease in *Pue's Occurrences*, a Dublin newspaper, probably gets closest to the truth: 'The Efficacy of which Medicine is certain and safe, that one out of a Thousand cannot fail of being cured' – which was tough luck on the other nine hundred and ninety nine.

Richard Steele described the quack medicine men as 'imposters and murderers'. Some were also known as 'the grave-diggers' friend'. There was more than an element of truth in this. Some of the best-selling pills and powders contained arsenic or antimony. They killed the disease by killing the patient. Oliver Goldsmith's death is thought to have been accelerated by the use of Dr James's Powders. Even so, there was less risk of an untimely death from taking quack medicine than from placing oneself in the hands of the surgeons.

In the 1730s, the *Grub-street Journal* ran a campaign against Joshua Ward's Pill and Drop by printing the case histories of those alleged to have been made worse or even killed as a result of taking Ward's medicines: 'A single *Pill*, taken by a poor Fellow for a venereal nocturnal Head-ach, after a most violent vomiting for some Hours, gave near 70 Stools, with the most imminent Danger' (14 December 1734).

The *Grub-street Journal* suggested that the war on the continent could be settled by giving three pills each to the soldiers on both sides; the side that withstood them the best should be declared the winner. It also suggested, at a time when suicides were buried at the crossroads and their property was forfeited to the state so their next of kin could not inherit, that Dr Ward's medicines could be used as an inconspicuous but certain form of suicide. After a series of attacks of this nature, a correspondent urged the *Journal* to desist:

> The learned Mr *Ward's* Abilities and great Success are too well known amongst the Undertakers, Coffin-Makers, and Sextons of this City to be blasted by your

slanderous Pen. Let the Man alone, and if he has the Art to kill, by one *Drop* only, while others must fill Vials, and sometimes quart Bottles, before they can do it, it shews him to be the greater Artist. You may say your Pleasure; but I say, a *Quack* is a very useful Person in a Common-wealth, especially when it is too populous.

*Grub-street Journal*, 9 January 1735

Stories about the uncertain effects of quack medicine continued through the century:

The following odd affair happened last week at the West end of the town: A person of fortune having taken a medicine prepared by his apothecary, was soon seized with a violent sickness, and being convinced there had been some mistake in the composition, ordered the apothecary to attend him, who no sooner came than the patient locked the chamber door, drew his sword, and pouring out the remaining draught, obliged the apothecary to drink it; and it is said they both still continue very ill.

*The Craftsman; or Say's Weekly Journal*, 21 February 1767

## Books, Pamphlets and Magazines

Next to advertisements for quack doctors' medicines, publishers' notices are the most numerous. Early-eighteenth-century newspapers advertise a wide range of books from the sacred to the profane. Advertisements for books of sermons mingle with advertisements for books like *Onania*:

Newly published, the 5th Edition of

Onania; or the heinous Sin of Self-Pollution, and all its frightful Consequences in both Sexes considered; with Spiritual and Physical Advice to those who have already injured themselves by that abominable Practice. To which is subjoined, a Letter from a Lady to the Author, (very curious) concerning the Use and Abuse of the Marriage-Bed; with the Author's Answer … The whole necessary to be perused by all Sorts of People of both Sexes, old as well as young, guilty or not guilty, in the Opinion of several learned and pious Divines, as their Letters inserted shew.

*Mist's Weekly Journal*, 20 August 1720

Other examples of the literature advertised in newspapers include:

ROUND ABOUT OUR COAL FIRE: Or, CHRISTMAS ENTERTAINMENTS. Containing Christmas Gambols, Tropes, Figures, &c. with abundance of Fiddle-Faddle-Stuff; such as Stories of Fairies, Ghosts, Hobgoblins, Witches, Bull-beggars, Raw-heads and Bloody-bones, merry Plays, &c. for the Diversion of Company on a cold Winter Evening, besides several curious Pieces relating to the History of old Father Christmas: setting forth what Hospitality has been, and what it is now. Very proper to be read in all Families. Adorned with many curious Cuts.

*Craftsman*, 15 January 1731/32

Just Published. Price SIX Pence.
The Third Edition Of
A CAP.
TEN to *One* but it FITS.
*When* CAPS *Amongst A Crowd Are Thrown*
*What Fits* YOU *best, take for* YOUR *Own.*

Being Suited to *All* the Following Cases. – Viz.
A *Venereal Running, Heat & Smarting of Urine, Cordee*, a GLEET, or other *Weakness*, Either in the Back, Or, *Loins*, Or in the *Seminal*, Or *Urinary Vessels, Sore Urinary Part, Scrotum, Or Groin*, Also of *Night Work*, and LOOSE *Women.*
And How A Person May be *Severely Infected* by An *Entire* SOUND *Woman*, Let Her Say Whatever SHE Will.
With a *Sure Remedy* Against being *Deceived* SO, Another Time.
And An Immediate Riddance of Venereal Warts, and *Crab Vermin.*
Also of *Self Defilement*, (that Accursed *School of Wickedness*). With a Sure Preservative against EVER Doing that most Wretched Unhappy Action again, as long as they Live.
And How to Renew MANHOOD, and *Virility* almost Ruined by it.
And of *Preposterous Venery* with *Machines.* With the *Machine* itself, and its UGLY Use Described, and the Dangers of it Discovered.
All which Articles are Distinctly Treated in this Book, but with such a *Freedom of Expression*, as is in PRIVATE Only to be Read.
This Book is Sold Up One Pair of Stairs, At the Sign of the Famous ANODYNE NECKLACE for Children's *Teeth, Fits, Fevers, Convulsions*, &c. Over Against Devreux Court, Without Temple Bar.

*Common Sense*, 3 April 1742

The LIFE and OPINIONS of
JEREMIAH KUNASTROKIAS,
Doctor of Physic.
(Adorned with a curious Genealogical Frontispiece)

*Lloyd's Evening Post*, 4 July to 7 July 1760

Surprisingly, Robert Raikes, proprietor of the *Gloucester Journal* and the founder of the Sunday School movement, saw fit to accept an advertisement for *Harris's List of Covent Garden Ladies*, a guide to the whores of London, in 1761.

The popularity of the weekly journals in the 1720s and the magazines in the 1730s showed that there was a strong market for serial publications. People who might balk at the idea of spending several shillings, or indeed pounds, on a book were quite happy to spend sixpence on a magazine. The publishers identified this market, and from around 1724 onwards began to issue part-works in quantity. This enabled the buyer to spread the cost of the purchase over several months, and sometimes years, and it allowed the publisher to spread his investment as well, as he had only to finance the printing and distribution of one part at a time. In some cases a limited number of copies of the publication would be issued complete in book form and the remainder would be printed in stages as a part-work. Part-works were particularly popular in the provinces where they could be sent cheaply through the post in the same way as newspapers and magazines, or distributed by the printers of provincial newspapers.

Part-works were extensively advertised in the tri-weekly evening posts, which had a strong circulation in the provinces, and in the provincial newspapers themselves. The *General Evening Post* for 29 November 1755 has six advertisements for part-works, including Samuel Johnson's *Dictionary*, to be published in 165 weekly parts at the affordable price of 6d. each, or the whole work 'compleat, in 2 vols fol. Price 4l. 10s. bound'.

The advertisements also show that the 'instant book', quickly produced with minimal effort to cash in on some newsworthy event, has its forebears in Grub Street. Shortly after the great storm of 26–27 November 1703 that destroyed the Eddystone Lighthouse, killed the Bishop of Bath and Wells when his house collapsed, and was said to have drowned thousands of people by the flooding of the Thames and the Severn, as well as at sea, Daniel Defoe placed this advertisement in *The London Gazette* for 6 December 1703:

> To preserve the Remembrance of the late dreadful Tempest, an exact and faithful Collection is preparing of the most remarkable Disasters which happened on that Occasion, with the Places where, and Persons concerned, whether at Sea or on Shore. For the perfecting so good a Work, 'tis humbly recommended by the Author to all Gentlemen of the Clergy, or others, who have made any Observations on the Calamity, that they would transmit as distinct an Account as possible, of what they have observed, to the Undertakers, directed to John Nutt near Stationers-Hall, London. All Gentlemen that are pleased to send any such Accounts, are desired to write no Particulars but what they are well satisfied to be true, and to set their names to the Observations they send, which the Undertakers of the Work promise shall be faithfully recorded, and the Favour publickly acknowledged.

By the beginning of the nineteenth century, when newspapers had become the preserve of the comfortable classes, auctioneers had overtaken quack medicine vendors and booksellers as the biggest advertisers. The best part of one page of the four-page *Morning Chronicle* for 6 September 1814 is taken up by auctioneers' advertisements, mainly for sales of property, including the entire village of Great Tew.

## Transport

Advertisements of the eighteenth and nineteenth centuries illustrate the social and cultural changes of those two hundred years. Take transport, for example. Advertisements trace the development from the pioneer days of coaching when the condition of the roads was such that the York and London stagecoaches considered it an achievement to perform the journey in five days, 'which is a day less than usual' (*Daily Advertiser*, 5 April 1734). The *Daily Advertiser* for 4 April 1758 carries an advertisement for what must have been an exciting ride through the night, in the hands of an exhausted coachman, braving the dangers of Hounslow and Bagshot Heaths:

> Blandford Machine, by Robert Porter, begins flying next Sunday Night, sets out from the Rose Inn at Holborn-Bridge, London, every Sunday Night at Eleven o'Clock, gets to the Antelope in Salisbury on Monday Evening, and to the Crown in Blandford on Tuesday in the Forenoon, stays there till One, and returns the same Day to Salisbury, and to London on the Wednesday; sets out again from London every Wednesday Night at Eleven, and gets to Salisbury on Thursday, and to Blandford on Friday in the Forenoon, and returns to Salisbury the same Day, and to London on Saturday. Porter drives himself, and calls at the Black Bear and White Horse Cellar, Piccadilly, going and coming.

During the coaching age proper, roads had improved and advertisers in the London papers provided long lists of coaches leaving the London coaching inns with their destinations, while rival coaching proprietors fought each other in the advertising columns of the provincial papers. In the nineteenth century, advertisements reflected the growth of the railways (the offer of shares in railway companies, the appearance of timetables in the advertising columns of local papers – Figure 6.3 – and advertisements for excursions to the races or the seaside) and the introduction of private mechanized transport in the form of the penny-farthing bicycle and ultimately the safety bicycle.

## Entertainment

In the brief wave of moral panic following the two London earthquakes of 1750, the Bishop of London, in his *Letter to the Clergy and People of London and Westminster On Occasion of the late Earthquakes*, complained:

> While I was writing this I cast my Eye upon a News-Paper of the Day, and counted no less than fifteen Advertisements for *Plays, Operas, Musick*, and *Dancing*, for Meetings at *Gardens*, for *Cock-fighting, Prize-fighting*, &c. Should this Paper (as many of our News-Papers do) go abroad, what an Idea must it give to all the Churches abroad, of the Manner in which *Lent* is kept in this Protestant Country?

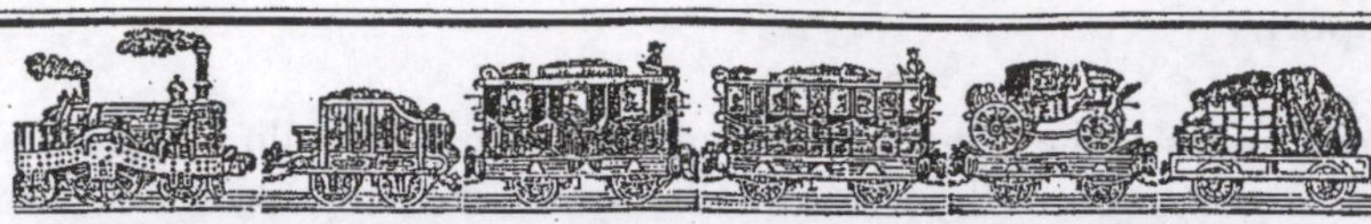

# NORFOLK RAILWAY.

## OPENING OF THE LINE.

THE Public are respectfully informed that this Railway will be opened in connexion with the Cambridge Line, on WEDNESDAY, the 9th JULY, for Passenger Traffic and Light Goods, to and from London, Norwich, and Yarmouth.

The Trains will run as follows :—

| DOWN. | A.M. | A.M. | A.M. | A.M. | P.M. |
|---|---|---|---|---|---|
| | H. M. | H. M. | H. M. | H. M. | H. M. |
| From LONDON ...................... | — | — | 8 0 | 11 30 | 5 0 |
| " ELY............................ | — | 7 30 | 11 5 | 1 50 | 7 50 |
| " NORWICH.................... | 8 30 | 10 45 | 2 15 | 4 30 | 11 0 |
| Arriving at YARMOUTH........... | 9 15 | 11 30 | 3 0 | 5 15 | 11 45 |

| UP. | A.M. | A.M. | P.M. | M.P. | P.M. |
|---|---|---|---|---|---|
| | H. M. | H. M. | H. M. | H. M. | H. M. |
| From YARMOUTH.................. | 5 30 | 9 30 | 3 15 | 6 30 | 8 30 |
| " NORWICH..................... | 6 45 | 11 0 | 4 30 | 8 0 | 9 15 |
| " ELY............................ | 9 0 | 12 50 | 6 45 | 11 30 | — |
| Arriving at LONDON ............ | 12 30 | 3 31 | 10 0 | — | — |

### FARES FOR STOPPING TRAINS.

| LONDON | 1st Class. | 2d Class. | 3d Class. |
|---|---|---|---|
| To NORWICH ...................... | £1 2 6 | £0 16 0 | £0 10 6 |
| To YARMOUTH .................... | 1 6 0 | 0 18 6 | 0 11 9 |

### FARES FOR QUICK TRAINS.

| LONDON | 1st Class. | 2d Class. |
|---|---|---|
| To NORWICH ...................... | £1 7 0 | £0 18 0 |
| To YARMOUTH .................... | 1 10 6 | 1 0 6 |

Fish and Light Goods will be conveyed to London by the 6 . 30 P.M. Up Train from Yarmouth, and arrive in London at 3 . 30 A.M.

Trains for Heavy Goods will be put on shortly.

By Order, RICHARD TILL,
Secretary.

**6.3** Railway timetable, *Bury and Suffolk Herald*, 25 June 1845

… We have turned this Season appointed for serious Reflexions, and Humiliation of Body and Spirit, into a Time of Mirth and Jollity, of Musick, Dancing, and riotous Living.

The advertisement columns of the newspapers give some idea of the variety of public entertainments on offer. The following advertisement in the

*Craftsman* for 2 December 1738 encapsulates the, often inappropriate, juxtaposition of the high-brow and the low-brow that was typical of eighteenth century theatre:

AT THE
THEATRE ROYAL in DRURY-LANE
on Thursday the 14th of December, will be presented,
The Tragedy of
HAMLET Prince of *Denmark*
With several Entertainments of Dancing.

None the less, this mixture of high taste and low taste seems to have given good value:

SALISBURY THEATRE
Will open on Wednesday Evening the 17th Inst. with (not acted here these two years) Dr Goldsmith's Comedy, called

SHE STOOPS TO CONQUER;
Or, the MISTAKES of a NIGHT.
After the Play will be exhibited
TUMBLING, ROPE DANCING
And Astonishing FEATS of ACTIVITY

By those capital performers Messrs MENUIE, DUPUIS, and RICHE, from Sadler's Wells; and the same were engaged at the Bath and Bristol Theatres in the course of last winter.
After which Mr SCALIONI will exhibit the wonderful and astonishing

DANCING DOGS
Being the same as performed last Summer at Sadler's Wells upwards of Two Hundred successive Nights.

Boxes 3s. – Pit 2s. – Gallery 1s.

*Salisbury and Winchester Journal*, 15 November 1784

Newspapers, in particular daily papers, were providing a useful service to the theatre-going public by printing advertisements at the head of the first column of the front page showing the cast lists of the plays in the main London theatres. As it was considered that many people bought newspapers solely for this purpose, newspapers paid the theatres for the privilege of printing their advertisements – the *Public Advertiser* paying £100 per year. With the loss of many original playbills, newspaper advertisements have become an invaluable record of the theatrical history of the eighteenth century.

Like the theatre, musical performances also contained a mixture of the serious and the sensational, as in this notice in the *Gazetteer and London Daily Advertiser* for 13 March 1762:

> For one night only, by particular desire of several persons of distinction, for the benefit of Mr TENDUCCI, at the New Theatre in the Hay-Market, on Tuesday next the 16th Instant, will be performed a concert of vocal and instrumental music. The vocal parts by Mr Tenducci and Mr Peretti who will sing (by Dr Arne's permission) the favourite songs in Artaxerexes. The first violin with a concerto and a solo by Mr Piffet, (being his first public performance in England.) A concerto on the German flute by Mr Florio, and a solo on the violoncello by Mr Siprutini. After which will be performed a pantomime, and a grand dance, in which will be introduced the real ghost of Cock-lane. The child itself shall appear on a table, uncovered; then disappear, and appear again; then (by the conjuror's art) the room shall change to a beautiful transparency of Chinese fireworks, without any crackers, bounces, noise, smell of powder, or the least possibility of danger or accident to the spectators; the whole appearing to them as a beautiful variety of shining colours.

Travelling showmen placed advertisements in the papers of the towns they were visiting:

> *This is to acquaint the Ladies and Gentlemen*
>
> THAT Mr. POWEL, the celebrated FIRE EATER, is come to this City and hopes the Gentlemen &c. will favour him with their Company, this and the following Evenings this Week at the White Hart in the Southgate-street; where he will exhibit his extraordinary and astonishing Performances which much surpass any Thing he ever performed here before.
>
> He will exhibit the following Articles, 1st. He eats red-hot Coals out of the Fire as natural as Bread. 2dly, He licks with his naked tongue red-hot Tobacco Pipes flaming with Brimstone … 5thly, He fills his Mouth with red-hot Charcoal, and broils a Slice of Beef or Mutton on his Tongue; and any Person may blow the Fire with a Pair of Bellows at the same Time. And lastly, He takes a Quantity of Rosin, Pitch, Bees-wax, Sealing-wax, Brimstone, Allum and Lead, melts them together over a Chaffing-Dish of Coals, and eats the said Combustibles with a Spoon, as natural as a Porringer of Broth, (which he calls his Dish of Soup) to the great and agreeable Surprize of all the Spectators. Every Article above mentioned is justly performed without Fallacy.
>
> He displaces Teeth or Stumps of Teeth so easy as scarce to be felt. – This Advertisement does not mention half that he performs.
>
> *Glocester Journal*, 3 February 1766

The rough nature of country entertainment is illustrated by advertisements such as this from the *Reading Mercury* for 18 July 1774:

> This is to give Notice, to all Gentleman Gamesters, and others, that CHAPPEL

ROW REVEL will be on Monday the 1st of August; and for the Encouragement of the Gamesters, there will be given, an exceedingly good GOLD LACED HAT, of Twenty-seven Shillings Value, to be PLAYED at CUDGELS for; the Man that breaks most Heads to have the Prize; the Blood to run an Inch. Also Two Shillings for every Man that breaks a Head, for the first Twelve Heads that are broken.

**Situations Vacant, Lonely Hearts and Agony Columns**

The eighteenth-century equivalent of the situations vacant column offer a host of opportunities, including joining the crew of a privateer, becoming an apprentice to a surgeon, and sometimes both at the same time. In the provincial papers there is sometimes a rare glimpse of the pay on offer. It is clear that no one was going to make a fortune as a teacher in Shropshire. The post of teacher at Oswestry Charity School is advertised at £6 per year (*Aris's Birmingham Gazette*, 11 March 1761) and for a 'School Master to teach the Children to Read' at the Orphan Hospital, Shrewsbury, 'The Salary will be Ten Pounds per Ann. with Diet, Washing and Lodging' (*Aris's Birmingham Gazette*, 27 July 1761). The post of Apothecary at Birmingham General Hospital is advertised at £35 per year, and the post of Governor of the Wolverhampton Workhouse at £30 per year (*Aris's Birmingham Gazette*, 7 March 1785). At the lower end of the scale, a vacancy for a porter at Salisbury Infirmary offers £8 per year (*Salisbury and Winchester Journal*, 4 April 1785). The following are typical situations vacant advertisements of their time:

WANTED
A Servant Maid;
She must be able to boil and roast, and keep a clean House, must have had the Small-Pox, and produce a good Character from her last Place.

*Western Flying-Post*, 26 October 1761

WANTED
A Young Lad, from 14 to 18 Years old, to run of Errands, clean Knives and Shoes &c. and do other Work in and about House; he must have had the Small-Pox, and bring a good Character for Diligence, Honesty and Sobriety.

*Northampton Mercury*, 10 January 1763

Advertisements from those seeking employment are common. At the time when it was not safe for young men to walk the streets for fear of being kidnapped by press gangs, this advertisement in the *Daily Advertiser* for 20 March 1758 is particularly sad:

WANTS a Wet-Nurse's Place, a young Woman, Twenty Years of age, has had the Small-Pox, and is willing to serve any good Family. My Husband being press'd away from me obliges me to offer as above. Any one may see the Child, if required, being a very proper one. Can have a good Character. Please to direct for N.Z. at Mrs Child's, in Neal's Court, in the Minories.

The many advertisements seeking the return of runaway apprentices raise the question whether they were maltreated starvelings escaping from an unjust or cruel master, or idle apprentices setting off for a life of crime. I would liked to have known more about Mary Lee, alias Baxter,

run away from her Master, the 10th of August last, with a dark bay Mare. She is a lusty tall Woman, pretty red Complection, a Dimple in her Chin, dark brown Hair, apt to drink and smoak, sometimes she'll sit on the Mare's back and sing Ballads.

*Evening Post*, 4 September 1714

Another form of situations vacant advertisement was placed by lonely hearts. It is unlikely that the following lonely heart received many responses:

TO THE FAIR SEX

A PERSON of Character, 26 Years of Age, of a genteel profession, and of moderate fortune, wishes to engage in the Hymenial State, with an agreeable, good-tempered LADY, in AGE inferior to himself, in FORTUNE equal, or nearly so; but, in GOODNESS, as superior as Emulation CAN excite. – One having no Objection to enter a Public Line, or Shop-keeping, would be preferred; And it would be no Object of Denial, if she happens to have a fortune of MORE Capital than required. – Any Lady this may suit, may depend on a punctual Answer by addressing (Post paid) for T.H. to be left at the Printers till called for.

*Aris's Birmingham Gazette*, 7 March 1785

The personal column of the *Times*, the so-called 'agony column', contained a jumble of peculiar paragraphs that allow the imagination of the casual reader to roam free. As Sherlock Holmes remarked to Watson in *The Adventure of the Red Circle*, 'What a chorus of groans, cries, and bleatings! What a rag-bag of singular happenings! But surely the most valuable hunting-ground that was ever given to a student of the unusual!'

Are these coded messages the work of spies, or criminals planning the robbery of the century, or are they simply the work of married lovers arranging their next illicit tryst?

S.B. is a STRICT Disciplinarian, and not afraid of a rather unruly Pupil.
21 June 1845

NO DOORMAT TONIGHT
24 March 1849

NORTH KENT LINE, Sept. 20, 7.10 p.m. Up. – Dear Harriet, was it you, or your ghost? Reply. – Blackheath Park.
22 September 1854

W.P. – You were SEEN LAST NIGHT. Hawks are abroad. – 25th July.
27 July 1855

J.B.R. The MONKEY is HOME. Where is the Man of Ross. G.G.
6 October 1855

HAMPSTEAD HEATH ENCLOSURE. Look out! The Weasel is not asleep!
1 April 1856

THE BLACK VELVET DRESS, which was sent back by rail and coach in a very compressed parcel slightly covered with brown paper, and unaccompanied by any letter, has arrived as safely as under the circumstances was possible.
24 February 1857

A slightly less obscure announcement appeared in the *Times* on 10 September 1861:

S to L, the 2 Rs and W. CHARLES URQUARDT NEWPORT TINSLEY has not suffered from the eels.

This unsubtle disguise was sufficient to fool the management of the *Times* into accepting the message, which, when converted into an acronym, must have offended most of its Victorian readers. But it must have been a great relief to L, the 2 Rs and W to know that S hadn't given them the eels, although I do wonder whether L, the 2 Rs and W were hitherto aware of each other's existence.

## Public Apologies

Perhaps the most amusing type of personal advertisement is the public apology that was prevalent in the provincial papers in the eighteenth century. They were inserted to publicly retract a slanderous statement as an alternative to prosecution. If anything, they gave wider circulation to an accusation, which was probably made only once as a jest one drunken night and forgotten the next morning by those few who had heard it. The Bristol publican who insisted that this apology was inserted in *Farley's Bristol Newspaper* on 7 August 1736 might have been better advised not to have given wider publicity to the admission that

… I did say in the presence of several people, That Antony Collier, living at the Sign of the Ship and Dove in the Pithay, in Bristol, was sent to Newgate for putting LIVE TOADS into his Beer, in order to fine it.

Here are two more examples:

> I THOMAS MARSH, of Wellington in the County of Somerset, being informed that I am charged with declaring and uttering certain defamatory Expressions at the Bell Inn in Taunton to the Prejudice and Disadvantage of Mr. WILLIAM KENNAWAY, late of Wellington, but now of Crewkern in the County aforesaid, Surgeon and Apothecary, do hereby certify the Public, That I could have no Reason or Cause for uttering any thing disrespectfully of the said Mr. Kennaway, whom I verily believe to be a skillful and judicious Person in his Profession, as a Surgeon and Apothecary, and very well qualified and disposed to do Justice, and give Satisfaction to his Patients.
>
> *Western Flying-Post*, 26 October 1761

> WHEREAS I ISAIAH MULLETT, of Shaftsbury, in the County of Dorset, have lately, in a public manner, propagated a scandalous and defamatory report, in the presence and hearing of several persons, that NICHOLAS JOYCE, of the same place, did, some years since, attempt to commit a detestable and unnatural crime with me; which expressions I do hereby own and acknowledge are false, abusive, and groundless, and were spoken and uttered by me without any reason, consideration, or cause, and merely out of wantonness; on which the said Nicholas Joyce hath very justly commenced a prosecution against me; but through the interference of many friends, and my voluntarily begging his pardon, and agreeing to put this advertisement in the Salisbury and Sherborne Papers, he hath withdrawn the prosecution, for which I return him my thanks.
>
> *Salisbury and Winchester Journal*, 15 March 1784

## Alcohol

Provincial advertising papers, the forerunners of today's freesheets, were created to meet the demand for advertising in the provinces. *Gore's Liverpool General Advertiser* (1765–1876; Figure 6.4) is an early example. The issue for 14 February 1793 contains a small section of mainly shipping news, and the rest of the paper is taken up by advertisements. These include 42 shipping advertisements, each with a small woodcut of a sailing vessel. In addition there are advertisements for property auctions, legal notices, lotteries and tontines, magazines, patent medicines, and the Royal Mail Coach, 'with a Guard all the way' which 'goes in THIRTY hours' from Liverpool to the 'Swan With Two Necks, in Lad-Lane, London – Fare 3l.3s.', a considerable advance on the five days it took to travel from York to London sixty years earlier. There are five notices placed by clubs and societies, including the Association of Hair Dressers, protesting about the rise in the price of a quart of ale from 4d. to 5d., resolving

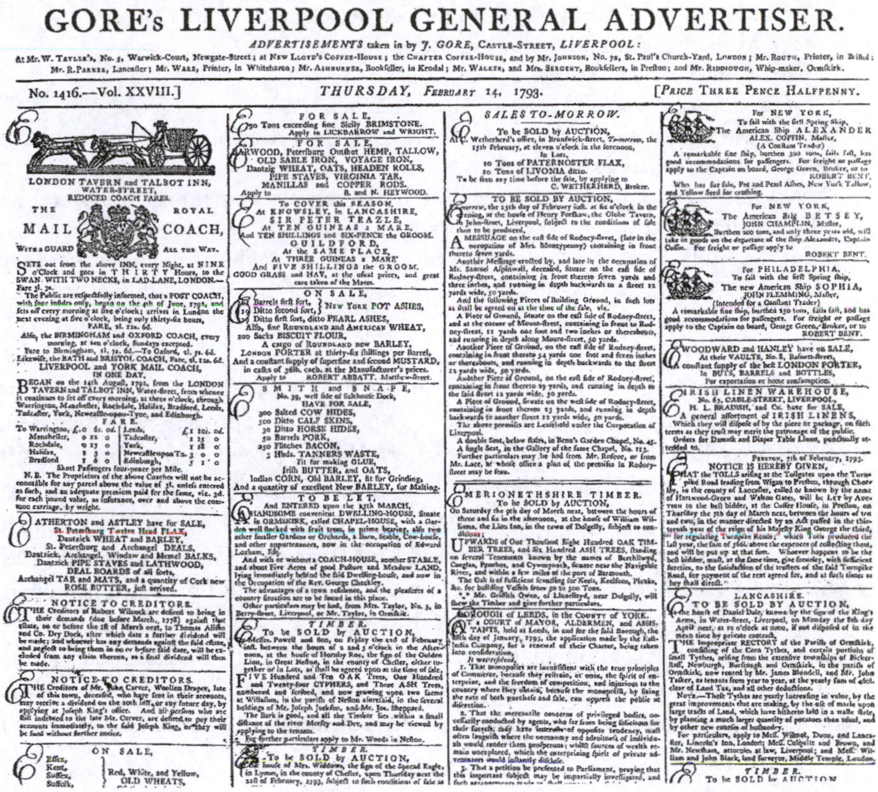

# GORE's LIVERPOOL GENERAL ADVERTISER.

*ADVERTISEMENTS* taken in by *J. GORE*, Castle-Street, *LIVERPOOL*:

At Mr. W. Tayler's, No. 5, Warwick-Court, Newgate-Street; at New Lloyd's Coffee-House; the Chapter Coffee-House, and by Mr. Johnson, No. 72, St. Paul's Church-Yard, London; Mr. Routh, Printer, in Bristol; Mr. R. Parkes, Lancaster; Mr. Ware, Printer, in Whitehaven; Mr. Ashburner, Bookseller, in Kendal; Mr. Walker, and Mrs. Sergent, Booksellers, in Preston; and Mr. Riddiough, Whip-maker, Ormskirk.

No. 1416.—Vol. XXVIII.] *THURSDAY*, February 14, 1793. [*Price* Three Pence Halfpenny.

LONDON TAVERN and TALBOT INN, WATER-STREET,
REDUCED COACH FARES.
THE ROYAL MAIL COACH,
With a GUARD All the Way.

SETS out from the above INN, every Night, at NINE o'Clock and goes in THIRTY Hours, to the SWAN WITH TWO NECKS, in LAD-LANE, LONDON.—Fare 3l. 3s.

The Public are respectfully informed, that a POST COACH, with four insides only, began on the 4th of June, 1792, and sets off every morning at five o'clock; arrives in London the next evening at five o'clock, being only thirty-six hours,
FARE, 2l. 12s. 6d.

Also, the BIRMINGHAM and OXFORD COACH, every morning, at ten o'clock, Sundays excepted.
Fare to Birmingham, 1l. 7s. 6d.—To Oxford, 2l. 5s. 6d.
Likewise, the BATH and BRISTOL COACH, Fare, 2l. 12s. 6d.

LIVERPOOL and YORK MAIL COACH, IN ONE DAY.

BEGAN on the 14th August, 1792, from the LONDON TAVERN and TALBOT INN, Water-street, from whence it continues to set off every morning, at three o'clock, through Warrington, Manchester, Rochdale, Halifax, Bradford, Leeds, Tadcaster, York, Newcastle-upon-Tyne, and Edinburgh.

FARE.

| | £ | s. | d. | | £ | s. | d. |
|---|---|---|---|---|---|---|---|
| To Warrington, | 0 | 6 | 0 | Leeds, | 1 | 10 | 0 |
| Manchester, | 0 | 12 | 0 | Tadcaster, | 1 | 15 | 0 |
| Rochdale, | 0 | 17 | 0 | York, | 1 | 18 | 0 |
| Halifax, | 1 | 3 | 0 | Newcastleupon Ty. | 3 | 0 | 0 |
| Bradford | 1 | 6 | 0 | Edinburgh, | 5 | 1 | 0 |

Short Passengers four-pence per Mile.

N. B. The Proprietors of the above Coaches will not be accountable for any parcel above the value of 5l. unless entered as such, and an adequate premium paid for the same, viz. 3d. for each pound value, as insurance, over and above the common carriage, by weight.

ATHERTON and ASTLEY have for SALE,
St. Petersburg Twelve Head FLAX,
Dantzick WHEAT and BARLEY,
St. Petersburg and Archangel DEALS,
Dantzick, Archangel, Windaw and Memel BALKS,
Dantzick PIPE STAVES and LATHWOOD,
DEAL BOARDS of all sorts,
Archangel TAR and MATS, and a quantity of Cork new ROSE BUTTER, just arrived.

NOTICE TO CREDITORS.

THE Creditors of Robert Wilcock are desired to bring in their demands (due before March, 1778) against that estate, on or before the 1st of March next, to Thomas Alison and Co. Dry Dock, after which date a further dividend will be made; and whoever has any demands against the said estate, and neglect to bring them in on or before said date, will be excluded from any claim thereon, as a final dividend will then be made.

NOTICE TO CREDITORS.

THE Creditors of Mr. John Carver, Woollen Draper, late of this town, deceased, who have sent in their accounts, may receive a dividend on the 20th inst. or any future day, by applying at Joseph King's office. And all persons who are still indebted to the late Mr. Carver, are desired to pay their accounts immediately, to the said Joseph King, or they will be sued without further notice.

ON SALE,
Essex, Kent, Sussex, Suffolk, } Red, White, and Yellow, OLD WHEATS,

FOR SALE,
90 Tons exceeding fine Sicily BRIMSTONE.
Apply to LICKBARROW and WRIGHT.

FOR SALE,
BARWOOD, Petersburg Outshot HEMP, TALLOW,
OLD SABLE IRON, VOYAGE IRON,
Dantzig WHEAT, OATS, HEADEN ROLLS,
PIPE STAVES, VIRGINIA TAR,
MANILLAS and COPPER RODS.
Apply to B. and N. HEYWOOD.

To COVER this SEASON,
At KNOWSLEY, in LANCASHIRE,
SIR PETER TEAZLE,
At TEN GUINEAS a MARE,
And TEN SHILLINGS and SIX-PENCE the GROOM.
GUILDFORD,
At the SAME PLACE,
At THREE GUINEAS a MARE
And FIVE SHILLINGS the GROOM.
GOOD GRASS and HAY, at the usual prices, and great care taken of the Mares.

ON SALE,
[illegible] Barrels first sort, } New York POT ASHES,
19 Ditto second sort, }
[illegible] Ditto first sort, ditto PEARL ASHES,
Also, fine Roundland and American WHEAT,
200 Sacks BISCUIT FLOUR,
A cargo of Roundland new BARLEY,
London PORTER at thirty-six shillings per Barrel,
And a constant supply of superfine and second MUSTARD, in casks of 36lb. each, at the Manufacturer's prices.
Apply to ROBERT ABBATT, Matthew-street.

SMITH and SNAPE,
No. 39, west side of Salthouse Dock,
HAVE FOR SALE,
300 Salted COW HIDES,
500 Ditto CALF SKINS,
30 Ditto HORSE HIDES,
50 Barrels PORK,
250 Flitches BACON,
3 Hhds. TANNERS WASTE,
Fit for making GLUE,
Irish BUTTER, and OATS,
Indian CORN, Old BARLEY, fit for Grinding,
And a quantity of excellent New BARLEY, for Malting.

TO BE LET,
And ENTERED upon the 25th MARCH,

A HANDSOME convenient DWELLING-HOUSE, situate in ORMSKIRK, called CHAPEL-HOUSE, with a Garden well stocked with fruit trees, in prime bearing, also two other smaller Gardens or Orchards, a Barn, Stable, Cow-house, and other appurtenances, now in the occupation of Edward Loxham, Esq.

And with or without a COACH-HOUSE, another STABLE, and about Five Acres of good Pasture and Meadow LAND, lying immediately behind the said Dwelling-house, and now in the Occupation of the Rev. George Checkley.

The advantages of a town residence, and the pleasures of a country situation are to be found in this place.

Other particulars may be had, from Mrs. Taylor, No. 3, in Berry-street, Liverpool, or Mr. Taylor, in Ormskirk.

*TIMBER.*
To be SOLD by AUCTION,

By Messrs. Powell and Son, on Friday the 22d of February inst. between the hours of 2 and 5 o'clock in the Afternoon, at the house of Hornby Roe, the sign of the Golden Lion, in Great Neston, in the county of Chester, either together or in Lots, as shall be agreed upon at the time of sale,

FIVE Hundred and Ten OAK Trees, One Hundred and Twenty-four CYPHERS, and Three ASH Trees, numbered and scribed, and now growing upon two farms at Willaston, in the parish of Neston aforesaid, in the several holdings of Mr. Joseph Jackson, and Mr. Jos. Sheppard.

The Bark is good, and all the Timber lies within a small distance of the river Mersey and Dee, and may be viewed by applying to the tenants.

For further particulars apply to Mr. Woods in Neston.

*TIMBER.*
To be SOLD by AUCTION,

At the house of Mrs. Widdows, the sign of the Spread Eagle, in Lymm, in the county of Chester, upon Thursday next the 21st of February, 1793, subject to such conditions of sale as

*SALES TO-MORROW.*

To be SOLD by AUCTION,

At C. Wetherherd's office, in Brunswick-street, *To-morrow*, the 15th February, at eleven o'clock in the forenoon,
In Lots,
10 Tons of PATERNOSTER FLAX,
10 Tons of LIVONIA ditto.
To be seen any time before the sale, by applying to
C. WETHERHERD, Broker.

TO BE SOLD BY AUCTION,

To-morrow, the 15th day of February inst. at six o'clock in the evening, at the house of Henry Forshaw, the Globe Tavern, in John-street, Liverpool, subject to the conditions of sale then to be produced,

A MESSUAGE on the east side of Rodney-street, (late in the occupation of Mrs. Moneypenny) containing in front thereto seven yards.

Another Messuage erected by, and late in the occupation of Mr. Samuel Aspinwall, deceased, situate on the east side of Rodney-street, containing in front thereto seven yards and three inches, and running in depth backwards to a street 12 yards wide, 50 yards.

And the following Pieces of Building Ground, in such lots as shall be agreed on at the time of the sale, viz.

A Piece of Ground, situate on the east side of Rodney-street, and at the corner of Mount-street, containing in front to Rodney-street, 11 yards one foot and two inches or thereabouts, and running in depth along Mount-street, 50 yards.

Another Piece of Ground, on the east side of Rodney-street, containing in front thereto 54 yards one foot and seven inches or thereabouts, and running in depth backwards to the street 12 yards wide, 50 yards.

Another Piece of Ground, on the east side of Rodney-street, containing in front thereto 29 yards, and running in depth to the said street 12 yards wide, 50 yards.

A Piece of Ground, situate on the west side of Rodney-street, containing in front thereto 23 yards, and running in depth backwards to another street 12 yards wide, 50 yards.

The above premises are Leasehold under the Corporation of Liverpool.

A double Seat, below stairs, in Benn's Garden Chapel, No. 45.

A single Seat, in the Gallery of the same Chapel, No. 113.

Further particulars may be had from Mr. Roscoe, or from Mr. Lace, at whose office a plan of the premises in Rodney-street may be seen.

MERIONETHSHIRE TIMBER.
To be SOLD by AUCTION,

On Saturday the 9th day of March next, between the hours of three and six in the afternoon, at the house of William Williams, the Lion Inn, in the town of Dolgelly, subject to conditions;

UPWARDS of One Thousand Eight Hundred OAK TIMBER TREES, and Six Hundred ASH TREES, standing on several Tenements known by the names of Berthllwyd, Caeglas, Penrhos, and Cywmynach, situate near the Navigable River, and within a few miles of the port of Barmouth.

The Oak is of sufficient scantling for Keels, Keelsons, Planks, &c. for building Vessels from 50 to 300 Tons.

*** Mr. Griffith Owen, of Llanelltyd, near Dolgelly, will shew the Timber and give further particulars.

BOROUGH of LEEDS, in the County of YORK.

AT a COURT of MAYOR, ALDERMEN, and ASSISTANTS, held at Leeds, in and for the said Borough, the 28th day of January, 1793, the application made by the East-India Company, for a renewal of their Charter, being taken into consideration,

*It was resolved,*

1. That monopolies are inconsistent with the true principles of Commerce, because they restrain, at once, the spirit of enterprize, and the freedom of competition, and injurious to the country where they obtain, because the monopolist, by fixing the rate of both purchase and sale, can oppress the public at discretion.

2. That the mercantile concerns of privileged bodies, necessarily conducted by agents, who far from being solicitous for their success, may have interests of opposite tendency, must often languish where the oeconomy and adroitness of individuals would render them prosperous; whilst sources of wealth remain unexplored, which the enterprizing spirit of private adventurers would instantly disclose.

3. That a petition be presented to Parliament, praying that this important subject may be impartially investigated, and such arrangements made as shall

For NEW YORK,
To sail with the first Spring Ship,
The American Ship ALEXANDER
ALEX. COFFIN, Master,
(A Constant Trader)

A remarkable fine ship, burthen 300 tons, sails fast, has good accommodations for passengers. For freight or passage apply to the Captain on board, George Green, Broker, or to
ROBERT BENT,

Who has for sale, Pot and Pearl Ashes, New York Tallow, and Yellow Seed for crushing.

For NEW YORK,
The American Brig BETSEY,
JOHN CHAMPLIN, Master,
Burthen 200 tons, and only three years old, will take in goods on the departure of the ship Alexander, Captain Coffin. For freight or passage apply to
ROBERT BENT.

For PHILADELPHIA,
To sail with the first Spring ship,
The new American Ship SOPHIA,
JOHN FLEMMING, Master,
(Intended for a Constant Trader)

A remarkable fine ship, burthen 250 tons, sails fast, and has good accommodations for passengers. For freight or passage apply to the Captain on board, George Green, Broker, or to
ROBERT BENT.

WOODWARD and HANLEY have on SALE,
At their VAULTS, No. 8, Basnett-street,
A constant supply of the best LONDON PORTER,
In BUTS, BARRELS and BOTTLES,
For exportation or home consumption.

IRISH LINEN WAREHOUSE,
No. 67, CABLE-STREET, LIVERPOOL,
H. L. BRADISH, and Co. have for SALE,
A general assortment of IRISH LINENS,
Which they will dispose of by the piece or package, on such terms as they trust may merit the patronage of the public.

Orders for Damask and Diaper Table Linen, punctually attended to.

Preston, 7th of February, 1793.
NOTICE IS HEREBY GIVEN,

THAT the TOLLS arising at the Tollgates upon the Turnpike Road leading from Wigan to Preston, through Chorley, in the county of Lancaster, called or known by the name of Hartwood-Green and Walton Gates, will be Let by Auction to the best bidder, at the Coffee House, in Preston, on Thursday the 7th day of March next, between the hours of ten and two; in the manner directed by an Act passed in the thirteenth year of the reign of his Majesty King George the third, "for regulating Turnpike Roads;" which Tolls produced the last year, the sum of 566l. above the expences of collecting them, and will be put up at that sum. Whoever happens to be the best bidder, must, at the same time, give security, with sufficient sureties, to the satisfaction of the trustees of the said Turnpike Road, for payment of the rent agreed for, and at such times as they shall direct.

LANCASHIRE.
TO BE SOLD BY AUCTION,

At the house of Daniel Dale, known by the sign of the King's Arms, in Water-street, Liverpool, on Monday the 8th day April next, at 12 o'clock at noon, if not disposed of in the mean time by private contract,

THE Impropriate RECTORY of the Parish of Ormskirk, consisting of the Corn Tythes, and certain portions of small Tythes, arising from the extensive townships of Bickerstaff, Newburgh, Burscough and Ormskirk, in the parish of Ormskirk, now rented by Mr. James Blundell, and Mr. John Talker, as tenants from year to year, at the yearly sum of 460l. clear of Land Tax, and all other deductions.

Note.—These Tythes are yearly increasing in value, by the great improvements that are making, by the use of marle upon large tracts of Land, which have hitherto laid in a waste state, by planting a much larger quantity of potatoes than usual, and by other new courses of husbandry.

For particulars, apply to Mess. Wilmot, Dunn, and Lancaster, Lincoln's Inn, London; Mess. Colquitt and Brown, and Mr. Newsham, attornies at law, Liverpool; and Mess. William and John Black, land surveyor, Middle Temple, London.

*TIMBER.*
To be SOLD by AUCTION

**6.4** *Gore's Liverpool General Advertiser*, 14 February 1793

not to comply with the present exorbitant demand of five pence per quart for ale; but are determined to drink nothing but grog or porter.

The imposition of a measure so injurious to all working mechanics, has determined us in our resolve not to drink FIVEPENNY ALE so long as our West India islands can supply us with Rum.

These are followed by the following unsigned announcement:

To The PUBLIC

A variety of advertisements having appeared in Gore's Liverpool newspapers, against the present advance in the price of ALE, I wish to appeal to the calm sense of the public on this occasion. I will tell you how the brewers are at present circumstanced.

Coals, formerly 2d. halfpenny, now 5d. halfpenny.

Malt, ditto 3s.6d. to 4s.6d. now 7s.4d. to 7s.9d.

Barley, 2s.2d. to 2s.6d. now 5s. to 5s.8d. and not very good for malting.

> Servants' wages, formerly 7s.6d. to 9s. per week, now 11s. to 15s.
> Hay, formerly 3d. to 3d. halfp. per stone, now 8d. to 12d.
> Barrels, ditto 12s. now 18s.
> Hops, ditto 2l.10s. to 3l. now 4l.10s. to 7l.7s.
>
> Every brewer gives a quantity of small beer, which is distributed by the publican gratis to the poor labourer.
>
> Now, let every thinking man weigh well the above statement of things and he will find that good wholesome ale cannot be brewed for less than 5d. per quart, and if the public were to consider the matter with that coolness and attention they ought, they would readily subscribe to the opinion of one who wishes every man to live by his business.

Advertisements for alcohol are fascinating, if only for the prices. The era of 'Drunk for a Penny, Dead Drunk for Twopence', is captured by advertisers like William Mills, Distiller, advising readers of the *Penny London Post* in 1749 that at the 'Grape and Raisin-Brandy Warehouse in Leadenhall-Tripe-Market, near the Back Gate of the Spread-Eagle-Inn', Fine Old Grape and Raisin Brandy are for sale at 3s. 6d. per gallon, 'Three Pence per Gallon to be allowed to those who take half a Hogshead and upwards', and 'Full Proof English Malt Spirits' would be delivered on board ship at '15d. Per Gallon'. Brandy is advertised at 4s. per gallon in the *London Courant* in 1746. Even as late as 1864, according to an advertisement in the *Tewkesbury Weekly Record*, it was possible to stroll into the Farriers Arms in Tewkesbury and order gin at 10 shillings per gallon.

## The Effects of Advertising

The growth in the volume of advertisements and the increased number of newspaper titles meant that advertising has become an industry in its own right. From the early nineteenth century advertising agencies were formed to act as intermediaries between advertisers and newspapers. National advertising campaigns were started for products such as J. W. Benson's watches, Pears' Soap, Player's Navy Cut, Cadbury's cocoa, Beecham's Pills, Spratt's dog biscuits and Atora suet, which were distributed and sold throughout the country. Printing blocks advertising these products were cut centrally and sent to the London papers and provincial papers.

The income from advertising contributed to the development of the independent press, freeing it from dependence on bribes from governments or subsidies from opposition. However, it can be argued that newspapers simply exchanged one master for another. Control switched from politicians to advertisers whose financial power could influence the content of the newspaper to the extent that newspapers were inhibited from opposing advertisers' commercial or political interests. This was particularly so with provincial papers in the nineteenth century when a small number of local advertisers could have a disproportionate influence on the editorial policy of the paper. It was also true to some extent of the national press. The initial radicalism of *Reynolds's Weekly Newspaper* had to be toned down in order not to alienate advertisers. In the 1880s, some advertisers boycotted *The Pall Mall Gazette* as a result of the 'Maiden Tribute' case to the extent that its advertising income fell by £2,500, and the *Daily News* lost advertising because of its support for Home Rule for Ireland.

These examples show the power of the advertiser to restrain the freedom of the press. Paradoxically, the wider range of goods and services advertised, and the competition between advertisers selling the same type of product – those factors that made the press dependent on advertising – ensured that the power of advertisers was limited. Provided advertisers were satisfied that the readers of a particular newspaper could afford to buy their products, that newspaper had little to fear if it offended those advertisers. If one set of advertisers withdrew their custom, others could be found to take their place.

## Chapter 7

# Robberies and Bloody Murders: Home News

> This Article call'd Home News is a new Common Hunt, tho' upon a cold scent after Casualties; the Miseries of Mankind are the chief Materials, such as Death and Marriage in the first Class; the Disasters of Families, such as Robberies and Bankrupts, that's the second Class; the Jail Deliveries, either to or from the Gallows, that's the third Class. If indeed a flaming Rogue came upon the Stage, such as a Sheppard, a Gow, a Jonathan Wild, or a Blueskin, they are great Helps to us, and we work them, and work them till we make Skeletons of the very Story, and the Names grow as rusty as the very Chains they are hang'd in.
>
> Daniel Defoe, *Applebee's Original Weekly Journal*, 21 August 1725

The newspaper is the ultimate in ephemera – to be read once and then be discarded. The old newswriters were in business simply to try to sell that day's paper and quickly move on to the next. But, in compiling their hastily produced paragraphs of news, they were unknowingly writing for posterity. Those few newspapers that have survived from 200 or 300 years ago can tell us more about what was important to their readers, and the pleasures and dangers of the life of their times, than any other source. Nowhere is this more true than in 'this Article call'd Home News'.

The main fascination of old newspapers lies not in their accounts of great events, but in their bread-and-butter reports of day-to-day news – highwaymen, footpads, smugglers, pirates, Newgate and the gallows. Newspapers provide the social backcloth to their times. If Hogarth painted the picture of eighteenth-century life, the newspaper supplied the text.

'We writers of diurnals are nearer in our styles to that of common talk than any other writers', wrote Richard Steele in the *Tatler* in 1710. But what were these common talkers saying to their readers through the columns of their newspapers? According to Eustace Budgell, writing in the 1730s, the domestic columns of newspapers were filled with

> Robberies, bloody Murders, Accounts of Draymen's Carts that have run over People, with the Adventures of Post-Boys, Tide Waiters, and Messengers, &c. The Promotions, Deaths and Marriages of the Nobility, Gentry and Clergy, and of the Days when some of the Royal Family go to the Play House, or take the Air.

## Highwaymen and Footpads

Before the end of the eighteenth century, when the highwayman was rendered obsolete by the crackdown on the licensing of safe houses, the reduction in the wild heathland resulting from the rapid extension of the enclosure system and increasing urbanization, and changes in banking practices which no longer made it necessary for people to carry large sums of money with them on their travels, accounts of the adventures of highwaymen were a standard feature in newspapers, encouraging a belief, amounting to a moral panic, that England, and London in particular, was in the stranglehold of the highwaymen:

> On *Friday* last *Reading*-Coach was robb'd upon *Hounsloe*-Heath, and the loss amounted to above 50l. Some days before, *Exeter*-Coach was robb'd near the same Place, and the Passengers amongst them lost the value of 400l. And it is reported that not a Coach hath passed or repassed that Road any time this ten days, but hath been robb'd.
>
> *Protestant (Domestick) Intelligence*, 8 February 1681

> So many robberies were committed this morning and the night before, on passengers from *London* to *Wandsworth*, *Putney* and *Richmond*, that this evening most of the people coming thence to *London*, assembled at *Wandsworth*, and came home in companies.
>
> *Gentleman's Magazine*, September 1751

An instance of how close to London the highwaymen operated is given in this report:

> This Morning about Three o'clock, the Post-Boy with the *Bristol* Mail was stopped by three Men on Horseback, well-mounted, and a fourth on Foot, between *Knightsbridge* and *Kensington*, who opened the Mail, and took out the *Bath* and Bristol Bags. It is thought, they chose those Bags at this Time, as believing there were several *Bank* Bills for the Company at the *Bath*. In the *Bristol* Bag was a reprieve for a Man condemned for Sodomy there. A second Reprieve was hereupon sent; but the Fellow had been hanged before its Arrival.
>
> *London Magazine*, September 1738

Stories of gentlemen highwaymen were common. Here are two examples:

> On Sunday last, between one and two o'clock, David Stone, Esq; of the Custom-house, was robbed in a post-chaise on Wimbledon-common, near Lord Spencer's park, by a single highwayman, (well mounted, without boots, and in white stockings) of his gold watch and money, who told him he was neither tradesman nor a servant, but a gentleman in distress.
>
> *General Evening Post*, 21 November 1769

On Tuesday Night Farmer Golden, of Upton St. Leonard's, was robbed between this City and his own House by a Man on Horseback. Golden told the Man he was a poor Farmer in great Distress, and had only Six Shillings in his Pocket, which he hoped he would not take from him. – 'I am in great Distress too, said the Robber, however, I will be content with Two Shillings; and perhaps I may one Day return to you as many Pounds.' Golden then gave him the Two Shillings, with which he rode off.

*Jackson's Oxford Journal*, 4 January 1783

While the newspapers showed a kind of grudging admiration for highwaymen, footpads (street robbers) were generally feared and loathed. Without a horse, they were unable to escape from the scene of their crime as easily as the highwaymen. They had no compunction about killing their victims to avoid capture. The following is, therefore, a rare example of a gentleman footpad:

A most extraordinary robbery was committed on Thursday morning last on Finchley Common, by a single footpad, who stopped a Gentleman's coach, in which there were two Ladies, a Counsellor of eminence, and a Captain of foot. The fellow had no weapon but a large clasp knife, which he thrust into the coach, and swore instantly to Prod, as he called it, into the Gentlemen, if they made the least hesitation in delivering their purses; the Counsellor gave him five guineas, and the officer three and a half. The Ladies were all the time in the greatest agitation for fear the fellow would commit some barbarity, and held their money out, begging he might be content with it, and go about his business; but he had no sooner done with the Gentlemen than he removed their uneasiness, by saying, 'Nay, Ladies, don't be frightened. I never did the least injury to a woman in my life, nor ever will, damme; as for your money, keep it to yourselves; all that I shall ask from you will be a kiss a-piece, and if you grudge me that, I am sure you are neither sensible nor good-humoured.' The Ladies having complied, he took his leave very civilly, declaring that was the first robbery he ever committed, and should be the last; that he served on board one of his Majesty's ships the whole war, but that being foolish and extravagant, he had spent all his wages, and was utterly destitute of employment and bread.

*Lloyd's Evening Post*, 6 February 1764

This report is more typical:

A Gang consisting of five Pickpockets, infest the Strand and Temple Bar every afternoon, from four o'clock, until the Watchman goes on duty: The principal of the Banditti is a tall, lusty man who, in order to attract the attention of the person they intend to rob, runs against him, and damning him, asks if he does not mean to let him pass, this usually has the desired effect; meanwhile the associates of this rascal, plunder him of his watch, money, &c. – By this new mode of robbery, three gentlemen lost their watches and money a few evenings ago, and all of these thefts were committed in the space of an hour, between Temple Bar and St. Clements Church. – The robbers are well dressed, and therefore are not suspected.

*Maidstone Journal*, 12 January 1790

## The Watchmen

It is surprising that those pickpockets felt obliged to desist when the watchman came on duty. By all accounts the watchmen were an ineffectual crew. They were paid very little, so their posts tended to be filled by people whose physical or mental or moral deficiencies rendered them otherwise unemployable. It is little wonder, therefore, that reports such as these were quite common:

> *March* the 9th, in the Morning about 3 o'Clock, a Watchman, who lodged in *New Bond-street*, going his Rounds pick'd up a Woman of the Town, and took her Home to his Habitation; but while the careful Watchman was beating the Hour of Four, the crafty Jilt heated a Poker, with which she burnt a Hole through the Chest of Drawers in order to rob her Gallant, by which she not only set Fire to the Apparel contained therein, but likewise to the Furniture of a Bed, and alarmed the Landlord, who, after extinguishing the Flames, carried them before a Magistrate, and they were by him committed to *Bridewell*.
>
> *Political State of Great Britain*, April 1739
>
> Last Week some Rogues took the Opportunity, while the Watchmen were asleep, to strip the Lead off the Piazzas adjoining the Watch-House at St. Margaret's-Hill, Southwark; but an Outcry of Thieves being made by some of the Neighbours prevented their carrying it off. This is a true Specimen of the Watchmens Care, and the Benefits the Publick receive from their Night Attendance.
>
> *Old England*, 2 April 1743
>
> Notwithstanding the complaints which are so generally and loudly made of the negligence with which the WATCHMEN conduct themselves down THE STRAND, and of the number of WOMEN OF THE TOWN who consequently resort to that place, to the extreme disgust and great inconvenience of the inhabitants, the nuisance remains exactly the same, and will certainly continue unless the Magistrates should vigorously interpose.
>
> It is impossible to describe the impudence, clamour and indecency which prevail among these women, insomuch that no modest woman can pass without being terrified, shocked and insulted in a great degree.
>
> It is a very common circumstance, so regardless are the men who are appointed to preserve peace and decency, to see the watchmen, at the time they are not employed in crying the hours, deeply engaged in conversation with these women, close to their boxes, up a passage, or at the corner of a street.
>
> There can be no doubt, that the watchmen are paid by these wretches for permitting them to parade to a certain extent, which they must not exceed because

they would trespass upon the territories of other watchmen, who have also a number of females upon whom they levy a nightly contribution.

It is but fair to suppose, that men who thus violate their duty, and so shamelessly pervert the purpose for which they are employed, may be equally in league with the HOUSE-BREAKER, whom, for a suitable requital, they may leave to the unmolested exercise of his villainy; and if the inhabitant should luckily be disturbed in his repose, and the ruffian be likely to be secured by proper assistance, connive at his escape, as they would have shared in the profits of his success.

The only remedy to prevent the probable consequences of the scandalous proceedings which now prevail, and remove the women who thus lie in wait to entrap unwary youth, corrupt its morals, and lead it to destruction, is to discharge the watchmen who shall be found most evidently guilty of lending their authority to these practises; if not, it does not need much sagacity to perceive that the town will soon be over-run in all parts with iniquity, danger and misery.

*Morning Post*, 20 September 1788

That the system of law enforcement in the eighteenth century was inadequate in virtually every particular is self-evident from a glance at the newspapers of the period. Take this 'wanted' notice in *The London Gazette* on 29 October 1705, for example:

John Childs, aged about 26 years, born near Wisbich in the Fenns, a thin Faced and Bodied Fellow, of a middle Stature, wearing his own blackish lank Hair, is slow of Speech, and goes often on his Heels, having lost some of his Toes, if not all of them, which makes him lame when he travels, broke out of Her Majesty's Gaol at Bedford on Thursday night the 18th Instant.

Or this notice from the *Reading Mercury* on 26 November 1770 for William Varndall who 'made his Escape from the Persons who had him in Custody'. Varndall was described as

a tall, thin, pale-looking Fellow, about forty Years of Age who stoops his Walk, very badly made about the Legs, which are thin, is knock-knee'd and splay-footed, with his Ancles hanging over his Shoes.

If people like that could make their escape, what chance had the authorities against the able-bodied? Perhaps in order to maintain a conviction the authorities picked on the very young:

Yesterday Ann Hill, a child of no more than six years old, was committed to Clerkenwell Bridewell, by John Girdler Esq; for stealing a lawn apron.

*Lloyd's Evening Post*, 14 March 1764

Yesterday, Charles Earle (a boy about 14 years of age) and … [five others] … all young men, were taken in two carts from Newgate, and executed at Tyburn.

*London Chronicle*, 19 November 1772

There were a number of measures to try to reduce the high rate of crime in the eighteenth century,

> The desperate gangs of housebreakers, by which both town and country are infested, has made every precaution necessary for the security of private families; among a variety of others that have been proposed, none seems as likely to answer the purpose effectually, as having a number of hand-grenades always in readiness. These, lighted, and thrown among any number of these villains, would instantly clear the house of them; nor would they ever be hardy enough to make a return.
>
> *Gentleman's Magazine*, January 1775

Newspaper advertising was a less self-destructive method of trying to combat crime. Sir John Fielding, the Bow Street magistrate, placed this notice in the *Public Advertiser* for 22 December 1766:

> From The POLICE
>
> The extensive Sale of The PUBLIC ADVERTISER, (joined to the *Variety* of Channels thro' which it passes) has always been the Means *detecting of many* ROBBERIES, and of *apprehending so many* OFFENDERS, that it may be proper to give THIS PUBLIC NOTICE, That, for the Future, all Information of this Kind, sent to BOW-STREET, will be *constantly inserted in* THIS PAPER: And if SUCH INFORMATIONS are *properly* attended to, by PAWNBROKERS, JEWELLERS, SILVERSMITHS, STABLE-KEEPERS, BUYERS OF SECOND-HAND CLOATHS, *&c. few Robberies will escape Detection*; especially *if* ALL PERSONS ROBBED *make use of* THIS PAPER *to advertise their Losses in.*

Fielding recognized that crime was no respecter of the boundaries of magistrates' jurisdiction. Under his General Preventative Plan of 1772, he arranged for provincial magistrates to send details of wanted criminals and stolen property to Bow Street for collation and transmission all over the country. Some provincial newspapers placed notices from local justices and private prosecutors together in an eye-catching position (Figure 7.1). Fielding's system was further developed by the *Hue and Cry; or, Police Gazette* in 1791. The *Hue and Cry*, 'Published by Authority', was not a newspaper as such. It was an official list of wanted notices printed in newspaper format under headings such as ARSON AND WILFUL BURNING, HOUSE-BREAKING, HORSE AND CATTLE STEALING, LARCENY and A LIST AND DESCRIPTION OF DESERTERS FROM HIS MAJESTY'S SERVICE.

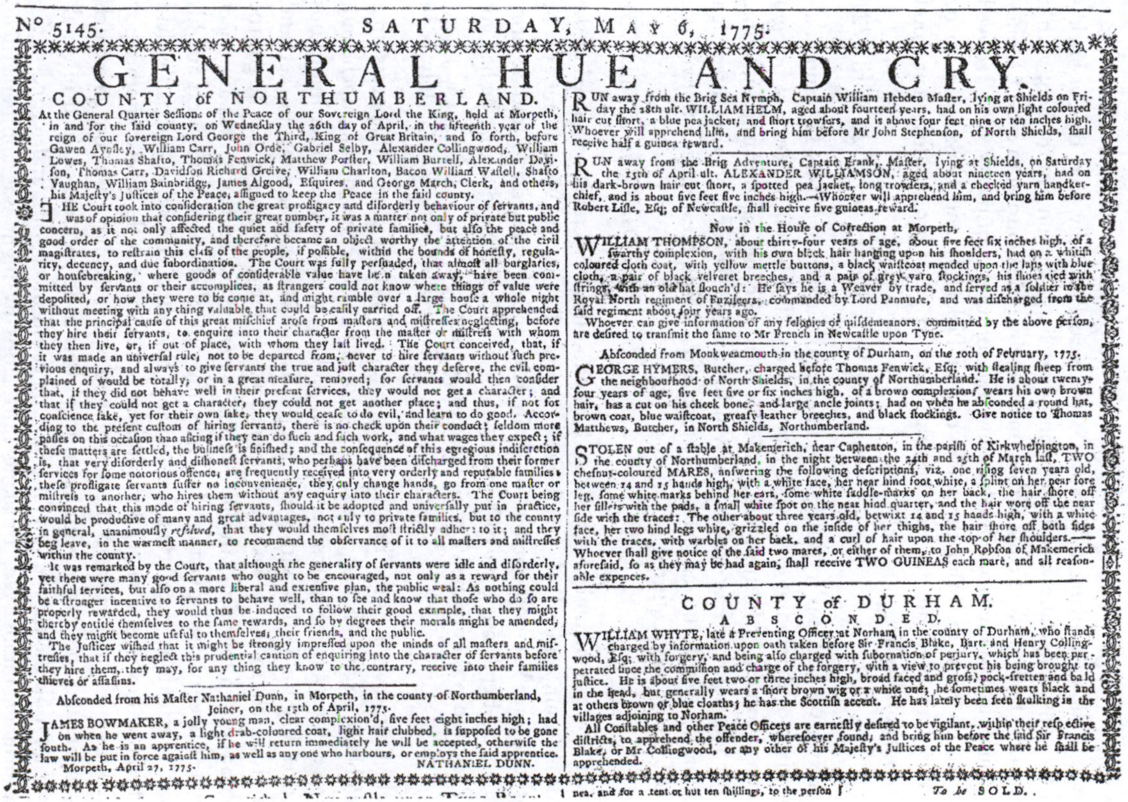

N° 5145. SATURDAY, MAY 6, 1775.

# GENERAL HUE AND CRY.

## COUNTY of NORTHUMBERLAND.

At the General Quarter Seſſions of the Peace of our Sovereign Lord the King, held at Morpeth, in and for the ſaid county, on Wedneſday the 26th day of April, in the fifteenth year of the reign of our ſovereign Lord George the Third, King of Great Britain, and ſo forth, before Gawen Aynſley, William Carr, John Orde, Gabriel Selby, Alexander Collingwood, William Lowes, Thomas Shafto, Thomas Fenwick, Matthew Forſter, William Burrell, Alexander Daviſon, Thomas Carr, Davidſon Richard Greive, William Charlton, Bacon William Waſtell, Shafto Vaughan, William Bainbridge, James Algood, Eſquires, and George March, Clerk, and others, his Majeſty's Juſtices of the Peace, aſſigned to keep the Peace in the ſaid county.

THE Court took into conſideration the great profligacy and diſorderly behaviour of ſervants, and was of opinion that conſidering their great number, it was a matter not only of private but public concern, as it not only affected the quiet and ſafety of private families, but alſo the peace and good order of the community, and therefore became an object worthy the attention of the civil magiſtrates, to reſtrain this claſs of the people, if poſſible, within the bounds of honeſty, regularity, decency, and due ſubordination. The Court was fully perſuaded, that almoſt all burglaries, or houſebreaking, where goods of conſiderable value have been taken away, have been committed by ſervants or their accomplices, as ſtrangers could not know where things of value were depoſited, or how they were to be come at, and might ramble over a large houſe a whole night without meeting with any thing valuable that could be eaſily carried off. The Court apprehended that the principal cauſe of this great miſchief aroſe from maſters and miſtreſſes neglecting, before they hire their ſervants, to enquire into their character from the maſter or miſtreſs with whom they then live, or, if out of place, with whom they laſt lived. The Court conceived, that, if it was made an univerſal rule, not to be departed from, never to hire ſervants without ſuch previous enquiry, and always to give ſervants the true and juſt character they deſerve, the evil complained of would be totally, or in a great meaſure, removed; for ſervants would then conſider that, if they did not behave well in their preſent ſervices, they would not get a character; and that if they could not get a character, they could not get another place; and thus, if not for conſcience ſake, yet for their own ſake, they would ceaſe to do evil, and learn to do good. According to the preſent cuſtom of hiring ſervants, there is no check upon their conduct; ſeldom more paſſes on this occaſion than aſking if they can do ſuch and ſuch work, and what wages they expect; if theſe matters are ſettled, the buſineſs is finiſhed; and the conſequence of this egregious indiſcretion is, that very diſorderly and diſhoneſt ſervants, who perhaps have been diſcharged from their former ſervices for ſome notorious offence, are frequently received into very orderly and reputable families: theſe profligate ſervants ſuffer no inconvenience, they only change hands, go from one maſter or miſtreſs to another, who hires them without any enquiry into their characters. The Court being convinced that this mode of hiring ſervants, ſhould it be adopted and univerſally put in practice, would be productive of many and great advantages, not only to private families, but to the county in general, unanimouſly *reſolved*, that they would themſelves moſt ſtrictly adhere to it; and they beg leave, in the warmeſt manner, to recommend the obſervance of it to all maſters and miſtreſſes within the county.

It was remarked by the Court, that although the generality of ſervants were idle and diſorderly, yet there were many good ſervants who ought to be encouraged, not only as a reward for their faithful ſervices, but alſo on a more liberal and extenſive plan, the public weal: As nothing could be a ſtronger incentive to ſervants to behave well, than to ſee and know that thoſe who do ſo are properly rewarded, they would thus be induced to follow their good example, that they might thereby entitle themſelves to the ſame rewards, and ſo by degrees their morals might be amended, and they might become uſeful to themſelves, their friends, and the public.

The Juſtices wiſhed that it might be ſtrongly impreſſed upon the minds of all maſters and miſtreſſes, that if they neglect this prudential caution of enquiring into the character of ſervants before they hire them, they may, for any thing they know to the contrary, receive into their families thieves or aſſaſſins.

Abſconded from his Maſter Nathaniel Dunn, in Morpeth, in the county of Northumberland, Joiner, on the 13th of April, 1775.

JAMES BOWMAKER, a jolly young man, clear complexion'd, five feet eight inches high; had on when he went away, a light drab-coloured coat, light hair clubbed, is ſuppoſed to be gone ſouth. As he is an apprentice, if he will return immediately he will be accepted, otherwiſe the law will be put in force againſt him, as well as any one who harbours, or employs the ſaid apprentice.

Morpeth, April 27, 1775. NATHANIEL DUNN.

RUN away from the Brig Sea Nymph, Captain William Hebden Maſter, lying at Shields on Friday the 28th ult. WILLIAM HELM, aged about fourteen years, had on his own light coloured hair cut ſhort, a blue pea jacket; and ſhort trowſers, and is about four feet nine or ten inches high. Whoever will apprehend him, and bring him before Mr John Stephenſon, of North Shields, ſhall receive half a guinea reward.

RUN away from the Brig Adventure, Captain Frank, Maſter, lying at Shields, on Saturday the 15th of April ult. ALEXANDER WILLIAMSON, aged about nineteen years, had on his dark-brown hair cut ſhort, a ſpotted pea jacket, long trowſers, and a checked yarn handkerchief, and is about five feet five inches high.—Whoever will apprehend him, and bring him before Robert Liſle, Eſq; of Newcaſtle, ſhall receive five guineas reward.

Now in the Houſe of Correction at Morpeth,

WILLIAM THOMPSON, about thirty-four years of age, about five feet ſix inches high, of a ſwarthy complexion, with his own black hair hanging upon his ſhoulders, had on a whitiſh coloured cloth coat, with yellow mettle buttons, a black waiſtcoat mended upon the laps with blue cloth, a pair of black velveret breeches, and a pair of grey yarn ſtockings, his ſhoes tied with ſtrings, with an old hat ſlouch'd: He ſays he is a Weaver by trade, and ſerved as a ſoldier in the Royal North regiment of Fuzileers, commanded by Lord Panmure, and was diſcharged from the ſaid regiment about four years ago.

Whoever can give information of any felonies or miſdemeanors, committed by the above perſon, are deſired to tranſmit the ſame to Mr French in Newcaſtle upon Tyne.

Abſconded from Monkwearmouth in the county of Durham, on the 10th of February, 1775.

GEORGE HYMERS, Butcher, charged before Thomas Fenwick, Eſq; with ſtealing ſheep from the neighbourhood of North Shields, in the county of Northumberland. He is about twenty-four years of age, five feet five or ſix inches high, of a brown complexion, wears his own brown hair, has a cut on his cheek bone, and large ancle joints; had on when he abſconded a round hat, brown coat, blue waiſtcoat, greaſy leather breeches, and black ſtockings. Give notice to Thomas Matthews, Butcher, in North Shields, Northumberland.

STOLEN out of a ſtable at Makemerich, near Capheaton, in the pariſh of Kirkwhelpington, in the county of Northumberland, in the night between the 24th and 25th of March laſt, TWO cheſnut-coloured MARES, anſwering the following deſcriptions, viz. one riſing ſeven years old, between 14 and 15 hands high, with a white face, her near hind foot white, a ſplint on her near fore leg, ſome white marks behind her ears, ſome white ſaddle-marks on her back, the hair ſhore off her fillets with the pads, a ſmall white ſpot on the near hind quarter, and the hair wore off the near ſide with the traces: The other about three years old, betwixt 14 and 15 hands high, with a white face, her two hind legs white, grizzled on the inſide of her thighs, the hair ſhore off both ſides with the traces, with warbles on her back, and a curl of hair upon the top of her ſhoulders.—Whoever ſhall give notice of the ſaid two mares, or either of them, to John Robſon of Makemerich aforeſaid, ſo as they may be had again, ſhall receive TWO GUINEAS each mare, and all reaſonable expences.

## COUNTY of DURHAM.

### ABSCONDED.

WILLIAM WHYTE, late a Preventing Officer at Norham in the county of Durham, who ſtands charged by information upon oath taken before Sir Francis Blake, Bart. and Henry Collingwood, Eſq; with forgery, and being alſo charged with ſubornation of perjury, which has been perpetrated ſince the commiſſion and charge of the forgery, with a view to prevent his being brought to juſtice. He is about five feet two or three inches high, broad faced and groſs, pock-fretten and bald in the head, but generally wears a ſhort brown wig or a white one; he ſometimes wears black and at others brown or blue cloaths; he has the Scottiſh accent. He has lately been ſeen ſkulking in the villages adjoining to Norham.

All Conſtables and other Peace Officers are earneſtly deſired to be vigilant, within their reſpective diſtricts, to apprehend the offender, wheresoever found, and bring him before the ſaid Sir Francis Blake, or Mr Collingwood, or any other of his Majeſty's Juſtices of the Peace where he ſhall be apprehended.

nea, and for a tent or hut ten ſhillings, to the perſon

*To be* SOLD.

7.1 General Hue and Cry, in the *Newcastle Courant*, 6 May 1775

## Crime ...

The following extracts from eighteenth-century newspapers give a flavour of the way different types of crimes were reported:

> This Day se'nnight Nathaniel Bridgeman, an Attorney, and Jane Symonds, a Woman of ill Fame, living in Windmill-street near Pickadilly, were try'd at Hick's-Hall for conspiring falsely and maliciously to charge Simon Smith, Esq; with a Rape on the Body of Willielma Weale, and thereby endeavouring to exhort Money from him; they were accordingly convicted of the Conspiracy, and received Sentence to be whipt from the lower end of Pickadilly and back again, to be committed to Newgate for six Months, and to find Sureties for their good Behaviour for Twelve.
>
> *Mist's Weekly Journal*, 29 April 1721

> Yesterday a Woman was try'd before the Bench of Justices at Hick's-Hall, upon an indictment of defrauding one Mrs. Newton of 12l. 13s. on pretence of being a Cunning Woman, or Fortune-teller, and, as such, of being capable to bring home safe her Son from the East-Indies in a Whirlwind; and also of procuring three Men to fall in Love with the said Mrs. Newton: After a long Hearing of the Evidence the Defendant was acquitted.
>
> *Daily Post*, 15 July 1731

> William Townshend and Henry Long, for Sodomitical Practices, convicted of the Misdemeanour, order'd to stand once in the Pillory at Warminster, to be imprison'd one Year without Bail or Mainprize, and Townshend to find Security for his good Behaviour for two Years. At their Trial Long pleaded that he had got the Piles, and was only shewing his Case to Townshend.
>
> *London Evening-Post*, 27 July 1738

> On the Examination of the Boy admitted evidence against others, it appears, that the Publican in custody had an association, or club, where they drank punch, and, at proper intervals, he instructed them in picking pockets, and other iniquitous practices, beginning first with picking a handkerchief out of his own pocket, and next his watch, so that at last the evidence was so great an adept, that he got the publicans watch four times in one evening, when he swore that he was as perfect as one of twenty years practice. The pilfering out of shops was the next art; his pupil's instructions were, that at as many chandlers, or other shops, as had hatches, one boy was to knock for admittance for some trifle, whilst another boy was lying on his belly, close to the hatch; who, when the boy came out, the hatch was on jar, and the owner withdrawn into their little parlour, crawled in on all fours, and took the tills, or anything else he could meet with, and retired in the same manner, unobserved. Breaking into shops by night was another article, which was effected thus; as walls of brick under shop windows are very thin, two of them were to lay under a window as destitute beggars, asleep to passers by, but when alone, were provided with pickers to pick the mortar out of the bricks, which soon tumbled, and so on till they had secured a hole big enough to go in,

when the other lay as if asleep before the breach, till they had accomplished their wicked purposes.

*Stamford Mercury*, 4 April 1765

Saturday last was committed to Aylesbury gaol, Henry Boddy, of Chesham, upwards of 76 years of age, charged with having committed bestiality with a she ass.

*Reading Mercury*, 22 August 1774

Among the criminal trials at Glasgow, there was one for a rape and robbery. The only witness examined was the woman herself. After stating that the Prisoner had first violated, and then robbed her of six shillings and a bottle of whiskey, she stated as a reason for not immediately complaining of his conduct, that she was 'so sorry about the shillings and the whiskey, that she clean forgot the rape!'

*The Globe*, 17 October 1817

On Tuesday last, about ten at night, as a young surgeon had just quitted one of the brothels in New-Church-Lane, he was attacked by two men, one of whom presented a pistol to his breast, whilst the other rifled his pockets of his watch, seventeen shillings and six-pence, and a silk handkerchief; they also took from him *The Memoirs of a Woman of Pleasure*, which he had clandestinely taken from the Lady with whom he had been; and afterwards cut him across the face in a most shocking manner, so that one of his eyes is entirely lost.

*Reading Mercury*, 31 October 1763

This reference to John Cleland's *Memoirs*, or *Fanny Hill*, is an indication of the fame of contemporary pornographic books. The writer appears to have assumed that the Berkshire farmers who read the *Reading Mercury*, and who needed to be told that Paris was 'the capital town or city of France', were familiar with the work and needed no further explanation.

With only four pages to play with, and at least one of those taken up by advertisements, there was little scope to devote much more than one paragraph per case. In very rare instances, other news was dropped to produce verbatim reports of major trials, such as the trial of Admiral Keppel in 1779. In even rarer cases, some surprisingly obscure trials were reported in full, as in the case of the murder of the wife of an alehouse keeper in Berkshire which took up eleven pages of the *Political State for Great Britain* for May 1737 and was headed 'From the Reading Journal'. Here is an extract:

| | |
|---|---|
| Q. | Had she any Wounds about her? |
| Eliz. Winch. | Wounds! Yes, an't please your Lordship, a many: She had a great Gash in her Skull, big enough to put your three Fingers into her Head, and her Kekker was cut quite in two with a Hatchet that lay a-cross her Arm. |
| Q. | Was the Hatchet bloody? |
| Eliz. Winch. | Yes, an't please your Lordship, and there was something upon it that looked like Brains. |

If the eighteenth-century reader was not satisfied with the sparse offerings in the newspapers, verbatim reports were available in the sixpenny pamphlets of the *Proceedings of the King's Commissioner of the Peace, Oyer and Terminer, and Gaol Delivery* that were printed for Catherine Nutt and other purveyors of street literature.

It was not until the nineteenth century, with the advent of the broadsheet newspapers and the wider use of shorthand that court cases were regularly reported at length.

## … and Punishment

Most newspapers carried at least one item about hanging. Generally this was either the report of a trial resulting in the death sentence or the report of the execution itself. The number of offences attracting the death penalty rose from about fifty in 1688 to about 225 in 1815. They ranged from sheep stealing to sodomy. In practice many of those sentenced to death had their sentences commuted to transportation, and for those awaiting the gallows there was the possibility of a last-minute reprieve. So whether one was hanged or not was something of a lottery. Also, sentencing policy was inconsistent. Punishments varied wildly from court to court.

Hanging days were regarded as holidays. The long journey from Newgate to Tyburn attracted large crowds thronging the highway to take a last look at the condemned men they had read about in the newspapers. The biggest crowds were at Tyburn itself to watch the execution and hear the dying speeches. As with all occasions that attracted large numbers of people, professional pickpockets were out in force, undeterred by the example dangling in front of them.

The executions themselves were often bungled. It was common for the executioners to misjudge the length of the rope in relation to the body weight – too short a rope meant a slow death by strangulation, too long a rope meant decapitation. Ownership of the body after death was often hotly debated between the friends of the deceased and the anatomists. The following extracts combine most of the elements of the eighteenth-century execution and its aftermath:

> A most extraordinary affair we hear happened some time ago in Dublin; A surgeon's son, with four other young fellows, being capitally convicted for a highway robbery, and ordered for execution; the surgeon went the evening before they were to suffer, to take leave of his unfortunate boy; but carried a preparation in his pocket, which he left with the lad, to prevent the infamy of a public death; the son took it after the father's departure, and it just began to operate as a reprieve was brought for him and his companions, he expired however in a short time and

the rest were pardoned. The father was so affected at the circumstances, that he died within a fortnight, not without suspicion of having hastened his end by some such potion as he had prescribed for his son.

*The Craftsman; or Say's Weekly Journal*, 1 August 1767

Yesterday the following Convicts under Sentence of Death in Newgate, were executed at Tyburn pursuant to their Sentence. – In the first Cart went John Holt and Andrew Carleton, for breaking open the Warehouse of the White Horse Inn, Cripplegate, and John Meadows, for robbing Ann Maxwell on Finchley Common, of Two Guineas; in the second Cart, Robert Allen, and John Milbourne, for a Burglary in the House of John and Richard Ottlay in Holbourn; and Henry Scott, for robbing John Higgins in the Green Park, of a Silver Watch, Stock-Buckle, and 3s. In the third Cart, Lyon Lyons, for a Burglary.

At the Place of Execution, the Housebreakers and Lyons confessed themselves to be guilty, and the other two continued in asserting their Innocence, calling God to Witness the Truth of their Declarations in the last Gasp of Life.

Among the Number of Spectators who made a Holiday to see so dreadful a Sight, was the noted William Bolton, alias Billy the Flat, who was detected by a Gentleman following his Vocation. He had picked the Gentleman's Pocket of his Handkerchief, but it was too quickly conveyed away to be recovered; however, as the Gentleman saw it in his Hand, he secured Billy, who was conducted to Bow-Street, where he denied the Fact, saying, a Handkerchief was too mean an Object for his Pursuit.

*Jackson's Oxford Journal*, 24 October 1778

FRIDAY, 19.

Being the day appointed for the execution of Matthew Dodd, coachman to Kitty Fisher, for ravishing Anne Dutnell, a farmer's daughter, the prisoner was brought down to prayers about ten o'clock, and received the sacrament. Soon after this a tumultuous and daring mob surrounded the New Gaol in the Borough, and would not suffer the cart to drive up to the gaol door to carry the prisoner to execution, but drove it away by force. The constables, by a warrant from the justices, pressed another cart; but when the prisoner was brought out of the gaol to be put into it, the mob rose in a violent threatening manner, and a rescue being apprehended, the keeper very prudently ordered the prisoner into gaol again, and immediately applied to one of his majesty's principal secretaries of state, who sent an order to the war office for a military power; and about six in the evening a command of 150 men, with their bayonets fixed, attended by their officers, came from the Tower to the New Gaol, and the prisoner was then put into the cart, and carried to execution, amidst the greatest number of spectators ever known on such an occasion. When he came out of the gaol, his wife, who was at a house adjoining, made several hideous shrieks, which greatly alarmed the unfortunate man, and raised the compassion of the populace. The execution was not over till half an hour after seven at night. He denied the fact for which he suffered.

*London Magazine*, August 1763

On Monday last was executed, Robert Hyne and Samuel Baxter, for committing several Robberies on the King's Highway. At the Place of Execution, their

Behaviour was suitable to their Unhappy Circumstances, as their Confession of the Crimes for which they suffered was attended with an earnest Exhortation to Youth to take Warning by them, briefly desiring them particularly to avoid the Company of lewd Women, Drunkeness, Sabbath-breaking, and Disobedience to Parents, the fatal Inlets to all their Misfortunes.

*General Advertiser*, 27 August 1747

*Paul Lewis*, *John Rice*, and *Hannah Dagoe*, were carried from Newgate, and executed at *Tyburn*. *Dagoe* was a strong masculine woman, had been an old offender, and once stabbed a man in *Newgate*, who was evidence against her. At the place of execution, getting her hands loose, she struggled with the executioner, and gave him such a blow on the breast, as almost beat him down. She disposed of her hat, cloaths and cardinal in despite of him; and as soon as the rope was fixed about her neck, pulling a handkerchief over her eyes, she threw herself out of the cart with such violence, that she broke her neck, and died instantly.

*Gentleman's Magazine*, May 1763

After the execution, a young woman, who had a wen on her neck, was held up in a man's arms, and the hand of one of the hanging malefactors was several times rubbed over it with much ceremony: so that, if it shall please God to remove this complaint, a miracle will be imputed to the wonder-working hand of a dead thief.

*Gentleman's Magazine*, October 1759

Yesterday the Malefactor mention'd in our last was carry'd to Tyburn, where having pray'd and sung Psalms, was turn'd off, and being thought dead, was cut down by Jack Catch as usual, who had procur'd a Hole to be dug at some Distance from the Gallows to bury him in: But just as they had put him into his Coffin, and were about to fasten it up, he thurst [*sic*] back the Lid, and to the great Astonishment of the Spectators, clapt his Hands on the Sides of the Coffin in order to raise himself up. Some of the People in their first Surprise were for knocking him on the Head; but Jack Catch thinking that foul Play, insisted on hanging him up again, when the Mob taking a different turn, cry'd Save his Life, and fell upon the poor Executioner (who stickled hard for fulfilling the Law) and beat him in a most miserable Manner. They carried the Prisoner to a House at Acton, where he was put to Bed; he vomited about three Pints of Blood, and 'twas once believ'd he would recover, but it was afterwards reported, that on giving him a Glass of Wine he died. The Sheriff's Officers believing the Prisoner dead, were retir'd from the Place of Execution before he was cut down.

*Old Whig*, 29 July 1736

There was a great Contest at Tyburn, Yesterday, between a Surgeon's Mob and the Populace, about the Body of one of the Malefactors, which the latter, however, brought off in Triumph, and delivered to his Friends for Burial.

*St. James's Chronicle*, 10 January 1765

As Tyrie was conducting to execution, he said to the jailor 'At this place I was to have been rescued, could I have raised money enough, for the smugglers had offered to do it, but demanded a sum greater than was in my power to give.' He afterwards said, there was one man living yet, who furnished intelligence to the

French; and while he lived, the navy of Great Britain would never be successful. After he was executed and buried in the sand, the sailors dug him up, pulled him to pieces, lapped his fingers and toes in rags to make tobacco stoppers of, and carried his entrails in triumph on a stick.

*Chelmsford Chronicle*, 6 September 1782

Cornelius Saunders, Lewis Makely, William Holloway, James Geary and Thomas Murphy were executed at Tyburn. As soon as the execution was over, the body of Cornelius Saunders, who was executed for stealing about 50l. out of the house of Mrs White in Lamb-street, Spitalfields, was carried and laid at the prosecutrix's door; where great numbers of people assembled, and were so outrageous that a guard of soldiers was sent for to stop their proceedings; notwithstanding which, they forced open the door, fetched out all the salmon tubs, most of the household furniture, piled them on a heap, and set fire to them; and, to prevent the guards from extinguishing the flames, the populace pelted them off with stones, and would not disperse till the whole was consumed.

*London Magazine*, August 1763

Fuller accounts were to be found in the threepenny or sixpenny broadsheets of Dying Confessions that were hawked about the streets after, and sometimes during, the execution. Many of these were the work of the Ordinary or Chaplain of Newgate. The Ordinary would try to obtain a full account of the life and crimes of the prisoner in the condemned cell under the pretence that the prisoner ought to confess all his sins to make his peace with God. If that did not work, he would travel in the cart with the condemned man from Newgate to Tyburn to try to wring some serviceable copy out of him. Naturally, the publicity value would not be so great if the prisoner was reprieved. The Rev. James Villette once tried to prevent the last-minute reprieve of a fifteen-year-old boy by telling the hangman to get on with it, as it was too late to worry about such details.

The judicial repertoire was not restricted to hanging, imprisonment and transportation. In some cases the phrase 'hanging is too good for them' was taken literally,

Isabella Condon, whose crime was high treason … for coining and counterfeiting shillings … was hung on a separate gallows, and was not turned off till about a quarter of an hour after the other convicts.

The solemnity of the occasion drew tears from the most obdurate heart, and the concourse of persons seemed all to feel the rude barbarity of that law, which condemns the softer sex to a punishment so much more horrid, and dreadful in idea, than the male. When the unfortunate female was turned off, a quantity of faggots was piled around her body, and in about twenty minutes fire was set to them. The poor creature's sense of feeling was beyond the reach of this fresh torture, but those of the spectators were agitated in the most exquisite degree. They felt the horrors of the scene, but they suffered more for the ignominy of the law that gave rise to it, than the creature who fell a sacrifice to its savage partiality.

*General Advertiser*, 28 October 1779

Thomas Rounce … was sentenc'd to be drawn on a Hurdle to the Place of Execution, there to be hang'd, but cut down before he is dead, his Privities to be cut off, his Head sever'd from his Body, his Bowels taken out, and then to be quarter'd, which Quarters are to be put up where his Majesty shall please to appoint.

*Aris's Birmingham Gazette*, 20 December 1742.

Later, from the *London and Country Journal* for 12 January 1743: 'We hear that Rounce, who was lately found guilty of High Treason, is so very ill in Newgate, that he has not being [*sic*] able to attend the Chappel for Several Days past.' Which was hardly surprising with the thought of what was in store for him.

Other punishments seem almost medieval in their cruelty,

At the Assizes at *Lewes* in Sussex, a Man who pretended to be dumb and lame, was indicted for a barbarous Murder and Robbery. He was taken up on Suspicion, several spots of Blood, and Part of the Goods being found upon him. When he was brought to the Bar, he wou'd not speak or plead, tho' often urged to it, and the Sentence to be inflicted on such as stand mute was read to him: Four or five Persons in the Court swore they had heard him speak, and the Boy who was his Accomplice and apprehended was there to be a Witness against him; yet he continued mute: Whereupon he was carried back to *Horsham* Gaol to be press'd to Death, if he wou'd not plead. They laid on him first 100 Weight, then added 100 more, and he still continu'd obstinate; they then added 100 more, and then made it 350lb. yet he wou'd not speak; then adding 50lb. more he was just dead, having all the agonies of Death upon him: Then the Executioner, who weighs about 16 or 17 Stone, lay down upon the Board which was over him, and, adding to the Weight, kill'd him in an Instant.

*London Magazine*, August 1735

and upon the 10th of this Month, the said *Japhet Crook* stood on the Pillory at Charing-Cross; after which he was set in an Elbow Chair, and the Common Hangman executed the Sentence against him, by cutting both his Ears off, slitting both his Nostrils, and searing them with a red hot iron, which Sentence he underwent with a great deal of Courage and Resolution, never so much as winch'd or stirr'd but put on his Cap, and tuck'd up his Hair under it himself. He had a Surgeon to attend him to stop the Effusion of Blood. And its said, that after the Execution he turned and laugh'd at his Prosecutors, who were at a House against the Pillory to see the Sentence put into Execution.

He was afterwards carried to the *Ship Tavern* at *Charing Cross*, where he dined, and was in as good Humour as any one of the Company, from whence he was carried to the *King's-Bench* Prison, where he is to remain for Life.

*Political State of Great Britain*, June 1731

Japhet Crook got off lightly. He was convicted of forgery, which normally carried a mandatory death sentence as in the famous cases of John Ayliffe who was executed in 1759; the Perreau brothers, who were undoubtedly innocent, in 1776; and Dr William Dodd in 1777.

The pillory was intended to publicly shame the offender, to make him suffer the scorn and insults of his neighbours. Sometimes the authorities misread the public mood. In 1703, Defoe was cheered in the pillory and, instead of being pelted with rotten fruit, he was presented with flowers. When Parsons, the instigator of the Cock Lane Ghost (see Figure 7.2), was pilloried in 1762, the crowd made a collection to pay his debts.

Thief-takers and homosexuals did not fare so luckily. Charles Hitchen, a former confederate of Jonathan Wild who combined thief-taking with homosexuality, would almost certainly have been killed by the mob had he not been rescued by the sheriff's men before his hour in the pillory was over.

The fate of the MacDaniel Gang was recorded in the *Gentleman's Magazine* for March 1756:

> FRIDAY, 5.
>
> *Berry and Macdaniel*, two of the thief-takers, were put in the pillory, opposite the end of *Hatton Garden*, pursuant to their sentence, and were severely pelted by the populace, many of whom suffered by the greatness of the crowd. *Macdaniel* received a terrible wound in his forehead with a stone, and *Berry*, who was weak before, was scarce able to survive.
>
> MONDAY, 8.
>
> *Egan* and *Salmon*, the other two thief-takers, stood in the pillory at *Smithfield*, when the former soon received a mortal wound, of which he soon after died, and the latter many miserable bruises.

The three survivors died of their wounds in Newgate shortly afterwards. One of the 'two wretches convicted of an infamous crime' in 1780 suffered the same fate:

> Yesterday about twelve o'clock in the forenoon the plaisterer and coachman were brought from the new jail, Southwark, to St Margaret's hill, and set in the pillory according to their sentence. A vast concourse of people had assembled upon the occasion, many by seven o'clock in the morning, who had collected dead dogs, cats, &c. in great abundance, which were plentifully thrown at them; but some person threw a stone, and hit the coachman on the forehead, and he immediately dropped on his knees, and was to all appearance dead. He was taken out and laid upon the pillory until his time had expired, when he was carried back to the new jail without any signs of life. The plaisterer was also severely handled.

It seems that the authorities played no small part in his death. The deceased was

# Lloyd's EVENING POST,

AND

VOL. X.] **BRITISH Chronicle.** [Numb. 706.

To be continued every MONDAY, WEDNESDAY, and FRIDAY.

From WEDNESDAY, JANUARY 20, to FRIDAY, JANUARY 22, 1762.

THURSDAY, JANUARY 21.

COUNTRY NEWS.

*Gloucester, Jan.* 16.

ON Thursday last one of Owner Hill's trows, laden with goods for this city from Bristol, was cast away upon a rock at the mouth of this river. It is said this accident was occasioned by the wind's falling short, by which means the vessel would not answer her helm, and was driven by the rapidity of the tide against the rock, where she was immediately dashed to pieces. The loss is very considerable. We are told that nothing had been saved but some wool, wine, and oil, which floated.

*Newcastle, Jan.* 16. Friday se'nnight a horse belonging to George Robson, of Stockton, lost both his hind feet in riding between this town and Chester le Street: they came off at the pastern joint.

LONDON.

Yesterday the Right Hon. the House of Peers waited on his Majesty at his palace at St. James's, with their Address of Thanks for his most gracious Speech from the Throne.

It is said there will be a Lottery for 1,200,000l. the prizes and blanks to be long annuities for a term of years, and the tickets to be 10l. The preference to be given to the subscribers of the last loan to the Government.

The hopes of a Congress at Augsburg being vanished, Count de Pergen, who was appointed Plenipotentiary from the Court of Vienna to that meeting, is gone to his former post at Frankfort on the Mayn.

The Minister of the Duke of Mecklenburgh has been greatly caressed by the French Court; and his most Christian Majesty has presented him with a watch of curious workmanship, embellished with his own picture in minature.

His Majesty's ship Africa, and some fireships, have joined Admiral Saunders. The convoy that sailed from Torbay the 25th of November, was arrived at Gibraltar.

We hear that six more men of war and two bombs are going to join Admiral Saunders.

Tuesday morning came the agreeable news that the Swiftsure man of war, commanded by the Hon. Sir Thomas Stanhope, was put into Torbay.

On Thursday and Friday last seven companies of Lord Loudon's regiment from Belleisle, marched into Salisbury from Portsmouth.

Letters from Lyons in France say, that the Sieur Burgarett, a French Physician, has obtained a licence for erecting an hospital to cure all distempers in horses, cows, sheep, and other beasts.

Late on Tuesday night last, Essex Merrick Lilly, alias Edward Somerset Howard, was brought to town from Basingstoke in Hampshire, where he was apprehended, and committed to New Prison, Clerkenwell, by Sir John Fielding, charged with several forgeries and publications of the same, as well in Middlesex as in Liverpool, Bristol, Bath, and other places, to a very considerable amount.

Yesterday afternoon, about four o'clock, a Washerwoman was robbed in Barn-Fields near the hay-ricks, a small distance from the Queen's Head in the lower street at Islington, of a large bundle of cloaths, and 4s. 6d. in money, by a short fellow in a blue coat and black wig.

On Friday night Mr. Sadler, a Lighterman, was drowned as he was going with his lighter thro' London-Bridge. Seven men have been drowned within these ten days.

On Saturday last the man, who was stabbed by a Portuguese sailor at the Black-Boy, a publick-house, at Saltpetre Bank, died of his wounds in the London Infirmary, Mile-End.

On Sunday last as Mr. Spurling, Parish Clerk at Stretham, Surry, was chiming the bells, he was seized with a fit of apoplexy, and expired in a few minutes.

Tuesday morning, about three o'clock, a hackney coach, by the carelessness of the driver, was overturned in the deep ditch near the windmill in St. George's Fields; both the horses were killed, and the coach broke in pieces, but the coachman escaped with little hurt.

*The Story of the Apparition in* Cock Lane, *continuing still much the subject of discourse, we presume, it will not be disagreeable to our Readers, to collect together the following accounts.*

On Monday night last four Gentlemen sat up to examine into the reality of the above report. Upon going up stairs, they were desired to make no noise, for fear of disturbing the Spirit, who had already began to scatch; upon their setting down, a woman in company thus addressed herself to it: Are you come, my dear? Pray tell me what it is o'clock. A scratch followed, which implied displeasure. The woman again said, Do, my dear, don't be ill-natured, tell me what it is o'clock; on which ten knocks were given. She was then asked, How much after? One knock was given, signifying one quarter. [Here the Spirit was mistaken, it being thirty-five minutes after.] A Gentleman present got up, stamped with his foot by the bedside; on which she scratched; which they continued for some time, stamping and scatching. At last the Gentleman sat down. She, beginning to knock, was asked, If she would answer any questions? One knock, signifying Yes. When she was asked, If Mr. ------ was in the room? one knock was given. 2. Whether she had been seen by any body? one knock. 3. Whether she had been seen by Mr. P---- and his daughter, and Mr. F----? one knock. 4. If she had been seen by them, whether she could not be seen by the persons present? two knocks, signifying No. 5. If Mr. ------ was to be left in the room alone, whether she would appear to him? two knocks. 6. If he went out, would she appear to the persons present? two knocks. 7. If she was the wife of Mr. ------? two knocks. 8. If she died naturally? two knocks. 9. If by poison? one knock. 10. If any other person but Mr. ------ administered it? two knocks. 11. If it was given in water-gruel, beer, or any other liquor? the knocks were given for beer. A Gentleman observing she drank no beer, but loved purl, asked her, Whether it was given her in beer or purl? knocked for purl. 12. How long she lived after receiving it? three knocks, signifying three hours. 13. Whether one Carrots knew of her being poisoned? one knock. 14. Whether Mr. ------ should be taken up? one knock. [Here a Gentleman took up a candle to look under the bed to examine, but saw nothing.] 13. Whether Mr. ------ should speak to her? no answer. The woman in company said she was gone, and that the candle was the cause, she not loving light. In less than five minutes the scratching came again. 14. How many Clergymen were present? one knock. [Here the Spirit was again mistaken, for there were two; but this was cleared up by a Gentleman's observing, that the second Clergyman was a stranger to her.] 15. How many persons were present? six knocks; right. 16. Whether she would answer to Mr. ------? scartching hard, angrily; but being again intreated, gave one knock. 17. Mr. ------ asked, if she was Fanny ------? one knock. 18. If Mr. J----- or Mr. S----- was not her Apothecary? no answer, but scratching; but

[Price Two-pence Halfpenny.]

**7.2** Cock Lane Ghost, *Lloyd's Evening Post*, 20 January to 22 January 1762

a short man … [who] … complained of the pillory being too high for him … being seized with a giddiness and fainting, from the extreme severity he received from the populace, lost the strength of his legs, and hung by his head. The jury brought in their verdict, 'Strangled in the Pillory.'

*Salisbury and Winchester Journal*, 17 April 1780

## Accidents

Budgell used 'Accounts of Draymen's Carts that have run over People' as an example of reports of accidental death which were a standard feature of eighteenth century newspapers, especially the cut-price press.

The *Penny London Post*, as befits its name, was a cheap publication, printed on inferior paper with a worn typeface. It advertised that

Any Gentleman, Shopkeeper, Tradesman, or other Person, who has Occasion for any Advertisements, small Hand Bills, or Shop Bills, of any Kind whatsoever, to be printed, are hereby acquainted that the same will be performed much cheaper than by any other Person in England. Please to enquire at the Printer's of this Paper. [one of the earliest examples of the Greengrocer's Apostrophe].

It specialized in stories of crime and violent death:

On Tuesday Morning early as an old Woman, who lived at the Bible at Fleet Ditch, was leaning out of a Window three Stories high, to see the Dog-Skinner, after whom a great Number of Dogs were barking, she unhappily miss'd her Hold, and, falling to the Ground, dash'd her Brains out on the Spot.

10 March 1748/9

In the same issue there is another dog story. An apprentice lad wishing to read the inscription on the collar of a dog was bit in the hand for his inquisitiveness. Some months later, he was 'seized with such a violent Disorder, that a Physician was sent for', where upon it was discovered that

the Dog was killed on a Supposition of being mad, and that he had bit a Horse, who having some Symptoms of Madness, was also knock'd on the Head. The Youth died last Friday Morning in the most violent Agonies, bound in his Bed.

This may caution Persons how they meddle with strange Dogs.

This piece of homespun advice, the extension of a straightforward report to include a moral at the end, was a common feature of eighteenth-century newspapers. Despite good intentions, they nearly always ended in bathos:

An extract from a Letter from one of the Crew belonging to the Goodfellow, a Ship Trading to the Streights, to his Friend in London:

I have had no Cause of Uneasiness since I came on board this Ship, but what has arisen from the following accident ... two of our Crew, having the Boat to attend them, went into the Sea to wash themselves, one got into the Boat and was dressing himself, when he heard his Companion give a lamentable Shriek, towards whom he row'd the Boat with the utmost Expedition, and found him in the dreadful Jaws of a voracious Shark, (accompany'd by another of that devouring Species) which he discern'd had already torn out his Bowels. He endeavour'd with his Boat-Hook to recover the Body, but upon catching hold of the upper Part of it, he found it separated from the lower.

This, its hop'd, will serve as a Warning against washing in the Sea, there being no Security against one of those Monsters of the Deep.

*London Evening-Post*, 1 April 1738

One *Hitchins* who had been disordered in his senses for some time, going into the house of *Thomas Bedworth*, of *King's-Wood* near Birmingham, and finding only three children all in bed, took one of them, a girl about three years old, cut off its head, arms and feet, ripped open its belly, and put some part of the body on the fire: while he was employed in this horrid barbarity, a brother who had been abroad, came in, and being terrify'd, alarmed the neighbours with his cries, who asking the wretch why he had committed such an act of cruelty, said, that he had killed the child to eat it, and that he would serve all the little girls so.

This is inserted as a caution against suffering persons disordered in their senses to wander at large without a keeper.

*Gentleman's Magazine*, September 1759

Some few Days since a large Quantity of Gunpowder took fire, in the Time of Market, in a shop at Buckingham; which did much Damage, greatly alarmed the Neighbourhood, and (what was worst of all) the Wife of the Shopkeeper was most miserably burnt, her Life being despaired of. – This ought to be a Caution not to keep Gunpowder near a Forge.

*Northampton Mercury*, 20 February 1769

Monday afternoon the Coroner's jury sat on the body of the man who was killed on the top of the stage-coach, as it was going out of the gateway of the Four Swans inn, in Bishopsgate-street, on Thursday morning last, and brought in their verdict accidental death. The misfortune happened by his not stooping low enough, by which neglect his head struck with violence against the beam at the extremity, and fractured his skull, of which he languished a short time. It is a pity but people on the tops of the coaches were properly cautioned against the like danger on coming out of the gateway, or not being permitted to get upon the carriage till it came into the street.

*Morning Chronicle*, 11 August 1779

## Death and Marriage

Eustace Budgell included the marriages and deaths of the nobility, gentry and clergy in his list of subjects that filled the domestic columns of the newspaper. This, from the *London Evening-Post* for 13 November 1746, is a typical report of a society wedding:

> On Tuesday last Anthony Allen, Esq; one of the Masters of the High Court of Chancery, was married at St. Bride's Church in Fleet-Street to Miss Rebecca Collyer, A young Lady of fine Accomplishments, with a handsome Fortune; after the Ceremony was over they set out for her Mother's Seat at Ponder's End to consummate their Nuptials.

Couplings from other classes also made the news:

> A few days since an elderly gentleman of fortune coming to town from Hackney, met a buxom young girl going to the said town with a basket of mackerel to sell, with whom he was so enamoured, that he immediately offered her marriage, which the girl as readily accepted, and, it is said, they were married this morning.
>
> *London Chronicle*, 2 June 1759

> Last week a woman of Langly-dale, near Middleton, was brought to bed of a daughter. She is upwards of 56 years of age, was never married, and has procured two fathers for the child, who have mutually agreed to bring it up in common as their own.
>
> *Reading Mercury*, 2 September 1765

> *Cambridge, Sept. 18.* Last week died the wife of one Goodwin, a labouring man, at Little Shelford in this County. The sorrowful widower, unable to bear the thoughts of a single state, set off the next morning, and was married to a woman at Linton. At their return in the evening to Shelford, the dead wife was removed from his bed into a coffin, to give way for the new-married couple to celebrate their nuptials. The coffin continued in the room all night.
>
> *The Craftsman: or Say's Weekly Journal*, 26 September 1767

Newspapers also offered scenes from married life, including the story of the man who tried to blow up his wife because she hadn't cooked his dinner and the couple who couldn't afford a chastity belt:

> A man who lodged in Earl-street, Seven-Dials, went home in expectation of having his dinner ready, but found his wife on the bed intoxicated with liquor, on which he placed a train of gunpowder, with the diabolical resolution to blow her up, but in setting fire to the same, he was so terribly burnt that he was carried to the hospital with little hopes of recovery. The woman escaped unhurt.
>
> *Gentleman's Magazine*, February 1767

An odd Trial came on at Leicester Assizes, the Case being thus; one Baggerley being hired to work about 5 Miles from Grooby, and being jealous of his Wife, was afraid to leave her to her own Inclinations, therefore put into Execution a most villainous and barbarous Design, which the Wife told her Mother and Sisters of, and they the Neighbourhood, who released the Woman from her great Pain, and took him up. His Indictment was as follows. That he, George Baggerley, on Oct. 15. with Force and Arms at Grooby, against the Peace of our Sovereign Lord the King, then and there did make an assault; and that the said George Baggerley a certain Needle and Thread into and thro' the Skin and Flesh of the Private Parts of the said Dorothy in Divers Places then and there wickedly, barbarously and inhumanely did force; and the said private Parts of her the said Dorothy Baggerley, with the Needle and Thread aforesaid, did then and there sew up, to the great Damage of the said Dorothy, and against the Peace of our Sovereign Lord the King, his Crown and Dignity.

To which Indictment the Prisoner pleaded Guilty, and the Court gave him a very severe Reprimand; but considering his great Poverty, fin'd him 20 s. and to be imprison'd for two Years. As he was carrying from his Trial to the Goal, the Women fell upon him, and scratch'd him terribly, calling him all the ill Names they could think of.

*London Magazine*, April 1737

The lists of deaths generally showed no more than the name of the deceased and the date of death. But sometimes they mentioned how the person died:

July 21st, Suddenly, at his House in *King-street, St. James's*, Brigadier Cockburn. His Death is said to be occasion'd by eating Cucumbers, and drinking Cyder after them; for he was well at Dinner and dead before Night.

*Political State of Great Britain*, July 1738

Lately died at Dunston Green, Oxon, after twelve days painful illness, Mr. C. Langford, formerly an eminent farmer and grazier of that place. His death was occasioned by eating a large quantity of cherries, and very imprudently swallowing the stones, which produced an obstruction in his bowels terminating in a mortification. Thus fell a hearty, hale constitution, a woeful sacrifice to the incautious use of fruit.

*London Chronicle*, 13 September 1796

Rev. Mr *Richards*, parson of the *Hay*, *Herefordshire*, as supposed suddenly. His friends seeing his body and limbs did not stiffen, after 24 hours, sent for a doctor, who upon bleeding him, and not being able to stop the blood; told his friends that he was not dead, but in a sort of trance, and ordered them not to bury him, which, however, they did the next day. A person walking along the church yard, hearing a noise in the grave, ran and prevailed with the clerk to have the grave opened, where they found a great bleeding at the nose, and the body in a profuse sweat; whence 'tis conjectured that he was bury'd alive, tho' they were now obliged to let him remain, as all appearance of recovery was vanish'd by his internment.

*Gentleman's Magazine*, January 1751

A note in brackets referred readers to the issue for December 1747 in which a correspondent suggested that in order to prevent 'that most barbarous of murders, that of burying alive', people should 'have the patience to wait 'til the body sends forth a cadaverous smell, or shews any evident mark of putrefaction'.

Deaths from lower social groups were only deemed worthy of reporting if they arose from accidents or misadventure:

> Sunday last in the afternoon some boys got into an inclosed orchard belonging to Bamber Gascoyne, Esq; at Barking, in which an elk was kept, and opening the gate of the orchard, they drove the beast about the grounds till at last the animal was so enraged that he ran after them, and gored a lad about 15 years of age so terribly that he died within an hour afterwards.
>
> *Reading Mercury*, 22 February 1768

In many accounts of deaths, the victim came to a sticky end. This was particularly true of Robert Myres, who shit himself to death:

> DIED. At his House in Clare Market, Mr. Robert Myres Jun. a wealthy Butcher. He dined on Friday with some Friends at a Tavern on Mock-Turtle, when two of the Company wantonly put a Quantity of Jalap in his Plate, which operated so violently as to occasion his death.
>
> *Aris's Birmingham Gazette*, 22 April 1771

Suicides could usually be guaranteed a fairly full report. Here are two contenders for the title of the world's most inefficient suicide:

> On Tuesday one Robinson a Journeyman Goldbeater in Little Britain, being disordered in his Senses, stabb'd himself with an Iron Scewer, then cut his Throat, and afterwards hanged himself with his Apron Strings, but the Cellar wherein he committed the horrid Fact, being low, he did not fully execute his Design, and was cut down alive. He had attempted some Violences the Night before, but he was prevented.
>
> *Chester Weekly-Journal*, 22 February 1726/27

> Yesterday Morning the following remarkable and unhappy Circumstance of Suicide happened: Capt. Bruce, of Holles-street, Cavendish-square, (as is supposed in a Fit of Insanity) drew a Pair of Pistols from his Pocket, and shot himself in the Head, but finding that he did not immediately expire, he drew his Sword and fell upon it, which struck against a Bone and broke. His Groans alarmed his Footman, who in vain attempted to force open the Door of the Room, but was obliged to get in at the Window and alarm the House: a Surgeon who lived next Door was sent for, who drew the Part of the broken Sword from the Wound, dressed him, and put him to Bed, and left him in a seeming Composure: But as soon as he found himself alone, he took a large Knife and stabbed himself, and, strange as it

appears, the Blade of the Knife broke; the Surgeon again dressed those Wounds, and after a Time he was left as before. He then got to his Pocket, took out a Penknife, cut his Throat, laid the Knife by his Side, and laid himself down and died.

*Jackson's Oxford Journal*, 10 April 1779

Even after death, nothing was safe:

On Saturday last was committed to New Prison, Clerkenwell … John Fowler … on suspicion of removing the dead body of Ann Vicars out of the burying-ground belonging to the parish of St. Giles, Cripplegate; and also on suspicion of taking and carrying away the coffin and shroud; on Monday he impeached an accomplice, whose house was searched by virtue of a warrant from the Bench of Justices … when a box, full of human bones, and three skulls was found. The man is absconded, but his wife is taken up. – It is remarkable, that this man keeps a number of wild beasts, but it is not known with what he feeds them.

*Reading Mercury*, 13 May 1765

## Ghosts and Witchcraft

Stories about popular superstitions show that, while the newspapers themselves did not subscribe to a belief in ghosts or witches, in some sections of society those beliefs remained:

A Report having been spread that a House near *Artillery-lane*, in *Bishopsgate-street* was haunted; a Tradesman of Credit and good Sense went thither, in order to satisfy his Curiosity, and to detect the Cheat if there was any, but he returned to his House frighted, speechless, and is since run mad, notwithstanding he had the assistance of an eminent Physician. If it should come out that there is any Knavery in this Business, it will be hard to say whether this last mentioned Fact is the worst; indeed there is such a spirit of Levity as well as Knavery at present predominant amongst us, that it were to be wished, Parents and Housekeepers would endeavour to correct those under their Care, and to do their utmost to restore that Sobriety and Purity of Manners for which the Inhabitants of the City of *London* especially were formerly distinguished.

*Political State of Great Britain*, February 1737

*July 30.* At *Hertford* assizes was condemned *Tho. Colley* for the murder of *Ruth Osborne* near *Tring*. Such was the folly and superstition of the crowd, that when they searched the work-house for the supposed witch, they even looked into the salt-box, supposing that she might have concealed herself within less space than would contain a cat. Having wrapped the deceased and her husband in two different sheets, first tying their great toes and thumbs together, the most active of the mob dragged the deceased into the water by a cord which they had put round her body, and she not sinking, the prisoner *Colley* went into the pond, and turned her over several times with a stick; after a considerable time she was hawl'd to shore, and the old man was dragg'd into the pond in the same manner; and this they repeated to each three times. The deceased after she was dragg'd in the third time, being pushed about by the prisoner, slipt out of the sheet, and her body was exposed naked; notwithstanding which the prisoner continued to push her on the breast with his stick. After using her in this manner till she was motionless, they dragg'd her to shore, and laid her on the ground where she expired; and then the prisoner went among the spectators, and collected money for the pains he had taken in showing them sport.

*August 24. Thomas Colley* for the murder of *Ruth Osborne* was executed at *Gubblecot Cross*, and afterwards hang'd in chains on the same gallows near 30 miles from the place of his confinement; the people about Marston Meere having petitioned against hanging him near their houses. He was escorted from *Hertford* gaol by the sheriff and his officers, and a guard of 108 men, 7 officers, and 2 trumpets belonging to the regiment of horse blue. The infatuation of the country people was so great that many thousands stood at a distance to see him go, grumbling and muttering that it was a hard case to hang a man for destroying an old wicked woman who had done so much mischief by her witchcraft.

*Gentleman's Magazine*, August 1751

A very extraordinary circumstance has lately attracted the notice of the inhabitants of Colchester. A widow woman, (Mrs. B.) who kept a farm in the neighbourhood, frequently complained of her house being haunted. Strange noises were heard in the dead of the night; the furniture of the kitchen and the bed-chambers was thrown about the floors; the milk turned in the dairy, and many other alarming incidents took place. Crowds of people went from most parts of Essex to be witness of the devastations committed by this mischievous apparition. Several people sat up during the night, and were convinced how well-founded Mrs. B's complaints were. A worthy clergyman, however, on Friday last developed the whole mystery, by bringing the Lady of the Mansion to a confession that the demon who haunted it was no other than herself, who had found means to make the above disturbance, in order to prevent a young woman (to whom her son s going to be married) from coming to live at the farm. The above, we are assured from concurring testimonies, is absolutely fact.

*Salisbury and Winchester Journal*, 2 August 1784

Reports of sea monsters and other strange creatures crop up infrequently. Generally, the newspapers distanced themselves from the stories by attributing the source without comment:

From *Exeter* by Letters dated the 21st of *July*, came an Account that on the 12th instant, just without *Exmouth* Bar, by *Robert Heath* (the Person who caught 2 Fishes, by People in general called *Mermaids*, on *Sept.* 9, 1737. the other *May* 6, last) was taken a strange or stranger Fish, supposed by many to be the Triton, or *Merman*, of the Ancients, being 4 Feet and a half in Length, having a Body much resembling that of a Man, with a Genital Member of considerable Size; together with jointed Legs and Feet, extending from his Belly 12 or 13 Inches, with Fins at his Thighs, and larger ones like Wings, in the Form of which those of Angels are often painted, at his Shoulders, with a broad Head of very uncommon Form, a Mouth 6 Inches wide, Smellers, or kind of Whiskers at his Nostrils, and two Spout-holes behind his Eyes, through which he ejected Water when taken, 30 or 40 Feet high.

*Political State of Great Britain*, August 1738

## Ballooning

Newspapers frequently carried reports of scientific inventions. In the last quarter of the century, experiments with balloons caught the imagination, and newspapers were full of accounts of the aeronauts. *Jackson's Oxford Journal* for 15 November 1783 carried a story about one Joseph Fathom who built an experimental balloon which he tied to a barge horse with 50 yards of cable in the expectation that 'he might be towed along at Pleasure in this Aerial Vehicle':

> Up he flew – flew indeed! for alas, at the very Instant of his Departure, an unfortunate Puff of Wind taking off his Hat, he in snatching at it, let go the Moderating String of the Machine, which, being quite full of inflammable Air, rushed upwards with such Impetuosity as to force not only him, but the Horse too, into the upper regions of the Atmosphere. The Weather being clouded over, the Machine and its Appendages were soon out of Sight. Messengers have been dispatched along every Direction in which the Wind has blown ever since that dreadful Accident, and it is said that last Night one of them returned with Advice that the Horse had fallen on a House, with about 20 Yards of the Cable which appeared to have given Way: Upon which Report our Philosophers assure us, that the Loss of so much Weight by forcing poor Fathom up a Mile or two higher into Air utterly unfit for Respiration, must have put an immediate End to his Existence.

SALISBURY, AUGUST 23.

An air balloon, 15 feet in circumference, was launched from Milford, near this city, on Monday evening, by Robert Lampard, an ingenious young man there, to the entire satisfaction of a very large number of spectators. It continued visible nearly eight minutes, travelling almost due East, and was at length lost in the clouds. The next morning it was found in Farley Wood, near Winchester, by Capt. Ford, of the 7th regiment, and carried to the Shakespeare's Head, St. Cross, where a live cat was affixed to it, and a good market made of the credulity of the public, by shewing it and the animal as having made an aerial voyage together.

*Salisbury and Winchester Journal*, 23 August 1784

## The weather

News about the weather usually mentioned extremes of heat or cold, unusually high winds, heavy rain causing flooding and loss of life or unseasonably good weather causing the early or late flourishing of crops. The following extracts show how newspapers reported the great Uxbridge hailstorm of 1738, the floods of 1748 and the severe cold winter of 1789:

> Last Tuesday, between the Hours of Twelve and One at Noon, there happen'd at Uxbridge one of the most dreadful Hurricanes of Hail, accompany'd with Wind and Lightening, that has been known in the Memory of the oldest Person living; the Hail-stones were of so prodigious a Size, and flew with such Velocity, that they broke many of the Windows in the Town, and split the Tiles on Houses, wounding divers Passengers and Horses on the Road, tearing large Branches off the stoutest Trees, and destroying vast Quantities of Fruit; Numbers of People ran about Uxbridge with bloody Hands and Faces cut with the Stones. Mr Sarjeant at the Crown-Inn had three large Chickens and two Pigeons kill'd in his Yard, besides all the Glasses that cover'd his Beds in the Garden broke to pieces, together with the Windows of his Cupola, his Damage alone being computed at 20l. The Birds were struck dead in the Air in vast Numbers, and the Horses took fright and run away on the Road. In a Word, all Nature that beheld it stood shock'd and amaz'd. The Storm continu'd about a Quarter of an Hour, and was felt about a Mile and half round the Place. The Hail-stones being gather'd up, some of them were found to measure seven or eight inches round, and to be of a harder Consistency than even Ice itself: The Inhabitants have taken Care to preserve many of them for the Satisfaction of the Curious.
>
> *London Evening-Post*, 27 July 1738

> There have been the greatest floods on the edge of *Cheshire* and *Derbyshire* that ever were known: the river *Goit* overflowed, and carried all the bridges, mills, and several houses away, besides washing out of their graves, at *Hawfield* church-yard, 14 bodies, which were found hanging upon hedges some miles from the church.
>
> *Gentleman's Magazine*, August 1748

> The scene on the Thames this week has been really entertaining, from Putney-Bridge upwards, the river being completely frozen over, and people walking to and from the different villages on the face of the deep. – Booths have been erected, and a fair kept on the river. – Puppet-shews, round-abouts, and all the various amusements of Bartholomew-fair exhibited.
>
> At Shadwell the Thames was likewise frozen quite over, several booths were fixed on the ice, and on Wednesday an ox was roasted whole, and sold to the people who were skaiting and sliding.
>
> Yesterday about two o'Clock as some people were drinking on the ice, a little below London-bridge, that part of the ice the tent was upon broke from the main body, and floated with the tide almost to one of the arches of London-bridge, where the people were taken out in boats.
>
> *Wheeler's Manchester Chronicle*, 17 January 1789

## Elections

Hogarth's four election prints show that parliamentary elections were corrupt and often violent. In the constituencies where contested elections took place, each candidate had a great deal at stake. For the City of London merchant who sat for Parliament there was the opportunity to snap up contracts to supply government departments at inflated prices and take part in debates that decided which duties should be charged on what goods. For the younger son of the landed gentry, there was the possibility of landing a valuable sinecure as a reward for voting the right way. For both, there was the possibility of receiving monetary and other favours for using their influence to advance the commercial interests of groups or individuals outside Parliament. Money laid out in buying sufficient votes to secure election could produce a sizeable return on the investment. For the unsuccessful candidate, there was the prospect of bankruptcy if the bribes were too high for his means, but not high enough to buy the majority of the voters. For the voter, a contested election provided a wonderful excuse to get drunk at someone else's expense and take part in a pitched battle. And for the newspaper, there was a good supply of news stories:

> We hear from Northampton, that last week two men drank to such excess of the liquors given to the populace on account of the ensuing election, that they died in a few hours after; that the lower sort of people, being continually heated with liquor, assemble in large bodies, and go about the town in a riot, knocking people down, &c. One man, a few days ago, received so violent a blow on the head, as killed him on the spot: and that it is dangerous for persons to go about their business.
>
> *The Craftsman; or Say's Weekly Journal*, 28 November 1767

> A letter from Tregony in Cornwall mentions, that at the contested Election there, nine People were killed in the Mob.
>
> An opulent Elector, in a certain Borough in the West, was lately offered 50l. a Year and 700 l. in Money, for his Vote and Interest, which he nobly refused.
>
> *Chelmsford, March 30.* The Mob Yesterday Afternoon at this Place, both during the Time of the Poll, and after the closing of it, were extremely riotous and outrageous, breaking almost all the Windows, knocking one another down, and behaving in such a Manner that the Inhabitants were afraid to stir out of their Houses. Two Men lost their Lives; another was run over by a Coach, and had both his Legs and one of his Arms broke. In short, so dismal a Scene has not been known here for many Years.
>
> *St. James's Chronicle*, 31 March 1768

> At Salisbury assizes last week, were tried three several actions depending against one Bye, an agent to one of the candidates at the late Hindon election, who gave money to the electors through a hole in the wall.
>
> *Reading Mercury*, 14 August 1775

At Chelmsford assizes on Wednesday se'nnight, a cause was tried ... wherein a capital innkeeper at Colchester was plaintiff, and an unsuccessful candidate at an election was defendant. The action was brought by the plaintiff to recover the sum of 640l. being the amount of two bills delivered for provisions, liquor, and entertainment, furnished by the plaintiff to the defendant and his friends at the two last elections for Members to serve in Parliament.

*Salisbury and Winchester Journal*, 21 March 1785

At Nottingham there were dreadful riots on account of the Election. The Candidate was knocked down three times in going from the Cross to his own house, and it is thought he was killed; an attempt was then made to pull down his house, in which one of the mob was shot. Several of the men were killed, and several dangerously wounded. Two thousand pounds will not repair the damage done to the different houses. Peace was at length restored by a party of the light horse, which the Magistrates were obliged to call in, having previously read the riot-act to very little purpose.

*Kentish Gazette*, 29 June 1790

## Women

Evidence of the condition of women in eighteenth-century life was more implicit than explicit in the newspapers. There was much discussion about the reform of prostitutes in the pages of the chronicles at the time of the opening of the Magdalen Houses in the 1760s, and examples of women criminals throughout the century. But these were not representative of the condition of women as a whole. Even less representative were the rare examples of lesbianism in the newspapers. While society had a barbaric response to male homosexuality, lesbianism left it confused and uncertain of how to respond:

At a quarter sessions of the peace, held at *Taunton, Somersetshire, Mary Hamilton*, otherwise *Charles*, otherwise *George Hamilton*, was try'd for pretending herself a man, and marrying 14 Wives, the last of which, *Mary Price*, deposed in court that she was marry'd to the prisoner, and bedded and lived as man and wife for a quarter of a year, during which time, she thought the prisoner a man, owing to the prisoner's vile and deceitful practices. After a debate about the nature of the crime, and what to call it, it was agreed that she was an uncommon, notorious cheat, and sentenced to be publicly whipt in *Taunton, Glastonbury, Wells* and *Shipton Mallet*, to be imprison'd 6 months, and to find security for as long time as the justices at the next quarter sessions shall think fit.

*Gentleman's Magazine*, November 1746

The newspapers give the general impression of women being mere chattels of their husbands, as in the criminal conversation (adultery) cases in high society, and the sale of wives in low society. Yet, on the other hand, there are examples of female entrepreneurs such as Mrs Mapp, the bone setter, whose talent for self-publicity at Epsom races and the London playhouses earned her considerable press coverage in 1736, and the quack doctor Mrs Stephens who was granted £5,000 by Act of Parliament in 1739 for divulging the secret of her cure for the stone. The advertisements in the provincial papers include many placed by female tradespeople who have taken over their late husband's business.

Occasionally, there is a glimpse of a totally independent woman, making the best progress she can by living dangerously on her wits:

> A few Weeks ago a genteel Woman, about 25 Years of Age, applied to a Farmer and Broom-Maker, near Hadleigh in Hants for a Lodging; telling him that she was the Daughter of a Nobleman, and forced from her Father's House by his ill Treatment. Her Manner of relating the Story so affected the Farmer, that he took her in and kindly entertained her. In the Course of Conversation, she artfully let drop that she had a Fortune of 90,000l. of which she should be possessed as soon as her Friends in London knew where she was. After some Days Stay, she told the Farmer, that the best Return in her Power for his Favours, would be to marry his Son Thomas (a Lad of about 18) if it was agreeable to him. The poor old Man was overjoyed at the Proposal, and in a short Time they were married; after which she informed her Father-in-Law she had great Interest at Court; and if he could for the present raise Money to equip them in a genteel Manner, she should procure a Colonel's Commission for her Husband. The credulous Farmer thereupon mortgaged his little Estate for 100l. and every Thing necessary being bought for the new-married Couple, they took the rest of the Money and set out for London, accompanied by three of the Farmer's Friends, and got to the Bear Inn in the Borough on Christmas Eve; where they lived in an expensive Manner; and she went in a Coach every Morning to St. James's End of the Town, on Pretence of solliciting for her Husband's Commission, and to obtain her own Fortune: but it was at length discovered that the Woman was an Impostor; and the poor Country People were obliged to sell their Horses by Auction, towards defraying the Expenses at the Inn, before they could set out on their Return Home, which they did on Foot last Saturday Morning. Before the fatal Discovery, the Company were greatly pleased with the Woman's behaviour, as she was not only very sprightly and engaging in Conversation, but sang and played on the Guitar to Perfection. By the Description given, she is supposed to be the same Woman who has for near two Years past obtained Money, by imposing on the Compassion and Credulity of different Persons in Town and Country.
>
> *St. James's Chronicle*, 10 January 1765

She turns up again, two years later:

> At the general quarter sessions held for the borough of Devizes, on the 9th instant, one Sarah Boxall was convicted upon the vagrant act, and adjudged a vagabond: She declared her maiden name was Wilson, and that about two years since she was

married to Farmer Boxall, of Frensham in Surrey, her own relations living in London. – It seems this woman has for some time past been travelling through almost all parts of the kingdom, assuming various roles and characters. At different times and places she has pretended herself to be of high birth and distinction, as well foreign as English, and accordingly stiled herself a Princess of Mecklenbourg, Countess of Normandy, Lady Vicountess Wilbrahammon, &c. and under some or other of such names made promises of providing, by means of her weight and interest, for the families of the lower class of people, at the same time borrowing money from them, and giving notes in payment. Unto those of higher rank she has represented herself to be in the greatest distress, abandoned by her parents and friends of considerable family, either on account of an unfortunate love affair, or of religion, pretending to be a Protestant against the will of her relations, Roman Catholicks, and always varying the account of herself, as she chanced to pick up intelligence of the characters and connections of those she intended to impose upon. – A description of the person of this woman was published in the evening posts of July 1, and July 15, 1766, dated from Coventry, and Great Budworth in Cheshire. Since that she has been mostly in the North of England upon the like errand, till July last, when she thought proper to direct her travels for the Western counties, and in these parts gone about to the houses of divers families; among others, she had the impudence to visit Lord Bottetourt, in Gloucestershire, and attempted the like civility to the Countess of Shelburne, while in Wiltshire, but endeavouring to impose false and crafty representations of her distress on sundry persons in the Devizes, information thereof was made before Charles Carth, Esq.; who issued a warrant for her apprehension; in consequence whereof, she is to be conveyed, by a pass, to Frensham (sworn by her to be the place of her husband's settlement) after the time of her punishment ordered upon her conviction is expired. – She is a short, slender woman, of a pale complexion, somewhat deformed, has a speck or kell over one eye, and dresses in a lightish coloured riding habit.

*Say's Weekly Journal*, 24 October 1767

Would that she had lived forty years earlier, she would have made a wonderful model for a novel by Defoe!

## Entertainment

The use of humour is a common feature of the eighteenth-century newspaper. In order to retain the readers' interest, the newspaper writers tried to make their news as entertaining as possible, selecting items that were likely to amuse as well as inform:

A few days since a very remarkable affair happened at a lady's house in Grantham. As the maid-servant was going through the dining-room she saw a man's legs hanging down the chimney, which she had the presence of mind not to take any further notice of till she got down stairs, when she alarmed the family and neighbourhood, and having got proper assistance, they entered the room with fire-arms, and pulled the man from out of the chimney, who, to their great surprise, they found to be a young gentleman that Venus had blindly misguided.

*General Evening Post*, 9 November 1765

One Day last Week the Master of a certain Tavern, not a Mile from Garlick Hill, caught one of his Waiters in Bed with his Wife, and in the Day Time; he called all the Servants up to be Witnesses of this Scene of Matrimonial Impiety. One of his Neighbours by Way of Comfort told him, 'That now he was in the Fashion; 'twas Marriage A-la-mode, as performed at the West End of the Town among Persons of Quality.'

*Aris's Birmingham Gazette*, 4 November 1771

Last Week two Men came into a Publick-House at Stadhampton in Oxfordshire, one of them pretended to be deaf and dumb, and the other assumed the Character of his Servant, who took an Opportunity of informing the Company, that his Master was the most extraordinary Gentleman in the Universe for his wonderful Knowledge in Medicine, having, as he termed it, a peculiar Faculty assigned him by Providence for curing every Kind of Distemper, however obstinate, by taking only two small Phials of his Preparation, which were delivered at the small Price of 5s. The Bait was swallowed, and the Doctor supported the Dignity of his Character for some Time, till at length he became elevated with Liquor, and unwarily discovered that he possessed a peculiar Fluency of Speech, which so irritated some Countrymen present, that they determined to prescribe for the Doctor, and it was agreed that a Cudgel should be immediately applied, which was laid on so heartily, that he narrowly escaped without broken Bones.

*Daily Advertiser*, 27 October 1772

As far as domestic coverage went, the writers of early newspapers and their readers had broadly the same news values as today. Only the detail was different, because society was different: the highwayman no longer comes riding, riding; they no longer send six-year-old girls to Bridewell or hang 14-year-olds; and the secret ballot has meant that spending a fortune in passing money through the wall and getting whole communities drunk in exchange for votes is no longer necessary. In these respects the past *is* another country, through which the newspaper can serve as our guide. But the interest in crime and the light-hearted attitude to sex is timeless. The human-interest stories of the old news-writers show that the newspaper readers of previous centuries were, like us, curious about the lives of others and willing to laugh at their misfortunes, and yet, where appropriate, as in the case of Isabella Condon, to feel sorrow and anger on their behalf.

# Chapter 8

# Foreign News, Wars and Shipwrecks

> It will be found from the Foreign Prints, which from time to time, as Occasion offers, will be mention'd in this Paper, that the Author has taken Care to be duly furnish'd with all that comes from Abroad in any Language. And for an Assurance that he will not, under Pretence of having Private Intelligence, impose any Additions of feign'd Circumstances to an Action, but give his Extracts fairly and Impartially; at the beginning of each Article he will quote the Foreign Paper from whence 'tis taken, that the Publick, seeing from what Country a piece of News comes with the Allowance of that Government, may be better able to Judge of the Credibility and Fairness of the Relation: Nor will he take it upon himself to give any Comments or Conjectures of his own, but will relate only Matter of Fact; supposing other People to have Sense enough to make Reflections for themselves.
>
> *Daily Courant*, 11 March 1702

Foreign news was the main feature of the early newspapers. In the days of the corantos, it was the only news. Even during the first decades of the eighteenth century, foreign news dominated the papers. Home news was the poor relation, comprising little more than a short paragraph or two tucked away at the back of the paper.

## Translations from Foreign Newspapers

No change was signalled by the first daily paper. The editorial advertisement, quoted above, in the first issue of *The Daily Courant* (Figure 8.1) made it clear that translations from the continental newspapers were going to be the mainstay of the new publication. This emphasis on foreign news indicates that the early-eighteenth-century newspapers were aimed at an informed and educated readership – politicians, London merchants and others in the City who had an interest in the economic and political consequences of the shifting balance of power in Europe. There was little to attract the general reader interested in domestic happenings.

It was standard practice to take the news straight from the continental newspapers or *The London Gazette* with little or no editorial intervention, save that of selection. The following extracts are representative of the style of the newspapers of the period:

Numb. 8132

# The Daily Courant.

Thurſday, November 2. 1727.

*Bon*, October 17.

THE Elector of Cologn is thought to be by this Time at Florence, and they ſpeak now with more Certainty of his Journey to Rome; the rather, ſince he travels incognito under the Name of Count de Wertern.

*Vienna*, Oct. 18. Some Days ago a Courier was diſpatched to Petersbourg, for which Place, M. de Hochholtzer, the Imperial Reſident, ſet out Poſt the 16th. His Imperial Majeſty has now offered Count de Wratiſlau, his late Ambaſſadour at Warſaw, the Embaſſy to the Ruſſian Court. There is no more Talk of the Duke of Holſtein's coming hither. Count de Thaun, Governour of Milan, giving but little Hopes of his recovering, and the ill State of Health of Count de Metſch, Ambaſſadour to the Circle of Lower Saxony, increaſing every Day, thoſe two Poſts will in all Likelihood ſoon become vacant. The Pamphlet publiſhed ſome Years ago, entituled, *Political Diſcourſe upon the great Power of the Electoral Houſe of Brandenbourg, &c.* having been lately reprinted and publiſhed in this City, the Pruſſian Envoy has made heavy Complaints thereupon to the Emperour in the Name of the King his Maſter, the rather, ſince that Writing contains Reflexions diſreſpectful to his Majeſty, and tending to ſet him at Variance with the Roman Catholick Powers. Advices from Hungary inform us, that Biſhop Jani was ſet upon in his Way to Semendria, his new Biſhoprick, near Belgrade, by Highwaymen in a Wood, who murdered him and his Coachman, but his two Heyducks found Means to eſcape.

*Zurich*, Oct. 18. The Romiſh Cantons wait with the utmoſt Impatience for the Arrival of the Marqueſs de Bonac the French Ambaſſadour, in hopes of having not only their Penſions renewed, but alſo of ſeeing the Affair of Reſtitution brought again upon the Carpet, or at leaſt of obliging the Cantons of Zurich and Bern to admit them as Partners in the Regency of the County of Baden; but the Proteſtant Cantons are of a quite different Opinion, being firmly perſwaded that the ſaid Miniſter does not come into Switzerland upon thoſe Accounts, but on purpoſe to negociate ſomething of Moment with the Proteſtant Cantons: Which ſuppoſed, it is not at all likely that he will propoſe any Thing contrary to a ſolemn Treaty concluded with the Mediation of a French Ambaſſadour; the rather, ſince the Court of France is very well ſatisfied that Zurich and Bern will not ſo much as hear of annulling the Treaty of Arau. They write from Rochelle, that in thoſe Parts abundance of People are carried off by Diſtempers which are very rife there.

*Schaffhauſen*, Oct. 23. The Family of the Marqueſs de Bonac, the French Ambaſſadour, is arrived at Solothurn, where his Excellency is expected next Week. We have an Account from Coire, that ſince the foreign Proteſtants ſettled in the Valteline and Cleef have reſolved to depart from thence, they impatiently expect now what will be the Fate of the native Proteſtants, and what the Majority of the Commonalties will determine in that Matter. Baron de Reiſenfels and his Party labour indefatigably by their Repreſentations, to prevail with the Commonalties to expel alſo out of the ſaid Countries the native Proteſtants, in Execution of the laſt Capitulation; but the Sentiments of the latter are drawn up in ambiguous Terms, in order to ward off, or at leaſt to ſuſpend for a while the final Reſolution on that Head.

*Francfort*, Oct. 23. On the 21ſt, Prince Alexander of Wurtemberg arrived here from Ludwigsberg, where he paid a Viſit to the reigning Duke. Our Magiſtrates ordered the Cannon to be fired at his Arrival, and complimented him afterwards by their Deputies, but he would not accept of the Company of Foot appointed to wait upon him, and Yeſterday Morning he ſet out for Bruſſels under the Diſcharge of our Artillery. The Meeting of the Circle of the Upper Rhine has been deferred to the latter End of the Month of November, but that of Suabia is aſſembled at Ulm, there to confer upon a Moderation of their Contingent. 18 Barrils full of Money lie ready here to be carried to Luxembourg.

*Mentz*, Oct. 24. As the preſent Juncture of Affairs is ſuch, that it is hard to gueſs whether we ſhall have Peace or War, our Elector endeavours to put off the ſending circular Letters to the Circle of the Upper Rhine for their Meeting, till he ſees clearer what Turn the Affairs of Europe will take, in order to concert then more effectual Meaſures at the Meeting of the Circle.

*Liverpool*, Oct. 27. Since my laſt arrived here the Whitehaven from Bremen; Katherine from Norway; Lawrel and May-Flower, both from the ſame Place; Scipio from Maryland; Oliver and Ann from Stockholm; Lawrel from Jamaica; Two Brothers from Riga; Virginia Merchant from Archangel.

*Deal*,

**8.1** Foreign news in *The Daily Courant*, 2 November 1727

*Vienna*, Feb. 6. N. S.

OUR last Letters from Constantinople are dated the 5th of the last Month, and inform us, That the Declaration of War against the Republick of Venice, publish'd on the 8th of December, had occaision'd divers Alterations in the Ministers of the Ottoman Porte; the Mufti, the Captain Bassaw, and several other Officers, having been depos'd. The same Advices say farther, That the Command of the Navy was conferr'd upon Gianum-Chogia; who being a Native of the Morea, was look'd upon as the fittest Person to be entrusted with the Management of an Enterprize against his own Country. His Fleet will, according to their Accounts, consist of about 300 Sail. The Bassaw of Belgrade is order'd to go to Jeni-Kalai; and Kiuproli-Oghlu-Numan Bassaw, Son of the late Grand Visier, who was kill'd in the Battle of Salankement, is appointed to succeed him. As for the Venetians that were settled at Constantinople, all the Merchants are to go on board two Ships of their Republick, which are ready to sail out of the Harbour: But the Bailo, or Ambassador, is detain'd in Custody, with all his Domesticks. The Express which arrived here some Days ago from the Elector of Cologn, is sent back to Liege, with a favourable Answer to his Electoral Highness's Dispatches. The Equivalent to be given to the Elector-Palatine, in lieu of the Upper Palatinate, is at last agreed upon.

*Post Boy*, 17 February 1714–15

Hamburgh, July 25. We have Letters from Petersburg which say, that a certain Resident there was arrested in his own House, and his Papers brought into the Russian Chancery, upon Pretence that he had written things that were not agreeable to Truth; and that the Vice-Chancellor Baron Schasiroff had let the other Ministers know, that this Accident ought not to give them Disturbance, the Rights of Nations not being thereby infring'd, but on the contrary, well taken Care of, and secured. They have no news at Petersburg from Aland.

[Read's] *Weekly Journal or, British Gazetteer*, 9 August 1718

The striking thing about these news items is their staleness, especially considering the eleven days difference between the continental New Style (N. S.) and the English Old Style calendars. The story in the *Post Boy* was translated from a newspaper over 20 days old, quoting from letters that were a month older.

## Interpreting the News

By the 1720s, the livelier weekly journals, aimed at a wider audience, acted as an intermediary between the raw material in the continental papers and the reader in a way that would have dismayed the writer of *The Daily Courant*. They presented the foreign news in the form of a commentary or extended essay. Where the raw material was confusing or contradictory, they would say so.

As the North is barren of News, so what they send is of Information; and they rather leave us to guess at their Designs, than tell us what they are. We are kept much in the dark about the Affairs of Sweden and Muscovy; one Week they amuse us with Hopes of Peace, the next they contradict it all, and tell us, War is resolved on; so that, in short we are at the utmost loss what to conclude.

*Mist's Weekly Journal*, 24 December 1720

The Turks and Poles have had a *Skirmish*, upon the Borders of the two Nations, near *Choezin*, but who has had the Best of it we can't learn; and what may be the Consequences of it is still harder to come to the Knowledge of. The Action happened within the Turkish Territories, upon which the Poles had entered, in order to make Reprisals for much the same Sort of Visit made to them some little Time before, by the Turks, when the Latter plundered the Country, and carried away the Inhabitants: Each Side calls the other Aggressors, and they mutually complain of Injustice, and demand Satisfaction, but which of them will be obliged to make it, Time can only discover.

*London Journal*, 4 February 1720

## Entertainment and Sensationalism

At this time, the range of foreign news, hitherto restricted to largely uninformative diplomatic intelligence and the movements of continental armies, expanded to include more sensational items designed to entertain and provide a talking-point in coffee-house and tavern:

We have received an Account from Amsterdam that it was observed by the Populace there, that sixteen Coffins were carried from their City-House, or Guildhall, which Coffins were supposed to contain Bodies that had been privately executed for Sodomy, of the richer Sort of People; and that Morning about 29 Persons, of mean Extraction, were to have been publickly executed for the like Crime, but the Populace arising in Arms, and demanding publick Execution of the Rich as well as of the Poor, (there then being about 300 of all Ranks in Prison in that City, accused of that Crime, and some of them of great Note and Substance) the Magistrates were obliged to send to the Hague for Assistance to quell this Mob, which was very outrageous; upon which 1000 Soldiers were sent to their Assistance. A List is published of those vile Wretches that are now in Custody. Several Gentlemen that were gone to their Country Seats, were returned to their Places of Abode, partly to take Care of their own Affairs, in this dangerous Time, and partly to convince People of their being free from any Fear or Apprehension. The same Cause had occasioned the like Tumults at the Hague, Rotterdam, &c. We hear, that, hoping to appease the People, the Magistrates promised a Number of Persons of Distinction should be publickly executed, at the same Time a Parson was to be burnt alive at Rotterdam.

*The Craftsman*, 20 June 1730

We have received certain Advice of a sort of Prodigy lately discovered in *Hungary*, at a Place called *Heyducken*, situate on the other Side of the *Tibiscus*, or *Teys*; namely, of *dead Bodies* sucking, as it were, the Blood of the *Living*; for the *latter* visibly dry up, while the *former* are filled with Blood. The Fact at first Sight seems to be impossible and even ridiculous; but the following is a true Copy of a Relation, attested by unexceptionable Witnesses, and sent to the Imperial Council of War.

*Medreyga* in *Hungary*, 7 Jan. 1732

Upon a current Report, that in the Village of *Medreyga* certain dead Bodies (called here *Vampyres*) had killed several Persons, by sucking out all their Blood, the present Enquiry was made by the Honourable Commander in Chief; and Capt. *Goschutz* of the Company of *Stallater*, the *Hadnagi* Bariacrar, and the Senior Heyduke of the *Village*, were severally examined; and unanimously declared, that about five Years ago a certain Heyduke named *Arnold Paul* was killed by the Overturning of a Cart Load of Hay, who in his Life-time was often heard to say, that he had been tormented near *Caschaw*, and upon the Borders of *Turkish Servia*, by a *Vampyre*; and that to extricate himself he had eaten some of the Earth of the *Vampyre's* Graves, and rubbed himself with their Blood.

That 20 or 30 Days after the Decease of the said *Arnold Paul*, several Persons complained that they were tormented, and that, in short, he had taken away the Lives of four Persons. In order, therefore, to put a Stop to such a Calamity, the Inhabitants of the Place after having consulted their *Hardnagi*, caused the Body of the said *Arnold Paul* to be taken up, 40 Days after he had been dead, and found the same to be fresh and free from all Manner of Corruption; that he bled at the Nose, Mouth and Ears, as pure and florid Blood as ever was seen; and that his Shroud and Winding Sheet were all over bloody; and lastly his Finger and Toe Nails were fallen off and new ones grown in their Room.

As they observed from all these Circumstances, that he was a *Vampyre*, they according to Custom drove a Stake through his Heart; at which he gave a horrid Groan, and lost a great deal of Blood. Afterwards they burnt his Body to Ashes the same Day, and threw them into his Grave.

These good Men say farther, that all such as have been tormented, or killed by the *Vampyres*, become *Vampyres* when they are dead; and therefore they served several other dead Bodies as they had done *Arnold Paul's*, for tormenting the Living.

*London Journal*, 11 March 1732

Advices from SPAIN and PORTUGAL

A Gentlewoman having some Years disguised herself, under the ecclesiastical Habit, had several Church Benefices conferred upon her; and as Women are generally good Sollicitors, a Quality which in a Priest seldom goes unrewarded, the Lady was soon promoted to be Dean of the Cathedral of *Origuella*, in the Kingdom of *Mercia*, so that she was in a fair Way to arrive at the Mitre, and perhaps at the Triple Crown; but unluckily she took it into her Head to play with her Page, not at Leap-frog, as *Hudibras* says, but at a game much more natural, and consequently less criminal: How long she had continued at this Game is not known, but at last the Reverend Dean became pregnant, and was brought to bed of two Daughters in the City of *Origuella.* This news extremely surprised the Bishop of that Diocese, and raised in him a Suspicion against the whole Chapter, so that he immediately summoned a Jury of Matrons, and made all the Brotherhood undergo a strict Examination: but the Matrons declared, that none of them had any Children in their Bellies whatever they might have any where else, which made the Bishop a little easy.

*Political State of Great Britain*, June 1736

*Warsaw, August 19.* The Plague has spread into several villages in Podolia, where it carries off great Numbers of People. Many die of it also in the Palatinate of Kaminiec; but the Inhabitants ascribe it to a Cause which is perfectly ridiculous; for they have a mighty Notion of the Power of the Vampyres, and being persuaded that these Blood Suckers are the only Authors of the Mortality, they have such a tender Regard for all their deceased Relations and Friends, that they won't let them rest in their Graves, but take them out of the Ground, drive a Stake through their Hearts, and then cut off their Heads, as a Sovereign Remedy against the Vampyres: But notwithstanding this Precaution, and the Repetition of it several Times, above 47 Persons have died in Kaminiec in the Space of three Weeks, who the Inhabitants protest that every Man of them was suck'd to Death by those Leaches the Vampyres.

*Warwick and Staffordshire Journal*, 14 September 1738

They write from Macon, a Place upon the River Seine, that two Grave-diggers being at Work in a Church-yard there, dug up a Skull which they had laid down upon the Grass; but a little while after, perceiving that it stirred, they hasten'd to the Parson of the Parish, and told him that some Saint was certainly buried in the Place where they had been at Work. The Parson immediately repair'd thither, and to his great surprize saw the Skull moving, upon which he and all the Spectators cried out, *A Miracle! A Miracle!* And in order to shew the utmost Respect to so precious a Relick, he ordered the Cross, Holy Water, Surplice, &c, to be brought; he caused the Bells to ring, and call'd the Parishioners together; he then gave Directions for a Dish to be brought, in which he put this Skull, cover'd it up with a Napkin, and carried it in Procession to the Church; during which Time there were warm Debates amongst the People, each claiming Kindred to the Skull. As soon as they came to the Church, and had placed it on the High Altar, the Curate began to sing *Te Deum*; in the midst of which, a Mole was observ'd to run out of the Skull, that had been the Cause of its Motion; upon which the Priest left off singing, the Congregation went home, and the Skull was buried again.

*Warwick and Staffordshire Journal*, 3 May 1739

## News from Different Sources

At the beginning of the eighteenth century, most foreign news that did not originate in the continental newspapers came from official sources – reports from diplomats, or war news from commanders in the field or the Admiralty or from *The London Gazette*. Over time, these official reports, which tended towards the bland, were augmented by letters from private correspondents. An example of this, and of the way news travelled slowly, can be seen from one newspaper's accounts of the Lisbon earthquake.

Although the earthquake happened on 1 November 1755, the story did not reach England until the end of the month. Reading the *General Evening Post* for 29 November 1755, one can see the news coming in from different sources – continental newspapers, diplomatic communiqués, merchants' letters and other private letters, messages from ships' captains – just as the newspaper was going to print:

> *Since our last arrived a Mail from* France.
>
> *Madrid, Nov.* 4. The 1st instant we had one of the most violent Shocks of Earthquake that has been known here these many Years.
>
> *Paris, Nov.* 22. We learn by Letters from Cadiz of the 4th that the Earthquake was felt there, but did no great Damage. The Sea indeed rose so high that the whole City was in Danger of being laid under Water. The Waves beat down the Parapet of the Wall from the Gate de la Galette to Fort Catherine. The greatest Damage done in the Neighbourhood of the Town was the carrying away the Causeway leading to the Island from the Land Gate to the Cantarelle, with all the Carriages, and about 200 Persons who were on it all perished.
>
> An Express which arrived at Madrid on the 8th brought Advice that the Earthquake began at Lisbon about Nine in the Morning, and hath thrown down half the City, with all the Churches and Royal Palaces. Happily the Royal Family, who were at Belem, received no Hurt; tho' the Palace there suffered. When the Express came away they were still in Barracks, and lay in Coaches, and had been twenty-four Hours without any of their Officers or any Thing to eat. That Part of the City which continued standing had taken Fire, and was burning at the Departure of the Courier.
>
> The Nuncio at Lisbon writes to the Nuncio in this City that three of his Servants were killed, and dates his Letter, *From the Place where Lisbon stood.*
>
> 'Tis computed that 50,000 Souls, at least, have perished at Lisbon. The Shocks continued ten Hours, and had not ceased when the Courier came away.
>
> The Account of the Earthquake at Lisbon contained in the Paris A-la-Main of the 22d inst. is as follows 'His Majesty hath received a Letter from his Ambassador at Portugal with Advice that on the 1st instant there had been such a terrible Earthquake at Lisbon, that the greatest Part of the Public Edifices and Houses of that superb Capital are destroyed and upwards of 100,000 Persons buried in the Ruins. The Spanish Ambassador was crushed to Death by the Gate of his Palace falling on him as he was coming out. The French Ambassador wrote this Account in his Tent in the Fields. To add to the Misfortune, the City took fire in several Places.
>
> LONDON
>
> An Express arrived on Thursday Night from Madrid, with letters from Mr. Keene, his Majesty's Ambassador at that Court, relative to the Earthquake which has happened at Lisbon.

We hear that there are Letters in Town, by the way of France, which advise, that on the 5th instant a second Earthquake happened at Lisbon, which destroyed the Remainder of that Place, and that the same was felt at St. Ube's, whereby great Part of that Town was destroyed, and several of the Inhabitants perished.

*Extract of a Letter from a Merchant at Cadiz, dated Nov. 4. to his Correspondent in London.*

'On Saturday the first instant we had here a Violent Shock of an Earthquake, attended with the most terrible consequences. The Sea drove with great Violence against the City, particularly on the West-Side, where it threw down the Walls, so that many different Parts thereof were laid under Water, by which many Persons were either drowned or crushed to Death by the Weight of the Waters. Amongst the unfortunate Number were two very eminent French Merchants, as also several other very considerable Persons. We hear likewise of much Mischief done in many other Parts fifteen or twenty Leagues distant from hence. Particulars are not yet known.'

Capt. Clark, of the Mary, arrived from Denia, reports, that on the 1st inst. between Nine and Ten in the Forenoon, in Lat. 36. 24. they felt an Earthquake at Sea, which shattered the Ship in such a Manner as overturned the Compass in the Binacle, and broke most of their Earthen-ware, China and Bottles, and strained the Ship very much, as if she had been striking on the Ground, and cracked the Seams of the Deck, which afterwards leaked, tho' quite tight before.

SUPPLEMENT

LONDON, November 29

*Abstract from a Letter from Sir Benjamin Keene to Mr. Arthur Sturt, Merchant in London, dated Madrid, Nov.* 10.

'On the 8th inst. arrived a Courier from Lisbon with the most dreadful Accounts ever heard of from Naples or Sicily in any Age. All is demolished in Lisbon; the Palace, Patriarchal, and the great Houses, fell in five Minutes; the Fire consuming the rest, and no one to resist it. The People who have escaped with their Lives are in the Country, without Houses, Cover, or Victuals, many of them without Clothes… I dread the first Accounts of my poor English Factory, the Death of many of them, and the ruin of many more.'

A Ship is arrived at Falmouth in seven Days from Gibraltar, which brings an Account that the Earthquake was felt there, tho' no Damage done; but they did not, when this Ship came away, know of the dismal Affair at Lisbon; which is a strong Proof that the Shipping there must have suffered greatly: and, besides, we don't hear of any Ship being sailed from Lisbon to any Place since the Misfortune; at which Time many Ships of all Nations must have been in the Harbour. The Dutch Convoy arrived there but the Day before. The Brazil Fleet was all there, but not loaded.

The Dutch Mails to day bring no fresh Particulars of the dreadful Calamity at Lisbon.

## Ship News

In addition to the accounts of sea battles that were an occasional feature of the newspapers of the seventeenth and eighteenth centuries, and sometimes illustrated in the magazines (Figures 8.2 and 8.3), most papers carried a number of short paragraphs under the heading, 'Ship News', listing the arrivals and departures from London and the other ports, and the ships lost at sea. By this means, ship owners, merchants and insurers could keep track of their investments, and families could learn of the safe arrival, or otherwise, of their loved ones. The massive human tragedy caused by the losses of ships was reduced to one sentence per ship:

> The Young William, Clancy, from Malaga, for Dublin, is lost on the Coast of Lancashire, and all the Crew except the Master and one Boy, perished.
> The Isabella, Jordan, from Leith, to Plymouth, is lost.
>
> *General Evening Post*, 29 March 1755

On very rare occasions, readers were given a first-hand account from a survivor of a shipwreck. The following narrative which appeared in both the *Gentleman's Magazine* and the *Political State of Great Britain* for July 1737 is worth quoting in full:

> about the same Time the following most extraordinary Account came to Hand.
>
> *An Account of the Voyage of the Ship* Mary *from* Lisbon *to* Cutchoe *in* Guinea, *and of her Foundering at Sea. Likewise the Sufferings of the Ship's Crew, related by* Simon Mac-Cone, *and* Thomas Thompson, *the only surviving Mariners belonging to the said Vessel, as follows,* viz.
>
> Our original Commander's name was *John Rawlinson*; we sailed from *Lisbon* freighted by a *Portugese* Merchant; in our Passage to *Guinea*, we stopped at the *Cape de Verd Islands*, from thence we sailed to *Cutchoe* in *Africa*, and in five Months and odd Days we got our Cargoe of Slaves, Bees-Wax, and some Ivory. Here it was our said Captain died, and his Wife, who he had carried the Voyage with him, died also. And then our Chief Mate, one *William Rye*, was made Captain; we then sailed, intending for *Lisbon*, but stopt again at the *Cape Verd Islands* to recruit ourselves and Slaves; but sailing from thence, our second Captain died; and then *William Cook*, who was at first our second Mate, was made Captain, and remained so; for about three or four Days after he was made Captain, our Ship sprung a Leake, and our Carpenter dying on the Coast of *Africa* at *Cutchoe*, we were in a very bad Condition with our Ship. The Leake growing larger, and the Water increasing, we were several Days hard put to it, to keep the Ship above Water: At length being all tired out, by standing so hard to the Pump, we were obliged to let the Negroes out of Irons to assist us in pumping the Ship, and save our Lives, which they did for some Days; but being extreamly short of Provision and Water, they could not possibly hold out long; the Leake still increasing, we found we must prepare for the best we could, in our poor small Boat; and so we got to work upon

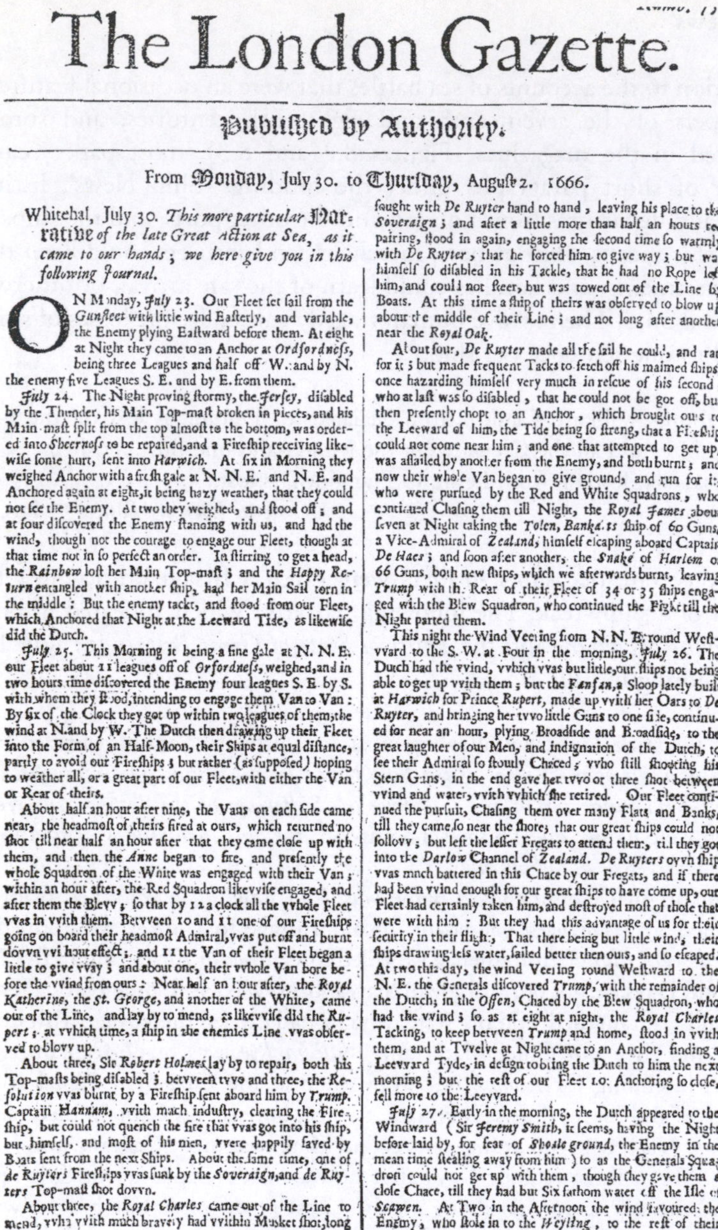

# The London Gazette.

**Published by Authority.**

From Monday, July 30. to Thursday, August 2. 1666.

Whitehal, July 30. *This more particular* Narrative *of the late Great Action at Sea, as it came to our hands; we here give you in this following Journal.*

ON Monday, *July* 23. Our Fleet set sail from the *Gunfleet* with little wind Easterly, and variable, the Enemy plying Eastward before them. At eight at Night they came to an Anchor at *Ordfordness*, being three Leagues and half off W. and by N. the enemy five Leagues S. E. and by E. from them.

*July* 24. The Night proving stormy, the *Jersey*, disabled by the Thunder, his Main Top-mast broken in pieces, and his Main mast split from the top almost to the bottom, was ordered into *Sheernoss* to be repaired, and a Fireship receiving likewise some hurt, sent into *Harwich*. At six in Morning they weighed Anchor with a fresh gale at N. N. E. and N. E. and Anchored again at eight, it being hazy weather, that they could not see the Enemy. At two they weighed, and stood off; and at four discovered the Enemy standing with us, and had the wind, though not the courage to engage our Fleet, though at that time not in so perfect an order. In stirring to get a head, the *Rainbow* lost her Main Top-mast; and the *Happy Return* entangled with another ship, had her Main Sail torn in the middle: But the enemy tackt, and stood from our Fleet, which Anchored that Night at the Leeward Tide, as likewise did the Dutch.

*July* 25. This Morning it being a fine gale at N. N. E. our Fleet about 11 leagues off of *Orfordness*, weighed, and in two hours time discovered the Enemy four leagues S. E. by S. with whom they stood, intending to engage them Van to Van: By six of the Clock they got up within two leagues of them, the wind at N. and by W. The Dutch then drawing up their Fleet into the Form of an Half-Moon, their Ships at equal distance, partly to avoid our Fireships; but rather (as supposed) hoping to weather all, or a great part of our Fleet, with either the Van or Rear of theirs.

About half an hour after nine, the Vans on each side came near, the headmost of theirs fired at ours, which returned no shot till near half an hour after that they came close up with them, and then the *Anne* began to fire, and presently the whole Squadron of the White was engaged with their Van; within an hour after, the Red Squadron likevvise engaged, and after them the Blevv; so that by 12 a clock all the vvhole Fleet vvas in vvith them. Betvveen 10 and 11 one of our Fireships going on board their headmost Admiral, vvas put off and burnt dovvn vvithout effect; and 11 the Van of their Fleet began a little to give vvay; and about one, their vvhole Van bore before the vvind from ours: Near half an hour after, the *Royal Katherine*, the *St. George*, and another of the White, came out of the Line, and lay by to mend, as likevvise did the *Rupert*; at vvhich time, a ship in the enemies Line vvas observed to blovv up.

About three, Sir *Robert Holmes* lay by to repair, both his Top-masts being disabled; betvveen tvvo and three, the *Resolution* vvas burnt by a Fireship sent aboard him by *Trump*. Captain *Hannam*, vvith much industry, clearing the Fireship, but could not quench the fire that vvas got into his ship, but himself, and most of his men, vvere happily saved by Boats sent from the next Ships. About the same time, one of *de Ruyters* Fireships vvas sunk by the *Soveraign*, and *de Ruyters* Top-mast shot dovvn.

About three, the *Royal Charles* came out of the Line to mend, vvho vvith much bravery had vvithin Musket shot, long fought with *De Ruyter* hand to hand, leaving his place to the *Soveraign*; and after a little more than half an hours repairing, stood in again, engaging the second time so warmly with *De Ruyter*, that he forced him to give way; but was himself so disabled in his Tackle, that he had no Rope left him, and could not steer, but was towed out of the Line by Boats. At this time a ship of theirs was observed to blow up about the middle of their Line; and not long after another near the *Royal Oak*.

About four, *De Ruyter* made all the sail he could, and ran for it; but made frequent Tacks to fetch off his maimed ships, once hazarding himself very much in rescue of his second, who at last was so disabled, that he could not be got off, but then presently chopt to an Anchor, which brought ours to the Leeward of him, the Tide being so streng, that a Fireship could not come near him; and one that attempted to get up, was assailed by another from the Enemy, and both burnt; and now their whole Van began to give ground, and run for it; who were pursued by the Red and White Squadrons, who continued Chasing them till Night, the *Royal James* about seven at Night taking the *Tolen*, *Bankarts* ship of 60 Guns, a Vice-Admiral of *Zealand*, himself escaping aboard Captain *De Haes*; and soon after another, the *Snake* of *Harlem* of 66 Guns, both new ships, which we afterwards burnt, leaving *Trump* with the Rear of their Fleet of 34 or 35 ships engaged with the Blew Squadron, who continued the Fight till the Night parted them.

This night the Wind Veering from N. N. E. round Westvvard to the S. W. at Four in the morning, *July* 26. The Dutch had the vvind, vvhich vvas but little, our ships not being able to get up vvith them; but the *Fanfan*, a Sloop lately built at *Harwich* for Prince *Rupert*, made up vvith her Oars to *De Ruyter*, and bringing her tvvo little Guns to one side, continued for near an hour, plying Broadside and Broadside, to the great laughter of our Men, and indignation of the Dutch, to see their Admiral so stoutly Chaced; vvho still shooting his Stern Guns, in the end gave her tvvo or three shot between vvind and water, vvith vvhich she retired. Our Fleet continued the pursuit, Chasing them over many Flats and Banks, till they came so near the shore, that our great ships could not follovv; but left the lesser Fregats to attend them, till they got into the *Darlow* Channel of *Zealand*. *De Ruyters* ovvn ship vvas much battered in this Chace by our Fregats, and if there had been vvind enough for our great ships to have come up, our Fleet had certainly taken him, and destroyed most of those that were with him: But they had this advantage of us for their security in their flight, That there being but little wind, their ships drawing less water, sailed better then ours, and so escaped. At two this day, the wind Veering round Westward to the N. E. the Generals discovered *Trump*, with the remainder of the Dutch, in the *Offen*, Chaced by the Blew Squadron, who had the vvind; so as at eight at night, the *Royal Charles* Tacking, to keep betvveen *Trump* and home, stood in vvith them, and at Tvvelve at Night came to an Anchor, finding a Leevvard Tyde, in design to bring the Dutch to him the next morning; but the rest of our Fleet not Anchoring so close, fell more to the Leevvard.

*July* 27. Early in the morning, the Dutch appeared to the Windward (Sir *Jeremy Smith*, it seems, having the Night before laid by, for fear of *Shoale ground*, the Enemy in the mean time stealing away from him) so as the Generals Squadron could not get up with them, though they gave them a close Chace, till they had but Six fathom water off the Isle of *Scawen*. At Two in the Afternoon the wind favoured the Enemy, who stole in to the *Weyling*, to the rest of their

Ffff Fleet.

**8.2** The St James's Day Fight, *The London Gazette*, 30 July to 2 August 1666

**8.3** Sea Battle, *Gentleman's Magazine*, April 1760

her, and got into her seven Stone Bottles of Water, and five Bottles of Brandy, which was all we could get, for when we got any Provision upon Deck to throw into the Boat, the Slaves being in Number two or three hundred, and Provision very short, they seized upon it, and eat it from us; and then the Slaves got what liquor they could find, and perceiving us to be very much confused, they took the Opportunity to get drunk, and forsook the Pump, which we seeing, and observing nothing but Death like to ensue, we got into the Boat, eight in Number, being two *Portugese* and six white Men, and veered her a-stern of the Ship about the 8th of *November*, 1736, at Night, the Ship being then upon sinking as we thought, and finding the rest of the Ship's Company wanted to jump into the Boat, which must have sunk her; we remained a-stern, not daring to pull along Side of the Ship; and next Morning, being the 9th of November, we left the Ship to the Hand of Providence, and so went to Sea in the Boat, believing ourselves near the *Canary-Islands*; but being Leeward of them, we were obliged to bear away for some of the *West-India* Islands, which were at least five or six hundred Leagues from us. Our Boat's Crew were two *Portugese*, four *English*, one *Irish*, and one *Rhode Island* Man born; the two latter whereof are the Authors of this Declaration.

Fifteen white Men we left on board the said Ship, which we believe perished with her. After we left the said Ship, we sailed in the Boat to and fro for several Weeks, until the 8th Day of *December* last to the best of our Remembrance, at which Time we saw a Sail, which was a Snow, and which revived us very much, and we hoisted a Signal of Distress, and the Snow lay by, until we were so near to her, that we could discern the Men on the Deck; and then she made Sail, and went away from us, without speaking to us; they being afraid, as we imagined, when they saw so many of us in the Boat. Our Hunger being then intolerable, we were forced to kill one of our Company to eat, and so agreed together to begin with one of the *Portugese*, who we accordingly killed out of pure Necessity, and cut his Flesh into small Pieces and hung it up to dry in the Sun, until it was hard, and so eat it, though but very sparingly; and then we were forced to do with four more of the Crew out of the eight: We also killed the sixth Man, but was forced to do so, because he would have kill'd me, *Simon Mac-Cone*, (one of these Declarants) for he struck me with the Tiller of the Boat, and had just bereaved me of Life, when this my Comrade, *Thomas Thompson*, came to my Relief, and we were forced therefore to kill him, though we flung him over-board, for he was just rotten with the Dry-pox, so that we could eat no Part of him.

We the said *Simon Mac-Cone*, and *Thomas Thompson*, being the only Survivors of all the Crew that left the said Ship, were determined to live and die the one by the other, and not to destroy the one the other, but to leave all Things to the Almighty Providence of God, expecting nothing less than Famine, for we lived several Days without eating any Thing, saving one small Flying-Fish that flew into the Boat, and some small Barnakles that grew on the Boat, which we were forced to eat raw. At last we espied Land, which happened to be the Island of *Barbados*, where we had like to have been cast on Shore, which was on *Wednesday* the 19th of *January*, we being so extreamly weak, that we could not work the said Boat. But Providence, who works all Things according to his blessed Will and Pleasure, prevented it, by a Schooner belonging to the said Island, standing along Shore to

Windward, the Capt. whereof was called *Glanveil Nicholas*, who was so kind as to take us up, and brought us to the chief Harbour or Bay, in the said Island of *Barbados*, called *Carlisle Bay*, and landed us at *Bridge-Town* in the said Island.

Our first Captain, Mr. *Rawlinson*, said he belonged to *London*, and the Ship also, but who were his Owners we cannot tell; but Captain *Rawlinson* said, he had been up the *Streights* in the said Ship for three or four Years, before he shipt us at *Lisbon* for the Voyage aforesaid.

We both remember, that Captain *Rawlinson* had a Dog, who had a Brass Collar round his Neck, with this Inscription on it, *John Rawlinson*, of *Wapping, London*.

The said *Simon Mac-Cone* was born in *Drogheda* in *Ireland*; and the said *Thomas Thompson* was born in *Rhode-Island* in *North America*.

*Given under our Hands*
*in* Barbados, *Feb. 1737*.

N.B. *The foregoing Account has been attested upon Oath by the said* Mac-Cone *and* Thompson; *the latter is since dead, being in a very weak Condition, and not able to stand upon his Legs when he came in here; the other I am told went on board the* Oxford *Man of War*.

## Pirates

Encounters with pirates provided exciting stories for the newspapers:

> We have an Account from Portsmouth, that the Mary and Martha, a Ship of twelve Guns, Capt. Roger Franklyn Commander, is arrived there from Malaga; and that being becalmed in her Passage, she was attacked by three Sallee Rovers; upon which the Captain ordered some Barrels of Powder to be placed in his Cabbin; and as soon as the Moors to the Number of fifty, boarded him, he sprung his Mine, and blew up above half of them; the Crew at the same Time laid about them most manfully with their Cutlasses, so that the rest were cut in Pieces, the Captain killing four with his own Hands.
>
> *Mist's Weekly Journal*, 23 July 1720

The *Political State of Great Britain* for August 1724 printed a copy of the letter from Captain Hawkins to the owner explaining the loss of his ship. In his letter he describes how the pirate vessel, the *Delight*, formerly a man-of-war, under the command of the pirate, Captain Spriggs, captured his ship. It gives the first recorded instance of the term 'Jolly Roger':

> [They] … hoisted *Jolly Roger*, (for so they call their black Ensign, in the Middle of which is a large white Skeleton, with a Dart in one Hand, striking a bleeding Heart, and in the other an Hour Glass) … When they fight under *Jolly Roger*, they give Quarter, which they do not when they fight under the Red or Bloody Flag.

Hawkins describes life on board the pirate vessel:

> The Pirates being then very merry, as is customary for them at that Time of Night, they unanimously agreed to set my Ship on Fire; and in less than three Quarters of an Hour she was all of a Blaze, and down she went. After this they wanted a little more Diversion, for Mischief is their sole Delight: I was sent down to the Cabbin to Supper; what should be provided for me but a Dish of Candles, which I was forced to eat, they having a Pistol at my Head, and a naked Sword to my Breast, whilst others beat me with Swords call'd Tucks … Then they consulted for more Diversion, which was to sweat me: it was agreed on, and all Preparations made thereto. The manner of a Sweat is thus: Between Decks they stick Candles round the Mizen-Mast, and about twenty five Men surround it with Points of Swords, Penknives, Compasses, Forks, &c. in each of their hands: *Culprit* enters the Circle; the Violin plays a merry Jig; and he must run for about ten Minutes, while each Man runs his Instrument into his Posteriors.

## The War of Jenkins's Ear

The sailor's narrative which had the most impact, and which showed the power of the press in stirring up hatred towards another country to the extent that a reluctant government eventually declared war, was the account of Robert Jenkins, Master of the *Rebecca.* His narrative was printed in most newspapers. Here is an extract from the *Grub-street Journal* for 24 June 1731:

> Near the Havanna, a Spanish Guarde Costa came up, rowing with 16 oars, and firing several shot … their number amounted to about 50 men: who broke open all her Hatches, lockers and chests … their Lieutenant ordered Capt. Jenkins hands to be tied, and his Mates, and seized them to the fore-mast. Then they cut and violently beat a Mulatto boy … they put a rope about his neck, and another about the Captain's, which fastening together, they hoisted them up to the fore-yard … they let the Capt. fall down on the deck, and asked him, if he would confess where his money was… one of them search'd his pockets, took his silver buckles off his shoes; and then he was hoisted up again, and kept hanging 'till he was quite strangled; after which they let him fall down the fore-hatch upon the casks, which bruised him very much; from thence he was dragged by his neck upon the deck, where he lay to appearance dead for near a quarter of an hour. When he recover'd, their Lieutenant, with pistols and a cutlass, went to him, crying, Confess or die. He told him he had no more money than he shew'd him at first, being 4 guineas, 1 pistole, and 4 double doubloons; which being commanded he gave him. No sooner had he done this, but the Lieut. took hold of his left ear, and with his cutlass slit it down; and another took hold of it and tore it off, but gave him the piece, bidding him carry it to his Majesty King George.

Throughout the 1730s, the anti-ministerial papers inflamed public opinion by printing reports of cruelties allegedly perpetrated by the crews of the Spanish guard ships on British seamen. Walpole tried to resist the popular clamour for war by attempting to reach an accommodation with Spain in the Convention of Pardo. The newspapers responded by printing a list of the Members of Parliament who had voted for the Convention, 'shewing the Places which they or their Relations enjoy, besides what secret Favours may be conferr'd on them'. The list showed that the number of sinecures and other employments enjoyed by those who voted for the Convention amounted to 234, with an annual value of almost £213,000.

By 1738 war seemed inevitable and the newspapers were full of stories of the activities of the press gangs. The first story managed to combine two topical subjects in one: the effects of the unpopular Gin Act where informants were paid large rewards; and the press gangs kidnapping recruits for the expected war with Spain:

> On Thursday last a Victualler in St. James's Street, being informed against for selling Spirituous Liquors, and having paid the Penalty, the Informant went into a House in the Neighbourhood to meet others of the Profession, to divide the Spoil: The Victualler by Accident met with a Press-Gang, telling them that several young Fellows had hid themselves in that House for fear of being press'd, the Lieutenant immediately entered the House, and press'd them into His Majesty's Service.
>
> *Warwick and Staffordshire Journal*, 10 August 1738

> The Men of Wars Boats passing through Bridge on Tuesday Night for impressing, it seems, was only a Feint to lull the Watermen into Security, and cover a real Design, which was, on the said 7th of *July*, successfully executed; for about Eight o'Clock 12 Gallies stoutly mann'd went up the River, as it were in a Fleet, taking at once both Shores, and the Stream, and swept off a great Number of Hands, regarding only the strongest Protections. It would have moved the rocky hearts of Neptune's most daring Sons to see the Distress of the Ladies, floating on the merciless Waves without a Pilot to steer their Wherries; on the other Hand it was a pleasing Scene to view many of the *Petit-Maitres* obliged to put their milky hands to the Oar, and with sorrowful Face and blister'd Fingers aukwardly pulling their Boats to Shore.
>
> *Political State of Great Britain*, July 1739

War was eventually declared in October 1739. On 22 November 1739 the British captured Porto Bello. Due to the slow passage of news, this information did not reach England until 13 March 1740. It was published in the *London Gazette* on 15 March. The following month, the *Gentleman's Magazine* printed a 'true copy' of a letter from a sailor press-ganged into one of the ships in Admiral Vernon's squadron:

My Dear Wife,

When I left you hevens noes it was with an akin hart for i thout it very hard to be hauld from you by a gang of rufins but hover i soon overcome that when I found out that we were about to go in ernest to rite my natif contry, and against a parcel of impodent Spanards, by whom I have often been ill treted and god nows my hearrt I have longed this fore Years past to cut of some of their Ears, and was in hopes I should haf sent you one for a sample now, but our good Admiral God bless him was so merciful we have taken Port Belo with such coridge and bravery that I never saw before, for my own Part my heart was rasd to the clouds and woud ha scaled the Moon had a Spaniad been there to come at him, as we did the Batry Jack cox is my mesmate he was always a hevy ased dog and sleepy headed, but had you seen him clime the Wals of the Batry, you woud never forget him for a cat coud not xceed him in nimbleness, and so in short it was with all of us I belefe I myself cod now overcum ten Spanards, we shall now make them kno we are the Cox of the Seas for our Admiral is of true Game breed had you se us english Salor, now what altration what contnances what bravry can xceed us we shall meet a French Squadron by am by but i wish it may be so And by G-d well jurch um Our dear cok of an Admiral has true english blood in his vains an thank god all our captins and officers have to a Man now we ar in earnes but lying in harbors and letting our timber rot and our provision to be devoured with Rats as bad as I haf sene, When our Canons had left of firing by order our men cou'd hardly forbear going on. My Dere I have got some token of Suces to show you I wish I could have sent some of them to you Our dear Admiral ordered every Man some Spanish Dollers to be imediately given which is like a Man of honor, i am and so is every Man of us resolved either to lose our lifes or conker our enemys. true british spirit revives and by G-d we will support our King and contry so long as a drop of blood remains Jo Wilks is as good a Sailor as the best of um, and can now bear a hand with an Able Sailor and has vowed never to take the Shittle in hand till we have reduced the pride of Spain help them who will the more the better true blews will never flinch I cant help mentoning the Solders we took with us from Jamaco who were as harty cox as ever took Musket in hand and behavd with glorious coridge but all for the honour of England. I wish we coud se one of those Plundrers the garda costaes especially him by whom I was once met with when i lost 16 months wages if i did not cut of the captain's ears may I be damd my dear i am well getting money Wages secure, and all Revenge on my Enemies, fiteing for my King and Country

i am Your for ever.

The slow and uncertain nature of the news of the war presented many problems for the newspapers. If news reached their offices, they would want to be the first to print it, but, at the same time, they wished to maintain a reputation for reliability. So they tended to qualify those reports that were unsupported by eye-witness accounts or official confirmation, as in this from the *London and Country Journal*, 6 May 1741:

> Yesterday a Rumour was spread, with some Industry, and prevail'd at Change, that the British Fleet, under the Command of Admiral Vernon had taken Carthagena, defeated both French and Spanish Land-Forces there, made Prize of the Galleons, and sack'd the Town. This important Account was pretended to be brought by a Ship arriv'd at Exeter from Guernsey, who had it from the Scarborough that she met with at Sea bringing the Express to England, but being a light fleet Ship she outsail'd her. This wants confirmation.

Confirmation came when Captain Laws of the sloop, *Spence*, arrived in London on 17 May bringing letters from Admiral Vernon at Cartagena dated 1 April describing his victory. These were printed in the *London Gazette* on 19 May. When the *Gentleman's Magazine* for May 1741 reprinted the letters from the *London Gazette*, it added this comment:

> A Paper on this Occasion so acceptable to the Public, that the Press could not keep Pace with the Demand; the Sale continuing (in some Places at an additional Price) till the setting out of the Post at One next Morning. Such an Incident formerly wou'd have contributed much to the making a Printer's Fortune; but since the Multiplicity of News-Papers published every Week, and the Custom of transcribing from one another, the Publisher of any important Account, however dearly purchased, has the Benefit but of one Day's Sale, the common News-Presses being immediately set to Work upon it. And yet, ridiculous as it may seem, some concerned in these Practices, are the People who, if they barely imagine that Reprisals are made upon them, raise the greatest Outcry.

Throughout the War of Jenkins's Ear the newspapers were full of short paragraphs listing the British ships that had been taken by Spanish privateers or Spanish ships taken by British privateers. It was only when letters from sailors were printed in the papers that these feats of derring-do on the Spanish Main came to life:

> *Extract of a Letter from Capt. Richard Baker, Commander of the Golden Sarah, dated Plymouth, March 28.*
> After having been chas'd 16 Hours by a Spanish Privateer, and finding I could no way clear myself of him, on Friday the 5th Instant I sheer'd my Ship about for him to come up with me, having taken in all my small Sails and furled my Main-sail; and at half an Hour past Twelve he came up to my Quarter, and gave me his two Chase Guns, and then his Larboard Broadside of nine more, being all six-Pounders; at the same Time I gave him my Broadside of four Three-pounders from my Lower-Deck, and my four small Quarter-Deckers. The Engagement was very warm till past two o'Clock, when he shear'd out of reach of my Guns, and got his Boat out, to stop, as I suppose, a Hole between Wind and Water, when I embrac'd this Opportunity to give my brave Men a hearty Drink of Wine. In a Quarter of an Hour his Boat was in again, and at us he came within Musketshot, and discharged all his Force, Small Arms and all, and we gave him a warm Reception,

our Guns being double charg'd, and we continued our Engagement as fast as ever we could load and discharge, and we generally got two Discharges of our great Guns to his one, but his Swivels he discharged faster than we: Thus we continued till past Four, when he sheer'd a little from us, which gave me Time to mount three of my Quarter-Deckers, which had been dismounted, and at us he came again, with his Guns all pointed forward. I saw his Design was to keep under my Stern, and take me fore and aft, so I put my Guns into a Position to gall him, if possible, as much; but my Ship being so much by the Stern, I could not fall the Metal of my lower Chase to hurt him, so closed my Chase Ports, and by that time he began, and discharged his two Broadsides, and I mine, but was forc'd to sheer the Ship so about to bring them to bear, he keeping right at my Stern, that I chose he should rather come on board me than lose my Mark, which he did at the Starboard Quarter, and call'd on us to strike, which we refus'd; so he back'd his Main-topsail, and then rang'd again along side, and run his Bolt-sprit among our main Rigging; we still refusing to strike he back'd a-stern and boarded me again at the Fore-chains, but not one of those Villains dar'd enter. All the Time he was on Board we fir'd two Broadsides with desir'd Success, for we had but just Length for our Guns clear of his Side. He then down'd Fore-Tack, and sat his Fore-top Gallant-sail, being on the Lee Side and ran away. I then got all my poor little Number, 23 Souls together, and to the Praise of God, and my great Surprize, had but three slightly wounded; but to look on the Ship, sure such a Wreck never was seen, I believe it will cost 200l. to repair the Damage she has received. Never did any Men behave with more Courage than mine did during the whole Action, which lasted upwards of three Hours and three Quarters; nor is it possible for me to express the Satisfaction I had, to hear them declare, one and all, they would die with me rather than strike. The Privateer was a new three Mast Ship, about 200 Tons, 20 Six-pounders, 16 or 18 Swivels, and there appeared to be 120 or 130 Men.

*Common Sense*, 3 April 1742

**News from America**

As the century progressed, foreign news was no longer dominated so much by the affairs of Europe. Colonial news took up an increasing proportion, starting with news from America and the West Indies, usually headed 'PLANTATION NEWS', moving on to India and Ceylon.

The type of news from America varied enormously. It included reports of the Indian Treaties, such as the Treaty between the King of the Delaware Indians and the Governor of Pennsylvania recorded in the *Political State of Great Britain* for September 1728. In return for 'Two Guns, six Strowd Water Coats, six Blankets, six Duffel Match Coats, and four Kettles', the Indians agreed to release their claim on the land between 'the two Rivers of *Delaware* and *Susquehannah*, from Duck-Creek to the Mountains'.

At the end of the negotiations, evidently concluding that he had obtained the best part of the deal, the Governor asked the Indians to send some

> trusty People amongst the neighbouring *Indians*; and, if you can, to the Five Nations, to acquaint them with what has passed between us: And I give you these Shoes and Stockings (presenting six pair of each) for the Use of those who are to travel, that they may better bear their Journey. I shall also give you Bread, Pipes, and Tobacco with five Gallons of Rum, to comfort and support you in your Return home.

Often, the editorial selection of American news was no different from the news values that determined the selection of domestic stories, with the emphasis on gruesome accounts of violent deaths, as in this report from the *Gentleman's Magazine* for August 1755:

> We have the following shocking and melancholy account from *Kats-Kill*, near *Albany*, viz. that some short time ago a servant woman in that neighbourhood absconded from her master, the better to consummate her nuptials with her lover, against whom we are told he was extremely averse, and sent out two *Indians* to bring her back. They overtook her on the road, and demanded her return, which she readily consented to, and was met soon after by her master on horseback, who, not apprehending the consequence, tied her cross-handed to his horse's tail, which presently after taking fright, flung his rider, and tore the poor creature limb from limb, nothing being found hanging from his tail but her two hands and part of her arm after he had run seven miles.

By 1765, the English papers provided news of the unrest over taxation that was to culminate in the American War of Independence and exposed the divisions in English opinion about imposing the Stamp Act on America. One commentator in the *Gentleman's Magazine* for December 1765 argued that the claim of no taxation without representation was built on a fallacy. The charters of the American colonies ('these charters, Sir, are solemn deeds to which the colonists are parties, and by consequence they cannot be allowed to contradict them') granted the Americans the same privileges as if they were born in England. Therefore, Americans were

> subject to that parliament which gives the law to, and taxes all *Englishmen* … If then, Sir, these colonists are to be considered to be born in *England*, *America*, their place of birth, must be esteemed to lie in *England*; and since all *England* is represented in parliament, *America*, the place of birth of our colonists, must be there represented also … Their day labourers have higher wages, and live at a cheaper rate than ours; they have land for almost nothing, and commerce there yields more profits than here: Why then should they not be taxed as well as we?

An opposing view in the same issue of the *Gentleman's Magazine* warned that the 'insolence, contempt and abuse' and 'the gentle terms of *republican race, mixed rabble of Scotch, Irish and foreign vagabonds, descendants of convicts, ungrateful rebels, &c* in the English newspapers, 'which are unfortunately reprinted in all *their* papers', were unlikely to induce the Americans to bear the tax with greater patience. The writer continued:

> The *Americans*, I am sure, for I know them, have not the least desire for independence; they submit, in general, to all the laws we make for them … [but they should not be taxed without their consent.]

The *Glocester Journal* for 3 February 1766 defended the Stamp Act:

> The whole taxes in all the American provinces do not amount, upon an average, to more than eight-pence per head per ann. on every individual person, including men, women and children; whereas the taxes to pay the interest only of the money spent in Great-Britain to defend America amount to twelve shillings per ann. on every individual in Great-Britain.

When resistance to taxation resurfaced in America in the 1770s, the English newspapers again provided a platform for opposing views. The topic was discussed in all three 'Letters to the Printer' in the *Public Advertiser* for 3 January 1775. The first dismissed the claim that the Americans had the right '*common to every British subject* of being taxed *only* by his Representatives … [This is not the common right of Britons. Due to the limited franchise] … Millions in England are without it'.

The second letter warned British merchants engaged in the American trade that those who 'may tend to encourage the (already misled) Americans' in their

> … vain mistaken Notion of their own Sufficiency and Importance, and presumptuous delusive Hopes of intimidating Britain by their empty Bravados and nugatory Parade, having taken her Lenity and Forbearance for Fear and Impotence … that whoever joins them in their unnatural Cry becomes an Accomplice in their Disloyalty, widens the Breach, and contributes to impede the general Harmony, Peace and Prosperity of the British Empire … It seems to be absolutely necessary for Britain to use some effectual Means of bringing the Americans under that Degree of Subordination, and due Acknowledgement thereof, which every civilised Colony owes to, and is the inherent Right of the Parent State, and upon which the Safety and Welfare of both mutually depend.

The third letter supported the Americans:

> The Question at present is not whether we have a Right or not to tax the Colonies … and by a Claim of Parliamentary Sovereignty alter the Forms of their Government, deprive them of their Charters, and establish a military and despotic Power in America. No, Sir, the sole point to be considered now is the Importance

and Usefulness of the Colonies to Great Britain, and whether we should lose all Advantages we gain from them by pushing Matters to Extremity … Would not a wise and honest Administration endeavour to make the most of the Industry of the Inhabitants, and the Produce of their Climate, rather than be continually contriving Methods to cramp their Genius and lower their Spirits? … The Ministry have pursued all imaginable Methods to dishearten the Colonies, and to render the Mother Country odious to them … no Part of this vast Empire should be deprived of the Benefit of those Laws and Liberties which the other enjoys. What would the people of Yorkshire say if they were deprived of the Benefit of the Habeas Corpus Act, while all the rest of the Kingdom enjoys it? Would they not have reason to murmur? If the Americans feel their Strength, and act with becoming Vigour, it is no more than what our own and their Ancestors have done before them … Let us not blame the Americans for imitating the Virtues of our Ancestors, and for seizing a right Opportunity to withstand the Oppressions of a dastardly, bribing, base and weak Administration that, not knowing true Wisdom, is scorned abroad, and lives on Tricks at home.

Six months later, the *Reading Mercury* for 12 June 1775 was full of reports of the action that took place in Lexington and Concord in April, taken from the *London Gazette* and other sources:

Lieutenant Colonel Smith finding, after he had advanced some miles on his march, that the country had been alarmed by the firing of guns and ringing of bells, dispatched six companies of Light Infantry, in order to secure two bridges on different roads beyond Concord, who, upon their arrival at Lexington, found a body of the country people drawn up under arms on a green close to the road; and, upon the King's troops marching up to them, in order to inquire the reason of their being so assembled, they went off in great confusion, and several guns were fired upon the King's troops from behind a stone wall, and also from the meeting-house and other houses, by which one man was wounded, and Major Pitcairne's horse shot in two places. In consequence of this attack by the rebels, the troops returned the fire, and killed several of them; after which the detachment marched on to Concord … [where] … great numbers of the rebels assembled in many parts, and a considerable body of them attacked the light infantry posted at one of the bridges, on which an action ensued, and some few were killed and wounded.

On the return of the troops from Concord, they were very much annoyed, and had several men killed and wounded by the rebels firing from behind walls, ditches, trees and other ambushes … and kept up in that manner a scattering fire during the whole of their march for fifteen miles; and such was the cruelty and barbarity of the rebels, that they scalped and cut off the ears of some of the wounded men, who fell into their hands.

Another ship is arrived at Bristol from New-York. She brings advices, that when the people of New-York were informed of the skirmish at Concord, they rose in a body, went to the Town-house, where the arms of the troops were deposited, and directly seized them. In the harbour there were two ships laden with stores for

General Gage, which they seized and unloaded. The Provincial troops of New-York immediately began their march for Boston.

The reason that so many more of the King's troops were wounded than killed in the late Action in New England, is, the Americans use a small shot called *buck shot*, which is much smaller than the soldiers' bullets.

By the several accounts from America, the Provincials in all parts are advancing in great numbers to Boston with a resolution to engage the King's troops, so that in all probability a bloody action has ensued by this time.

This was a fairly accurate prediction. The Battle of Bunker's Hill was fought five days later on 17 June. As the news arrived after the normal paper had been printed, the *Bristol Gazette* printed an Extraordinary edition on 29 July, following the example of the *London Gazette Extraordinary* which appeared when important news arrived that could not wait until normal publication day:

By the Grace, Capt. Bunday, who arrived here this morning from New-York in twenty-five days, we have the following account of the late action between his Majesty's troops and the Provincials.

From the NEW YORK GAZETTE.
NEW YORK, June 26, 1775.

Last night arrived an express from the provincial camp, near Boston, with the following interesting account of an engagement at Charles Town, between about 3000 of the regulars, and about half the number of provincials, on Saturday the 17th instant.

On Friday night, June 16. 1500 of the provincials went to Bunker's Hill in order to intrench there, and continued intrenching until Saturday ten o'clock, when two thousand regulars marched out of Boston, landed in Charles Town, and plundering it of all its valuable effects, set fire to it in ten different places at once; then dividing their army, one part of it marched up in the front of the provincial intrenchment, and began to attack the provincials at long shot; the other part of the army marched round the town of Charles Town, under cover of the smoak occasioned by the fire of the town. The provincial centries discovered the regulars marching upon their left wing : upon notice of this given by the centry to the Connecticut forces posted on that wing, Captain Nolton of Ashford, with 400 of the said forces, immediately repaired to and pulled up a post and rail fence, and carrying the posts and rails to another fence, put them together for a breast work. Captain Nolton gave orders to the men not to fire until the enemy were got within fifteen rods, and then not until the word was given : at the word being given the enemy fell surprisingly.

It was thought by the spectators who stood at a distance, that our men did great execution. The action continued about two hours, when the regulars on the right wing were put in confusion, and gave way. The Connecticut troops closely pursued them, and were on the point of pushing their bayonets, when orders were received from General Pomeroy, for those who had been in action two hours to fall back, and their places to be supplied by fresh forces. These orders being mistaken for a direction to retreat, our troops on the right wing began a general retreat, which was handed to the left, the principal place of action, where Captains Nolton, Clark and Putnam had forced the enemy to give way, and retire before them for some considerable distance; and being warmly pursued, the enemy were with difficulty persuaded to retire; but the right wing, by mistaking the orders, having already retired, the left, to avoid being encircled, were obliged to retreat also with the main body. They retreated with precipitation across the causeways to Winter Hill, in which they were exposed to the fire of the enemy from the shipping and floating batteries. We sustained our principal loss in passing the causeway: the enemy pursued our troops to Winter Hill, where the provincials being reinforced by General Putnam, renewed the battle with great spirit, repulsed the enemy with great slaughter, and pursued them till they got under the cover of their cannon from their shipping, when the enemy retreated to Bunker's Hill, and the provincials to Winter Hill, where after entrenching and erecting batteries, they on Monday began to fire upon the regulars on Bunker's Hill, and on the ships and floating batteries in the harbour when the express came away : the number of the provincials killed, is between 40 and 70, and 140 wounded; of the Connecticut troops, 16 were killed : no officer among them was either killed or wounded, except Lieut. Grosvenor, who was wounded in the hand : a Colonel, or Lieut. Colonel of the New Hampshire forces, is among the dead. It is also said, that Doctor Warren is undoubtedly among the slain. The provincials lost three iron six pounders, some intrenching tools and knapsacks. The number of regulars that first attacked the provincials on Bunker's Hill was not less than 2000. The number of provincials was only 1500, who, it is supposed, would soon have gained a complete victory, had it not been for the unhappy mistake already mentioned. The regulars were afterwards reinforced with 1000 men. It is uncertain how great a number of the enemy were killed or wounded; but it was supposed by spectators who saw the whole action, that there could not be less than 4 or 500 killed. Mr. Gardner, who got out of Boston on Sunday evening, says, that there were 500 wounded men brought into that place the morning before he came out.

This account was taken from Capt. Elijah Hide, of Lebanon, who was a spectator on Winter Hill during the whole action.

Yesterday Mr. Paul Reviere passed through this city on the way to the Continental Congress.

Saturday evening last an express arrived here from Albany, with advice, that the Caghnawaga Indians, of Canada, had actually taken up the hatchet, and, it is supposed, they intended to act against the colonies.

This report was reprinted in the *Reading Mercury* for 7 August 1775 with much additional information from America:

A private letter from Boston says, 'No words can describe the dreadful scene of misery of that unhappy town. The shrieks of the women, the cries of the children, the dying groans of the wounded, and the want of provisions, would extort a tear from even the eye of Nero.'

*Extract of a letter from Philadelphia, dated June 20.*
The grand congress in this city are making every necessary preparation to act with vigour … They have passed a vote to strike off two millions of dollars, 7s. 6d. our currency, to answer present exigencies. Col. George Washington, a delegate from Virginia, is, at the particular request of the people in New-England, and with the unanimous consent of the Congress, appointed commander in chief of the continental forces.

*Extract of a letter from a gentleman in Charles-Town, South-Carolina, to his correspondent in Bristol, dated June 17.*
I mentioned to you in my last the effects the engagement that happened in New-England had upon the people in New-York. Every arrival from thence confirms the concurrence of this province with the rest of the continent; nay, they seem to act like real converts, and endeavour to out-do the rest of the provinces; they have driven almost all the Tory party out of town … The inhabitants of Georgia are about to do the same; a letter from thence yesterday mentions there having had another meeting, when the Whig party went armed with full determination to drive the Tories who would not join the rest of the continent, out of the province … We all most earnestly wish for peace and reconciliation between Great-Britain and America, upon just, honourable, and constitutional principles; but are determined to have it upon no other. If any on your side of the water imagine America will grow tired and give up the matter, they are greatly mistaken.

Reports of the American War of Independence proved the old adage that journalism is the first draft of history. Like many first drafts, subsequent amendment becomes necessary as more facts come to light. This was particularly so when communications were slow and methods of newsgathering were haphazard, as shown by this premature account of the death of George Washington:

Saturday last arrived at Whitehaven, the Mary and Betty, Boadle, from Youghall, with whom came passengers two gentlemen, the mates of the Lively of Maryport, and the Snow John of Kirkudbright. – We are informed that they left Boston the 2d of February; a few days before which a Captain in the Provincial service wrote to a person in Boston, giving some account of a general engagement happening in the Jerseys; these passengers do not remember the day, but think it was the 25th or 26th of January; that the battle was long, bloody, and obstinate, but at length decided in favour of the King's troops; that Gen. Washington, in the conflict, was mortally wounded by a shot through the body.

*York Chronicle and General Advertiser*, 21 March 1777

## Foreign Correspondents

Following the French Revolution, continental news dominated once more as

British eyes turned to events in Europe. At about this time, the casual arrangements for gathering foreign news began to be replaced by professional foreign correspondents resident in the major capitals, supplemented by special correspondents sent out by their editors to cover topical events. Many of the special correspondents doubled as war correspondents, taking great risks to follow the wars around the world.

George Borrow, author of *Lavengro* and *Romany Rye*, moonlighted as a foreign correspondent for the *Morning Herald* from 1837 to 1839 while officially working as the British and Foreign Bible Society's representative in Spain. In his book, *The Bible in Spain*, Borrow described the war correspondents he encountered:

> There they stood, jotting down what they saw in their notebooks, as unconcernedly as if reporting a Reform meeting in Finsbury Square or Covent Garden, while in Spain they accompanied the Carlist and Christino guerillas in some of their most desperate expeditions, sleeping on the ground, exposing themselves fearlessly to hostile bullets, to the inclemency of winter, and the fierce rays of summer's burning sun.

Seven war correspondents were killed covering the revolt of the Mahdi in the Sudan campaigns of 1883–85 and are commemorated by a tablet in the crypt of St Paul's Cathedral. John Cameron of the *Standard*, who reported the rout of the British at Majuba Hill in 1881 during the First Boer War, was killed with Algernon Herbert of the *Morning Post* at the battle of Abu Kru. Frank Viztelly, the artist and special correspondent of the *Illustrated London News* and the *Graphic*, and Edmund O'Donovan of the *Daily News* both died when the Dervishes massacred Hicks Pasha's column outside El Obeid in November 1883. Young Frank Powers of *The Times* was another victim of the Sudan campaigns.

Powers had set off with Viztelly and O'Donovan to report Hicks Pasha's expedition. He escaped the massacre at El Obeid by suffering a severe bout of dysentery. Unable to walk or ride, he was strapped to a gun barrel in 127 degrees of heat before being shipped down river to join Gordon at Khartoum. Powers alerted Britain to the plight of General Gordon by telegraphing news reports to *The Times*. His last report, before the Mahdi cut the telegraph line, was sent to *The Times* on 7 April 1884. No longer able to communicate with Britain, Powers escaped from Khartoum with the aim of reaching Cairo to appeal for reinforcements. He was killed in an ambush at the age of 24.

**Reuters**

The invention of the electric telegraph transformed communications. News that took six months to arrive from India, subject to shipwrecks and wayward winds, could now travel at the speed of electricity. In 1815, news of the battle of Waterloo had taken five days to reach the newspapers. In 1896, a telegram sent from the paper's Washington correspondent arrived at *The Times* in London within two minutes.

The first telegraphic message to appear in an English newspaper came from Windsor Castle announcing the birth of Queen Victoria's second son. It was printed in *The Times* on 6 August 1844 in an edition that went to press 40 minutes after the birth. The main benefits of the telegraph, however, applied to reporting foreign news. With the aid of the telegraph, news from any part of the world connected to a telegraph cable could be in the following morning's paper.

During the second half of the nineteenth century, the telegraph and Reuters were synonymous. Reuter opened his Submarine Telegraph Office in 1 Royal Exchange Buildings in 1851, the year that the telegraph cable was laid between Dover and Calais, initially to provide London and Paris with the stock exchange prices in both capitals. He tried to get *The Times* interested in providing a news service, but was rebuffed as *The Times* had the most extensive network of foreign correspondents.

In 1858, Reuter managed to persuade James Grant, editor of the *Morning Advertiser*, to take his service. By the end of that year, all the leading London dailies, including *The Times*, and some of the provincial dailies, including the *Manchester Guardian*, were taking Reuter's service. The *Birmingham Journal* for 13 October 1860 commented, 'Reuter is not only the man of the time, but the master of time.'

Reuters came to the fore reporting news of the American Civil War. Reuter struck a deal with the Associated Press of New York to exchange news from Britain and the rest of the world in return for American news. In addition Reuter's agent in New York scanned the American press for items for transmission.

In the absence of a transatlantic cable (which was not successfully laid until 1866), American news was telegraphed to the ports and placed in special canisters on board the steamships bound for England. As the ships passed Crookhaven on the Irish coast, a Reuters boat would set out to meet them. The canisters were thrown overboard to be picked up in nets attached to long poles. At night, the canisters were lit by phosphorous and thrown into the sea. When the canisters were opened, the messages were telegraphed along a line Reuter had specially laid from Crookhaven to Cork, and from thence to Reuter's office in London for delivery to the British press and for further transmission to Reuter's agents in Europe.

When Abraham Lincoln was assassinated on the evening of 14 April 1865, a message datelined New York, 15 April, 9 am, was put on board the SS *Nova*

*Scotian.* The message was taken ashore to the telegraph station at Greencastle, near Derry on 26 April at 9.45 am and reached the London papers by 11.30 am.

The English newspaper reader was offered a window on the world with instant snippets of 'hard' news from Reuter's telegrams, political comment and background analysis from the papers' resident foreign correspondents and the personal testimonies of the special correspondents and war correspondents. Newspaper readers could thus flatter themselves that they were part of an informed élite. From the comfort of their drawing rooms, they were empowered by having immediate access to distant events in faraway lands.

The technology shaped the news. The preference for instant news by telegraph over belated news sent by letter, and the high per-word cost of telegrams, meant that the descriptive prose of the correspondent took second place to the compact messages of the telegraph. The Victorian newspaper reader could discover a great deal about the foreign policy of a country and the diplomatic questions concerning it, but little about the country itself. Thanks to the telegraph, the wheel had turned full circle, with the foreign news items resembling those of the early eighteenth century in their brevity, subject matter and lack of any attempt at depicting local colour.

## Objectivity

How objective were the foreign reports? There were many factors that could compromise objectivity. One factor was the policy of the paper itself. *The Times*, for example, for the most part reflected the views of the Foreign Office. In conflicts where the British were non-combatants, many papers had a bias towards one side over another. During the American Civil War, the *Daily News* and the *Morning Star* supported the North, and the *Standard* and the *Morning Herald* supported the South. Another factor was that the reports came from far away, outside the control of the editorial office. The paper had no means of knowing what external forces were influencing the reports they were receiving.

The main aims of the resident foreign correspondents were to obtain and report the news, preferably before anyone else; to produce an informed commentary on the political and diplomatic background to the news; and to provide an intelligent prediction of the likely impact of the news on future events. As foreigners in a strange land, they naturally gravitated towards the company of other British nationals and the staff of the British embassies with whom they generally enjoyed close relations. Inevitably their reports were coloured by their reliance on British official sources for their reports.

They also cultivated the company of local politicians. There was an unspoken bargain between the correspondent and the politician to use each other for their own ends. The politician wanted favourable British publicity and the correspondent wanted information. To retain the trust of the local politician, the correspondent would be careful not to include material that might antagonize his source. Similarly, accredited war correspondents were dependent on the protection of the armies to which they were attached, and on the armies' goodwill for granting access to the telegraph. The newspaper reader, therefore, did not always get the full story.

Perhaps the most objective reports came from an unlikely source. The personal, eye-witness reports of the special correspondents, for all their tendency towards self-dramatization, were probably more objective than the apparently detached, analytical briefings of the resident foreign correspondent. With no long-term commitment to the places they were reporting from, they owed no obligation to their hosts and, while they may have been guilty of exaggeration, there was little incentive to disguise the truth of what they saw.

The papers' solution to these problems was to make their own attempts at analysis in their leading articles and comments pages. As for the news itself, they printed the telegrams and letters from foreign correspondents raw, contradictions and all, with minimal editorial intervention other than arranging them on the page. In so doing, they were adopting the policy of *The Daily Courant* nearly 200 years before, relying on their readers 'to have Sense enough' to be 'able to Judge of the Credibility and Fairness of the Relation'.

# PART THREE
# Fleet Street

## Chapter 9

# *The Times*, the Fourth Estate and the Sunday Paper

> A News-Paper, conducted on the true and natural principles of such a publication, ought to be the Register of the times, and faithful recorder of every species of intelligence; it ought not to be engrossed by any particular object; but, like a well covered table, it should contain something suited to every palate.
>
> Manifesto for the *Daily Universal Register*, 1 January 1785

By far the most successful newspaper for most of the nineteenth century was *The Times* (Figure 9.1). It was founded by John Walter as the *Daily Universal Register* in 1785. Because the title was so long, people tended to ask for 'the Register', and were likely to end up with the *Weekly Register*, or the *Annual Register*, or even *Harris's Register*, the list of Covent Garden whores. So in 1788 Walter renamed his paper *The Times*.

When John Walter II took over the paper in 1803, he inherited a respectable, but far from large, circulation of 1,700. He began the task of transforming *The Times* into the most influential paper of the nineteenth century. At a time of great interest in the progress of the Napoleonic Wars, Walter built up a large network of foreign correspondents, including Crabb Robinson who gave the account of the death of Sir John Moore at Corunna. In order to be first with the news, Walter hired a team of special couriers, and even used smugglers to carry the news ashore. On at least one occasion the Foreign Office had to ask *The Times* for the latest news from the continent, official sources being so slow.

Walter's investments in printing technology helped to keep *The Times* ahead of its rivals. Having the largest sales, *The Times* had both the need and the capital to invest in the new technology. The Koenig steam press which Walter bought in 1814 was capable of printing 1,100 sheets per hour, while other newspaper presses, which had changed little since the days of Caxton, could still only print 250 impressions, or 125 double-sided newspapers, per hour. This meant that late news, which other papers had to leave over until the following day, could be printed in *The Times* shortly before it was due to hit the streets. This policy of being in the forefront of the latest developments in information technology continued. *The Times* bought Applegarth and Cowper's presses in 1828 which were capable of 4,000 sheets per hour printed

The Times.

No 5216 SATURDAY, SEPTEMBER 19, 1801. PRICE SIXPENCE.

**9.1** *The Times*, 19 September 1801

both sides, and a Hoe rotary press in 1858 which could print 20,000 sheets in an hour.

Walter was essentially a businessman. He did not see *The Times* as a vehicle for propagating his own views. His role was to establish the necessary infrastructure to enable the paper to expand, and to leave journalism to the journalists. In appointing Thomas Barnes as editor in 1817 and giving him full rein, he ensured the supremacy of *The Times*.

## Barnes

Barnes's philosophy was to let the paper reflect, and give voice to, majority public opinion. Like Mass Observation one hundred years later, he instructed his local correspondents to keep him informed of the state of public opinion throughout the country. Having collected and analysed this material, he articulated it as forcefully as possible. 'Newspaper writing', he once said, 'is in literature what brandy is to the beverage.'[1] In addition, he encouraged the use of *The Times*'s correspondence columns so that private opinion could also be heard.

Under Barnes *The Times* became the voice of middle-class England, in favour of reform, but fearful of violent revolution. Although *The Times* occasionally clashed with authority, in those clashes Barnes usually made sure that he had middle-class support behind him. The first clash took place in 1819. He had sent his chief reporter, John Tyas, to cover the mass meeting due to be addressed by the radical 'Orator' Hunt in St Peter's Fields, Manchester. Tyas introduced himself to Hunt beforehand and earned himself a seat on the platform. He was thus able to produce a vivid account of the Peterloo Massacre supported by a powerful leading article showing how 11 peaceful demonstrators were killed and over 60 injured in an unprovoked attack by the Manchester Yeomanry on the orders of the local magistrates.

*The Times*'s report and leader sent a shock wave across middle-class opinion. Hitherto *The Times* had the reputation of being a Tory paper. William Cobbett, the radical, called it 'the bloody and stupid old *Times*'. Its editorials had been hostile to Hunt and it was against the calling of the Manchester meeting. Almost overnight, the cause of parliamentary reform had become respectable. However, lest it be thought that Peterloo caused universal revulsion in the press, it is worth recording the comment made by the Tory *St. James's Chronicle*:

> What has long been desired by every friend of order has at length taken place. The strong arm of the law has been put forth to put, we trust, a final stop to the assemblage of the ignorant and the seditious.

The following year, sensing that public opinion was behind the 'wronged Queen', Barnes became the main champion of Queen Caroline while *The Morning Post*, which opposed Queen Caroline, had its offices stormed by the London mob. By taking the popular side once again, Barnes increased the circulation of *The Times* by 15,000. He assisted the Duke of Wellington in his attempts to secure Catholic Emancipation and, again siding with the popular view, he opposed the Duke by supporting the Reform Bill. In the issue for 29 January 1831, *The Times* urged 'the people – the people everywhere ... [to] ... come forward and petition, ay, thunder for reform' – hence *The Times*'s nickname, 'The Thunderer'.

By the middle of the 1830s there was a general disenchantment with the Whig government and Barnes, as usual, moved with the tide. *The Times* declared that it would no longer accept prior intelligence from government sources (usually given in return for editorial support) because the practice was inconsistent with 'the pride and independence of our journal'.[2] With the biggest advertising revenues, *The Times* could afford the biggest news team and dispense with the services of government spin-doctors. In setting out his conditions for supporting a new party, Barnes helped to draft Peel's Tamworth Manifesto, which gave rise to the modern Conservative Party. William Hazlitt, a former *Times* writer, summed up the character of the *Times* under Barnes as

> the greatest engine of temporary opinion in the world. It is the witness of the British metropolis; the mouthpiece, oracle and echo of the Stock Exchange, the organ of the mercantile interest. It takes up no falling causes; fights no uphill battle; advocates no great principle. It is ever strong upon the stronger side.[3]

The influence of *The Times* led the Lord Chancellor, Lord Lyndhurst, to describe Barnes as 'the most powerful man in the country'.[4] At the time of Barnes's death in 1841, he had increased the sales of *The Times* from 7,000 copies to 28,000, more than double that of the nearest daily rival.

The size of *The Times* also more than doubled under Barnes, and the range of its content widened to fulfil the first John Walter's vision of the paper as 'the Register of the times'. *The Times* for 12 September 1838 is a typical example of the paper towards the end of Barnes's editorship. A formidable broadsheet of eight closely typeset pages of six columns each, the front page and most of page two and the back page are full of small advertisements with the remaining five pages providing news, correspondence, features and editorial comment.

Page three begins with a two-column review of Loudon's *Suburban Gardener and Villa Companion.* Other features include a summary of the annual report of the Military Board in Calcutta of the progress of Public Works in India, a review of Dr Ure's *Dictionary of Arts, Manufactures and Mines,* and a four-column extract of the report of the Select Committee appointed to inquire into the System of Transportation, its efficacy as a punishment, making the point that most transported women were

> ... drunken and abandoned prostitutes ... A convict woman, frequently the only one in the service, perhaps in the neighbourhood, is surrounded by a number of depraved characters, to whom she becomes an object of indecent pursuit ... It can easily be imagined what a pernicious effect must be produced upon the character of the rising generation of the Australian colonies, in consequence of the children of settlers being, too frequently, in their tenderest years, under the charge of such persons.

As to the news, with Parliament in recess, the main domestic story that day was the Coroner's inquest into 'the late fatal steam-boat accident' (two persons drowned). Other stories included reports of the harvest all over the country taken from the county papers, the prize winners at the meeting of the South London Floricultural Society, the Money Market and City Intelligence and two and a half columns of reports from the police courts. Foreign news is taken from the overseas press and from 'private correspondence' – *The Times*'s own correspondents in Milan and Lisbon.

Letters to the Editor are dotted around the paper wherever there is convenient space. Subjects include the insolence of employees of the London and Birmingham Railway, the inefficiencies of Her Majesty's Colonisation Commissioners for South Australia, the Statues of the Metropolis, the high rates of Life Assurance Premiums and the operation of the New Poor Law:

> conceited upstarts, who, wielding a little brief authority as guardians of the poor, conceive themselves the mighty men of the earth ... persons not possessed of any education, and ignorant of the common courtesies of life, love to show their authority when they have any authority to show.

The fact that the letters are dotted around the paper is typical of the make-up of *The Times* and the other papers of the period. Apart from the advertisements and the leading articles, there are very few fixed points in the paper to which one can immediately turn in the knowledge that a certain kind of item will be in that place. This lack of direction in the design of the paper makes it difficult to read.

The contrast between *The Times* of 1838 and *The Times* of 1798 could not be more striking. The 1798 paper was an insubstantial publication of four tabloid pages with very little worthwhile content, but it was elegant, easy on the eye and closely modelled on the format of John Bell's *World*. In short, it was a printer's paper, strong on visual quality but weak on journalism. The 1838 paper was a journalist's paper, strong on content but with very little visual appeal.

Paper duties, stamp duty and the financial pressures to devote sufficient space for profitable advertisements meant that news and features had to be crammed into the smallest available space. *The Times* and its competitors were striving to be papers of record, especially when Parliament was sitting. The look of the paper took second place to the quality and quantity of the editorial material. If the size of the print had to be reduced to provide a detailed report of the debates in Parliament and a full foreign news service, then so be it.

## Delane

Barnes's successor, John Thaddeus Delane, the model for the all-powerful Tom Towers in the Barchester novels, increased the circulation of *The Times* to around 65,000 copies per day. Under Delane *The Times* became the only paper that was essential reading on political matters. Delane enjoyed the company of politicians and other Establishment figures, habitually dining, as Richard Cobden noted, at tables where 'every other guest but himself was an ambassador, a Cabinet Minister or a Bishop'.[5] At a time when Britain was governed by loose alliances of political groupings, most politicians were happy to give Delane information in order to advance their own personal interest and to try to gain his goodwill. *The Times* was thus privy to more confidential information than any of its competitors. And because the information came from so many different sources, no individual or political faction could lay claim to any special influence over *The Times*. Unlike the other dailies, which were generally politically partisan, *The Times* was regarded as being independent, so its political news and views were considered to have a unique authority.

The authority of *The Times* was strengthened by the inside knowledge of Delane's chief leader writers, Henry Reeve and Robert Lowe. Reeve was Clerk of Appeals to the Privy Council and a personal friend of many of the leading politicians. Working so close to the heart of government, Reeve was one of the best-informed men in the country. Robert Lowe was an active politician who later became Chancellor of the Exchequer.

By the mid-1850s, *The Times* was selling over seven times as many copies as its nearest rival daily paper and more than twice the five morning papers put together. Only the *Morning Advertiser* with its guaranteed sales to licensed victuallers and the *Daily News* were selling over 5,000 copies. *The Morning Chronicle*, *Morning Post* and *Morning Herald* were selling around 3,000 copies each. It is unlikely that the four evening papers, *The Sun*, *Globe*, *Express* and *Standard*, were selling as much as this.

The success of *The Times* led to accusations of monopoly over the daily press. In a leading article on 11 February 1850 it argued:

> Our monopoly is the monopoly of BARCLAY and PERKINS porter, of TWINING'S tea, of Mr. COBDEN'S agitation, and of FORTNUM and MASON'S hams. It is the monopoly of nothing but the first place, won by fair fighting and held against all comers on the same terms.

In its sales and influence, *The Times* had become the embodiment of the fourth estate.

## The Fourth Estate

The concept of the newspaper as the fourth estate of the realm first took root in Barnes's time. Instead of simply being the mouthpiece of ministerial or opposition groups, as was the case in the eighteenth century, the press, and

*The Times* in particular, was now an independent and powerful fourth estate – the channel between public opinion and the governing institutions.

As in the words of Henry Reeve, 'non-electors are more numerous than electors', Parliament was unrepresentative of the people. Also, Parliament only sat for half the year and was so overwhelmed with details of business that it could not reflect or react to the mood of the people, whereas newspapers, particularly *The Times*, could reflect and direct public opinion, and were thus an unofficial part of the constitution which politicians could ignore at their peril.

Newspapers served the establishment by being a means of social control, deflecting grievances into the peaceful, 'constitutional' medium of the newspaper column, and they served democracy by acting as a security against despotism. In practice, the virtual monopoly of *The Times* meant that the views that acted as a check and an influence upon government were largely those of *The Times*'s natural constituency, the powerful and newly enfranchised middle classes.

The newspapers' power to confirm or unseat governments led the Prime Minister, Lord Derby, to claim that, 'as the English Press aspires to share the influence of statesmen, so also must it share the responsibilities of statesmen'. *The Times* replied with the famous leader of 6 February 1852, defining the role of the fourth estate:

> We cannot admit that its purpose is to share the labours of statesmanship, or that it is bound by the same limitations, the same duties, the same liabilities as that of Ministers of the Crown. The purposes and the duties of the two powers are constantly separate, generally independent, sometimes diametrically opposite. The dignity and the freedom of the Press are trammelled from the moment it accepts an ancillary position ... The first duty of the Press is to obtain the earliest and most correct intelligence of the events of the time, and instantly, by disclosing them, make them the common property of the nation ... The Press lives by disclosures; whatever passes into its keeping becomes a part of the knowledge and the history of our times; it is daily and forever appealing to the enlightened force of public opinion – anticipating if possible the march of events – standing upon the breach between the present and the future, and extending its survey to the horizon of the world ... For us, with whom publicity and truth are the air and light of existence, there can be no greater disgrace than to recoil from the frank and accurate disclosure of facts as they are. We are bound to tell the truth as we find it, without fear of consequences.

The next day, *The Times* developed that theme:

> The duty of the journalist is the same as that of the historian – to seek out truth, above all things, and present to his readers not such things as statecraft would wish them to know but the truth as near as he can attain it.

Here we see the ideology of the fourth estate: the journalist as a professional and objective seeker after truth, performing a public service to make truth the common property of the nation. The flaw in this 'public service' concept of the fourth estate lay, ironically, in the technological advances that had helped to secure *The Times* its independence. New titles now needed tremendous amounts of capital to get off the ground. Generally, the only people with the means and the will to provide sufficient capital had other motives, mainly party-political, for wishing to own and control a newspaper. So, instead of acting as an independent fourth estate, representing public opinion to try to influence the political establishment, newspapers came to represent sections of the political establishment trying to influence public opinion.

*The Times* as the embodiment of the fourth estate reached its height in the mid-1850s when Delane sent William Howard Russell and Thomas Chenery to the Crimea. Russell, who provided the famous eye-witness account of the Charge of the Light Brigade, exposed the inefficiencies of the supply system and the incompetence of the generals. Chenery described the horrors of the hospital at Scutari, which led to the expedition of Florence Nightingale. Only one in five deaths were caused by battle. Disease accounted for the remaining four-fifths. In six months, cholera, fever and other diseases killed 35 per cent of the total strength of the British army.

In bringing the realities of war to the breakfast table, Russell's dispatches had a similar impact on the British public in the 1850s as the televising of the Vietnam War had on the American public in the 1960s, the difference being that *The Times* had its own agenda. Delane was carrying forward the class war that Barnes had begun on behalf of the middle classes against aristocratic maladministration in politics. That battle won, the target turned to aristocratic maladministration in the army.

*The Times*'s contempt could not have been plainer than in its leading article on 23 December 1854:

> The noblest army ever sent from these shores has been sacrificed to the greatest mismanagement. Incompetency, lethargy, aristocratic hauteur, official indifference, favour, routine, perverseness, and stupidity reign, revel and riot in the camp before Sebastapol, in the harbour of Balaklava, in the hospital of Scutari, and how much nearer home we dare not venture to say.

These attacks were bitterly resented by authority. Prince Albert, in a reference to Russell, declared that 'the pen and ink of one miserable scribbler is despoiling the country'. Sidney Herbert, the Secretary of State for War, expressed the hope that the army would lynch Russell. *The Times*'s reports led to a motion in the House of Commons demanding an inquiry into the condition of the army. The motion, which was treated as a vote of no confidence in the government, was supported by 305 votes to 148. The government resigned and Lord Palmerston became Prime Minister.

In 1855, the year after *The Times* had annoyed the Establishment with its reports from Crimea, the Establishment took its revenge. To find out how, we have to go back and trace the rise and fall of the radical press.

## Radical Papers

The father of the radical press was William Cobbett, whose *Political Register*, founded in 1802, attacked corruption in high places, the Establishment generally, and government-supporting newspapers which he claimed were published to serve the interests of 'court-sycophants, parasites, pensioners, bribed-senators, directors, contractors, jobbers, hireling lords, and ministers of state'.

The increase in stamp duty in 1815 forced the price of the *Political Register* up to one shilling and a halfpenny, way beyond the reach of the individual working-class reader. Some enterprising publicans bought copies for their customers to read, but the authorities reacted by threatening to withdraw their licences if they did not stop taking the paper. Hawkers were also intimidated. A Shropshire magistrate ordered two men to be flogged for distributing the *Political Register*. 'Since when', claimed the magistrate, 'I have heard of no others being circulated in the neighbourhood.'

As a means of avoiding the tax, in 1816 Cobbett produced an unstamped version of the paper commenting on the news, but with the news itself omitted. Cobbett's *Twopenny Trash* was an instant success with sales reaching almost 70,000, at a time when *The Times* was selling only 7,000 copies. The *Twopenny Trash* was so popular because it reflected the discontent of the majority of the poorer people at the time. The class divide was greater than ever before. On the one hand were the comfortable classes who had profited from the Napoleonic Wars, especially those receiving interest from the National Debt, and the beneficiaries of 'Old Corruption' – placemen, sinecurists and absentee parsons enjoying the income from two or more livings. On the other hand, a growing landless underclass, some evicted from their homes by the Enclosure Acts, and others thrown out of employment by the mechanization of industry, were drifting to the towns. Their numbers were swelled by returning soldiers with no homes and no jobs to go to, whose country had no further use for them.

Unemployment and starvation were the twin legacies of the Napoleonic Wars. Wages fell for those in work, just at the time when the Corn Laws of 1815 increased the price of food. The condition of the poor was further aggravated by increased taxes on the necessities of life that were levied to swell the coffers of the holders of the National Debt. The poor were being taxed to pay the rich and were kept in check by a repressive government with an artillery of weapons at its disposal – the Combination Acts, *agents provocateurs*, the suspension of Habeas Corpus, and a vast extension of the criminal laws, particularly the Game Laws, which were aimed specifically at the starving poor. This social background, and the success of the *Twopenny Trash*, gave rise to a number of other, generally more radical, publications. Chief among them were T. J. Wooler's *Black Dwarf*, William Hone's *Reformists' Register*, and *Sherwin's Weekly Political Register*, all founded in 1817.

According to the *Spectator*, sedition was 'universal and organic', the result of 'teaching people to read and neglecting their well-being, or to put it another way, one that arose from the incompatibility of democratic newspapers, which the government could not suppress, with near-starvation wages'. Worried by the popularity of the radical press and fearful of a backlash after the Peterloo Massacre, ministers reacted with alarm. Lord Eldon declared that the radical press was 'the most dangerous and formidable enemy to the Constitution ... there is scarcely a village in the Kingdom that had not its little shop in which nothing was sold but blasphemy and sedition'. And so the government brought in the Six Acts of 1819. Two of these Acts were aimed directly at the radical press. One allowed magistrates to seize blasphemous and seditious literature. The other, the Newspaper Stamp Duties Act, extended the Stamp Act to all pamphlets and papers issued more than once a month and costing less than sixpence, irrespective of whether they contained news, thus plugging the loophole in the law exploited by Cobbett's *Twopenny Trash*. In addition, as a security against sedition, the laws required bonds of £300 for London papers and £200 for provincial papers to be placed with the authorities before a newspaper could be published.

Despite *The Times*'s attitude to Peterloo, the Six Acts is a measure of how the mainstream newspapers, and the government's attitude towards them, had changed. They were no longer seen as a threat. Lord Ellenborough made this clear in his speech introducing the Newspaper Stamp Duties Act: 'It is not against the respectable press that this Bill was directed, but against the pauper press.'

As intended, the Six Acts destroyed the radical press. Liable to seizure, and unable to be sold for less than sixpence, radical papers were priced out of the market. They ceased to be an important force until the emergence of the illegal unstamped papers of the 1830s.

## The Great Unstamped

Richard Carlile fired the first shot in the war of the unstamped in November

1830 when he published an unstamped paper called the *Prompter* ('Down with kings, priests and lords, whose system is a system of murder, plunder, and spoliation').

A flood of unstamped publications followed in the *Prompter*'s footsteps, the best known of which was Henry Hetherington's *Poor Man's Guardian* (Figure 9.2), 'A Weekly Paper for the People. Published in defiance of "Law", to try the Power of "Right" against "Might", Price 1d.' In place of the official duty stamp, it printed an imitation stamp showing a printing press with the caption 'Knowledge is Power'.

The Bow Street magistrates summoned Hetherington for publishing a paper without a fourpenny stamp. Instead of attending court, he went on the run, and toured the country promoting the sale of his paper with the police hot on his trail. On one occasion, in Manchester, he escaped out of a window just as the police were entering the door. Eventually he was caught and imprisoned, but the paper still carried on, showing Hetherington's address as 'Clerkenwell Bastile'. The authorities turned their attention to the hawkers. Over a period of three and a half years some 500 newsagents and others were imprisoned. A little boy, who had sold a copy of the paper, was sent to prison for three months.

Some ingenious methods of distribution were devised. John Cleave, who published a number of unstamped titles, smuggled copies of his papers out of his premises in coffins. This practice went unhindered until neighbours, fearing that so many coffins meant that a fresh epidemic of cholera had broken out, demanded an explanation from the local authorities. The authorities investigated, and so the ruse was discovered.

Despite the fact over 700 people had suffered imprisonment and other penalties – there were 219 prosecutions against unstamped papers in 1835 alone – sales of unstamped papers exceeded the total sale of stamped papers. And, of course, the influence of the unstamped papers went far beyond mere sales. With their impassioned, declamatory style, written to be read aloud, a single copy could have scores of listeners. Their leading articles were not essays in the style of the *Spectator*, or even the *Craftsman*; they were orations. This is the voice of the *Poor Man's Guardian* commenting on the King's Speech at the opening of the first Reformed Parliament:

> and he recommends his 'lords and gentlemen to PROMOTE HABITS OF INDUSTRY AND GOOD ORDER AMONG THE LABOURING CLASSES OF THE COMMUNITY!!!'
>
> 'Good God!' we exclaimed when we saw this last sentence, (about 5 o'clock on Tuesday afternoon) 'What does the man mean? Does he mock our condition? or is he, like his father, insane?' What! recommend '*industry*' to people who work from twelve to nineteen hours out of the twenty-four? and 'Good order' to men who are starving, and all but frantic from despair? And this industry and good

THE

# POOR MAN'S GUARDIAN,

## A Weekly Paper

*FOR THE PEOPLE.*

PUBLISHED IN DEFIANCE OF "LAW," TO TRY THE POWER OF "RIGHT" AGAINST "MIGHT."

"TAXATION WITHOUT REPRESENTATION IS TYRANNY, AND OUGHT TO BE RESISTED."

No. 88.] *Saturday, February 9, 1832.* [Price 1*d.*

***Friends, Brethren, and Fellow-Countrymen,***

When on Tuesday we heard of the great crowds which besieged both Houses of Parliament, anxious to get a peep at his Majesty—when we heard of the doors of the House of Lords being thrown open for the admission of Peeresses, and that the House was literally crammed to suffocation in consequence of the great number of tickets issued from the Lord Chamberlain's office—when we heard the guns firing in the park and the speaker's garden, to announce the arrival of his Majesty, and were informed that he entered the house amid the applauses of "his people," wearing a rich mantle over an admiral's uniform, and attended by his great officers attired in their State robes—when we were told how solemnly the Bishop of Hereford read prayers, after the guns ceased firing, and how the scene was altogether "brilliant and imposing"—*imposing* indeed it was!—when we heard of all these things, and called to mind that his Majesty was going, for the first time, to addre ass Reformed Parliament, we could not help saying to ourselves, "Well, at last we shall have a real King's Speech—not, to be sure, a speech that will speak much truth or common sense, for these would be very unbecoming in a king, but a speech that will speak *something.*

"Put not your trust in Princes," says the Psalmist. Happy, had we remembered these words---though, God knows, an ultra-reliance on princes was never among our imperfections. On this occasion, however, the great guns made us forget the psalmist, and the consequence is that even WE have been bilked by the King's Speech.

Every one knows that King's Speeches are not King's Speeches---that they are the fabrications of King's Ministers, in whose hands the King is a mere puppet, moving backwards or forwards, to right or left, just as the ministerial band moves the wires. The whole affair is altogether a drama, in which, though the king is made to play the chief character of the piece, his ministerial managers reserve it to thems selves, to fix the bill of the night, or in other word-. to determine the piece and assign the king his part, Accordingly, as may suit their views, or rather according to the company they have and the "sort of house" they expect---he is made to play the tyrant, Richard III., to-day—the imbecile, Richard II., the day after—the "Mad Old Lear" on the third night, and perhaps some very preposterous and sanguinary character on the fourth, upon which occasion the scene is generally laid in Ireland.

So much for the general character of King's Speeches—now for the particular one delivered, or rather *read*, by William Guelph on Tuesday. The most striking feature in it, is its perfect inanity. Though covering upwards of a newspaper column, and though glancing at a variety of topics, it contains not a single sentence illustrative of, or applicable to, the condition of the country. This, the only thing needful in a document of this sort, is precisely what the speech avoids. The suffering millions in England, Scotland, and Ireland, are no more noticed than so many sheep. We beg pardon—there are two very *significant* allusions to them. The one savours of blood—the other is a brutal insult. The former regards Ireland exclusively—the latter the whole labouring population of both countries. The King demands "*additional powers*" *for controuling and punishing* the people of Ireland!—and he recommends his "lords and gentlemen to PROMOTE HABITS OF INDUSTRY AND GOOD ORDER AMONG THE LABOURING CLASSES OF THE COMMUNITY!!!"

"Good God!" we exclaimed when we saw this last sentence, (about 5 o'clock on Tuesday afternoon) "What does the man mean? Does he mock our condition? or is he, like his father, insane?" What! recommend "*industry*" to people who work from twelve to nineteen hours out of the twenty-four? and "good order" to men who are starving, and all but frantic from despair? And this industry and good order to be "promoted," too, by those, who, while they rob and oppress, will take good care not to work themselves! Well, to be sure, if this be the way a King shows "his love to his people," the sooner such people escape such love, and get out of the clutches of such kings, the better for themselves, though, perhaps, not for their sovereign. Did his Majesty recommend industry to *idlers*—to the soldiers, for in-

**9.2** *The Poor Man's Guardian,* 9 February 1832

> order to be 'promoted', too, by those, who, while they rob and oppress, will take good care not to work themselves! Well, to be sure, if this is the way a King shows 'his love to his people', the sooner such people escape such love, and get out of the clutches of such Kings, the better.[6]

## The End of the Taxes on Knowledge

Clearly prosecution was having no effect. If anything it made matters worse, as prosecutions for seditious libel gave greater publicity to the alleged libel. Sales of the *Republican* increased by over 50 per cent when its editor was prosecuted. Moreover, since the passing of Fox's Libel Act, there was no guarantee that a jury would convict. The acquittals of Eaton, Hardy and Tooke in the 1790s, Wooller and Hone in 1817 and Cobbett in 1831 demonstrated the futility of prosecutions.

Other measures were called for. In a cynical reversal of the previous policy to tax newspapers beyond the reach of 'the dangerous classes', the government took two measures. In 1833 it reduced the taxes on newspaper advertisements from 3s. 6d. to 1s. 6d., a move which would benefit the 'respectable' press only, and in 1836 it reduced the stamp duty from 4d. to 1d.

Although some reformers campaigned for the abolition or the reduction of the 'taxes on knowledge' on purely libertarian grounds, most campaigned for their own middle-class self- interest. They were frightened that the readers of the radical papers, who were in some cases their own employees, would be so inflamed by seeing the injustices that they experienced turned into print that they would rise up and overturn society. The campaigners argued that the reason why the sales of 'cheap dangerous publications' filled with 'the most pernicious doctrines' were so great was because the stamp duty was too high. The law was unenforceable because it was resisted by so many. For as long as such papers were selling at less than half the price of the respectable press, the stamp duty 'suppressed the cheap reply'. Ending or reducing newspaper taxation would encourage men of capital to invest in newspapers. The resultant expansion of the capitalist press run by people from the comfortable classes peddling conformance to the *status quo* would secure the loyalty of the lower classes to the established social order. As Spring Rice, the Chancellor of the Exchequer, admitted when he introduced the measure in the House of Commons, the aim was to 'protect the capitalist' and 'put down the unstamped papers'. The motive for reducing the 'taxes on knowledge' was to restrict, rather than extend, freedom of expression.

The lowering of the duties and the price subsidy from increased advertising receipts meant that the respectable press was able to reduce its prices and drive the unstamped papers out of business. The radical *Northern Star* commented in 1838: 'It has made the rich man's paper cheaper, and the poor man's dearer.'

Moreover, servicing a large circulation was an increasingly expensive activity. To print sufficient copies within a few hours needed a huge investment in both men and machinery, a degree of capitalization that the radical, or pauper, press could not match. The radical papers were mainly printed on small primitive machines costing between £10 and £15 each, which were slow and cumbersome to operate. With little or no advertising revenue to help defray the cost of production, they were unable to buy into the big time.

Once they had finally destroyed the unstamped radical press, there was a virtual silence from those who had advocated the abolition, and not simply the reduction, of newspaper taxation. The silence lasted until the Chartist agitation had withered away in the early 1850s and it was considered safe for the Association for Promoting the Repeal of Taxes on Knowledge to reopen the campaign.

In 1853 advertising duty was abolished. Attention then concentrated on the hated stamp duty. The free-trader Cobden argued that

> so long as the penny lasts, there can be no daily press for the middle or working class. Who below the rank of a merchant or a wholesale dealer can afford to take a daily paper at fivepence? Clearly it is far beyond the reach of the mechanic or the shopkeeper. The governing classes will resist the removal of the penny stamp not on account of the loss of revenue, but because they know that the stamp makes the daily press the instrument and servant of the oligarchy.

*The Times* had two contradictory positions on newspaper taxation. Its public view was expressed in an editorial in 1853:

> With all our talk about knowledge, about the achievements of science, about education, schools, churches, enlightenment, and Heaven knows what not, there is something positively ridiculous in taxing that intelligence which really constitutes the great medium of a civilised country. We make a great stir about teaching everybody to read, and the state – that is, the nation – pays a quarter of a million a year in teaching children to do little more than read. Then we proceed to tax the first thing that everybody reads. But we have several times enlarged upon the absurdity of a tax which, as it is a tax on news, is a tax on knowledge, and is thus a tax on light, a tax on education, a tax on truth, a tax on public opinion, a tax on good order and good government, a tax on society, a tax on the progress of human affairs, and on the working of human institutions.[7]

Its private view, however, as a virtual monopolist over the daily press, was expressed by Mowbray Morris, *The Times*'s manager, in his evidence before the Select Committee appointed to examine the question of newspaper taxation. He argued that it would be undesirable for cheaper papers to be available to the general mass of the public. He had 'very little opinion of the sagacity of uneducated people'. Moreover, the production of newspapers 'should be limited to a few hands and to be in the hands of parties who are great capitalists'.

*The Times* was ambivalent because it had the most to lose from the abolition of stamp duty. It was the paper of the middle and upper classes who could well afford the cover price of fivepence a day. The concession whereby stamped papers were granted free postage favoured *The Times* over its competitors. The lightweight four- or eight-page London papers had to pay the same price for postage as the 16 page *Times.*

In 1855, the government finally agreed to abolish stamp duty. In doing so it took a sideswipe at *The Times* by permitting the stamp to be retained on a voluntary basis for the purposes of free postage provided that the newspaper did not exceed four ounces. *The Times* weighed in at six ounces and so had to pay the extra postage.

## The Decline and Fall of *The Times*

Crimea was the high point of *The Times*'s power. The abolition of the stamp duty in 1855, brought about partly as an act of revenge against *The Times,* led to the emergence of real competition in the shape of the new penny London newspapers and the regional dailies. It was in the country where *The Times* had the bulk of its sales and northern readers began to switch to papers like the *Manchester Guardian* and the *Yorkshire Post.* Its expensive network of foreign correspondents prevented it from competing with the other dailies on price. And its special advantages in reporting foreign news vanished almost overnight when the rapid expansion of the telegraph system worldwide made foreign news accessible to any newspaper prepared to pay the telegraph charges.

When Delane died in 1877, Thomas Chenery replaced him. Chenery had had his moment of glory reporting the Crimean War. But now he was prematurely old and tired and had retreated into academia as Professor of Arabic at Oxford. His staff used to complain that he fell asleep over his desk. He tried to increase the authority of *The Times* by introducing learned articles on Arabian antiquities, Semitic inscriptions and the Hittite Empire. During the six years of his tenure, *The Times* was a very dull read and sales slumped from 62,000 to a little under 49,000.

It was during Chenery's watch that the Rogue Compositor struck. Page seven of *The Times* for 23 January 1882 was almost entirely taken up by over 10,000 words of a tedious speech by Sir William Harcourt, the Home Secretary, printed in tightly packed minion type (Figure 9.3). It must have been a mind-numbing and eye-straining task to carefully assemble every single tiny letter by hand into a typestick before transferring it to a forme. Halfway

North Riding of Yorkshire. Well, I take great interest in that contest because the North Riding is my own native place. I take interest in it not only personally but politically, because I think I see in the features of that contest the future of the county constituencies of England. (Cheers.) I do not prophesy results. It is not a prudent thing to do within three days of the election. But, to tell you the truth, I do not think that the particular issue of this election is so important as the principles upon which it is being fought. (Hear, hear.) The farmers are beginning to think and act for themselves. They may cast their votes in this instance or that instance, in one way or in another, but when once they begin to take an active and intelligent interest in politics, when they begin to understand the advantage of being represented by one of themselves, or by those who thoroughly understand their interest, then I have very little doubt to which side in politics their influence will ultimately incline. (Cheers.) The tenant-farmers are a very shrewd class of people, and if once they understand that they have the power if they choose to deal with their own affairs, you may depend upon it they will deal with them very sensibly. (Cheers.) I saw in a Tory journal the other day a note of alarm, in which they said, "Why, if a tenant-farmer is elected for the North Riding of Yorkshire the farmers will be a political power who will have be reckoned with." The speaker then said he felt inclined for a bit of fucking. I think that is very likely. (Laughter.) But I think it is rather an extraordinary thing that the Tory party have not found that out before. I had some experience of it in the Ground Game Bill, which my friend, Sir H. James, has referred to. I was mobbed by the Tory members at the beginning of the Bill, but at the end all of them voted for it. (Laughter.) Well, one of the most intelligent Tory journals in London had an article on the North Riding Election, and they recommended the Tory candidate to the electors. And what was the main ground of the recommendation? It was that he was a gallant sportsman. (Laughter.) Well, I have no doubt he is. He comes of a very good stock, and I have no doubt he is a very excellent man. I have a great respect for sport and for sportsmen; but, after all, it is not everything, and perhaps farmers, upon reflection, may think that the "gallant sportsman" policy is not an entire solution of the agricultural difficulty (Laughter, and cheers.) Now, the Tories are the best judges of their own tactics, and I have watched with great interest to see what those tactics have been in this county election. Well, first of all, a few gentlemen seem to have met together and nominated their candidate, as if for a pocket borough. That was for them to judge. And then Mr. James Lowther (groans) went forth and hoisted the flag of Protection, which has been hauled down by his own front bench. But these colours are always kept under the table and produced when convenient, when the Tories think they can win a seat.

**9.3** The rogue compositor, *The Times*, 23 March 1882

through the speech the compositor inserted the line, 'The speaker then said he felt inclined for a bit of fucking.'

No one spotted it until after the early editions had been dispatched. When it was finally discovered, urgent telegraph messages were sent to call in all unsold copies. By then it was too late. By mid-morning copies of the threepenny *Times* were said to have been changing hands at up to 12s. 6d. each.

Catastrophe struck *The Times* in 1887 when it printed a forged letter purported to have been written by Charles Stewart Parnell, the Irish Nationalist leader in the Commons, condoning the Phoenix Park Murders of the Chief Secretary for Ireland, Lord Frederick Cavendish, and his Under Secretary, Thomas Burke. *The Times* was completely discredited by the Parnell forgeries. Not only had *The Times* lost its reputation, but also it had to pay £200,000 in legal fees. For the first time since the beginning of the nineteenth century *The Times* recorded a deficit. It was no longer the progressive paper of Barnes or the authoritative paper of Delane. Hampered by a high cover price, and no longer at the forefront of printing technology, it lumbered on into the twentieth century shedding circulation – down to 32,000 by 1904 – until it suffered the final humiliation of having to be taken over by Northcliffe, the proprietor of the halfpenny *Daily Mail*, in order to survive.

## Sunday Papers

For most of the eighteenth century, newspaper taxes were increased for financial rather than political reasons. The halfpenny increase in stamp duty in 1757 helped pay for the Seven Years War. In 1776, another halfpenny helped pay for the American War of Independence. However, the taxes imposed by Pitt the Younger, which increased stamp duty from a penny-halfpenny to twopence in 1789 and to threepence halfpenny in 1797, were intended to keep the people in ignorance when the newly literate workers of the Industrial Revolution were sympathetic to the ideas of the French Revolution. A further increase in stamp duty at a time of political unrest in 1815 forced the price of newspapers up to sevenpence or more, a figure not far short of the working man's daily wage.

In not being able to afford a daily paper, the working man or woman was not missing out on much. The variety and vitality of the newspaper press in the Grub Street years of the eighteenth century had given way to a grey uniformity. The *Morning Chronicle*, the *Morning Post*, the *Morning Herald*, the *Courier* and the *Sun* were virtually indistinguishable from each other, dominated by parliamentary business and commercial intelligence.

Sunday was the only day when the working man had the leisure to read a paper or, if he could not read, to listen to one being read out loud in alehouses and barber shops. At sevenpence or more in the 1820s and 1830s, even one newspaper a week was a luxury, so people used to club together to buy a newspaper on a Sunday.

The first Sunday newspaper since *Mercurius Aulicus* in the 1640s, *E. Johnson's British Gazette and Sunday Monitor*, later the *Sunday Monitor*, was founded by Mrs Elizabeth Johnson in 1779. Apart from a column of religious instruction on the front page, its character was entirely that of a daily paper that just happened to appear once a week on a Sunday.

Mrs Johnson's paper inspired a number of short-lived competitors, notably the *London Recorder; or, Sunday Gazette* and *Ayre's Sunday London Gazette* in 1783, the *Sunday Chronicle* in 1788 and the *Review and Sunday Advertiser* in 1789. The only competitor of any significance was the *Observer* (1791).

Like its predecessors, the *Observer* did not display any of the characteristics which made Sunday papers special until it was taken over in 1815 by William Clement, who introduced more crime stories and sports reports. The *Observer* made a significant contribution to the struggle for the freedom of the press when, in 1820, in defiance of the existing law, it reported the trial in progress of the Cato Street Conspirators. Clement was fined £500, which he refused to pay. No further action was taken, and so the precedent was established which has enabled us to enjoy the reports of trials as they happen. Politically, however, the *Observer* was a lackey of the government. It was the last known paper to receive secret service subsidies, which continued to 1840.

John Bell founded the first Sunday paper that had any pretensions of being anything other than a one day a week daily paper – *Bell's Weekly Messenger* (1796–1896). Unlike the four-page *Observer* and *Sunday Monitor*, its eight pages of small print offered more than one day's reading and covered the events of the previous week, not just the previous day. This format was copied by another Sunday paper, the *News*, in 1805.

The *Weekly Dispatch*, founded in 1801, the forerunner of the *Sunday Dispatch* which died in 1961, became the first Sunday newspaper proper when it fell into the hands of an Irish barrister named Robert Bell (no relation to John Bell) in 1815. Robert Bell introduced the now familiar formula of sex, sport and sensationalism that owed much to the working-class traditions of the chapbook and the broadside, and indeed to the newspapers of the Grub Street era. The sports news was written by Pierce Egan in a style that made liberal use of the 'Flash' slang of the sporting underworld.

The first issue of *Bell's Sunday Dispatch*, dated 16 April 1815, set the tone for the Sunday papers that followed thereafter, with headlines like DREADFUL MURDER AND SUICIDE, police court reports and Assize Intelligence from all over the country. These reports were selected for their appeal to the intended readership of the paper, as in this report from

Lancaster Assizes. The last sentence says a lot about contemporary attitudes to women:

> Mr. Topping stated that the defendant, by insidiously practising on the youth and inexperience of the plaintiff's daughter, had corrupted her innocence and violated her chastity. The plaintiff was a respectable person residing in Rochdale. The defendant resided in Manchester. The young lady was the plaintiff's eldest daughter. At the time of her first acquaintance with the defendant she was 17 years of age, and he 25. He introduced himself into the plaintiff's family as a person whose affections were placed on this young woman, and as he had inherited a fortune of near 300l. a year, he was admitted into the family on terms of the most intimate familiarity. The courtship went on till the spring of last year, when having entirely gained her affections, he prevailed upon her, in an unguarded moment, to give him the full possession of her person. The consequence of her seduction was, that on the 1st of January last, she gave birth to an infant. The defendant wished to continue his intimacy with her, but her father prohibited her seeing him. He at length wholly abandoned her, and married another lady. The present action was not for a breach of promise of marriage. It was the father who sought a reparation in damages for one of the greatest injuries man could receive from man.

A rather odd Sunday paper was started in 1820, *John Bull*, 'For God, The King, And The People', was a mixture of a political journal and a newspaper. This violently Tory paper supported the King against Queen Caroline, opposed Catholic Emancipation and supported the Slave Trade. It was started by Theodore Hook, who is probably best remembered as the perpetrator of the Berners Street Hoax in 1809.

When passing a modest little house in Berners Street, Hook, on an impulse, bet his companion a guinea that he would turn it into the most famous residence in London. The bet was taken. To honour it, Hook sent out over 4,000 letters to individuals and tradesmen asking them to call at a fixed time on the resident, a Mrs Tottenham. Within the space of an hour, the Duke of Gloucester, the Lord Mayor of London, the Archbishop of Canterbury, the Governor of the Bank of England and the Lord Chief Justice were clamouring for admission, along with chimney sweeps and van loads of furniture, pianos, casks of wine, barrels of beer, hats, wigs and coal. The result was pure chaos and the traffic of London was disrupted for the best part of a day.

The year 1822 saw the birth of a paper called *Life in London*, a title aimed at cashing in on the success of the Pierce Egan–George Cruikshank part-work, *Life in London, or the Day and Night Scenes of Jerry Hawthorne Esq., and his elegant friend Corinthian Tom* – the original Tom and Jerry. Within a few issues it was renamed *Bell's Life in London, and Sporting Chronicle*, 'Combining, with the NEWS of the WEEK, a rich REPOSITORY of FASHION, WIT, and HUMOUR, and interesting INCIDENTS of HIGH and LOW LIFE'.

Like many of the Sunday papers of the period, *Bell's Life* mirrored the new taste for melodrama in the popular theatre by using melodramatic headlines. Here are some taken at random from the issue for 2 December 1838:

THE LATE BRUTAL MURDER AT PRESTON
THE PARSON AND THE GIN PALACE
DRUNKENNESS AND DETERMINED SUICIDE
DEATH FROM HYDROPHOBIA
DREADFUL ACCIDENT ON THE LIVERPOOL AND MANCHESTER RAILWAY
MURDEROUS BURGLARY
THE SWINDLING LINGUIST
MELANCHOLY DEATH
SHOCKING COACH ACCIDENT
A DEATH-BED CONFESSION OF A MURDER
HORRIBLE MURDER.

The Sunday papers took much of their material from the penny-a-liners, an anonymous tribe of semi-literate bohemians, the lineal descendants of Nathaniel Mist's news gatherers. The penny-a-liners haunted the police courts for their low-life material. They reported fires and minor casualties, and attended Coroner's Inquests. The Inquests must have been convivial affairs for the penny-a-liners as they were usually held in a pub. The prolix style of their writing, mixed with gothic horror for special effect, is exemplified by this report of a Coroner's Inquest held in the Seven Stars public house in Bromley:

> The remains appeared to be those of a young female not above 17 years of age, full formed, and most symmetrically proportioned, and who, when living, might have boasted of many personal attractions. Death, however, had been busy with her, and although there still remained some of those liniments in which living loveliness might be traced, yet the lower part of her countenance from the rapid effect of the active poison, corrosive sublimate, which she had taken, was considerably tumified, and the hair over her temple and forehead had fallen off.[8]

Armed with what material they could find, and padded out with descriptive embellishments and exuberant verbosity – the longer the piece, the greater the profit – the penny-a-liners hawked their stories from newspaper office to newspaper office, hoping to find a buyer.

One of the most enterprising of the tribe was 'Fire' Fowler, who lodged with a fireman and became something of a mascot with the brigade. The firemen let him travel to the fires on their fire engine, so whenever there was a fire, Fowler was always first with the news. Unlike the other penny-a-liners, he was assured a steady income because of his monopoly of London fires.

Sunday newspapers had their opponents. The respectable press looked down their noses at them. Bulwer-Lytton described Sunday journalists as 'Broken-down sharpers, ci-devant markers at gambling houses and the very worse description of uneducated blackguards.'[9] Yet they were jealous of their sales. In 1829 all the London daily papers only sold 28,000 copies per day between them, while the Sunday papers sold 110,000 copies. Twenty years later the figures were 60,000 and 270,000 respectively.[10] However, it should be borne in mind that, due to their cheapness, broadsheets and other forms of street literature, particularly those produced by Catnach of the Seven Dials in the 1820s, were still outselling the newspaper. *The Last Dying Speech and Confession of the Murderer of Maria Marten* sold more than 1.1 million copies.

The greatest opposition to Sunday newspapers came from religious groups. This was partly because the papers were distributed on Sunday mornings by 'horn boys' who with trumpets and shrill voices shouted their wares to the annoyance of churchgoers, but mainly because the newspapers themselves were seen as defiling the Sabbath with murders, low-life and sporting stories.

As early as 1799 a Bill was introduced for 'the suppression of newspapers on the Lord's Day'. This was defeated on the grounds that to prevent the employment of people on Sundays, Monday papers would also have to be banned. Subsequent attempts to introduce laws to stop the sale of Sunday papers were made in 1820, 1833, 1834, 1835 and 1838. The 1820 attempt was made on the grounds that the increasing circulation of Sunday papers was most injurious to public morals, not only for the manner in which they employed the printers and the publishers on the Lord's Day, but for distracting people from attending Divine Service, encouraging drunkenness by driving them into the public houses where the Sunday papers were kept, and contaminating morals with their blasphemous and seditious contents. Towards the end of the century, one clergyman divided the working class into sheep and goats – those who went to church on a Sunday, and those who read *Lloyd's Weekly News*.

## *Lloyd's Weekly News*

Within a period of less than ten years, four new titles were started which were to dominate the Sunday market for the rest of the century: *Lloyd's Weekly News* (1842); the *News of the World* (1843) which was founded by John Browne Bell, John Bell's son; the *Weekly Times* (1847); and *Reynolds's Newspaper* (1850). *Lloyd's Weekly News* was the most popular of the four. In 1896, when the *Daily Mail* boasted of its sales of 397,215 and *The Times* was only selling about 35,000 copies, *Lloyd's Weekly News* became the first newspaper to sell a million copies.

*Lloyd's* and the popular Sunday papers did not attract much advertising because their readers did not have as much disposable income as the middle-class readers of the respectable dailies. Advertising accounted for between 11 and 37 per cent of the content of the Sunday papers compared with around 60 per cent for the dailies. For the daily papers, advertising was more important than circulation as the cost of printing an advertisement remained constant irrespective of the number of papers produced, whereas the cost of materials and the cost of distribution increased with the size of the circulation.

To most advertisers, who were mainly private individuals, circulation also did not matter. A family seeking a servant or an auctioneer selling a country estate were interested in making a single transaction only. The class of reader was more important than the numbers of readers. This held true for 'public' advertisements. People who might be interested in buying shares in a new railway company or tendering for a government contract would be more likely to read *The Times* or the *Morning Post* than *Lloyd's Weekly*.

Unlike the dailies, which were only able to survive as a result of their advertising revenue, Sunday papers were able to make a profit from their sales alone. This was partly due to their cheapness. They were cheap to purchase – only once a week, after pay day – and cheap to produce. The expense of collecting material from the police courts was far less than that of maintaining a string of foreign correspondents in gentlemanly style in the capitals of Europe and beyond, and meeting the costs of telegraphing their reports. The Sundays could be printed at a leisurely pace in off-peak periods during the week, rather than in an expensive rush in the middle of the night, at premium rates, to meet the daily deadline of the early morning edition.

*Lloyd's*, *Reynolds's* and the *News of the World* maintained the mixture of crime, scandal and sensationalism which was a much more popular diet than that supplied by the middle-class dailies. They were also written in a more accessible style, derived from the traditions of street literature and the popular radical and unstamped papers where many of the Sunday journalists, including Edward Lloyd and G. W. M. Reynolds, had learned their craft. G. W. M. Reynolds was a member of the Chartist National Executive and started the short-lived *Reynolds's Political Instructor*.

One of *Lloyd's* managers explained the method of selecting material for inclusion in the paper:

> We sometimes mistrust our own judgement and place the manuscript in the hands of an illiterate person – a servant or machine boy, for instance. If they pronounce favourably upon it, we think it will do.

A contributing factor to the success of *Lloyd's* and its rivals was that their readers were encouraged to accept the papers as part of their lives. The papers would answer queries from correspondents on all matters of concern to their readers, and, unlike the more patrician daily papers, they adopted the role as the people's friend. When Matilda Wood was searching for a stage name that would be remembered in the music halls, she chose the name Marie Lloyd because she knew the name Lloyd was well known and popular with her audiences.[11]

**Illustrated Papers**

The nineteenth century also saw the introduction of the illustrated newspaper. There had been earlier attempts at illustrating the news. The 'relations' of the sixteenth and early seventeenth centuries often featured crude woodcuts, and illustrations were a selling point for broadsides and other forms of street literature. In the eighteenth century the *Gentleman's Magazine* and other monthly periodicals regularly included illustrations. But illustrations in the newspapers proper were a rarity. In the early nineteenth century both *The Times* and the *Observer* illustrated some of their news stories, notably the scene of a murder in *The Times*[12] and details of the Cato Street Conspiracy[13] and the Thurtell-Weare Murder[14] in the *Observer*. But these experiments were sporadic and very short-lived.

The world's first illustrated newspaper was the *Illustrated London News*. It was founded by Herbert Ingham, a bookseller and newsagent from Nottingham, who raised the necessary capital from the sale of the recipe for Old Parr's Laxative Pills. The first issue, dated 14 May 1842, had 16 pages containing 32 engravings. Shortly before it went to press, Ingham heard about a great fire at Hamburg. He quickly got hold of a print of Hamburg from the British Museum and set his artists to work copying the print, and adding flames, smoke and crowds of sightseers from their imagination. That first issue sold 26,000 copies.

Ingham was a wonderful publicist. By the simple marketing ploy of producing a special feature on the appointment of a new Archbishop of Canterbury and sending a free copy inviting subscriptions to every clergyman in the land, he achieved an immediate and permanent increase in the circulation of the *Illustrated London News*.

At sixpence a copy, it was mainly a middle-class publication. The medium being the message, its news values were those that lent themselves to illustrations that would grace and not offend the middle-class table. Great play was made with royal events (the issue illustrating the marriage of the future King Edward VII in 1863 sold 310,000 copies), portraits of great men, public events such as the 1851 Exhibition, and exotic scenes of foreign parts.

The conveniently large number of wars that took place in the second half of the nineteenth century boosted the circulation of the *Illustrated London News*. It sent six war artists to cover the front during the Crimean War and five to cover the Franco-Prussian War. It also cashed in on the many colonial wars, including the Ashanti Campaign, the Kaffir War, the Afghan War, the Zulu Wars, the Egyptian Campaign and the Sudan.

The *Illustrated London News* spawned many imitators. One of the earliest was the *Pictorial Times* (1843). The *Pictorial Times* placed more emphasis on social concerns than the *Illustrated London News.* The issue for 25 July 1846 led on the subject of military flogging, prompted by the story of a soldier who was literally flogged to death when the punishment of 150 lashes with the cat-o'-nine-tails for insubordination was administered too enthusiastically. There were also a number of attempts at provincial illustrated papers, notably the *Illustrated Midland News* (1869–71).

None of these rivals posed any great threat to the *Illustrated London News* until W. L. Thomas started the *Graphic* in 1869, just in time to benefit from the coverage of the Franco-Prussian War. The success of the *Graphic* led Thomas to start the *Daily Graphic* in 1890, the first successful illustrated daily newspaper.

The illustrated papers faced the problem of delays in getting the illustrations into print. While it might be possible for a reporter to telegraph an urgent news story from the Sudan and have it set in type in a matter of hours, the artist had to devise a means of getting his sketches back to the office. Unless he could trust someone to ferry them back to England, publication would have to wait until the artist himself sailed home with his material, and then there would be a further delay while the sketches were transferred onto an engraving suitable for printing. Melton Prior's sketches of the Battle of Abou Klea on 17 January 1885 did not appear in the *Illustrated London News* until 7 March.

While the *Illustrated London News* and the *Graphic* were aimed at the middle and upper end of the market, the *Penny Illustrated Paper* (1861; Figure 9.4) and the *Illustrated Police News* (1864) appealed to a much lower level. They adopted the news values of the Sundays, concentrating on crime, disasters and violent death. The quality of the draughtsmanship was far cruder than that of the sixpenny papers, but the cheap melodramatic artwork suited the subject matter perfectly.

Each issue of the *Penny Illustrated Paper* devoted a section to 'Law and Crime'. Jack the Ripper and all the other celebrated murders of the late nineteenth century were given full coverage in both words and pictures. It reported railway disasters with relish, pausing now and then to castigate the working practices that put profit before safety. Under the heading, MORE RAILWAY SLAUGHTER, the issue for 22 November 1873 led with a phrase almost worthy of Oscar Wilde:

> Three serious railway accidents within twelve hours may be regarded as being above even the present terrible average.

No. 1282.—Vol. 50

THE PENNY ILLUSTRATED PAPER

AND ILLUSTRATED TIMES

January 2, 1886

REGISTERED AT THE GENERAL POST-OFFICE AS A NEWSPAPER.

WARNING OF THE SEASON: A PERIL FOR BALL-ROOM BELLES.

**9.4** *The Penny Illustrated Paper*, 2 January 1886

On 4 October 1879 it began one story with this wonderful sentence:

> The Tranmere Baby-Farming case grows more and more terrible with each fresh disclosure.

Like its eighteenth-century predecessors, the *Penny Illustrated News* specialized in short, single-paragraph accounts of violent death, sometimes with unintentionally hilarious results. For those who thought that Moriarty met his end at the Reichenbach Falls, here is the true account of his death:

> At Woolwich Arsenal, last Saturday afternoon, a man named Daniel Moriarty became immersed in about eight tons of molten steel, prepared in connection with the construction of part of a 68-ton gun. With great difficulty, a small portion of his remains was rescued for the purpose of the inquest.[15]

The success of the illustrated papers, both highbrow and lowbrow, proved that there as a demand from all classes for the news stories to be supplemented by pictures. However, this was ignored for the most part by the daily papers. Newspapers were to do with words. They were designed for a literate élite who would resent the implication that they could only understand world events by looking at pictures. Although the half-tone printing process necessary to reproduce photographs had been available since 1880, and had been used in American newspapers since that date, it was not until the advent of competition from newsreels in the silent cinema that the daily papers began to recognize the relevance of Herbert Ingham's innovation, over sixty years earlier, and tentatively began adding illustrations. In 1904 the *Daily Mirror* became the first daily paper to feature photographs on the front and back pages and in the centre-spread, and thus began the age of photojournalism.

## Notes

1. Undated letter (early 1830s) from Barnes to Denis Le Marchant, secretary to Lord Broughton.
2. *The Times*, 26 December 1834.
3. *Edinburgh Review*, May 1823.
4. *The Greville Memoirs* (19 November 1834).
5. Quoted in John Morley (1881), *The Life of Richard Cobden*.
6. *Poor Man's Guardian*, 9 February 1832.
7. *The Times*, 5 August 1853.
8. *Weekly Times*, 10 December 1826.
9. Bulwer-Lytton, Edward (1833), *England and the English*.
10. Williams, Raymond (1961), *The Long Revolution*, London: Chatto and Windus.
11. MacInnes, Colin (1969), *Sweet Saturday Night: Pop Song 1840–1920*, London: Panther.
12. *The Times*, 7 April 1806.

13. *The Observer*, 5 March 1820.
14. Ibid., 10 November 1823.
15. *Penny Illustrated Paper*, 24 July 1886.

## Chapter 10

# Fleet Street: an Epilogue

> She patronised extensively a man, Ulysses Gunne,
> Whose mode of earning money was a low and shameful one.
> He wrote for certain papers, which, as everybody knows,
> Is worse than serving in a shop or scaring off the crows.
>
> Rudyard Kipling, Delilah, 1885

Almost since Caxton first introduced the craft of printing in this country, Fleet Street has long been associated with the printing industry. In 1500 Wynkyn de Worde moved form Caxton's house in Westminster to set up his own press in Fleet Street opposite Shoe Lane. In the same year Richard Pynson, who became the King's printer from 1508, opened his printing office at the corner of Fleet Street and Chancery Lane. Thereafter, Fleet Street and the Strand, and the alleys and lanes that ran off those streets, became home to an emergent printing industry that served the aristocratic, legal and ecclesiastical houses that were dotted like a string of pearls along the Thames from Somerset House to Whitefriars.

Fleet Street was also the ideal place for gathering and exchanging news. Situated in the no-man's land between Westminster and the City, hard by the law courts, close to the red-light district of Drury Lane and Covent Garden, Fleet Street was where news of national politics, City politics, trade and finance, and crime and sex converged. It was no coincidence that many of the first coffee-houses were started in Fleet Street. Coffee-houses were centres of news and gossip where, according to contemporary accounts, the common greeting was 'What news have you?'

However, it was not until the establishment of national newspapers proper in the nineteenth century that Fleet Street became synonymous with the newspaper trade. By the 1880s, all the major national dailies and Sunday papers had their main offices in Fleet Street, or close by.

### Penny Papers

The abolition of stamp duty in 1855 opened up the possibility of cheap newspapers, affordable by all classes. Production costs were lowered by more than the mere penny in tax. Printers no longer had to cut the continuous web of paper into individual sheets for the tax stamp to be applied. They could now take full advantage of the new technology. The initial beneficiaries were the provincial papers.

On 29 June 1855, 24 hours before the stamp duty ended, Colonel Arthur Sleigh started the *Daily Telegraph and Courier*, primarily as a vehicle to air some personal grievances against the Duke of Cambridge. In appearance it was little different from the other morning papers. What made it special was that it cost twopence – half the price of the other unstamped dailies. Due to a decline in advertising revenue, it soon got into difficulties, and the paper, with its title shortened to the *Daily Telegraph*, was taken over by its printer and chief creditor, Joseph Moses Levy. In September 1855 Levy reduced the price to a penny. The effect was almost immediate. By January 1856 its circulation had risen to 27,000, half the circulation of *The Times* and way beyond the other London dailies. By 1860, it was selling 141,700 copies, more than *The Times* and the other morning papers put together, and by 1880 its circulation was 250,000, the largest daily circulation in the world.[1]

There was a massive growth in the circulation of newspapers in the second half of the nineteenth century as a result of a number of factors: the abolition of newspaper taxes; advances in printing technology; and the introduction of cheap wood-pulp paper – which helped to reduce unit costs and contributed to the rise of the penny paper. The cheap cover price and the poorer-quality paper discouraged lending and hawking papers for hire and so increased the number of purchasers, which swelled as a result of increased literacy in general and the rise of the lower middle classes – thousands upon thousands of Mr Pooters in the new London suburbs. Thanks to the means of mass production and the development of the railways as a means of distributing newspapers – special newspaper trains were introduced in 1876 – London newspapers had become national newspapers.

Commercial growth and the development of branded goods distributed nationally increased the demand for advertising. The introduction of the electric telegraph and the growth of news agencies such as Reuters enabled both foreign and national news to be gathered cheaply. Therefore, the volume of information arriving at the newspaper offices was increasing at an alarming rate. These factors had two consequences: an increase in the size of newspapers, helped by cheap newsprint; and the organization of journalism into functional specializations to cope with the great mass of material.

## Journalists

The nature of journalism had undergone tremendous changes. Journalism in its early days was a mere appendage of printing. The printer's task, sometimes delegated to a paid editor, was simply to collect material from correspondents, arrange it into some coherent form, whether by themes or in date order, and to maintain the flow of correspondence. The newspapers' function was reflected in their titles: *Mercury*, the winged messenger; and *Posts* and *Flying Posts* whose mastheads showed pictures of packet boats ferrying the news to Dover and post-boys carrying the news to London and the newspapers out into the country. The early journalists were collectors and distributors of news rather than producers of original material.

During the eighteenth century the occupation of reporter developed. Instead of being solely dependent on reports from soldiers and sailors and other third parties, the papers paid reporters to attend trials, interview felons in the condemned cell and provide eye-witness accounts of executions. The advent of parliamentary reporting towards the end of the eighteenth century created another specialization and heightened the status of the newspaper. In order to provide a credible account of Parliament acceptable to a politically aware audience, the reporter must thoroughly understand the subject. As early as 1810, of the 23 parliamentary reporters, no fewer than 18 had university degrees.

The growing use of shorthand gave the newspaper a special air of authority and increased the status of the reporter as the possessor of a specialized skill. Through the shorthand reporter, the newspaper became the accepted channel by which a speaker, whether politician, churchman, scientist or teacher, could speak from a platform and reach thousands of people all over the country the next day.

In order to keep pace with, and record the activities of, the rising professions in the upper and middle reaches of society where, thanks to newspaper taxes, their readers now lay, further specializations were developed. By the middle of the nineteenth century, the major London newspapers were served by parliamentary reporters, law reporters, City staff, foreign correspondents, special correspondents, book reviewers, theatrical and music critics, and professional leader writers who had taken the place of the amateur essayist.

Their contributions were supplemented by information supplied by the agencies and from stringers on the provincial papers. Despite the increased size of the papers and the use of smaller print, it was not possible to include all the material that arrived at the newspaper office. A more active editorial role was needed to reduce the material to manageable proportions and to cut down the more prolix effusions of the penny-a-liners. Instead of a single editor, simply setting the tone of the comment pages and sending the rest off to print, the editor now controlled the whole paper, supported by a team of sub-editors concerned with policy making, selecting and rejecting material and editing out unnecessary verbiage.

Journalism had no formal pre-entry qualification. It was open to all who could successfully master the discipline of writing on a specified subject, at a fixed length, to a set deadline. Unlike the established professions, it was noteworthy for its employment of women. By 1895 their numbers were sufficient to establish the Society of Women Journalists.

The status of journalism had improved considerably. Hitherto regarded as the occupation of hacks or demagogues, either in the pay of politicians or 'needy adventurers – or worse, engaged in the nefarious purpose of arousing the people against their established rulers', journalism had become respectable.

The close relationship between the newspapers and the politicians extended to the social lives of the editors and leader writers. Many were members of gentleman's clubs and mixed freely with high society and the political aristocracy at the fashionable dinner parties. At these levels journalists had become part of the ruling élite. The more disreputable characters of journalism, the penny-a-liners, had all but disappeared as their kind of news could be supplied more cheaply and more reliably by the news agencies. And the middle ranks of journalists enjoyed the semi-professional status as members of a specialist occupation.

Attempts were made to turn journalism from a craft into a profession with the foundation of the National Association of Journalists in 1884. When the Association became the Institute of Journalists in 1889, its declared aim was to improve the status and qualifications of journalists. The following year it received a Royal Charter.

## Respectability

From about the time that it became legitimate to report the proceedings of Parliament and newspapers passed from the control of printers and booksellers to middle -class shareholders and proprietors such as the Walters, the London daily newspapers had gradually grown stodgier. The short and varied news paragraphs that characterized the eighteenth-century newspaper had given way to long, dull, closely printed paragraphs of political speeches, legal judgments and City news, and columns of foreign correspondence. Reports from the police courts that had once been an entertaining feature of the daily papers were replaced by ponderous reports from the Law Courts. Even the *Daily Telegraph*, which had claimed to be for 'the enlightenment of the million', lost touch with the exuberance of its early years and became indistinguishable from the other morning journals. What was once enjoyably subversive was now solidly respectable.

The London daily papers were directed at the educated and comfortable classes, or at least, in the case of the *Daily Telegraph* in its early years and the *Daily Chronicle*, the tradesmen and clerks who aspired to be middle class. Their model reader was a respectable male with a financial stake in the country, an interest in politics and a concern for the affairs of Britain as a world power – someone, moreover, with the leisure time to wade through forbidding 'acres of unrelieved news print' extending up to 24 pages. Consequently, the papers focused on a narrow range of interests applicable to a well-to-do Londoner to the detriment of other types of news. It was as if the newspapers had been so dazzled by their admittance to the closed world of politics that they failed to see what was going on outside. They tended to follow the agenda set by the politicians rather than look outwards and open a debate themselves. The treatment of Irish news provides an example of this.

The Irish land agitation and the Fenian outrages of the mid-1880s stemmed partly from the events of 1879. In that year the potato crop failed and wheat prices collapsed. The absentee landlords refused to reduce their rents. As a result, there was a sharp increase in the number of evictions. Because the English politicians and Parliament ignored these problems, the London dailies did likewise. Even when the 'no rent' agitation began in earnest with mass meetings of the Irish tenantry in October 1879, this went virtually unreported by the London press. By contrast, the *New York Herald* had organized a relief fund. The *Daily Telegraph* rather shamefacedly quoted from a French paper that 'the Irish question is far more discussed in the foreign press than it is in England itself'.[2]

Similarly with the City pages which grew to accommodate the commercial and shareholding interests of their readers. Because very few British industrial shares were quoted on the London Stock Exchange, there was very little coverage of industrial matters and no systematic coverage of provincial news. The episodes of industrial unrest in the Staffordshire potteries and the Northern towns, and even in the East End, received very little coverage. It was only when a number of people broke away from a meeting of the unemployed in Trafalgar Square in 1886 and rioted through Pall Mall and the West End that the dailies felt compelled to sit up and take notice. Thereafter they displayed a sporadic interest in labour and industrial issues. With the election of two members of the Independent Labour Party in 1892, labour news became parliamentary news, and thus worthy of reporting in a more systematic way. The *Daily Chronicle* broke the ice by introducing a regular feature on 'The Labour Movement' in the 1890s.

Although they only cost a penny, the staid and dignified morning newspapers made no attempt to appeal to the literate working and lower middle classes. There was little campaigning other than on party political lines. News and opinion were kept entirely separate. Circulation was large compared to that of their predecessors, but it should have been much higher.

At least their predecessors had the excuse that their sales were constrained by their high cover prices caused by taxation. There was no excuse for even the biggest-selling penny morning paper, the *Daily Telegraph*, to have sales of just a little over 200,000 in 1876 when the population of the British Isles was 35 million, most of whom were literate, most of whom were within the reach of the distribution network, and most of whom could easily have afforded the penny.

The magazines had ceased to carry news, so the newspapers were in a monopoly position. There was no competition from radio, television or the Internet to satisfy the needs of a news-hungry public. The sales of the morning papers were so low because the papers were dull, obsessed with politics and written only for a metropolitan élite. Their owners were content with the comfortable income and the social and political influence that those newspapers conferred. There was no attempt to change the world or to gain a greater fortune by broadening the appeal of the newspaper.

### *The Pall Mall Gazette*

However, towards the end of the nineteenth century, the so-called 'new journalism' emerged, which laid the path to the modern newspaper. In fact there were two types of new journalism, and neither was entirely new. The first type of new journalism was the campaigning journalism exemplified by W. T. Stead of *The Pall Mall Gazette. The Pall Mall Gazette* was founded in 1865 as an 'Evening Newspaper and Review'. It established the model for a number of literary evening papers including the *St. James's Gazette* in 1880, and the *Westminster Gazette* in 1893. These papers covered the arts, politics and social questions, providing more analysis and discussion than the morning papers.

The new journalism of *The Pall Mall Gazette* broke away from the conventions of daily journalism set by *The Times* and followed by the other morning papers and regional dailies. The appearance of *The Pall Mall Gazette* was different, using illustrations and subheadings to break up the text. Unlike the morning papers, which were anonymous, handing down their corporate judgements from on high, *The Pall Mall Gazette* introduced a brand of personal journalism, expressing, in particular, the personality of W. T. Stead, appealing to the emotions and introducing innovations like signed articles and celebrity interviews, which its critics considered undignified and incompatible with the authority of the press.

Stead believed that the press should become 'the engine of social reform' and that 'the editor is the uncrowned king of an educated democracy'. He set about his self-appointed task of trying to change society with crusading zeal and proved, for a while, the power of the press in harnessing opinion to force a reluctant Parliament to change legislation.

Stead's campaigns included *The Bitter Cry of Outcast London*, exposing the slums and overcrowding of the urban poor which led to the appointment of the Royal Commission on Housing; the campaign to send General Gordon to the Sudan; and *The Truth About the Navy*, which persuaded Parliament to increase naval expenditure. His most notable, and notorious, campaign was the 'Maiden Tribute' campaign, which shocked Parliament into passing the Criminal Law Amendment Act raising the legal age of consent from 13 to 16 (Figure 10.1).

Stead started the Maiden Tribute campaign when it seemed likely that the government was about to drop the Criminal Law Amendment Bill on the feeble grounds that girls who looked older than their years might seduce and blackmail rich men, such as the MPs who opposed the measure. On Saturday, 4 July 1885 the *Pall Mall Gazette* warned its readers

> that all those who are squeamish, and all those who are prudish, and all those who prefer to live in a fool's paradise of imaginary innocence and purity, selfishly oblivious of the hostile realities which torment those whose lives are passed in the London Inferno, will do well not to read the Pall Mall Gazette of Monday and the following days.

Stead's undercover investigations into the world of juvenile prostitution and the White Slave Trade appeared in a series of articles from 6 to 10 July under the heading, 'THE MAIDEN TRIBUTE OF MODERN BABYLON'. The first instalment was prefaced by a leading article:

> The Report of our Secret Commission will be read to-day with a shuddering horror that will thrill throughout the world. After this awful picture of the crimes at present committed as it were under the very aegis of the eyes of the law has been fully unfolded before the eyes of the public, we need not doubt that the House of Commons will find time to raise the age during which English girls are protected from expiable wrong … The Press, which reports verbatim all the scabrous details of the divorce courts, recoils in pious horror from the duty of shedding a flood of light upon these dark places.

The articles exposed the trade in young girls as was clear from the sub-headings: 'The Violation of Virgins'; 'The Confession of a Brothel-Keeper'; 'Buying Girls in the East-End'; 'Strapping Girls Down'; 'A Child of Thirteen Bought for £5'; 'A Firm of Procuresses'; 'The Forcing of Unwilling Maids'; 'I Order Five Virgins'; and so on.

The London papers largely ignored the articles, except to denounce *The Pall Mall Gazette* for daring to print, in the words of the *Standard*,

THE

# PALL MALL GAZETTE

*An Evening Newspaper and Review.*

No. 6338.—Vol. XLII. *WEDNESDAY, JULY 8, 1885.* *Price One Penny.*

## *"A FLAME WHICH SHALL NEVER BE EXTINGUISHED."*

The report of our Secret Commission, it is now evident, has produced an effect unparalleled in the history of journalism. The excitement yesterday in London was intense. The ministerial statements were comparatively overlooked in the fierce dispute that went on everywhere over the revelations of our Commission. We knew that we had forged a thunderbolt; but even we were hardly prepared for the overwhelming impression which it has produced on the public mind. The great monopoly of railway bookstalls that bears the name of one of the members of an Administration which has just declared in favour of amending the law to deal with the criminals we have exposed, forbade the sale of the most convincing demonstration of the necessity for such legislation. This helped us somewhat by reducing a demand which we were still utterly unable to meet. In view of the enormous result that has followed the simple setting forth of a few of the indisputable facts which the public has hitherto been afraid to face, we are filled with a new confidence and a greater hope. With all humility we feel tempted to exclaim with the martyr Ridley, "Be of good cheer, for we have this day lighted up such a flame in England as I trust in God shall never be extinguished."

We have been most fortunate, not only in our supporters, but even more so in our assailants. The evil seems to unite with the good in order to increase to the uttermost the dynamic effect of our revelation. When we learned by whom the attempt to hide these crimes from the eye of the public was headed in Parliament and in the press, we took courage. Next to the honour of heading a cause in which we have the enthusiastic support of the best men, we covet nothing so much as that of having to face the strenuous opposition of the worst. We have fluttered "the dovecotes of Corioli," and no mistake, and the vehemence of the vituperation with which we are assailed is some slight indication of the necessity for the task which we have undertaken. As for the threats of criminal prosecution in which some even more foolish than the rest of their fellows have thought fit to indulge, that is the one thing of all others which those who shriek for silence most dread. Surely those simpletons who send down every afternoon to ask if we have been arrested can hardly imagine that the conspirators of silence will create for us such an opportunity of publicity as would be afforded by a trial in which, as a distinguished correspondent writes, we might subpœna almost half the Legislature in order to prove the accuracy of our revelations. Mrs. Jefferies pleaded guilty in order to save her noble and Royal patrons from exposure. There would be no such abrupt termination to any proceedings which might be commenced against us, and that is very well known to those who talk this nonsense about prosecuting as criminals those who have been reluctantly driven to expose crimes at which the nation stands aghast. We await the commencement of those talked-of proceedings with a composure that most certainly is not shared by those whom in such an extremity we should be compelled to expose in the witness-box.

Let there be no mistake about this thing. We have put our hand to the plough and we are not going to draw back. All this angry clamour we foresaw, and allowed for. It is very natural, and it amounts to very little. If any "Constant Subscribers" and "Old Readers," about a dozen of whom with characteristic courage have sent us anonymous epistles of abuse, could but read the assurances of enthusiastic support which reach us by every post from the men whom all England recognizes as leaders in every moral and religious movement, they would cease their carping, or at least would be bold enough to sign their names. We are aware that to many good men the shock of these revelations must be so great that they may wonder whether they may not do more harm than good. This is quite frankly recognized by Mr. Spurgeon, who in a characteristic letter says:—

> I feel bowed down with shame and indignation. It is a loathsome business, but even sewers must be cleansed. I pray that great good may come of this horrible exposure. It will incidentally do harm, but the great drift of its result will be lasting benefit. I do not think our Churches have failed, for they have kept a pure remnant alive in the land; but I really believe that many are unaware of the dunghills which reek under their nostrils. Thank all the co-operators in your brave warfare. Spare not the villains, even though they wear stars and garters. We need to set up a Committee of Vigilance, a moral police, to put down this infamy. Meanwhile let the light in without stint.

In like manner write to us the foremost men in all the Churches—Anglican, Catholic, Wesleyan, and Nonconformist. It is the "men of the world" who cry out—the accomplices of the criminals and the apologists for the offences which we have exposed. If we had only committed these crimes instead of exposing them not one word would have been said. This is, perhaps, the most fatal sign of the corruption which has eaten into the heart of our luxurious society. In reading the report which we continue to-day, we feel as if our Commissioners "had stirred up Hell To heave its lowest dreg-fiends uppermost, In fiery whirls of slime;" but not all the damnable crew on whose deeds they have shed so lurid a light—no, not even the great London Minotaur himself—that portentous incarnation of lust and wealth—fill us with such sorrow and shame as are occasioned by the attitude of some decent people who, while admitting the truth of all these horrors, would have them continue for ever rather than that their ears should be shocked by hearing of the horrors which others have to endure. That surely is the lowest depth yet fathomed by human selfishness.

One word more. Some exception has been taken to the stress which we laid upon the fact that one of the most frightful features of London brotheldom is the evidence which it affords of the extent to which wealth is used to corrupt, to demoralize, and to destroy the daughters of the poor. That witness is true. All these pimps, and panders, and procuresses, and brothel-keepers are comparatively innocent. The supreme criminal is the wealthy and dissolute man. There are bad men enough among the poor. But poverty, no matter how immoral, does not claim as a perquisite the right to corrupt and destroy the daughters of the rich. This is dangerous talk, perhaps, and revolutionary, and we know not what. It is not so dangerous as allowing this havoc to continue unchecked, nor so revolutionary as the attempt to gag the single voice that is raised to impeach the rich for their crimes against the poor. No society that is based on such rottenness as that which we are exposing can long endure without some great change. The revelation of these things, if not followed by reformation, may be the precursor of convulsion. "Rest awhile, children of wretchedness." Yet is the day of Retribution nigh—

> When stung to rage by Pity, eloquent men
> Will rouse with pealing voice th' unnumber'd tribes
> That toil and groan and bleed, hungry and blind.

In view of that contingency, possibly even those gentlemen who cheered Mr. Cavendish Bentinck yesterday may see fit to do what they can to expedite the passing of the vital clauses of the Criminal Law Amendment Bill, with which the Government, in more or less half-hearted fashion, intends to persevere.

## *THE MAIDEN TRIBUTE OF MODERN BABYLON.—III.*

### The Report of our Secret Commission.

The advocates of the Criminal Law Amendment Bill are constantly met by two mutually destructive assertions. On one side it is declared that the raising of the age of consent is entirely useless, because there are any number of young prostitutes on the streets under the legal age of thirteen, while, on the other, it is asserted as positively that juvenile prostitution below the age of fifteen has practically ceased to exist. Both assertions are entirely false. There are not many children under thirteen plying for hire on the streets, and there are any number to be had between the ages of thirteen and sixteen. There are children, many children, who are ruined before they are thirteen; but the crime is one phase of the incest which, as the Report of the Dwellings Commission shows, is inseparable from overcrowding. But the number who are on the streets is small. Notwithstanding the most lavish offers of money, I completely failed to secure a single prostitute under thirteen. I have been repeatedly promised children under twelve, but they either never appeared or when produced admitted that they were over thirteen. I have no doubt that I could discover in time a dozen or more girls of eleven or twelve who are leading immoral lives, but they are very difficult to find, as the boys of the same age who pursue the same dreadful calling. This direct evidence is by no means all that is available to show the deterrent effect of raising the age of consent. The Rescue Society, of

**10.1** The Maiden Tribute in *The Pall Mall Gazette*, 8 July 1885

> the most offensive, highly-coloured and disgusting details concerning the vicious ways of a small section of the population … we protest the streets being turned into a market for literature which appeals to the lascivious curiosity of every casual passer-by, and excites the latent pruriency of a half-educated crowd.

Even Frank Harris, self-styled sexual athlete and editor of the *Evening News*, in a classic case of the pot calling the kettle black and in an echo of the *Lady Chatterley* trial 80 years later, called for Stead to be prosecuted for broadcasting 'matter which we should have thought no man would willingly risk being read by his wife or daughter, or even his son rising to manhood'.

Members of the House of Commons declared the articles obscene and 'sensational statements of a filthy character'. W. H. Smith, who had a monopoly of railway bookstalls, refused to handle *The Pall Mall Gazette* for the week of the Maiden Tribute. It was alleged that women in the street were accosted by newspaper sellers crying, 'Come on Miss, 'ave a copy. This'll show you how to earn five pounds!'

However, the agitation in the country, helped by the provincial papers which were largely sympathetic to what Stead was trying to achieve, was such that Parliament was forced by pressure of opinion to proceed with the Bill, which was passed by a crowded House.

Unfortunately, the story under the heading, 'A Child of Thirteen Bought for £5', proved to be Stead's undoing. In order to show that it could be done, Stead purchased a 13 year-old virgin named Eliza Armstrong from her mother, a woman who was 'poor, dissolute, and indifferent to everything but drink', using Rebecca Jarrett, a reformed prostitute working for the Salvation Army, as a go-between. Stead arranged for Eliza to be examined by a known abortionist who certified her virginity. Eliza was taken to a brothel where she was given chloroform to make the supposed seduction easier. When Stead entered the room, Eliza screamed and, to quote from another master of sensational journalism, Stead 'made his excuses and left', arranging for Eliza to be sent to a safe house in France.

Stead fell victim to a technicality. He had failed to secure the formal consent of Eliza's father, and had been too naïve in accepting Rebecca Jarrett's assurances that Mrs Armstrong was fully aware that Eliza was being procured for immoral purposes. Stead was sentenced to three months' imprisonment for abduction.

The *Spectator* remarked that Stead's judgement had been confused by 'drinking champagne with women of bad character' and that the Maiden Tribute articles were 'the conception of an over-excited brain'.[3] Stead, a non-smoker and a teetotaller, had smoked cigars and drunk champagne during his investigations to make his cover as a connoisseur of vice more convincing.

The aftermath of the Maiden Tribute campaign exposed *The Pall Mall Gazette* to ridicule. Stead promised his proprietor there would be 'no more

Maiden Tributing', but turned from 'government by journalism' to 'justice by journalism' when in 1887 he ran a campaign to try to prove that Israel Lipski was innocent of the murder for which he was sentenced to hang. Lipski won a reprieve, and just as Stead was convinced that he had established the power of the press to correct miscarriages of justice, Lipski confessed that he was guilty after all and was duly hanged.

Tired of Stead backing his convictions to the proprietors' last penny – Stead's support for the illegal Trafalgar Square demonstrations in 1888 led to lost circulation and advertising – the proprietors decided that Stead should leave *The Pall Mall Gazette* on 1 January 1890.

Although Stead described the editor's chair of *The Pall Mall Gazette* as the 'only true throne in England', *The Pall Mall Gazette* and the other literary evening papers were only concerned to influence those who themselves had influence. They were small-circulation papers appealing to a limited cultivated audience in the Whitehall–West End Club circle. Maiden Tribute only managed to increase the sales of the paper from a pitiful 8,360 to a slightly less pitiful 12,250. Stead managed to change the law, but he could also have changed the face of 1880s journalism if he had chosen a more popular medium than the literary evening paper in which to demonstrate his innovations.

After Stead left *The Pall Mall Gazette*, he dabbled in spiritualism and in 1892 published a short story that bore an uncanny resemblance to what happened to *The Titanic* twenty years later, even to the extent of there being insufficient lifeboats. In so doing, Stead forecast his own death. He went down with *The Titanic* in 1912, and thus missed his greatest news story. When last seen, he was helping women and children to safety.

## The *Daily Mail* and the Popular Press

The foundation of the second type of 'new journalism', which gave rise to the popular press, is generally attributed to George Newnes. Newnes started *Tit-Bits* in October 1881 'from all the Most Interesting Books, Periodicals and Newspapers of the World', a weekly paper of simple, short, amusing and instructive paragraphs. Although this apparently new formula was a throwback to the eighteenth-century newspapers which had provided nuggets of news in short paragraphs, *Tit-Bits* was a runaway success, and an offer of free insurance against railway accidents increased its sales to 700,000 copies per week.

Inspired by the success of *Tit-Bits*, the *Star*, a halfpenny evening paper, was started in 1888. Pledged to be 'animated, readable and stirring' and to 'do away with the hackneyed style of obsolete journalism and verbose and prolix articles', the *Star* had news on the front page and specialized in large headlines and short, brisk articles full of human interest. Its first issue, in which the longest article was only half a column in length, was said to have sold 142,600 copies.

Meanwhile, Alfred Harmsworth, the editor of *Bicycling News*, a paper cashing in on the latest craze, was considering how to emulate the success of George Newnes:

> The Board Schools are turning out hundreds of thousands of boys and girls annually who are anxious to read. They do not care for the ordinary newspaper. They have no interest in Society, but they will read anything which is simple and is sufficiently interesting. The man who produced this *Tit-Bits* has got hold of a bigger thing than he imagines. He is only at the beginning of a development which is going to change the whole face of journalism. I shall try to get in with him.

He got in with him by becoming a contributor to *Tit-Bits*. But his ambition was to capture, in his own right, this potential market he had identified. Noticing that the 'Answers to Correspondents' column was one of the most popular features in the newspapers and magazines, in 1888 he started a weekly magazine, *Answers to Correspondents*, later shortened to *Answers*, which, probably unconsciously, adopted the formula devised by John Dunton's *Athenian Mercury* two hundred years earlier. When Harmsworth offered a pound a week for life for guessing the value of the gold in the Bank of England on 4 December 1889, 700,000 entries were received and sales increased from 48,000 to 352,000.

Harmsworth's first venture into daily journalism came about when he bought the ailing *Evening News* at a knockdown price. He installed Kennedy Jones as editor. Jones's motto was 'Don't forget that you are writing for the meanest intelligence.'[4] He presented the news in a simple, easily digestible form made vivid by the use of maps and illustrations, and turned the *Evening News* into the biggest-selling evening newspaper in the world.

The lessons learned from producing periodicals for the wider public and a popular evening paper, and the profits gained from their success, provided the springboard for Harmsworth to launch into morning journalism. The first issue of Harmsworth's *Daily Mail*, 'A Penny Newspaper for One Halfpenny', appeared on 4 May 1896 (Figure 10.2). It is claimed to have sold 397,215 copies. (All circulation figures quoted between the abolition of stamp duty in 1855 and the foundation of the Audit Bureau of Circulations in 1931 should be treated with caution, especially the quotation of 397,215 copies of the first issue of the *Daily Mail* that appeared in the second issue. Without the opportunity of assessing newsagents' returns, how could they tell?)

By the end of the century *Daily Mail*'s sales were approaching a million. Like the *Star*, eight years earlier, the *Daily Mail*'s manifesto announced a

A PENNY NEWSPAPER FOR ONE HALFPENNY.

# Daily Mail.

THE BUSY MAN'S DAILY JOURNAL

NO. 1. — LONDON, MONDAY, MAY 4, 1896. — ONE HALFPENNY.

BUSINESS NOTICES.

PRIVATE ADVERTISERS

RATES FOR ADVERTISEMENTS.

BIRTHS.

MARRIAGES.

PERSONAL.

HOTEL CECIL.

TRACKED BY A TATTOO.

THE WAR IN EGYPT.

CASSELL'S DICTIONARY OF COOKERY.

THE ILLUSTRATED CARPENTER AND BUILDER.

SWAN SONNENSCHEIN & CO.

JONES & HIGGINS, LIMITED.

THE CYCLE MANUFACTURERS' TUBE COMPANY, LIMITED.

**10.2** The *Daily Mail*, 4 May 1896

change from the style of the other morning papers: 'the note of the *Daily Mail* is not so much economy of price as conciseness or completeness. It is essentially the busy man's paper', or, as Lord Salisbury remarked, 'a newspaper for office boys, written by office boys'.

Like all those printers and journalists we have looked at in this narrative who took a leap in the dark to start a new newspaper for an unknown audience, Harmsworth had to imagine and construct the readership for his new title. Despite Jones's motto about the meanest intelligence, Harmsworth pitched the *Daily Mail* at the lower-middle and upper-working classes who had sufficient disposable income to attract advertisers; the man, and the wife of the man, who might be earning only £100, but considered himself 'tomorrow's £1000 a year man, so he hopes and thinks. He likes reading news about people who have succeeded. He sees himself as one of them eventually, and he's flattered.'[5] Tomorrow's £1,000 a year man wouldn't be seen dead going to work on the train reading a paper with headlines on the front page like a cheap, sporting evening paper, so Harmsworth insisted that, from the outside at least, the *Daily Mail* would have the appearance of a respectable morning journal with its front page covered with advertisements.

The main difference between the *Daily Mail* style of new journalism and the old journalism was that the new papers were more thoroughly edited. Instead of printing huge slabs of undigested verbatim reports, papers printed news rewritten to suit the perceived tastes and interests of their readers, and shortened so that more stories could be included and still leave room for advertisements that grew more profitable as the circulation expanded.

Unlike the old papers, which assumed that their readers had sufficient leisure to wade through the unedited report of a two-hour speech and sufficient education to decide for themselves which were the most significant passages, the new journalism increased the possibility of slanting the news by emphasis or omission to suit the political views of the proprietor.

Another feature of the mass circulation papers was highlighted by the *Daily Mail*'s manifesto:

> It is no secret that remarkable new inventions have just come to the help of the Press. Our type is set by machinery, we can produce 200 000 papers per hour, cut, folded and, if necessary, with the pages pasted together! Our stereotyping arrangements, engines and machines are of the latest English and American construction, and it is the use of these inventions on a scale unprecedented in any English newspaper office that enables the *Daily Mail* to effect a saving of from 30 to 50 per cent, and be sold for half the price of its contemporaries.

**Journey's End**

This shows how far the technical innovations started by *The Times* in 1814 had progressed. The abolition of stamp and paper duties, and the introduction of cheap paper made from wood-pulp shortly thereafter, led to the use of gigantic presses fed by continuous lines of newsprint which were capable of much faster and bigger print runs than could have been contemplated at the beginning of the century. Fleet Street had become one big heavily capitalized factory.

The need for capital to produce a mass-circulation newspaper meant that there was a growing concentration of ownership in fewer hands, with a consequential reduction in the number of alternative voices in the press. Even as late as the early nineteenth century, it was still possible to start a successful paper with very limited capital. The *Northern Star* was launched with a capital of £690 in 1837 and it broke even with sales of 6,200.[6] By contrast, the *Sunday Express* was running at a loss with sales of 250,000 and had to have nearly £2 million spent on it before it could be turned into profit.[7] The teeming multitude of Grub Street papers, which had cost next to nothing to produce, had given way to the oligarchy of a few highly capitalized papers with big sales and huge advertising receipts.

Not only had the press become big business; it had also become respectable. The close social contacts between those responsible for the policy of the newspapers and the political élite meant that newspapers had become the voice of the Establishment, unlike the Grub Street papers of two hundred years earlier which were feared and harassed by the Establishment as engines of sedition. Even the popular halfpenny papers were concerned with sport, snippets of news and romantic serials instead of the subversion and sedition of the popular radical and unstamped papers, which would have driven away the all-important advertisers.

The newspaper had not only become respectable, it had also grown more powerful. The power of the press to influence public, and even parliamentary, opinion, which Tudor monarchs, Roger L'Estrange and even Whig reformers had feared, had come to fruition. W. T. Stead may have been deluding himself, but only slightly, when he wrote in his article 'Government by Journalism' in the *Contemporary Review* in 1886:

> I am but a comparatively young journalist, but I have seen Cabinets upset, Ministers driven into retirement, laws repealed, great social reforms initiated, Bills transformed, estimates remodelled, Acts passed, generals nominated, governors appointed, armies sent hither and thither, war proclaimed and war averted, by the agency of newspapers.

When Edward Levy-Lawson of the *Daily Telegraph* became the first Baron

Burnham in 1903, and Alfred Harmsworth and his brother Harold became Lords Northcliffe and Rothermere respectively, the age of the Press Baron had arrived – a development that hustlers like John Trundle, Samuel Pecke, Nathaniel Mist and the writers of the *Grub-street Journal* could never have imagined in their wildest dreams. The journey from Grub Street to Fleet Street was now at an end.

## Notes

1. Wadsworth, A. P. (1955), 'Newspaper Circulations, 1800–1954', *Transactions of the Manchester Statistical Society*, March.
2. Quotation from *République Française* in the *Daily Telegraph*, 27 October 1879.
3. *Spectator*, 14 November 1885.
4. Jones, Kennedy (1919), *Fleet Street and Downing Street*, London: Hutchinson.
5. Clarke, Tom (1955), *Northcliffe in History*, London: Hutchinson.
6. Read, Donald (1961), *Press and People 1790–1850*, London: Edward Arnold.
7. Taylor, A. J. P. (1972), *Beaverbrook*, London: Hamish Hamilton.

# English Newspapers: a Brief Chronology

| | |
|---|---|
| 1513 | *The Trewe Encountre* published |
| 1538 | Licensing introduced |
| 1557 | Stationers' Company receives Royal Charter |
| 1620 | George Veseler's first coranto for the English market |
| 1621 | First corantos published in London |
| 1622 | *Weekely Newes* started |
| 1621–32 | Butter, Bourne and Archer's corantos |
| 1632 | Corantos prohibited |
| 1638 | Butter and Bourne allowed to print corantos by Royal Letters Patent |
| 1641 | Star Chamber abolished |
| | Samuel Pecke's first newsbook |
| 1641–55 | Proliferation of newsbooks |
| 1643 | *Mercurius Aulicus* and *Mercurius Britanicus* started |
| | Board of Licensers established |
| 1644 | Milton's *Areopagitica* |
| 1655 | Newsbooks suppressed |
| 1662 | Licensing Act |
| 1663 | L'Estrange appointed Surveyor of the Press |
| 1665 | *Oxford Gazette* started |
| 1666 | *Oxford Gazette* becomes *London Gazette* |
| 1665–79 | Virtual monopoly of *London Gazette* |
| | Manuscript newsletters |
| 1679 | Licensing Act lapses |
| 1679–82 | Proliferation of 'Popish Plot' news-sheets |
| 1685 | Licensing Act reintroduced |
| 1695 | Parliament fails to renew Licensing Act |
| | *Post Boy*, *Post-Man* and *Flying Post* started |
| 1701 | *Norwich Post* started, probably the first provincial newspaper |
| 1702 | *Daily Courant* started, the first successful daily newspaper |
| 1709 | *Tatler* started |
| 1711 | *Spectator* started |
| 1712 | Stamp Act levies duty of a halfpenny a sheet |
| 1715–25 | Six-page weekly journals |
| 1725 | Stamp Act applied to all newspapers, irrespective of length |

| | |
|---|---|
| 1726 | *Craftsman* started |
| 1727–42 | Popularity of four-page weekly journals |
| 1728 | Nathaniel Mist flees to avoid prosecution for seditious libel |
| 1730 | *Grub-street Journal* started |
| | *Daily Advertiser* started |
| 1731 | Edward Cave starts *Gentleman's Magazine* |
| 1731–41 | Walpole spends over £50,000 bribing newspapers |
| 1735 | Ministerial newspapers amalgamate to form *Daily Gazetteer* |
| 1738 | Publication of parliamentary debates suppressed |
| 1757 | Stamp duty increased to 1d. |
| | *London Chronicle* started |
| 1763 | John Wilkes publishes North Briton no. 45 |
| 1769–70 | Letters of Junius appear in *Public Advertiser* |
| 1771 | Publication of parliamentary debates reinstated |
| 1770–90 | The rise of the morning daily paper |
| 1776 | Stamp duty increased to a penny-halfpenny |
| 1779 | *British Gazette and Sunday Monitor* started, the first Sunday newspaper |
| 1785 | *Daily Universal Register* started, later to become *The Times* |
| 1787 | John Bell starts the *World* |
| 1788 | The *Star* founded, the first daily evening newspaper |
| 1789 | Stamp duty increased to 2d. |
| 1792 | Fox's Libel Act |
| 1797 | Stamp duty increased to threepence-halfpenny |
| 1802 | *Cobbett's Political Register* started |
| 1814 | *The Times* introduces Koenig steam press |
| 1815 | Stamp duty increased to 4d. |
| 1816–20 | The age of the radical press |
| 1817 | Barnes becomes editor of *The Times* |
| 1819 | The Six Acts, two of which are aimed at the radical press |
| 1821 | *Manchester Guardian* started |
| 1828 | *Times* installs Applegarth and Cowper's presses |
| 1830s | 'The Great Unstamped' |
| 1833 | Reduction in advertising duty from 3s. 6d. to 1s. 6d. |
| 1836 | Stamp duty reduced to 1d. |
| 1838 | *Northern Star*, the Chartists' newspaper, started |
| 1840s | Development of electric telegraph |
| 1842 | *Illustrated London News* started |
| | *Lloyd's Weekly News* started |
| 1843 | *News of the World* started |
| 1851 | Reuters opened in London |
| 1853 | Advertising duty abolished |

| | |
|---|---|
| 1855 | Stamp duty abolished |
| 1855–60 | *Daily Telegraph* and other penny papers started |
| | *Sheffield Daily Telegraph* and other regional dailies started |
| 1856 | Edward Lloyd installs Hoe rotary press |
| 1861 | Paper duties abolished |
| 1881 | George Newnes starts *Tit-Bits* |
| 1885 | 'Maiden Tribute' articles in *Pall Mall Gazette* |
| 1888 | Alfred Harmsworth starts *Answers* |
| 1896 | *Daily Mail* started |

# Select Bibliography


Aspinall, A. (1949), *Politics and the Press, 1780–1850*, London: Home and Van Thal.

Barker, Hannah (2000), *Newspapers, Politics and English Society, 1695–1855*, Harlow: Longman.

Black, Jeremy (1987), *The English Press in the Eighteenth Century*, London: Croom Helm.

Black, Jeremy (2001), *The English Press 1621–1861*, Stroud: Sutton Publishing.

Bond, R. P. (ed.) (1957), *Studies in the English Periodical*, Chapel Hill, NC: University of North Carolina Press.

Boston, Ray (1990), *The Essential Fleet Street*, London: Blandford.

Boyce, George, Curran, James and Wingate, Pauline (eds) (1978), *Newspaper History from the 17th Century to the Present Day*, London: Constable; Beverley Hills, CA: Sage Publications.

Brake, Laurel, Jones, Aled and Madden, Lionel (eds) (1990), *Investigating Victorian Journalism*, London: Macmillan.

Brown, Lucy (1985), *Victorian News and Newspapers*, Oxford: Clarendon Press.

Carlson, C. Lennart (1938), *The First Magazine. A History of the Gentleman's Magazine*, Providence, RI: Brown University.

Clark, Charles (1994), *The Public Prints: The Newspaper in Anglo-American Culture, 1665–1740*, New York and Oxford: Oxford University Press.

Clay, Alice (ed.) (1881), *The Agony Column of the 'Times'*, London: Chatto and Windus.

Cranfield, G. A. (1962), *The Development of the Provincial Newspaper*, Oxford: Clarendon Press.

Cranfield, G. A. (1977), *The Press and Society*, London: Longman.

Curran, James and Seaton, Jean (1981), *Power Without Responsibility*, London: Fontana.

Dahl, Folke (1952), *A Bibliography of English Corantos and Periodical Newsbooks, 1620–1642*, London: The Bibliographical Society.

Downie, J. A. and Corns, Thomas N. (eds) (1993), *Telling People What to Think: Early Eighteenth Century Periodicals from The Review to The Rambler*, London: Cass.

Escott, T. H. S. (1911), *Masters of English Journalism*. London: T. Fisher Unwin.

Ewald, William (1956), *The Newsmen of Queen Anne*, Oxford: Oxford University Press; Boston, MA: Houghton Mifflin.

Feather, John (1988), *A History of British Publishing*, London: Routledge.

Frank, Joseph (1961), *The Beginnings of the English Newspaper, 1620–1660*, Cambridge MA: Harvard University Press.

Griffiths, Dennis (ed.) (1992), *The Encyclopedia of the British Press*, London: Macmillan.

Haig, R. L. (1960), *The Gazetteer: 1735–1797*, Carbondale, IL: Southern Illinois University Press.

Handover, P. M. (1965), *A History of the London Gazette, 1665–1965*, London: HMSO.

Hanson, Lawrence (1936), *Government and the Press, 1695–1763*, Oxford: Clarendon Press.

Harris, Bob (1996), *Politics and the Rise of the Press: Britain and France, 1620–1800*, London: Routledge.

Harris, Michael (1984), 'Print and Politics in the Age of Walpole', in Black, Jeremy (ed.), *Britain in the Age of Walpole*, London: Macmillan.

Harris, Michael and Lee, Alan (eds) (1986), *The Press in English Society from the Seventeenth to the Nineteenth Centuries*, London and Toronto: Associated University Presses.

Harris, Michael (1988), *London Newspapers in the Age of Walpole,* London and Toronto: Associated University Presses.
Harrison, Stanley (1974), *Poor Men's Guardians,* London: Lawrence and Wishart.
Hart, Jim A. (1970), *Views on the News,* Carbondale, IL: Southern Illinois University Press.
Herd, Harold (1956), *The March of Journalism,* London: George Allen and Unwin.
Hillhouse, James T. (1928), *The Grub-street Journal,* Durham, NC: Duke University, reprinted New York: Benjamin Blom, 1967.
Hollis, P. (1970), *The Pauper Press,* Oxford: Oxford University Press.
Hudson, Derek (1943), *Thomas Barnes of the Times,* Cambridge: Cambridge University Press.
Hudson, Derek (1945), *British Journalists and Newspapers,* London: Collins.
Jackson, Mason (1885), *The Pictorial Press: Its Origin and Progress,* London: Hurst and Blackett.
Kitchin, George (1913), *Sir Roger L'Estrange,* London: Kegan Paul; reprinted New York: Augustus M. Kelley, 1971.
Koss, Stephen (1990), *The Rise and Fall of the Political Press,* London: Fontana.
Lake, Brian (1984), *British Newspapers. A History and Guide for Collectors,* London: Sheppard Press.
Lee, Alan (1976), *The Origins of the Popular Press, 1855–1914,* London: Croom Helm.
Morison, Stanley (1932), *The English Newspaper. Some Account of the Physical Development of Journals Printed in London Between 1622 and 1932,* Cambridge: Cambridge University Press.
Myers, Robin and Harris, Michael (eds) (1993), *Serials and their Readers, 1620–1914,* Winchester: St Paul's Bibliographies; New Castle, DE: Oak Knoll Press.
Nelson, Carolyn and Seccombe, Matthew (1987), *British Newspapers and Periodicals, 1641–1700; A Short-Title Catalogue of Serials,* New York: Modern Language Association of America.
Nevett, T. R. (1982), *Advertising in Britain: A History,* London: Heinemann.
Pinkus, Philip (1968), *Grub St. Stripped Bare,* London: Constable.
Raymond, Joad (1993), *Making the News: An Anthology of the Newsbooks of Revolutionary England,* Moreton-in-Marsh: Windrush Press.
Raymond, Joad (ed.) (1999), *News, Newspapers and Society in Early Modern Britain,* London: Cass.
Read, Donald (1961), *Press and People, 1790–1850,* London: Edward Arnold.
Read, Donald (1992), *The Power of News: The History of Reuters,* Oxford: Oxford University Press.
Rogers, Pat (1980), *Hacks and Dunces: Pope, Swift and Grub Street,* London: Methuen.
Richardson, Mrs Herbert (1933), *The Old English Newspaper,* London: English Association.
Schaaber, M. A. (1927), *Some Forerunners of the Newspaper in England, 1476–1622,* Philadelphia, PA: University of Pennsylvania Press, reprinted London: Frank Cass, 1967.
Scott, J. W. Robertson (1950), *The Story of the Pall Mall Gazette,* Oxford: Oxford University Press.
Siebert, F. (1952), *Freedom of the Press in England 1476–1776,* Urbana, IL: University of Illinois Press.
Smith, Anthony (1979), *The Newspaper. An International History,* London: Thames and Hudson.
Smith, D. Nichol (1965), 'The Newspaper', in Turbeville, A. S. (ed.) *Johnson's England,* Oxford: Oxford University Press.
Sommerville, C. John (1996), *The News Revolution in England,* New York and Oxford: Oxford University Press.
Steed, H. Wickham (1938), *The Press,* Harmondsworth: Penguin.
Sutherland, James (1986), *The Restoration Newspaper and its Development,* Cambridge: Cambridge University Press.
Symon, J. D. (1914), *The Press and its Story,* London: Seeley, Service.
*The Times* (1935), *The History of the Times: The Thunderer in the Making, 1785–1841,* London: *The Times* Publishing Co.

*The Times* (1939), *The History of the Times: The Tradition Established, 1841–1884*, London: *The Times* Publishing Co.

*The Times* (1947), *The History of the Times: The Twentieth Century Test, 1884–1912*, London: *The Times* Publishing Co.

Turner, E. S. (1952), *The Shocking History of Advertising*, London: Michael Joseph.

Westmancoat, John (1985), *Newspapers*, London: British Library.

Wiles, R. M. (1965), *Freshest Advices. Early Provincial Newspapers in England*, Columbus, OH: Ohio State University Press.

Williams, Francis (1957), *Dangerous Estate*, London: Longmans.

Williams, J. B. (1908), *A History of English Journalism to the Foundation of the Gazette*, London: Longmans, Green.

Williams, Keith (1977), *The English Newspaper. An Illustrated History to 1900*, London: Springwood Books.

Woods, Oliver and Bishop, James (1985), *The Story of the Times: Bicentenary Edition 1785–1985*, London: Michael Joseph.

The journal, *Media History*, and its predecessors, the *Journal of Newspaper History* (from 1984) and *Studies in Newspaper and Periodical History* (from 1993) contain many interesting articles on the pre-twentieth-century English press.

# Index

The page numbers in *italic* type are those of illustrations.